Economic Thinking in a Canadian Context
Volume 1 Microeconomics

Gordon F. Boreham
Professor of Economics
University of Ottawa

Richard H. Leftwich
Professor of Economics
Oklahoma State University

Holt, Rinehart and Winston of Canada, Limited
Toronto : Montreal

Preface

About a century and a half ago, Thomas Robert Malthus, a distinguished member of the classical school in economics remarked that:

> "Political economy is perhaps the only science of which it may be said that the ignorance of it is not merely a deprivation of good, but produces great positive evil."

I need hardly labour the point that modern economists share this same belief. However, what to teach beginning students in economics and how to teach it are perennial and unsolved problems.

Although this Canadian version of *An Introduction to Economic Thinking* (1969) by Richard Leftwich represents a major revision and rewriting of the U.S. edition, there has been no change in the approach to the problems of "what" and "how" to teach newcomers to economics. I fully subscribe to Professor Leftwich's view that we cannot cover the whole broad scope of the discipline of economics in depth in the principles course. But it appears that this is what our profession has been trying to do in recent years and, correspondingly, principles of economics books are becoming basic economic encyclopedias. To attempt to teach in depth all that is typically included is to invite frustration and disappointment on the part of both students and teachers. For most beginning students I suspect that extended discussions of methodology and of sophisticated analytical models are simply irrelevant and boring. In my judgment a thorough grasp of a limited number of elementary principles, together with the economist's way of thinking about things, will do much more toward building economic literacy in the land.

This, then, is not a complex book and there are indeed omissions of a number of topics that are currently fashionable in principles textbooks. Yet I believe it is complete enough to provide the fundamental background for a reasonably correct analysis of both our current and our recurring economic problems. Moreover, it is so organized as to present the material in an order designed to arouse the interest of the student in the subject matter. Needless to say, the book has been conceived and written with the Canadian student of economics in mind. I believe, too, that if the principles contained herein are mastered those desiring to do so will have little difficulty in moving into more advanced, complex, and sophisticated realms of analysis.

It is a pleasure to pay tribute to those who have helped me with this book. Unquestionably I owe most of all to Professor Richard Leftwich who has read the entire manuscript and provided numerous helpful suggestions, and for allowing me full freedom to adapt the U.S. original for Canadian use. Others whose comments on parts of the book are greatly appreciated include Miss Catherine Starrs, Economic Council of Canada (chapter 13); Mr. I. F. Furniss, Canada Department of Agriculture (chapter 14); Dr. Eugene Forsey, formerly of the Canadian Labour Congress (chapter 19); Dr. J. A . Galbraith and Miss A. L. Guthrie, The Royal Bank of Canada (chapters 21, 22 and 23); and Mr. Maurice Strong, Mr. Peter M. Kilburn and Mr. P. Slyfield of the Canadian International Development Agency (chapter 34). Nor can I easily forget the help received from my research assistant, Mr. Stephen Wiseman. Thanks are also due to Mr. Brian Carter, another graduate student, for his help in preparing the index. Finally, I owe an overwhelming debt to my wife and family for their patience and understanding while this work was in progress. None of the persons mentioned above are, of course, in any way responsible for the shortcomings of this book.

Gordon F. Boreham
Professor of Economics
University of Ottawa

August 1970

Richard H. Leftwich
Professor of Economics
Oklahoma State University

Preface

Like most academic disciplines, economics can be classified in several ways. Classified by content of economic activity, there are two broad types: microeconomics and macroeconomics. Microeconomics is concerned with the behaviour of individual economic units such as the household, the firm, the industry, or single commodities. Macroeconomics deals with the broad aggregates of economic activity. It is concerned with the economy as a whole. Prior to the Second World War, economics dealt mainly with microeconomics. Since then, however, an increasing emphasis has been placed on macroeconomics. Today we study both aspects of economic analysis.

With a view towards flexibility, *Economic Thinking in a Canadian Context* has been divided into two volumes. The order in which these two volumes are used is not crucial; each volume is an integrated unit. Thus they can be used interchangeably to meet the preference of instructors who teach macroeconomics first, as well as those who cover microeconomics first.

The focus of the present text is on microeconomics. It provides the student with the tools for analysing the composition of economic activity, which includes makeup of total output, structure of prices, use of productive resources, and the structure of rates of pay.

G.F.B.
Ottawa, Canada
June, 1971.

Contents

Part 1

An Overview of Economic Activity and Analysis

There are many facets to the study of economics. In order to achieve a depth of understanding, we shall examine each one in turn as we proceed through this book. But we shall find out that the analysis of any one area is not independent of the others, and that our grasp of each is enhanced by some knowledge of the others. Chapters 1–3 provide an overview of economic activity and analysis. Hopefully, they will give us a place to hang our hats—a place to which we can return time and again to make the apparently different aspects of economics fall into proper place within an overall framework of knowledge.

1

What Economics is About

You discovered long ago that what you have to spend is not sufficient to obtain as much as you would like to have of the many goods and services available. Your diet is probably varied but it is unlikely that you can afford champagne and gourmet food day in and day out. Your wardrobe is somewhat less than perfect for the kind of life you want to lead, and the room in which you live is not exactly a palace.

In short, you are confronted with the fundamental principle upon which economic activity rests – the wants of mankind are unlimited while the means available for satisfying those wants are not. Individuals and societies must determine how they are going to use the relatively scarce means available to them. They must determine which of their many desires they will apply their means to attain and the extent to which the chosen desires will be fulfilled. Steel used in making automobiles is not available for construction purposes and land used for growing wheat cannot at the same time produce corn.

Accordingly, Lionel Robbins' famous definition of economics as "the science which studies human behaviour as a relationship between ends and scarce means which have alternative uses"[1] is a good generalization of what economics is about. Or, to put the same point another way, economics is essentially a study of the logic whereby we choose among

[1]*Lionel Robbins,* An Essay on the Nature and Significance of Economic Science. *London: Macmillan Co., 1935, p. 16.*

alternative possible economic objectives. It is this decision making process that is the core of economics.

In this introductory chapter we shall consider the nature of economic activity, and we shall take a brief look at some of the economic problems that confront us from day to day. We shall then differentiate between the analysis of economic activity and the policies aimed at solving economic problems. Finally, we shall point out the relationship between economics and the other social disciplines.

Economic Activity

We devote much of our time to different kinds of economic activity. We earn our incomes by engaging in the production of the goods and services that society wants and in turn we use what we have earned to satisfy our own wants as fully as we can. In a society in which there are millions of people, almost as many different goods and services desired, and a great many different means of contributing to the processes of production, patterns of economic activity develop as an integral part of the social fabric. These patterns become exceedingly complex, frequently obscuring cause and effect relationships. Think of our task, then, as one of sorting out these relationships in order to understand how our economic system works, to determine its shortcomings, and to devise means of improving the operation of the system. The first step is to examine systematically the elements involved in economic activity. These are (1) human wants, (2) resources, and (3) techniques of production.

Human Wants

We have mentioned already that there are no limits to the range of goods and services that people want. We hear from time to time that we in Canada are surfeited with material things, but this is not so in any sort of absolute sense. Why do people want higher wages and salaries? Why do we have so many slums? Why is "a more concerted and purposeful attack on poverty urgently required now."[2] Not many people are so affluent that additional quantities of goods and services would add nothing to their satisfactions.

[2]*Economic Council of Canada, "The Challenge of Growth and Change"*, Fifth Annual Review. *Ottawa: Queen's Printer, 1968, p. 130.*

Human wants arise from several sources. Those of a biological nature are always in the foreground. We require certain minimum amounts of food and protection from the elements – shelter and clothing – in order to stay alive and to function. But a full stomach does not end our desires for food, nor does an eight-room house fully satisfy our wants for housing. Once our basic needs are met we want more variety and more elegance in the goods and services used to meet these needs. Consider the desire for variety in entertainment. Among university coeds, too, although there will be some degree of conformity in types of clothing worn, within those types every effort will be made to avoid duplications in patterns and colour schemes. Social pressure, too, generates wants. For example, the purchase of a colour television set by a neighbour makes us feel that we should have one too. Additionally, as we engage in the activities necessary to satisfy a given desire, new wants are born. Who wants to move into a new house without buying at least a few new pieces of furniture? Does the pursuit of a bachelor's degree create wants that would otherwise never have come into being for an individual?

These unlimited human wants are the mainsprings of economic activity. All economic activity is carried on for the purpose of fulfilling people's desires. It is directed toward satisfying as fully as possible the wants of individuals, of groups, and of the entire society.

Resources

The extent to which wants in any society can be fulfilled is determined largely by the availability of the ingredients that can be put into processes of production. What do you have that can contribute toward the production of goods and services desired by the society in which you live? You certainly are able to do physical labour and, given the opportunity, you may be able to put a little mental effort into the economic machine. You may also own a piece of land or other property that you can rent out to others. Or perhaps you own a few shares of stock, making you part owner of the assets of some corporation, and you let the corporation use your part of these assets to produce its products.

Resource Classifications

We call the ingredients that go into the production of goods and services *resources*, and for convenience we classify them into two broad categories: (1) *labour* and (2) *capital*. Each category contains a great many subcategories which may differ widely: corporation executives and garbage collectors, for example, both fall within the labour classification. While the classification is useful for many purposes, undue importance should not be attached to it. It is primarily a device to help us keep our thinking orderly when we consider resources.

Labour consists of all the muscular and mental effort that mankind can put into the productive processes. It includes what common labourers are able to do, but it is also made up of the capabilities of actors, musicians, artists, university professors, lawyers, accountants, railroad engineers, and so on. Labour, then, represents all productive efforts rendered directly by human beings.

Nonhuman resources are called *capital*. We include as capital all kinds of tools such as pencils, notebooks, hammers, pliers, and nails; machinery; and buildings. We shall place so-called natural resources in the capital category also, although some economists prefer to set these up in a third category called *land*. Natural resources consist of farm land, space for residential and industrial sites, mineral deposits, water, fish and wildlife, forests, and other such items. Inventories of goods comprise still another type of capital resource. For example, grocery inventories are a part of the capital resources of a supermarket and stocks of iron ore make up a portion of the capital resources of a steel mill.

A substantial part of the capital resources of the economy consists of *intermediate goods*—goods produced to be further used in production processes rather than directly by consumers. Steel, for example, is not consumed directly but is fabricated into any number of products that are then used by consumers. Thus resources may be used to produce other resources that are in turn employed to produce resources that are then used in the production of consumer goods and services. Pyramiding of this kind is common in the productive process.

Scarcity of Resources

We know from everyday experience that the quantities of resources available for producing goods and services are inadequate for fulfilling our unlimited wants. If resources were not scarce relative to wants they would not command a price; that is, they would be free like the air we breathe. That consumers and, in turn, producers are willing to pay to put resources into the productive process is evidence that they are scarce and are not to be had simply for the taking.

It is easy to see that there is an upper limit to the size of the labour force. The total population of an economy, if nothing else, would be the ultimate limiting factor. But there are a number of factors that restrict the labour force to something like one third of the total population. These include the age distribution of the population, its state of health, attitudes toward employment of women and children, whether or not aristocrats and would-be aristocrats are willing to get their hands dirty, and other factors of a similar nature.

The quantity of capital that an economy has available to place in production is also limited, but by a somewhat different set of factors. An economy may experience a paucity of natural resources—for example, many of the areas of North Africa and the Middle East. But scarcity of machines, buildings, tools, and other intermediate goods is even more significant. We might ask ourselves how an economy accumulates a stock of capital goods to put into productive processes. Generally, in order to do this, an economy must use existing resources that could have been used for the production of consumer goods to produce intermediate or capital goods instead. The production of intermediate goods thus involves a sacrifice of some quantities of consumer goods, unless unemployment of resources exists in the economy and these unemployed resources can be put to work. As consumers, we may not be willing to tighten our belts sufficiently to release the quantities of resources needed to bring about large relative increases in the economy's stock of capital. The poorer a country, the more difficult capital accumulation becomes.

Techniques of Production

The amounts of goods and services that can be produced with given quantities of labour and capital depend, of course, on how well those resources are used. Two students with the same degree of intelligence, the same books, and in the same surroundings may perform at different levels on an examination. The difference may well be in the techniques of study used by each. Similarly, with given quantities of resources one shoemaker may turn out a larger quantity of shoes than another because he employs superior techniques. In the same way, the general level of technological know-how varies among countries. The economies of Asia, Africa, South America, and the Middle East are behind those of western Europe and the United States and Canada in this respect.

By production techniques we mean the methods, knowledge, and means available for converting resources into want-satisfying goods. Engineering is generally thought of as the discipline most directly concerned with this process, which includes the development of new energy sources, improvements in construction methods, more efficient plant design and layout, development of new products, and anything else that increases the want satisfaction attainable from available resources. But we are also concerned with techniques of production in economics. Since resources are scarce relative to wants, we concern ourselves with whether or not the "best" techniques are used. The best techniques are those that enable given quantities of resources to yield the highest outputs of goods and services, or, to put it the other way around, those that permit given quantities of goods and services to be produced with the least expenditure of resources. We shall come back to these points again and again in a variety of contexts.

Goals of Economic Activity

The primary economic goal of most societies is to achieve a standard of living as high as its resources and its techniques of production will allow. Having made this statement, we must qualify it immediately. No society is likely to focus single mindedly on maximizing average living standards. There are other values to be achieved in "the good life," and the fulfillment of some of these objectives may require backing away from the achievement of the highest possible living standards. Preservation of a free as opposed to a totalitarian society, for example, may require that some resources be diverted from the production of want-satisfying consumer goods and services toward the production of armaments. Too, Canada has supported income-redistribution measures—the farm price-support program, progressive taxation, minimum wage legislation—which many people believe have held the total output of the economy below what it would be in their absence, in order to secure a greater measure of economic justice. But most modern societies most of the time are interested in continually raising the levels of want satisfaction they can achieve. Through newspapers, television programs, conversations, and other contacts with the rest of society we are reminded that the economic system operates imperfectly. Problems arise, the solutions to which make up a set of subgoals toward which economic activity is directed. What are some of a country's major economic problems? *Unemployment* is surely an important one. Another is *economic instability*. A third is *low levels of growth and development,* particularly in the poorer countries of the world. A fourth is presumed *injustices in income distribution*—in the way the economic system treats certain individuals and groups in the society as compared with others. A fifth problem centers around what *type of economic system* will best promote the goals toward which society wants to work. Let us examine the subgoals in greater detail in order to grasp more securely the dimensions of the problems that systematic economic analysis must attack.

Full Employment

The economy of Canada has experienced some difficulty in keeping its labour force and its productive capacity fully employed. During the depression of the 1930's, unemployment did not fall below 9.1 percent of the labour force. In the worst year, 1933, 19.3 percent of the labour force was unemployed. From 1957 to 1964, the unemployment rate was more than 4.5 percent. As individuals and as a society, we are concerned; unemployment implies hardship for ourselves and for fellow human beings. It also means that the economy is turning out smaller quantities of goods and services than it is capable of producing and that our standard of living is lower than it need be.

What are the causes of unemployment? What can be done to decrease it? Economists are not entirely in accord on either point, but they do agree that identification of the causes is a prerequisite to taking intelligent action to mitigate the problem. Unless we can diagnose the disease, we are not likely to get far in curing it.

Economic Stability

Economic instability, characterized by periods of recession and periods of inflation, is cause for much uneasiness in a society. A *recession* refers to a reduction in economic activity in which unemployment will increase, and it presents the possibility of becoming a serious depression such as that of the 1930's. *Inflation*, on the other hand, is characterized by rising prices and is ordinarily, but not necessarily, associated with high levels of economic activity. Both recessionary and inflationary periods have occurred in Canada since 1940, but none has been as severe as those of the 1870's, the 1890's or the 1930's.

Economists believe they have learned much in recent years about economic instability and how to control it. In fact, many feel that our present state of economic knowledge is such that there will never be another depression of the magnitude of the Great Depression. Other economists, however, are more cautious and maintain that although we may know how to prevent future depressions, the political climate may impede or even prevent the application of this knowledge. Nevertheless, we continue to have periods of inflation and of recession. At the very least, we must be able to prevent them from getting out of hand; hopefully we can make them less and less damaging. We must learn all we can about the causes and consequences of recession and inflation in order to decrease their adverse effects on living standards.

Economic Growth and Development

We expect modern economic systems to provide rising standards of living over time. We want growth and development to take place particularly in the poorer countries of Latin America, Africa, and Asia, but most of us anticipate that living standards in Europe and North America will rise as well. What are the forces that produce economic growth? What annual growth rate can reasonably be expected in Canada and in other countries? Why are growth rates so low in the underdeveloped nations? What, if anything, can be done to accelerate growth rates in the latter? Is economic aid from the advanced to the less advanced countries in order, and if so, how and in what quantities should it be provided?

There is much to be learned about the processes of economic growth and the obstacles that lie in its path. Growth processes as such should be amenable to economic analysis, but many of the factors that hinder economic development are outside the province of economics proper, lying rather in the fields of political science, sociology, psychology, and cultural anthropology.

Economic Justice and Economic Security

As individuals and as a society we are concerned with the twin problems of economic justice and economic security even though we are seldom clear as to what we mean by these terms. In a very broad sense, *justice*, or lack of it, is inferred from the treatment received by one person in economic affairs as compared with that received by others. *Security* refers to a guarantee of some minimum level of consumption. Some measure of security is ordinarily thought to be necessary for the individual in the interests of economic justice.

A great many questions arise with respect to what is just and what is not. Should people share equally in the economy's output or should they share in proportion to their contribution to the productive processes? If they are to share equally, what incentive does an individual have to make his maximum contribution? If they are to share in proportion to their contribution, security for many goes out the window. Many people do not own sufficient quantities of resources to earn a large enough share of the economy's output to keep them alive. Consider those who are permanently disabled and who own no capital. Problems of economic security and of economic justice cannot be solved with economic theory alone, although theory is an important ingredient in arriving at satisfactory solutions.

Ideas of what constitutes security and what constitutes justice depend upon the value judgments of individuals and groups in society, that is, upon their particular view of how things should be. We have not been able to reach a consensus in these areas and, consequently, in Canada we have a broad range of governmental and private arrangements designed to achieve some measure of security and justice. Among these are social security laws, the system of graduated income taxes, minimum wage laws, and laws providing for free public education. In the private sector we have insurance of many types. One of our main tasks from the point of view of economics is to subject such arrangements to thorough examination in order to determine whether or not they accomplish their objective. In addition, we need to assess their impact on the over-all level of economic activity.

Economic Systems

What type of economic system is most conducive to "the good life" as envisaged by people all over the world? Obviously people and societies hold widely differing opinions on this subject—indeed the Cold War has largely turned on this issue. Which will lead to the highest living standards, the socialistic system of the Soviet Union and Red China, the free enterprise system as represented by Canada and the United States, or some combination of the two? Which will come closest to fulfilling society's complex of economic and noneconomic goals?

Although we shall not define the terms "socialism" and "free enterprise" with precision at this point, let us consider the characteristics of each of these economic systems. In the *socialistic system* the economy is state directed, that is, the means of production are owned and controlled by the state. In the *free enterprise system* the means of production are owned privately. Economic activity is carried on through the volition of and under the direction of private individuals and groups. Neither the socialistic system of the Soviet Union nor the free enterprise system of Canada is pure in form. For example, recent evidence indicates that the U.S.S.R. is making increasing use of private ownership of some resources, while in Canada we find that some industries are socialized—the postal services and many provincial and municipal utility companies are cases in point. Further, half the railway system and more than half the airline system and the broadcasting system are government owned. Final choices of the type of economic system that will predominate have not been made in either sphere of influence and likely will never be made. But societies are continually making choices that move them in one direction or the other, and these choices should be made as intelligently as possible.

Economic Analysis and Economic Policy

Legislative bodies as well as groups of private individuals are constantly engaging in activities designed to remedy defects in the operation of the economic system. Some of these measures accomplish their objectives, but some produce results and by-products that are unexpected and unwanted. For example, for many years Parliament has been concerned with the problem of low average incomes in the agricultural sector of the economy, and thus a farm program built around price supports for key storable farm products has been built up in order to increase farm incomes relative to other incomes in the economy. The general public, as well as a number of members of Parliament, have expressed surprise that surpluses of a number of farm products have accumulated, and in addition, many are also surprised to learn that the wealthier farmers on the large farms receive the bulk of price support payments while smaller, poorer operators receive very little. The problem illustrated here is that those who attempt to remedy the economy's defects do not always understand how the economic system operates and thus the ramifications of their actions. For this reason we must distinguish clearly between economic analysis and economic policy. We need to understand both and to ground the latter on the former.

Economic Analysis

Economic analysis is the process of making sense out of economic relationships. Economists examine and record economic behaviour and economic events in order to establish causal relations among the data and activities they have observed. Some of their conclusions are reached through reasoning deductively from more general to more specific events. As an illustration, the Cold War requires military preparedness, which in turn requires the use of steel. Thus, economists reason, an increase in military activities will increase demand for steel. Other causal relationships are established inductively, with analysts inferring from a series of events that certain relationships must exist. Suppose that over a number of years it is observed that increases in prices and increases in the total money available for spending in the economy always occur simultaneously. Economists might then reason that these conditions are causally related, or perhaps that they have common causes.

Tentative statements of causal relationships are called *hypotheses*. Such statements need to be tested again and again in order to determine whether or not they are valid. They can be weighed for logical consistency and they can be tested empirically in the world of facts. As a consequence of testing they may be verified, modified, or rejected.

Hypotheses that have withstood repeated testing and that seem to be able to explain or to predict economic activity with a fair degree of accuracy become known as *principles*. It must be emphasized, however, that principles are not necessarily absolute truths but rather should be thought of as subject to correction and refinement.

The general body of economic analysis is made up of principles designed to explain causal relationships among what are believed to be the more important economic variables. All possible variables surrounding all possible economic events obviously cannot be taken into account because of the limitations of the human mind. Principles are essentially simplifications of complex relationships and are intended to indicate what will happen most of the time in most cases, but almost any principle is subject to exceptions.

Economic analysis serves three main purposes. First, by explaining relationships among various economic variables it is a valuable aid in understanding the operation of an economy. Second, it aids in predicting the consequences of changes in economic variables. Finally, economic analysis serves as the fundamental framework for economic policy-making—indeed, if wise policy-making is to occur, it must be based on correct economic analysis.

Economic Policy

Economic policy refers to conscious intervention in the economic processes by government or by private groups in order to affect the results of economic activity. Associations of employers may agree not to "pirate" each other's labour, that is, not to try to hire each other's employees, in order to prevent wages from rising; labour organizations may use coercion to raise the wage levels of their members; Parliament enacts laws that influence the behaviour of businesses, employees, and consumers. Such legislation includes antimonopoly laws, social welfare laws, farm legislation, tax laws, and many others.

Whereas economic policies of private groups in the economy are generally pursued with the intent of furthering the interest of those groups, we have every right to expect that government policies will be in the interests of the general public. To put it another way, we anticipate that government policies will increase economic efficiency. Although greater efficiency may result from a number of such measures, a healthy skepticism is in order, too. Individual members of Parliament often have different ideas of how the economy should operate—and so do their advisers and the witnesses at their hearings. In addition, their economic analysis is not infallible. This is not to say that governmental policy-making usually goes off on the wrong track but rather that the more sound the economic analysis underlying governmental policy-making, the more effective that policy-making is likely to be. Yet there will always be conflict in this area.

Economics and the Other Social Sciences

Social science is the broad field of study which includes all the disciplines that deal with man in his social or group relations. Economics centres its investigation of social relationships "on the activities and arrangements by which people provide services to create products, and are thereby entitled to other products". More simply, economics is concerned with those aspects of social organization and social behaviour involving trade—exchange of service for service, exchange of commodity for service, exchange of commodity for commodity, or exchange of financial instrument (such as money) for service or commodity.[3]

Quite obviously, economics overlaps with and is closely related to the other social sciences. It overlaps with sociology which studies the structure and functioning of social groups, from the family to the tribe, to local communities, to nations and international units. Since man reacts to other motives besides pecuniary ones, economics is closely related to psychology, especially social psychology which deals with the behaviour

[3]*For a more detailed discussion of economics as a social science, see Melvin A. Eggers and A. Dale Tussing,* The Composition of Economic Activity. *New York: Holt, Rinehart and Winston Inc., 1965, pp. 1-4.*

of the individual as it affects, and is affected by the behaviour of others. Since laws relating to taxation, to regulation of commerce and business behaviour, to commercial treaties and agreements with other countries, are the result of political and governmental decisions, it is also clear that economics overlaps with political science. Because each society has its distinctive habits, ideas, and attitudes, economics impinges on cultural anthropology which studies and compares both prehistoric and extinct cultures (archaeology) and living cultures of mankind (ethnology). Since economics deals with human acts, it is also related to philosophy, and in particular to ethics, a branch of philosophy that deals with morality of human acts.

Other important fields of study which should be mentioned are: (i) history, which describes and to some extent explains the past development of human societies; (ii) human geography, which places man in his physical setting and studies his relations with that environment. Economics also draws heavily on the studies of statistics and mathematics and on logic, the science of exact thinking.

Clearly, anyone who expects to acquire much depth of economic understanding must have some broad knowledge of the other aspects of man's social life.

Summary

This chapter introduces the study of economics. Economic activity stems from the unlimited range of man's wants and the comparative scarcity of means available for fulfilling them. Wants arise from many sources, including biological necessity, desires for variety, social pressures, and want-satisfying activity itself. The means available for fulfilling wants comprise the resources of the economy and its technology. Resources are the ingredients that go into the processes of production and can be classified into a labour category and a capital category. Labour includes all human efforts that contribute to production while capital consists of resources that are nonhuman in character. By technology we mean the know-how and the means available to a society for converting resources into want-satisfying goods and services. The level of want satisfaction, or the average standard of living, that a society can attain depends upon the quantities and qualities of its available resources as well as the level of its technology.

The ultimate economic goal of a society is ordinarily the achievement of a standard of living as high as its resources and production techniques will permit. A number of subgoals related to problems that arise in the operation of the economic system can be identified. These include full employment of resources, economic stability, economic growth and development, economic justice and security, and determination of the type of economic system that best serves the purposes of the society.

The relation between economic analysis and economic policy must be clearly understood. Economic analysis is concerned with the establishment of causal relations among economic events. Its purposes are to help us understand how the economy operates, to enable us to predict what the consequences of changes in economic variables will be, and to serve as the basis for economic policy-making. Economic policy refers to the conscious attempts of private groups and governmental units to make the economy operate differently than it would in the absence of those attempts. Wise economic policy must rest on sound economic analysis.

Since economics is primarily concerned with human behaviour in a group context, it is classed as one of the social sciences. And inasmuch as many of the vital factors which contribute to material well-being are social, cultural, psychological and political in character, economics overlaps with and is closely related to the other social sciences.

Exercises and Questions for Discussion

1. During the course of a day make a list of the things you would like or would like more of, but cannot afford. Why is your income (or your family's income) inadequate to make these purchases?
2. Per capita income, or average income per person, in India is less than $100 per year. What explanations can you offer for this relatively low standard of living?
3. Look through a current issue of your favourite news periodical, noting the articles pertaining to economic issues. Classify these articles under the five problem areas discussed in the chapter.
4. What do you think were the main causes of the relatively high rate of unemployment (over 5 percent of the labour force) between 1958 and 1963?
5. Which of the following are examples of socialism and why: (a) a municipally owned power plant; (b) Polymer Corporation Limited; (c) Bell Telephone Company of Canada; (d) the federal government's farm price-support program; (e) public medical care programs.
6. Evaluate this statement: "That may be all right in theory but not in fact."

Selected Readings

Boulding, Kenneth E., *Economic Analysis*, 4th ed., Vol. 1. New York: Harper & Row, Publishers, Inc., 1966, Chap. 1.

Heilbroner, Robert L., *The Making of Economic Society*. Englewood Cliffs, N.J.: Prentice-Hall, Inc., 1962, Chap. 1.

Lewis, B. S., "Economic Understanding: Why and What", *American Economic Review*, Papers and Proceedings, May 1957, pp. 653–670.

Daly, F. St. L., "The Scope and Method of Economics", *The Canadian Journal of Economics and Political Science*, May 1945, pp. 165–76.

Taylor, K. W., "Economic Scholarship in Canada", *The Canadian Journal of Economics and Political Science*, February 1960, pp. 6–16.

2

How an Economic System Works

Consider your morning coffee break. It had its origins some time ago with investment in a piece of land in Brazil, Colombia, or some other tropical country. Labour and machinery cleared the land and brought it under cultivation. Coffee trees were planted and cultivated, bearing fruit after some five years. The berries were picked and pulped, leaving only the seeds or beans. These were hulled, peeled, sorted, sacked, shipped to Canada, cleaned, blended, roasted, and ground. The student union purchased the ground product and made it into the brew you drink. In addition to the resources used in the direct production process sketched above, still others were needed for the containers, railway cars, trucks, and ships in which the coffee product was transported through its different stages of manufacture. Still other resources were needed to construct the machinery and the buildings that were used at every point in the production of the coffee you drink.

A modern economic system is enormously complex. Thousands of economic operations are required to produce almost any product, and all of these processes must be efficiently coordinated. We attempt in this chapter to strip away the complexities and get down to the bare essentials of economic activity so that we may begin to understand how an economic system works. We shall consider first the functions that every economic system must perform and we then shall take a brief, preliminary look at how different types of systems perform them. Third, we shall construct a simple model of a free enterprise system.

The Functions of an Economic System

Most economists list three basic functions that every economic system must perform. First, the system must determine what goods and services are to be produced as well as their order of importance. Second, it must organize productive effort so that the goods and services selected are produced in the proper quantities. Finally, it must determine how the finished output is to be shared among the members of the society. All societies are confronted with these same central functions, but the methods used to achieve them can differ widely.

Determining What is to be Produced

The fundamental economic problem of unlimited wants and scarce means of satisfying them makes it necessary for an economic system to have some method of determining not only what goods and services are to be produced but also their order of importance. We find two basic methods of performing this function in use in the world today. In the first instance the function is performed by the private action of the individuals making up the society and in the second by the state, that is, by the government or its agencies.

In a society that depends upon private action, consumers themselves determine the comparative values of goods and services through the price system. Individuals spend their available purchasing power however they wish, and each dollar spent is a vote on what is to be produced. The more urgently consumers want specific items, the higher will be the prices of these items relative to those of other items. Less urgently desired items command relatively lower prices. The more abundant the quantity available of any one product, the lower its price will be. Changes in consumers' preferences bring about changes in the prices of goods. For example, if the desires of housewives for television sets rise relative to their desires for dishwashers, they will channel their spending away from the latter toward the former and prices of television sets will rise while those of dishwashers will fall. The array of prices established for goods and services reflects the relative per unit values of the quantities currently available to consumers as a group.

In economies in which the state determines what is to be produced much detailed planning is necessary. In making estimates of future production needs, difficult questions arise concerning whether larger quantities of some products are in order. For example, a decision to step up automobile production is also a decision to increase the quantities of sheet metal, rubber tires, copper wire, batteries, and other items used in their manufacture. Since the resources of the economy are limited, additional quantities of these items can be had only if the quantities of other products are reduced. But by how much must they be reduced? Even with high-speed computers the task confronting the planners is a difficult one.

Government planning of what is to be produced may be based on (1) consumer desires, (2) governmental decisions as to what is best for the public, or (3) government aims and objectives apart from what the public wants. When governments attempt to plan in accordance with consumer desires, they may make use of a price system to register those desires, although it is not essential that they do so. Where government planning is based on governmental decisions as to what is best for the public, arbitrary decisions are made as to what is to be produced, and production quotas are established for each item in a vast array of goods and services. There is likely to be a move toward narrowing the types, models, and styles available in order to simplify planning—for example, a consumer may not be able to obtain the red necktie he desires. When government objectives are given priority, conflicts between these objectives and the desires of consumers are sure to occur. The government may find military strength essential to maintain itself in power when the public would prefer that more consumer goods be produced instead. Or the government, looking toward the future, may want to divert resources away from consumer goods and services at the present time in order to accumulate capital and increase future productive capacity while consumers want more goods and services now.

Actually, we see combinations of the two methods of determining what is to be produced in use throughout the world. In Canada consumer choice is the predominant method, but it is tempered by governmental decisions in a number of areas. For example, there are legal prohibitions against the sale of certain drugs; governmental units make decisions with regard to road building; and a number of other examples could be cited. In the Soviet Union government planning is the predominant method of allocating resources, yet even here consumer choice plays at least a limited role.

Organizing Production

Every economic system must have some means of mobilizing productive effort in order to turn out in appropriate quantities the goods and services desired. The organization of production has two main aspects.

One is the process of moving resources away from the production of goods where they contribute less to consumer desires and into the production of goods where they contribute more. The other is the attainment of the greatest possible efficiency by individual production units or business enterprises in the economy. Again we can think in terms of two alternatives. Private individuals can be left to organize production on their own or the state can undertake the task.

Can we avoid chaos if individuals are left to their own devices—to work wherever they desire and to place the capital they own in employments of their own choosing? Even if chaos can be avoided, the task of getting the right resources to the right place at the right time seems highly remote. But we have omitted the price system from our thinking. The price system and the profit motive, maligned as they are, perform the task of organizing production in an unobtrusive, automatic way. It is evident that businesses can make higher profits by producing goods that consumers want most rather than those that consumers want least. Further, the most profitable businesses pay the highest prices for labour and capital resources while the least profitable businesses are those that resource owners prefer to avoid. We, as resource owners, move our labour and capital away from the lower-paying areas toward the higher-paying ones. As production of what consumers want most is expanded and of what they want least is contracted, prices and profits fall in the former and increase in the latter, diminishing the incentive of resource owners to make further transfers.

The profit motive also provides the prime incentive to private businesses to operate efficiently. The greater the value of output that can be obtained from a given value of resources, the more efficient the production process. Or, what amounts to the same thing, the smaller the value of resource inputs necessary to produce a given value of product output, the more efficient the process. It follows that the more efficient an enterprise is in its operations, the more profit it will make; hence the quest for profit spurs a drive for efficiency.

Organization of production by the state will be neither automatic nor unobtrusive. The magnitude of the planning task is almost overwhelming simply by virtue of the millions of decisions that must be made. Suppose that the state planning agencies have determined what goods and services are to be produced and have established production quotas for each that are within the capabilities of the economy, given its resources and its level of technology. How can one get workers who prefer the seaside to work in the mines? How can one decide on the degree of mechanization to use in road building as compared with that to use in agriculture? How far should one go in producing intermediate goods, and what kinds of intermediate goods should be produced? What if someone makes a mistake with respect to the amount of natural rubber that can be imported and an insufficient number of tires are available for the automobiles that are being produced? Of course, these problems also arise under a price system, but the price system corrects them before they become critical.

What are the incentives for efficiency in the operation of individual production units in the state-planned economy? Bonus incentives and promotion possibilities for managers and workers can be and are used to some extent. It is also common for the state to establish production quotas and for penalties to be assessed if these quotas are not met. But individual units may not be free to obtain resources in the kinds and quantities that will contribute most to efficient operation. They are usually obliged to accept whatever they can get, that is, whatever is allocated to them.

In the organization of production most economies will use some combination of the two alternatives discussed above, although it is apparent that some rely more heavily on one than on the other. The economy of Canada is largely price directed, but at a number of points governmental decisions are superimposed on, or substituted for, the price mechanism. The Soviet Union illustrates the opposite emphasis.

Distributing the Product

Every economic system must provide a method of determining how its citizens are to share in the economy's output. This function too can either be performed by private enterprise or by the state.

Here too the private approach utilizes the price system as the controlling device. How does it work? You know that the part of the economy's total yearly output that you can claim depends on the yearly income that you earn. Your income, in turn, depends upon how much labour and how much capital you put into the production process and the prices (wage rates, interest, dividends, rents, and so on) you receive for them. Most of us believe that we are not paid enough for our resources, but by and large we receive for them about what they contribute to the value of the economy's output. If one employer is not willing to pay that much for them it will be profitable for another to do so. But a fuller explanation of this point must wait.

The distribution of the economy's output thus depends on the distribution of income. In turn, the distribution of income depends on the distribution of resource ownership and the prices individuals receive for placing their resources in production. People well endowed with capital and labour resources and who place these where they contribute much to the value of the economy's output will have large incomes relative to others and will receive large shares. The Rockefellers and the Fords are cases in point. People with few resources that they utilize poorly receive low incomes and small shares.

In the state-planned approach income distribution can be whatever the state wills it to be. As a first approximation it might think in terms of rationing equal quantities of each product to each member of the society, but this would not be a satisfactory arrangement. People differ in their preferences and in their consumption patterns for a variety of reasons— different ages and residence in different parts of the country are two important ones. Indeed, if all were to share equally in the economy's output, how could workers be induced to move from employments where they want to be into employments where they are needed?

Economies such as Canada that rely mainly on the private approach make considerable use of state-planned distribution measures. Similarly, state-planned economies such as the Soviet Union make some use of the private approach. In Canada the government redistributes income in a number of ways—through progressive taxation, free public education, farm subsidies, and others. In the Soviet Union equal sharing in distribution is not followed in practice. Distribution is partly fixed as the state determines what is to be produced—what parts of total output are to be military hardware, heavy industrial goods, consumer goods, and so on. Wages and prices are rather rigidly controlled, but there are differentials between skilled and unskilled workers. Sometimes certain managerial positions or certain professions carry bonuses in order to attract more persons into them. These differences in income make it possible for some people to obtain greater shares of what is produced than others.

Types of Economic Systems

The private approach to the three functions of an economic system is provided by a *free enterprise* type of economic system while the state-planned approach is typical of *socialistic* economies. Although a detailed discussion of these alternative types of systems is out of order at this point, we should have some grasp of the fundamental characteristics of each. The economic system that evolves in any particular society is not the consequence of decision-making on economic grounds alone. In fact, political and philosophical issues are likely to predominate—witness the Russian Revolution in 1918; and in some cases, such as Nazi Germany and Facist Italy of the pre-World War II days, personal aggrandizement on the part of an individual may be the molding force. But our concern here is with the economic aspects of the different systems.

The Free Enterprise System

The right of private persons and private organizations to own things is the foundation of a free enterprise economic system. We call this the *institution of private property*. Generally, legal guarantees are given to private individuals, partnerships, corporations, and other associations to own capital resources and consumer goods of almost all kinds. Individuals also own their own labour power, although this would not be so if slavery were permitted.

The fundamental methods by which such an economy operates are voluntary exchange and cooperation by private individuals and organizations. Why do people work 40 hours a week, week in and week out? They do so primarily because the time and effort they give up are worth less to them than the money they receive for working. The same proposition holds for the willingness of people to exchange capital resources for income. Producers who pay for the services of labour and capital must also feel that those services are worth more to them than what they pay out to resource owners. Unless both parties gain, the exchanges would never occur. Why do you give up purchasing power you have in exchange for goods and services? Again because the items you purchase must be worth more to you than the purchasing power you give up, otherwise you would not make the trade. The seller too must believe that the money he receives will be of greater benefit to him than the goods and services he gives up. Exchange occurs whenever and wherever two or more parties believe that they can benefit from the transaction.

Individuals or groups cooperate with each other whenever they believe they can gain more from working together than from working individually. You help your neighbour move his refrigerator; in turn he helps you haul a dead tree out of your yard. People in a society join their labour and their capital in more extensive productive efforts—in the manufacture of automobiles, houses, airplanes, and almost everything else that is needed.

In the exercise of voluntary exchange and cooperation there are three areas in which people are free to act either as individuals or in groups. First, as consumers people are free to purchase whatever goods and services they want within the limits of their income. Second, as resource owners they are free to sell or hire out their resources for income wherever they can find takers. Third, they are free to establish business enterprises for the production and sale of any desired product or service, and they can terminate those enterprises whenever they see fit to do so.

Largely because of its emphasis on individual freedom and voluntary exchange, many people conclude that the free enterprise system operates in a highly disorganized way. This, however, is not the case. As noted in the preceding section, prices and profits provide the guiding mechanism: the things that consumers value most highly are also those that it is most profitable to produce, and those valued least are produced at losses. The termination of enterprises and the contraction of productive capacity occurs in the latter while new enterprises and expansion of productive capacity occurs in the former. The profitable enterprises attract resources away from those incurring losses by paying more to resource owners. The mechanism is automatic, and although it is not perfect in its operation, neither is it chaotic.

The free enterprise system places a high premium on individual freedom of choice and action. Individuals are thought to be the best judges of the economic objectives of the society. Economic activity, guided and directed by prices, is motivated by the pursuit of self-interest. Each consumer attempts to spend his income in such a way as to maximize his individual well-being, and each business firm attempts to maximize its profits. Individuals as resource owners seek to maximize their incomes. Pursuit of individual self-interest in these ways is thought to lead to the greatest common economic welfare of the society as a whole.

The Socialistic System

Government ownership or control of the economy's resources underlies the socialistic type of economic system. The government owns such capital resources as land, buildings, and machinery, but since ownership of labour power is hard to separate from the individual who furnishes it, control of labour resources rather than outright government ownership is the usual case.

In the socialistic system government planning is used to organize economic activity. The government plans what is to be produced and it operates enterprises in different lines of production accordingly. Business enterprises can be established, labour resources can be directed, and capital resources can be allocated in whatever way government officials believe they will make their maximum contribution to the economic objectives specified by the state. Distribution of the product, too, will be in accordance with government's over-all economic plan.

The socialistic system is based on the philosophy that individual self-interest should be subordinated to the interests of the society as a whole. The government is thought to be the best judge of what constitutes the best interests of the society and, therefore, of its economic objectives. As a consequence, important restrictions may be placed on individual freedom. Consumers may find that their choices of some products, along with the quantities available for purchase, are curtailed when state objectives and consumer objectives are in conflict. The government may give planes higher priority than cooking utensils and may divert aluminum from the production of the latter into the construction of the former. Individuals may not be free to go into the occupations of their choice. Potential nuclear physicists may be diverted toward medicine or some other profession depending upon the number of physicists the government decides should be trained. Workers may not be able to move to the geographic area they desire because the state needs people with their qualifications elsewhere. On the face of it, there appears to be more compulsion by the state and less voluntary action on the part of individuals in the socialistic economy than in the free enterprise system.

Mixed Systems

In practice we find neither the free enterprise nor the socialistic economic system in its pure form. Canada leans heavily towards the free enterprise type of economy, but government regulation, control, and even ownership of production facilities are common. On the other hand, the Soviet Union, while predominantly socialistic, uses the market mechanism to accomplish some of its economic tasks.

In Canada governmental units influence in some way almost one third of the economy's output. Since some government action has the effect of redistributing income, patterns of consumer demand are affected. In addition, regulatory and control activities affect what many industries are able to produce and the prices they can charge. Regulation of railway, commercial air and merchant marine services by the Canadian Transport Commission, and of energy resources by the National Energy Board are examples. Furthermore, the government, having reduced consumer demand through taxes, spends those tax receipts to build roads, buildings, and dams and to provide services such as police protection and national defence, items that individuals might not purchase if they were free to spend the tax dollars directly.

In the Soviet Union almost all production facilities are state owned and operated. Workers are paid wages, however, and differentials have been established between professional and manual workers as well as between the skilled and the unskilled in order to provide incentives for developing labour potential. These measures, however, are supplementary to others taken in order to ensure that supplies of different kinds of labour are developed as the state desires. Goods are sold in state-owned stores at set prices, but the prices are controlled by the state and so do not perform the function of reflecting how consumers value different goods and services relatively. It has recently been proposed in the Soviet Union, notably by an economist by the name of Liberman, that production units should be given some form of profit motive in order to stimulate efficiency.[1]

A Model of a Free Enterprise System

In this section we shall develop a highly simplified model of a free enterprise system. Its purpose is to identify the main operating units of such an economic system and to explain how they interact. Hopefully it serves as an introduction to economic analysis. However, the model presented here is not intended to provide a complete explanation of how the economy works. Indeed, it does not take into account an important factor in the operation of a free enterprise system—the government—but rather embraces the private sector of the economy only.

Classification of Economic Units

There are two groups of economic units that interact or engage in economic activity. These are households on the one hand and business enterprises on the other. Both are familiar concepts. *Households* consist either of family units or of unattached individuals who do not live with families. *Business enterprises* include individual proprietorships, partnerships, corporations and cooperatives.

Since everyone in the economy belongs to some household unit, households play two roles in economic activity: (1) they are the consumers of the economy's output—its food, automobiles, houses, barbers' services, and books; and (2) they are the owners of the economy's resources—its labour and its capital. Much of the economy's capital is owned by corporations, but these are in turn owned by households, so that the entire available supply of capital is owned either directly or indirectly by households.

[1]*See* Time, *Vol. 85, February 12, 1965, pp. 23-29.*

Business enterprises are the units that carry on the production of goods and services at all levels and stages. They include the family farm, the supermarket, and companies turning out sophisticated computers or electronic devices. The production processes carried on by business enterprises consist of the processing or conversion of resources either into final usable form or into states closer to that form. The economic activity of this group of units includes buying or hiring resources, processing or combining them, and selling the resulting goods and services.

Not all of the economy's population is embraced in the business enterprise group of economic units. Many resource owners prefer not to operate firms but instead to sell or hire out what they own to those who do. Sometimes a household unit is also a business enterprise. A neighbour-

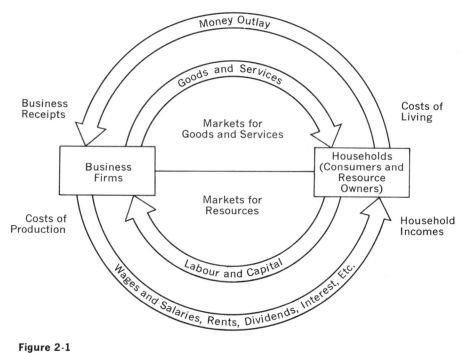

Figure 2-1
The circular flow.

hood grocery store and a family farm are cases in point. But these firms present no analytical difficulties. We simply view their activities as households in the same light as we look at other household units and we analyze their behaviour as business firms in the same way as we analyze other business firms.

Interaction of Economic Units

The well-known circular flow diagram of Figure 2–1 brings the two groups of economic units together and provides a convenient means for exploring the interaction that takes place between them. Consumer groups are represented by the box on the right and business firms by the one on the left. Resources or resource services flow from households to business firms and are converted into consumer goods and services.[2] Goods and services then flow to households in their role as consumers. As consumers pay for the goods and services purchased, a money flow is established in the opposite direction—toward business firms. The money flow continues around the circle from business firms to households as the former pay for the resources they use in the production of goods and services. Thus a physical flow of resources, goods, and services moves around the circle in one direction while a money flow moves around it the other way.

The money flow takes on different but closely related aspects at different points in the circle. As it is paid out by consumers for goods and services it is *costs of living*. As it reaches business firms the same flow becomes *business receipts*. Business receipts are paid to resource owners for the use of labour and capital in production. After materials, labour, and other operating costs are met, whatever is left of business receipts goes to the owners of enterprises in payment for the use of their physical plant and equipment. The money flow as it is paid out by business firms represents *costs of production*. When households receive it the same flow becomes *household incomes*, or what consumers have available to spend.

The Two Sets of Markets

Households and business enterprises interact in markets or places of exchange. These can be separated into two categories: (1) markets for goods and services, represented by the upper half of Figure 2–1, and (2) market for resources, represented by the lower half.

In the consumer goods market the physical flow of goods and services is linked to the opposite flow of money by prices. Prices of goods depend on the amounts that consumers are willing to spend for the goods and the quantities available for purchase. Suppose that 1000 identical auto-

---

[2]*In the interests of simplicity we shall ignore the possibility that some resources may be used to produce net additions to the economy's stock capital. In technical language we are working with a* stationary economy *in which productive capacity neither increases nor decreases.*

mobiles are sold and that a total of $3 million is spent for the entire lot. The average price per automobile obviously must be $3000. If more were spent—say, $4 million—the average price would be $4000. If only $2 million were spent, the average price would be $2000.

If we extend the analysis to cover all goods and services sold and all purchasing power spent for them, several simple but important propositions emerge. The total value of goods and services flowing from business firms to households must equal the money flow going in the opposite direction. If the money flow rises, that is, if households increase their rates of spending, but the physical volume of goods and services sold does not, then prices must rise. A decrease in household spending with no change in the physical volume of sales means that prices must fall. On the other hand, if the money flow is constant while the physical volume of goods and services declines, prices must rise, whereas if the volume of goods and services increases, prices must fall.

The same relations hold in resource markets. The flow of resources and their services to business firms is linked to the reverse flow of money by resource prices, although we seldom talk in terms of the "price" of resources. Generally we refer to the price of labour as *wages*. *Dividends* are prices paid to corporation stockholders for the complex of resources that they permit the corporation to use. *Interest* is the price paid for borrowing funds used by businesses to invest in capital equipment. In many instances when a firm uses resources that it does not purchase, for example, land and buildings, the prices for their use are called *rents*. But whatever name we give to the prices of different resources, a change in the spending of business firms on given quantities of resources will cause price changes to occur in the same direction as the change in spending. Given the total spending of business firms on resources, decreases in the quantities of resources made available will increase their prices while increases in the quantities will decrease their prices.

An Application of the Model

There are many uses to which the foregoing model can be put. Let us apply it to the problem of economic instability. As a starting point, suppose that the money flow around the circle is constant—that consumer outlays or cost of living are equal to consumer incomes and that business outlays or costs of production are equal to business receipts. Suppose also that initially the flow of goods and services from firms to households and the flow of resources and resource services from households to firms are constant. These conditions mean that average price levels are constant also.

What happens if the public develops a depression psychosis? Fear of depression induces people to save money for anticipated hard times ahead. In addition, if people believe that prices are going to fall in the near future, they will spend as little as possible at present prices, postponing purchases to the anticipated future period of lower prices. The reduction in household spending is a reduction in the money flow from households to business firms. Firms find their sales volumes lagging and inventories of goods building up. They reduce prices in order to limit the reductions in volume and the inventory build ups. Thus far, then, we find that a fear of depression reduces total household spending, which in turn reduces the volume of goods sold and the prices received for these goods.

When we turn to business firms we discover that since sales volume and business receipts have fallen, businesses desire to contract production. Since the promise of profits has faded and the funds available for obtaining resources have declined, firms want smaller quantities of resources.

Households now find that some of the resources they own are unemployed, so they reduce asking prices in order to limit the magnitude of unemployment. Some unemployment, coupled with lower resource prices, means that consumer incomes are decreased. Consumer spending is likely to be further reduced, and the decline in economic activity may become progressively worse.

The downward movement may eventually be halted and reversed, however. Suppose that the public, and particularly business enterprises, begin to feel more optimistic about the future of the economy. Businesses may then decide to expand production of goods and services. Since expansion requires higher levels of resource use, there may be some slight increase in resource prices as firms attempt to attract larger quantities of resources. However, if unemployment is serious, employment opportunities alone may be sufficient to put larger quantities back in production. In any case, the increased expenditures of firms generate higher consumer incomes, thus providing incentives for households as consumers to increase their spending on goods and services. Prices tend to rise, as does the volume of goods purchased. Greater spending by consumers means larger receipts for businesses, which in turn spark expansion of production and increased business expenditures on resources. Progressive expansion of economic activity occurs in much the same way as progressive contraction.

A special situation may develop in which increases in spending are reflected solely in price increases with no expansion in resource employment or in the output of goods and services. Suppose, for example, that

economic activity has expanded to the point at which all available resources are employed. Further increases in consumer spending on goods
and services can serve only to raise prices, since it is not possible to increase the quantities of goods available. Similarly, since further increases
in business spending cannot increase the quanties of resources available,
the prices of resources are driven higher.

Micro- and Macroeconomics

The circular flow model is useful in distinguishing between the two
main branches of economic theory: (1) *microeconomics,* or price and allocation theory, and (2) *macroeconomics,* or national income analysis. Both
are used extensively in the areas of study into which economics has traditionally been divided—money and banking, public finance, international
trade, economic development, industrial organization, manpower economics—the precise division depending upon who is doing the dividing.

Microeconomics, as the name implies, is concerned with parts of the
economy rather than with the economy as a whole. It is the economics of
individual units, households and business firms, as they carry on their
activities in the two sets of markets. The pricing and output of the goods
and services that make up the flow from firms to households are also the
concern of microeconomics, as are the pricing and employment of each
of the many resources that constitute the flow from households to firms.

Macroeconomics, on the other hand, examines the economic system
as a whole rather than in terms of individual economic units or specific
products, resources, and prices. As such, it is the aggregate flows in
Figure 2–1 that are important rather than the items that make up each
flow. Macroeconomics is particularly concerned with problems of
economic stability—with the causes and control of depression and
inflation—and is relevant to the aggregate level of employment. It is
concerned also with problems of economic growth and development.

Summary

All economies must perform three basic functions: (1) determine what
goods and services are to be produced and their priority; (2) organize
production; and (3) distribute the goods and services through some sort
of sharing arrangement. In the world today two methods are used to

perform these functions. One is the private approach while the other is the state-planned approach.

The private approach utilizes the price system and the profit motive to guide economic activity. The system works automatically, though not perfectly, as individual economic units engage in economic activity, trying to make the most of what they have. The Canadian and U.S. economies best illustrate the use of the private approach.

The state-planned approach is based on governmental decision-making. The system does not work automatically but requires detailed planning and coordination by a great many individuals and groups throughout the economy. A price system may be used to some extent to assist in the planning and organizing process. The Soviet Union and the socialist countries of Eastern Europe provide examples of the state-planned approach.

The private approach is that of a free enterprise type of economic system. Such a system rests on the institution of private property and accomplishes its ends through voluntary exchange and cooperation. It places a high value on individual freedom and employs self-interest as its primary motivating force.

The state-planned approach is that of a socialistic economy. In this system the government owns the capital resources of the economy, controls labour, and owns and operates its business enterprises. Rather than individual self-interest, the interests of society as a whole as the government conceives them are paramount.

In a simple circular flow model of a free enterprise economy, leaving the government out of account, economic units can be classified into two groups, households and business firms. A flow of resources and their services moves from households as resource owners to business firms. At this point resources are made into goods and services that then flow from firms to households as consumers. A flow of money moves in the opposite direction. The two flows are linked together by prices as households and business firms interact in markets for goods and services and in markets for resources. The model can be used to present a highly simplified analysis of economic instability and is also helpful in distinguishing between micro- and macroeconomics, the two main facets of economic theory.

Exercises and Questions for Discussion

1. What are some industries in Canada in which the government determines prices and organizes production?
2. Explain how the Canadian government redistributes income through progressive taxation, free primary and secondary education, the Agricultural Stabilization Act, and the Medical Care Act.

3. Classify each of the following situations as a micro- or a macroeconomic problem. explaining your answer in each case.
   a. The Ford dealer in your city sets a price on a Galaxie 500.
   b. The ABC Canning Company decides to lay off 1200 men during the winter slowdown in business.
   c. Uncle Harry debates whether or not to install a modern meat counter in his corner grocery store.
   d. The Bank of Canada decides to tighten credit.
4. How would a surtax of 10 percent on personal incomes affect the circular flow?
5. Who runs a free enterprise type of economic system?

Selected Readings

Boulding, Kenneth E., *Economic Analysis*, Vol. 1, *Microeconomics*. New York: Harper & Row, Publishers, Inc., 1966, Chap. 2.

Heilbroner, Robert L., *The Worldly Philosophers*, rev. ed. New York: Simon and Schuster, 1961, Chap. 2.

Lange, Oskar, and Fred M. Taylor, *On the Economic Theory of Socialism*, B. E. Lippincott, (ed.). Minneapolis: University of Minnesota Press, 1938.

Smith, Adam, *An Inquiry into the Nature and Causes of the Wealth of Nations*. New York: Random House, Inc., Modern Library edition. Book 1, Chap. 2.

Turgeon, Lynn, *The Contrasting Economics*, 2d ed. Boston: Allyn and Bacon, Inc., 1969.

3

Business Firms

Since business firms play a major role in the economic activity of a free enterprise economy, we must at this point examine the nature and functions of these institutions. What part do business firms play in overall patterns of economic activity? What is their organizational structure? What is the current business firm population in Canada? What is the general health of business firms in Canada as measured by the rate of failure? What are the broad underlying causes of business failure? What role do publicly-owned corporations play in the Canadian economy? What is the extent to which Canadian corporations are externally controlled? These are the questions considered in this chapter.

Economic Activity of Business Firms

In the preceding chapter we introduced business firms as the production units of the economy. But what does this mean? What constitutes production? The primary objective of economic activity is to satisfy man's wants as fully as possible from the limited means available—from the resources of the economy and from its usable technology. Production refers to any activity that moves or transforms resources from their current places or forms to places or forms that are either closer to the satisfying of wants or that make them more useful in accomplishing this objective. Schematically, production is often thought of in terms of using technology to transform resources into finished goods. With some refinements this conceptualization is essentially correct. When we think of an individual business firm we are usually considering only one link in a long chain of production processes, each of which brings raw and semi-finished materials closer to their ultimate users. But production for the economy as a whole is not complete until what is being produced is actually in the hands of its ultimate user. We call the outputs of processes farther removed from the ultimate consumer *lower-order goods and services* and those that are closer *higher-order goods and services.*

The extractive activities in the economy provide examples of firms producing lower-order outputs. Firms engaged in mining crude oil, iron and copper ore, lead, and zinc are typical, as are those engaged in agricultural pursuits. Most such outputs require further processing before they are ready to be consumed.

At the other extreme, retail stores produce higher-order outputs. Some people have difficulty thinking of a retail store as engaging in production at all, but its activity is fundamentally the same as that of a manufacturing firm. The resources it uses are items not yet accessible to the final user, and these include inventories in the hands of wholesalers and manufacturers, labour, and buildings and equipment. These resources are utilized to put products where they are accessible to consumers; that is, to complete the production process.

Between these extremes are firms operating at many different levels of production. Basic steel firms use iron ore and other resources to make steel ingots, which may be sold to processing firms and steel frabricators to be converted into forms useful in making many different products. Milling companies turn wheat into flour, cereal, feed for livestock, and other items that are further processed before being sold to consumers. The outputs of a great many firms are the resource inputs of a number of other firms as lower-order goods go through the many production processes necessary to make them useful to consumers.

Profit expectations provide the primary incentive for establishing and expanding business firms. Firms are born and flourish in areas where revenues from the sale of goods and services exceed the costs of all resources used in producing them. Where losses occur, that is, where revenues are less than the costs of all resources used, firms contract and die. The profit incentive may be tempered or supplemented by other incentives—the safety of diversification into several product fields, the desire to obtain a large sales volume, the prestige of ownership of a business, and others—but firms will not remain in areas where losses persist over long periods of time.

Forms of Business Firms

With respect to legal organization, there are four major types of profit-seeking firms in Canada: (1) the sole proprietorship, (2) the partnership, (3) the corporation, and (4) the co-operative. There are, of course, non-profit-seeking organizations that use resources to provide goods and services. These include religious, charitable, philanthropic, scientific, and educational institutions. This chapter focuses on the former, but it should be kept in mind that the latter exist also, frequently in the same four legal forms.

The Sole Proprietorship

Sole proprietorships are individually owned business firms. Many grocery stores, restaurants, gas stations, barber shops, doctors' offices, and farms are in this category. One individual owns most of the capital resources of such a business—its building, equipment, and inventories of goods in process—although lease or rental arrangements may be made for some. Usually the proprietor operates the business as well. As one of four alternative forms of organization, the sole proprietorship has its pros and cons.

The Pros

The most common reason for a businessman to choose the sole proprietorship form of organization is the *ease with which it can be established*. What does it take to establish a farm? Usually all that is required is a decision to do so plus the means of financing the minimum amount of capital resources necessary to get started. For a grocery store no more is required. Some entrepreneurs (e.g., tavern and cabaret owners) must have in addition a license or permit in order to set themselves up in business, although this requirement holds as well if the business is a partnership or corporation.

Proprietors have greater *freedom and flexibility* in making a wide variety of decisions than the managers of other forms of business organizations simply because there is no one other than themselves to whom they are accountable for their actions. The proprietor is free to switch from one line of business to another. He can withdraw money from the business for his personal use or he can invest more money in the business as he desires.

The Cons

The most important restraints placed on a sole proprietor are (1) his limited access to funds for investing in the business and carrying on its operations and (2) his inability to separate his business assets from his personal assets for liability purposes. A sole proprietor about to get a good thing going may find that he has *difficulties in securing funds* to convert his dreams into reality. To set up a business in the first place he must have money available to purchase the minimum amounts of capital resources —land, buildings, and equipment—necessary to operate. If he wants to expand the business, still more money is needed, both to increase his productive capacity and to pay the additional costs of operating at higher levels of output. He has access to two types of financing: (1) equity financing and (2) debt financing.

Equity financing refers to the financing of a business through the acquisition of ownership interests in it. The owner uses whatever savings he may have to purchase his plant and equipment and to operate it. Over time, if the business does well, some of the profits, or the excess of receipts over the costs of all resources used in the production process, can be used to finance expansion. The limitation on the equity financing available to the proprietor is set by the extent of his personal assets or his personal fortune.

Debt financing refers to funds that the owner of the business borrows. A single proprietor may go to a commercial bank, to the federal Industrial Development Bank, or to some other type of lending institution, but the amount that he can borrow will depend upon the lending institution's evaluation of him and his business prospects. Most proprietors are not able to obtain money in the way of long-term loans simply because their long-term prospects are uncertain.[1] Thus borrowing by proprietorships is largely in the form of short-term loans to carry on current operations, for example, to finance inventories.

Debt financing of a slightly different sort may be used also in carrying on current business operations. The proprietor of a grocery store may purchase canned goods on credit from a wholesaler, agreeing to make payment in 30, 60, or 90 days, depending upon the terms of the agreement. Short-term credit of this kind can be quite important for sole proprietors, but it may be largely offset by credit that the proprietor in turn extends to his customers.

---

[1] *A sole proprietorship lacks permanence because it ends with the financial, mental, or physical death of the owner. This is a serious defect in obtaining long-term credit as it may be impossible to sell the firm for anything near the amount it was previously worth as a going concern.*

Unlimited liability of the proprietor for debts of the business constitutes the second disadvantage of the sole proprietorship. The proprietor cannot separate claims by creditors upon his business from their claims on his personal belongings. If the proprietor does not pay his business debts, his creditors can legally attach not only his business property but also such personal property as his house and his automobile up to the extent of their claims. This creditors' weapon is double-barrelled. If the proprietor's wife runs up personal debts for mink coats, jewellery, and the like, her creditors can attach the business property. All provinces provide some relief for the debtor, however, by specifying a minimum value of property that is not subject to attachment.

The Partnership

As defined by the Partnership Act, a statute originally passed in 1890 by the British Parliament and subsequently adopted in all the provinces of Canada except Quebec, a partnership is "The relation which subsists between persons carrying on business in common, with a view to profit". Carrying on business in common means that the assets of the business are owned by the partners as a group rather than by the individual partners; one partner cannot pick out which specific assets are his and which belong to the other(s). Similarly, business liabilities are group liabilities. Operation of the business for profit means that this is the objective of the group, even though losses may in fact be incurred. Though somewhat more complex, the characteristics of the partnership are similar to those of the sole proprietorship.

The Pros

The partnership is also born easily, since its existence does not require approval by any governmental unit. Only an agreement among the partners is necessary. This may be written or oral; in fact, it may even be inferred from the activities of persons carrying on some business activity jointly. A written agreement drawn up by a lawyer is ordinarily used, since it provides some measure of protection to each partner from the others. Among other things, it spells out what each partner is to put into the business in the form of money, managerial effort, or capital goods, and it usually specifies the ratio in which profits or losses are to be shared as well as the distribution of business assets in the event of dissolution. If the agreement has been properly drawn up and one or more partners fail to live up to their specified obligations, the others can sue. Apart from such agreement, provincial and territorial laws require that partnerships must be registered with the appropriate authorities. Registration consists in filing a declaration containing the names of the partners, the firm name and the time during which the partnership has subsisted, and stating that the persons therein named are the only members of the partnership.

Another advantage of the partnership is that *it lends itself more to specialization of talents* than does the sole proprietorship. Partnerships are often formed to take advantage of complementary skills. A medical partnership may be formed by an obstetrician and a pediatrician; a legal partnership may include a skilled trial lawyer and one whose specialty is contracts and negotiable instruments; an accounting partnership may be formed by an accountant who directs the office work and a non-accountant with good public contacts. A partnership, taking advantage of complementary fields of specialization, may prosper where any one of the partners working alone would fare badly.

Compared with the single ownership, the partnership *permits enlarging the scale of operations* because it is able to draw on the financial resources of more than one person.[2]

The Cons

One of the most serious drawbacks to the partnership is *unlimited liability* of each partner for the debts of the firm. If a partner cannot meet his share of the obligations of the business, the remaining partner(s) are personally liable for the business debts. As in the case of the sole proprietorship, the personal property of any one co-owner can be attached by creditors to satisfy their claims against the business. Partners that are obliged to meet partnership debts from their personal assets have a right to recover from those members who have not borne their agreed share of the liability, but this in no way diminishes their individual responsibilities to creditors.[3]

---

[2]*It is worth noting here that four provinces limit the number of partners that a firm can admit. In Newfoundland, no unincorporated enterprise may have more than 10 members or partners. In Alberta, British Columbia and Saskatchewan, a firm must be incorporated if it consists of more than 20 persons in business for profit.*

[3]*Most provinces provide for "limited partnerships" which protect one or more of the partners from the unlimited liability feature of general partnership. A limited partnership is composed of one or more general partners who manage the business and have unlimited liability, and one or more persons, called special or limited partners, who contribute an amount in actual cash for the duration of the partnership, who take no part in the management or control of the business, and who are liable to the firm or to its creditors only to the extent of the capital they have agreed to contribute.*

Closely related to the unlimited liability principle is the *agency rule* of partnerships. In the general type of partnership arrangement, any one of the partners may act in the name of the firm, committing the firm to those actions. The firm is bound even though the partner acts without the consent of the others and even though the action is outside the area assigned to him by the partnership agreement. This statement should be qualified. If it has been agreed by the partners that certain restrictions shall be placed on the authority of any one or more of them to commit the firm, no act done in breach of the agreement is legally binding on the partnership with respect to persons having notice of the agreement.

Another weakness of the partnership form of organization is the fact that if a partner dies or wishes to withdraw from the firm, the remaining partners must either find someone else to take his place or purchase his share. Many times the death or retirement of a partner will seriously disrupt the affairs of an enterprise, especially if it is growing rapidly and is in need of all the capital and managing ability it can muster.

Partnerships encounter much the same kinds of *financing limitations* as sole proprietorships, although the partnership has an advantage in equity financing in that there are more co-owners to provide it. Debt financing, too, may be easier, since creditors know that they will have recourse to more than one individual should the firm default on its payments. Nevertheless, limits are set by the personal assets of the partners and by the fact that a dissolution of the partnership could occur at any time. An understandable reluctance to grow by taking in more partners arises in the business from the unlimited liability principle and from the doctrine of mutual agency.

The Corporation

Most large business enterprises are organized as corporations. A corporation can be thought of as an entity separate and apart from the individuals who own it. From a legal point of view in many ways it functtions like a person. It can contract debts or extend credit in its own name; it can hold title to property; it can be taxed; and it can sue and be sued. Since a corporation is a collective entity, not a single individual, it enjoys certain immunities that individuals do not. It cannot commit murder or treason. (As Pope Innocent IV explained, a corporation cannot be excommunicated because it lacks a soul.) It can act only through its members or through the directors and officers who manage its affairs. Let us now consider what makes this organizational form so attractive for large enterprises.

The Pros

One advantage of the corporation is that *ownership of the business can be transferred* among individuals independently of the life and operation of the business. When ownership of a sole proprietorship or any part of a partnership changes hands, the old business ceases to exist and a new one is established. Frequently the death of an owner will result in the liquidation of the assets of the firm. On the other hand, if one buys a share of Algoma Steel Corporation stock he becomes a part owner of the firm. The purchase of the share does not affect business operations and neither does its sale. Every stock market transaction is a transfer of ownership, and to a large extent the impact on business operations of the firms involved is either negligible or slight, since the stock purchased or sold is a small proportion of the total amount outstanding for any one firm. Stockholders do, however, elect boards of directors, and these in turn appoint the corporate officers. Obviously, the transfer of a large enough block of stock of a corporation can change the composition of management and the course of business operations, but the continuity of the firm's business —its legal obligations to others and their obligations to it—is unaffected.

Another attractive feature of the corporate form of business is the *limited liability* of owners for business debts. If the corporation's gross income is not sufficient to meet its expenses and its debt obligations, the most that a stockholder can lose is what he has invested in his stock. Business creditors have no claim on the personal assets of any owner. They can force the firm into bankruptcy and divide the proceeds from the sale of its assets, but this is as far as they can go. The corporate structure is an effective device for insulating any one owner from the actions of other owners or of management.

Corporations also possess a greater *capacity for obtaining financial backing* than do proprietorships and partnerships. Equity financing is accomplished partly through the sale of stock. Debt financing can come from loans to the corporation, credit extended to it, or the sale of the corporation's bonds. The ease with which shares of stock can be transferred and the limited liability of stockholders makes incorporation an attractive way of bringing together equity funds to start a business or to expand it. The firm can have a very large number of stockholders—Bell Telephone of Canada has over two hundred thousand—and the holdings of each can be almost as large or as small as the individual desires. It is not at all difficult for a successful company to issue and sell additional shares of stock to obtain money for expansion.

Corporations frequently use retained earnings to finance expansion; this too is a form of equity financing. After a firm has paid all of its expenses—costs of resources hired or purchased from others—whatever remains from its total receipts belongs to its owners. A corporation may pay all of these net earnings to stockholders as dividends, or it may elect to pay out a part of them only, holding the rest as retained earnings. If it follows the latter course, retained earnings may be used to finance expansion of the firm. Since these earnings really belong to the stockholders, their use for this purpose can legitimately be thought of as equity financing.

The corporation can also use debt financing to a greater extent than either proprietorship or the partnership. It has special capacities for obtaining loans from financial institutions and issuing and selling bonds. The greater stability of the corporation, arising out of its ownership structures and its equity-financing capabilities, makes it a better risk on the average and enables it to borrow more easily from banks or other institutions.

Bond sales provide an important source of borrowing for corporations. A *bond* is a promise to pay to its purchaser at the end of a stated period of time a certain sum of money, with interest to be paid on the sum at regular intervals. The purchaser of the bond is in effect making a long-term loan to the corporation. When the bond reaches its maturity date and is paid off, the debt of the corporation is, of course, cancelled.

The Cons

The corporation is *more difficult to set up* than the proprietorship or the partnership, but this frequently cited disadvantage should not be overemphasized. Governmental approval is required, but it is ordinarily automatic if the proper organizational steps have been completed. In Canada there are 11 general Companies Acts, one for incorporation under federal law and one each for incorporation under provincial law.[4] It may be generally stated that federal charter is usually preferable for a company intending to operate in more than one province. In practice, most corporations come into existence under provincial authority. In such cases the procedure is relatively straightforward. An application for a charter is made to the Provincial Secretary or the Registrar of Companies of the appropriate province by a minimum of three persons intending to incorporate. Among other things, the application contains the name of the corporation, the purposes for which the company is formed, the location of its head office, the amount of stock it is authorized to issue, and the class

---

[4]*Certain types of companies are created by special Act of the Federal Parliament or of the legislature of any one of the provinces. The formation of a public company by special Act is restricted mainly to banks, insurance companies, trust and loan companies, and railways.*

and number of shares to be taken by each applicant and the amount to be paid therefor. Upon approval by the appropriate provincial agency, the application becomes the corporation charter. Stock is issued and the first meeting of the stockholders is held. By-laws for the operation of the corporation are adopted and a board of directors is elected. The directors appoint the corporation officers and the corporation is ready to engage in the economic activities for which it was established. Since the provisions of the charter and of the by-laws can be amended easily, no great handicap is placed on the corporate form of business by legal organizational requirements; the process of organization is just more cumbersome than that for the other forms of businesses.

A more significant disadvantage of the corporation is the *treatment accorded it by tax laws*, both federal and provincial. Corporations pay corporate income taxes on their net earnings. When net earnings are distributed as dividends to stockholders, the latter pay personal income taxes on all dividends received except for a small exemption.[5] The owners of the corporation thus find two tax bites taken out of the income of their business. Proprietorships and partnerships pay no business income tax on their net earnings; rather, net earnings are taxed only as personal income of the owners.[6]

Another alleged disadvantage of the corporation is that *corporate management and corporate ownership are distinct from one another*. The managers may be owners or stockholders, but they typically hold a small minority of total shares outstanding. Thus, if they so desire, the managers can pursue courses of action contrary to that desired by stockholders. To whom is the possibility of separation of ownership and control a disadvantage? It probably plays little part in the initial decision of whether to organize a business as a corporation or as a proprietorship or partnership. In a large enterprise managers may take actions such as paying themselves large bonuses that benefit them at the expense of the stockholders, but by and large both groups are interested in making the firm a profitable enterprise. Much controversy surrounds the issue of ownership versus control, but not much in the way of definitive conclusions have been reached.

---

[5]*Under present Canadian law taxpayers are permitted a credit against personal tax due of 20 percent of dividends received from "taxable Canadian corporations".*

[6]*Much can be said on both sides about the "fairness" or "justice" of so-called double taxation of corporate net income. Most arguments for double taxation maintain that the privileges or advantages of doing business as a corporation justify it. Arguments against it are to the effect that all forms of business enterprise should be accorded the same tax treatment.*

Co-operatives

Legally, the co-operative is organized as a corporation to do business under a corporate name, but it has certain partnership characteristics that differentiate it from an ordinary business corporation.[7] The principal characteristics of a co-operative enterprise are as follows:

1. Common law voting. Each shareholder, or member, has but one vote, regardless of the number of shares he holds in the co-operative. Since every stockholder has an equal voice in determining policy, control is more democratic than in the ordinary business corporation.
2. Limited return on share capital. Each member receives a fixed rate of return on his monetary investment—perhaps 5 percent. The member who put in $50 will receive $2.50 a year on his investment and no more. This means that profits are not distributed to members on the basis of how much each invested in shares.
3. Distribution of net earnings by patronage dividends. In a co-op, profits are distributed to members on the basis of how much business each member transacts with the organization. If the directors elect to pay a 10 percent patronage dividend, member A who did $100 worth of business would be paid $10, whereas member B, whose purchases or sales amounted to $1,000, would get $100. Thus, those who contribute to the success of the concern by their patronage profit in proportion to their contribution.

To this list of principles many co-ops concerned with selling at the retail level add cash trading (because it is more economical) and trading at prevailing prices (in order to avoid a price war with other retailers).

Co-operatives may be classified into two main types on the basis of the kind of business they do. Those organized to sell something *to* their members are called consumers' co-operatives; those which sell something *for* their members are called producers' or marketing co-operatives. In Canada, consumers' co-operatives sell farm supplies (feed, fertilizers, spray materials, gas and oil, machinery, equipment and building materials) and also food products, auto accessories, hardware, clothing and home furnishings and many other consumer goods. Other consumers' associations provide fire, life, automobile, hail, general casualty, fidelity and medical insurance, electricity, housing and other services including water, transportation, telephone, cold storage and seed cleaning. Credit unions and

[7]*Nearly all Canadian co-operatives are organized under provincial law. There is not yet any general federal legislation for incorporation of co-operatives. However, a few co-operative concerns that operate in more than one province have been formed under the Canada Corporations Act, or special Act of Parliament.*

caisses populaires are a special class of consumers' co-operatives. Such associations enable groups of individuals with a common alliance (the parish, the place of employment, etc.) to combine their savings and thereby provide loan funds to members of the organization for good purposes at relatively low interest rates. Today credit unions and *caisses populaires* have more members and more assets than all other types of co-operatives added together. At the end of 1968, there were 4,663 credit unions and *caisses populaires*, with 3,953,200 members and total assets of $3.7 billion. It is also interesting to note that one out of every four Canadians is a member of a credit union or *caisse populaire*, and more than 10 percent of all consumer credit flows through such co-operative societies.

Producers' co-operatives are usually organized for the purpose of marketing primary products. In Canada co-ops are extensively used in the marketing of grains and seeds, dairy products, livestock and products, poultry and eggs, fruits and vegetables and fish. About one-third of all agricultural products sold commercially in Canada are sold through co-operative marketing associations. In dollar volume of business, the western grain elevator companies greatly exceed all other Canadian marketing co-operatives. Also deserving of mention is the fact that sometimes these marketing associations play a dual role and serve the needs of their members not only as producers but likewise as consumers. Farm supplies generally account for the greater part of Canadian co-operative purchases.

The Pros

Advocates of co-operatives maintain that wherever there are private concerns making monopoly profits the co-operative form of business organization *can obtain more favourable prices* for its members, whether they are producers or consumers. Also, this type of organization *permits large-scale operation* while preserving democratic control. A further advantage is that earnings paid out to members in the form of *patronage dividends are not subject to the corporation income tax.*

The Cons

The greatest weakness of the co-operative concern is the *difficulty it faces in raising large amounts of capital* in formation and in expansion. It cannot attract financial investors as an ordinary business corporation can. As a consequence, the co-op must rely on retained earnings the sale of shares to new members, and on loans from other co-operative ventures.

A potential drawback of this form of organization is that *management may not have sufficient control* to assure the success of the enterprise as a commercial business. Since the organizers of co-operatives frequently include people who are more interested in social reform than in financial gain, this makes it hard to follow policies which economic efficiency demands.

Importance of Business Forms

Having described the four major types of business organizations, let us now compare them with respect to their impact upon employment provided and business transacted. The census figures for 1961, shown in Table 3–1, reveal that in that year slightly more than one-half of all manufacturing establishments were organized as corporations. As for the other half, 34.4 percent were proprietorships, and 9.4 percent used the partnership. Other forms were but little used. What is more significant is that corporations employed 94.4 percent of all the production workers and produced 96 percent of the total value of products in the manufacturing industry.

TABLE 3–1
Relative Importance of Organizational Forms, 1961 Manufacturing Establishments

	Establishments		Employees		Sales (Millions of Dollars)	
	Number	Percent	Number	Percent	Amount	Percent
Proprietorships	11,160	34.4	38,210	2.9	425	1.7
Partnerships	3,058	9.4	20,195	1.6	231	1.0
Corporations	17,439	54.0	1,225,535	94.4	23,221	96.0
Co-operatives	758	2.2	13,862	1.1	366	1.3
Other forms*	—	—	—	—		
Total	32,415	100.0	1,297,802	100.0	24,243	100.0

Refers to charitable, religious, philanthropic, scientific and educational institutions.
Source; Based on Canada Census data for 1961.

In merchandising, the corporation also dominates the wholesale field, as shown in Table 3–2. While 52.3 percent of the number of wholesale establishments in 1961 were corporations, they enjoyed 77.7 percent of the total sales and accounted for 84.2 percent of the employees.

In the retail field, the sole proprietorship is the most important form of business organization insofar as the number of units is concerned with 72.4 percent of the total, but corporation units show the greatest volume

TABLE 3-2
Wholesale Establishments

	Establishments		Employees		Sales (Millions of Dollars)	
	Number	Percent	Number	Percent	Amount	Percent
Proprietorships	11,642	37.7	21,373	8.9	2,079	10.7
Partnerships	1,942	6.3	6,609	2.6	652	3.3
Corporations	16,136	52.3	201,909	84.2	15,117	77.7
Co-operatives	1,105	3.6	8,803	3.7	791	4.1
Other forms	30	0.1	1,339	0.6	814	4.2
Total	30,855	100.0	240,033	100.0	19,453	100.0

of sales and number of employees, as Table 3–3 reveals. Only 18.1 percent of retail establishments were incorporated, but they hired 67.8 percent of the employees and accounted for 58.5 percent of the total business volume.

TABLE 3-3
Retail Establishments

	Establishments		Employees		Sales (Millions of Dollars)	
	Number	Percent	Number	Percent	Amount	Percent
Proprietorship	110,642	72.4	148,735	25.3	4,964	30.9
Partnership	12,209	8.0	27,897	4.7	995	6.1
Corporations	27,262	18.1	398,010	67.8	9,391	58.5
Co-operatives	849	0.6	5,802	1.0	168	1.0
Other forms	1,294	0.9	6,934	1.2	556	3.5
Total	152,256	100.0	587,378	100.0	16,074	100.0

In the field of "service" enterprises, the individual proprietorship is still pre-eminent in terms of numbers, constituting 74.8 percent of the firms. However, in 1961 incorporated companies took in 50.3 percent of the receipts and employed 55.4 percent of the total labour force.

TABLE 3-4
Service Establishments

	Establishments		Employees		Sales (Millions of Dollars)	
	Number	Percent	Number	Percent	Amount	Percent
Proprietorship	63,543	74.8	96,177	31.2	1,066	35.8
Partnership	8,779	10.4	34,344	11.1	365	12.3
Corporations	11,715	13.8	171,009	55.4	1,500	50.3
Co-operatives	199	0.3	1,649	0.6	15	0.5
Other forms	529	0.7	5,286	1.7	33	1.1
Total	84,760	100.0	308,465	100.0	2,979	100.0

Only in agriculture is the corporation overshadowed by the other organization forms. The agricultural census figures for 1966 indicate that in that year there were 430,522 separate farm operating units in Canada, of which 72 percent were owner-operated; 23 percent were partly owned by the operator and party rented; and only 5 percent were operated by a tenant or manager.

To sum up, while the sole proprietorship still dominates the Canadian scene from the point of view of numbers, the corporation accounts for the greatest part of our production and employment. However, it should be pointed out that the relative importance of the corporate form of organization differs widely as between different industries.

Business Concentration

Although there are thousands of corporate enterprises in Canada, a relatively small number do a large fraction of the business transacted. At the end of 1968 Canada's top 100 industrial corporations, with sales of $25.3 billion and combined earnings of $1.6 billion, accounted for two-fifths of all sales in Canada (excluding merchandising and financial firms) and two-thirds of all earnings; in merchandising, the 11 largest firms made about 40 percent of all store sales; and the 25 largest financial companies, with combined assets of $55 billion, controlled 80 percent of assets held by all financial institutions.[8] The following table lists the 10 largest manufacturing, resource and utility companies in Canada in terms of sales. Separate rankings by assets and earnings are also given. The listing does not include government-owned companies.

The *FP* figures for 1968, shown in Table 3–5, reveal that Imperial Oil Ltd. ranks first in sales, Bell Canada in assets, and International Nickel Co. of Canada in earnings. It is worth noting here that Bell Canada's assets are greater than all except the three largest utilities in the United States and its operating revenues are exceeded only by American Telephone and Telegraph (A.T. & T.). Similarly, Canadian Pacific Railway has larger assets than all except three U.S. transportation companies. Significantly, the number of industrial corporations with sales over the half-billion dollar mark grew from 9 to 14 between 1966 and 1968. Before leaving the industrial front, however, it should be pointed out that some large firms are not members of the "Hundred Largest Club" because they do not publish

[8]*Statistics from* Financial Post, Survey of Large Companies, *1968. See also* Financial Post, *August 2, 1969, pp. 1, 9 and 10.*

TABLE 3-5

Canada's 10 Largest Industrial Companies: Ranked by Sales, Assets and Net Profits, Fiscal Year ending nearest to December 31, 1968

(Millions of Dollars)

Rank by Sales	Sales $	Company	Rank by Assets	Assets $	Rank by Net Income	Net income $
1	1,432[1]	Imperial Oil Ltd.	5	1,397	3	100
2	1,292	Ford Motor Co. of Canada	13	732	10	50
3	1,241	Bell Telephone of Canada	1	3,126	2	115
4	1,081	Alcan Aluminium Ltd.	3	1,954	4	71
5	925[2]	Canadian Pacific Railway Co.	2	2,155	6	61
6	917	Massey-Ferguson Ltd.	7	940	17	28
7	823	Int'l Nickel Company of Canada	4	1,497	1	154
8	789	Canada Packers Ltd.	55	164	48	8
9	730	George Weston Ltd.	24	397	20	23
10	622[1]	Shell Canada Ltd.	10	802	8	54

[1]*Excise Taxes excluded.* [2]*Estimate.*
Source: Financial Post, *August 2, 1969, p. 9.*

financial statements and reliable estimates are not available. These firms are mostly wholly owned subsidiaries of U.S. and other foreign companies —such as General Motors of Canada Ltd., Chrysler Canada Ltd., American Motors (Canada) Ltd., Canadian International Paper Co. and Canadian Johns-Manville Co. These five firms would undoubtedly rank among the industrial giants. As partial evidence of this, while Ford Motor Co. of Canada ranked second in sales, as shown in Table 3–5, the largest producer of automobiles in this country is General Motors of Canada. Some other very large corporations are excluded from the 100-largest group because almost all their operations and assets are outside Canada. These include Brascan Ltd. (formerly called Brazilian Light & Power Co.), Mexican Light & Power Co., Canadian International Power Co., and Seven Arts Productions Ltd.

Table 3–6 compares Canada's 10 largest merchandisers according to sales volume. Separate rankings are shown for assets and earnings. The list does not include the vast T. Eaton Co., which, since it is privately owned, does not disclose its financial position. According to the *Financial Post*, its sales in 1968 probably were about $900 million, which would put it in second place in terms of store sales.

It is interesting to note that seven Canadian merchandisers would qualify for the *Fortune* magazine directory of the 50 largest U.S. merchandising corporations.

TABLE 3–6

Canada's 10 Largest Merchandisers: Ranked by Sales, Assets and Net Profits, Fiscal Year ending nearest to December 31, 1968

(Millions of Dollars)

Rank by Sales	Sales $	Company	Rank by Assets	Assets $	Rank by Net Income	Net Income $
1	2,434	Loblaw Cos.[1]	1	571	5	10
2	604	Canada Safeway Ltd.	6	150	4	12
3	603	Dominion Stores Ltd.	7	126	6	9
4	541	Simpsons-Sears Ltd.	2	379	2	14
5	480	Steinberg's Ltd.	5	169	8	8
6	453	Hudson's Bay Co.	4	272	1	15
7	389	M. Loeb Ltd.	10	57	10	2
8	291	Oshawa Wholesale Ltd.	9	90	9	5
9	267	Simpsons Ltd.	3	279	3	14
10	258	Woodward Stores Ltd.	8	113	7	8

[1]*Data consolidates U.S. companies Loblaw-Inc. and National Tea Co.*
Source; Financial Post, *August 2, 1969, p. 9.*

In the financial field, the chartered banks dominate the area, as Table 3–7 reveals. In 1968, five banks had about 61 percent of the total assets of Canada's 25 largest financial institutions. Or, to put it another way, their combined assets of $33.5 billion were more than double the whole life insurance industry's Canadian assets of $14.5 billion. Another important point is this: any one of the three largest Canadian banks is bigger than 44 trust companies, including the three largest consolidated trust and mortgage loan firms. Furthermore, Canadian financial corporations compare well with their counterparts in the United States. Ranked by assets,

TABLE 3–7

Canada's 10 Largest Financial Institutions Ranked by Assets Fiscal Year ending nearest to December 31, 1968

(Millions of Dollars)

Rank by Assets	Assets $	Company	Net Income $
1	8,743	Royal Bank of Canada	35
2	8,343	Canadian Imperial Bank of Commerce	33
3	6,818	Bank of Montreal	18
4	5,217	Bank of Nova Scotia	15
5	4,378	Toronto-Dominion Bank	14
6	3,370	Sun Life Assurance Co. of Canada	*
7	1,838	Manufacturers Life Insurance Co.	*
8	1,485	London Life Insurance Co.	*
9	1,411	Banque Canadienne Nationale	5
10	1,387	Great-West Life Assurance Co.	*

*Insurance companies do not report profit figures as such.
Source: Financial Post, *August 2, 1969 p. 10.*

six Canadian insurance companies are as large as those of the 28 largest U.S. insurance firms. Five of our banks rate alongside the 15 biggest U.S. banks. In fact, two Canadian banks are among the top 20 in the world. At the end of 1968, the Royal Bank of Canada and The Canadian Imperial Bank of Commerce were the world's twelfth and eighteenth largest banks.

While credit unions and *caisses populaires* do not appear on the list of Canada's top 25 financial companies, their collective importance is evidenced by the assets represented by some of the regional associations. For example, the 1,300 *caisses* which make up La Fédération de Québec des Unions Régionales de Caisses Populaires have assets of $1,750 million. Similarly, the 1,500 credit unions which constitute the Ontario Credit Union League Ltd. have combined assets of $750 million.

Against this background, it is clear that the Canadian economy is well equipped to take advantage of modern large-scale production. However, many Canadians are worried about the implications of big business and business concentration for the operation of a market economy. Does bigness imply, for example, the existence of significant monopoly power? How big must firms in particular industries be in order to be able to produce efficiently? Can we have the efficiency we desire without at the same time generating adverse monopoly power? These are some of the questions for which we will be seeking answers in the chapters that follow.

Foreign Ownership and Control of Canadian Industry

No other characteristic of our economy has stirred as much controversy as the large degree of control exercised by foreign business firms—particularly by United States corporations—over certain key sectors of Canadian industry and commerce. Available information for 1963, presented in Table 3–8, indicates that 54 percent of the capital (long term debt plus shareholders' equity) employed in the Canadian manufacturing industry was owned by non-residents, of which 44 percent was owned in the United States. In the field of petroleum and natural gas, non-resident and U.S. ownership were 64 and 54 percent respectively, while in mining and smelting they were 62 and 54 percent respectively. Turning back to the manufacturing sector, non-resident ownership represented 91 percent of the automobile and parts industry, 87 percent of the rubber industry and 70 percent of the electrical apparatus industry. In each case the whole, or virtually the whole, of foreign ownership was American.

Corresponding figures measuring foreign control of Canadian industry indicate that 60 percent of the manufacturing sector as a whole in 1963 was controlled by non-residents, of which 46 percent was subject to U.S. direction.[9] Non-resident and U.S. control of the petroleum and natural gas industry were 74 and 62 percent respectively, whereas in mining and smelting they rere 59 and 52 percent respectively. Additionally, 97 percent of the total amount of capital invested in rubber and automobiles and parts was subject to foreign control, as was 78 percent in transportation equipment and chemicals and 77 percent in electrical apparatus.

TABLE 3–8
Ownership and Control of Selected Canadian Industries, December 31, 1963

Enterprise classification	Percentage of capital employed owned in				Percentage of capital employed controlled in		
	Canada	U.S.A.	U.K.	other	Canada	U.S.A.	other
Manufacturing							
Beverages	74	23	2	1	83	17	—
Rubber	13	81	6	—	3	90	7
Textiles	80	14	6	—	80	13	7
Pulp and paper	48	44	7	1	53	35	12
Agricultural machinery	51	46	1	2	50	50	—
Automobile and parts	9	91	—	—	3	97	—
Transportation equipment	41	25	34	—	22	33	45
Iron and steel mills	80	8	7	5	86	2	12
Electrical apparatus	30	62	5	3	23	66	11
Chemicals	37	47	13	3	22	54	24
Other	41	47	8	4	30	54	16
Sub totals	46	44	8	2	40	46	14
Petroleum and natural gas	36	54	5	5	26	62	12
Mining and smelting	38	54	4	4	41	52	7
Totals of above industries	41	48	7	4	36	52	12

Source, Dominion Bureau of Statistics. The Canadian Balance of International Payments 1963, 1964 and 1965 and International Investment Position, *August, 1967, p. 128.*

The general nature of the controversy about the international firm is suggested by the following comments:

1. "Many direct investment firms[10] in Canada, it is claimed, are run simply as extensions of the United States market, in contrast with overseas affiliates of the parent. Therefore, the opportunities for Canadians to secure positions among senior management and on boards of directors

[9]*In general a business firm is considered to be foreign controlled if 50 percent or more of its voting shares are known to be held in one country outside of Canada. Foreign controlled enterprises include unincorporated branches of foreign corporations operating in Canada, wholly or partially-owned Canadian subsidiaries of foreign corporations, and Canadian private or public companies which have no parent concern but whose stock ownership is held substantially in a country other than Canada.*

[10]*A direct investment company is either an unincorporated branch owned by non-residents, or a concern incorporated in Canada in which the effective control of voting stock is held, or believed to be held, by non-residents.*

are limited. The consequences of these two points are to limit the development of Canadian managerial resources, to ensure that resident managers from parent companies make decisions in the interests of the international firm, and regardless of the nationality of the managers, to limit greatly the range of decision-making permitted to them.

2. Except for firms established to supply raw materials and partly finished goods to the parent, direct investment companies are often not allowed to export, or can export only to markets where imperial preferences are available ... The result is to prevent exports which are either economically feasible or which could be if the subsidiaries were given the right to seek and develop foreign markets.

3. The development of Canadian production and of service industries is limited (whether within or outside the subsidiary) because of limitations on the sources from which the subsidiary may buy, and particularly because of requirements to buy parts, equipment, and services from the parent and its affiliates abroad or from their foreign suppliers.

4. The centralization of research and development facilities in the parent abroad, and the control over the size and purpose of such facilities in Canada, inhibit the development of this important expenditure in Canada, further restrict the sales potential of the subsidiary, and limit the development of technical and scientific personnel.

5. "The financial policies of such firms, particularly where they are wholly owned by non-residents, may reflect the requirements of parent companies more than those of the subsidiary, may lead to an underdeveloped state for some sectors of the domestic capital market, and may cause serious balance of payments problems."[11]

6. "The fact that a large part of non-resident equity investment in Canadian industry is in the form of wholly-owned subsidiaries and branches means that Canadians are unable to participate financially even through the growth in incomes and the consequent increase in domestic savings will make it increasingly possible for them to so do."[12]

7. Many foreign-owned concerns are relieved of the necessity of public disclosure of their financial situation by virtue of their status as private companies. On the basis of published data, it would appear that approximately 60 percent of foreign firms in Canada are private limited companies. Since the operations of many of Canada's leading corporations are of legitimate interest to several groups of the community, including labour unions, government departments and economic analysts,

[11]*A. E. Safarian,* Foreign Ownership of Canadian Industry. *Toronto: McGraw Hill, 1966, pp. 19-20.*
[12]*Canada, Royal Commission on Canada's Economic Prospects (Gordon Commission),* Preliminary Report, *Queen's Printer, December, 1956, p. 89.*

and to every individual as a consumer, it is claimed that freedom from publicity enjoyed by large foreign-owned private corporations is not in the public interest.

These and related views pose a conflict of interest between the aspirations of Canada and those of the international firm with its locus of operations in several nations. If these opinions are correct, they indicate what may be significant offsets to the advantages traditionally associated with external direct investment. However, as one might suspect the controversy between those who see direct investment in Canada as a necessary condition for our continued growth and those who identify foreign domination of our country's economy with the extent of foreign ownership and control of Canadian corporations has generated more heat than light. In all probability, the economic factors involved in assessing government policies toward foreign investment in Canada can only be decided in the light of one's judgment about the appropriate rate and nature of growth and development in the Canadian economy. Measures could be devised which might facilitate a larger degree of Canadian stock ownership in foreign-controlled concerns and which might more effectively channel Canadian savings into the resource and manufacturing industries thus far dominated by a relatively few foreign business firms. It would be possible as well to emphasize to non-resident controlled companies the real advantages to be gained by employing qualified Canadians in senior management and technical positions; taking an active and constructive part in community and national affairs; having independent Canadian directors on the board; publishing regular financial statements; fostering a distinct Canadian research effort; developing sources of supply in Canada; processing natural resources in Canada as far as possible; maximizing their market opportunities in other countries as well as in Canada; and by retaining sufficient earnings for growth after paying a fair return to owners. But such steps, however useful, do not go to the heart of the matter. It seems that the basic issues are first, can Canada restrain or reduce the flow of foreign capital investment in this country without undermining the process of economic growth that has been to a large extent based on this outside capital, and second, how high a price are the Canadian people willing to pay in the form of slower growth to secure a greater measure of control over their own destiny.

Government Enterprises

No account of business organization in this country would be complete without mention of the publicly-owned corporation. In Canada, business enterprises have been established by government at the federal, provincial, and municipal levels. Some are run as departments of government, while others are managed by boards or commissions which are responsible in varying degrees to the government concerned. Businesses of this type have been most prominent in the field of public utilities. In most cases they are operated as monopolies.

Abstracting from the propriety of public ownership, two observations are worth stressing. First, some fifty Crown corporations have been established under the Company's Act or by special Act of Parliament, nine of them since 1963. In this connection, it should be mentioned that there are three types of Crown companies—*departmental corporations* are accountable for administrative, supervisory or regulatory services of a governmental character. Examples are the Agricultural Stabilization Board, The Economic Council of Canada, and the Unemployment Insurance Commission. *Agency corporations* are responsible for the management of trading or service operations on a quasi-commercial basis or for the administration of procurement, construction and disposal activities on behalf of federal government departments and agencies, industry, universities and foreign countries. Examples of such agency corporations are Atomic Energy of Canada Ltd., the Canadian Commercial Corporation and the National Capital Commission. *Proprietary corporations* are (1) responsible for the supervision of lending or financial operations, or for the management of commercial or industrial operations involving the supply of goods and services to the general public, and (2) normally required to conduct their affairs without Parliamentary appropriations. Well known examples are the Canadian National Railways, the Canadian Broadcasting Corporation, Air Canada, Central Mortgage and Housing Corporation, Eldorado Mining and Refining Ltd., and Polymer Corporation Ltd. Like an ordinary business corporation, proprietary corporations pay taxes on income earned. Other enterprises owned by the federal government include the Bank of Canada, the Canadian Wheat Board and the Industrial Development Bank. Five prominent provincial proprietary corporations are the Liquor Control Board of Ontario, British Columbia Hydro and Power Authority, Saskatchewan Power Corporation, Alberta Government Telephone Company and the Nova Scotia Electric Power Commission. Examples at the municipal level are the Toronto Transit Commission and the Ottawa Hydro Electric Commission. Clearly some very important businesses are carried on by our three levels of government.

It should also be emphasized that the profit motive is not the only force at work in a publicly-owned corporation. Public concerns are impelled by other motives as well and these other considerations may often exert a perceptible influence over the conduct of their affairs. For instance, many crown corporations have had as their primary purpose the development of a particular product, service, industry, or part of the country. To argue that the public interest is not always served by the pursuit of profit most emphatically does not deny that public enterprises are subject to inefficiency nor does it deny the need to consider other ways of achieving the same ends. To put it differently, it is always proper for the economist to assess whether the public goals are best achieved through public enterprises and agencies or through private enterprises subsidized, if necessary, by the government.

Business Failures

One indicator of the business climate is the number of business failures (defined as concerns that are forced out of business with loss to creditors) per 10,000 firms in operation. Available information presented in Table 3–9, indicates that over the span of years since 1900, there has been an improvement in the general health of Canadian business firms as measured by the rate of failure. During the first three decades of this century, the failure rate exceeded that which has prevailed since then. Yet the failure rate has been generally trending upward since the end of World War II.

To look briefly at the picture for the past several years, Canadian business failures in 1968 decreased, falling to 1,697, the smallest number since 1959. The total dollar liabilities involved in 1968 mortalities fell to a five-year low of $130 million after reaching the all-time peak of $215 million a year earlier. While the average liability per business failure shrank to $76,652, it nevertheless was the second highest figure in history, exceeded only by 1967's record $109,638. Retail trade firms accounted for 42 percent of all business failures in 1968; the construction sector accounted for roughly 20 percent; the manufacturing group accounted for 16 percent; the commercial service group accounted for about 12 percent; and wholesale trade accounted for the rest. By province, the largest number of failures occurred in Quebec (859), Ontario (589), and British Columbia (91). The smallest number occurred in the Maritimes.

The causes of business failure may be divided into two groups—*internal* causes, which can be attributed to management, and *external* causes, over which management has little or no control. Dun & Bradstreet Ltd., the leading supplier of credit information, whose statistics on number and liabilities of business failures have the weight of Holy Writ, reports the cause of failure to lie in management: incompetence, lack of managerial experience, lack of experience in the given line of business, or an un-

TABLE 3–9
Canadian Business Failures 1900-1968

Year	Failure Rate per 10,000 Concerns*	Year	Failure Rate per 10,000 Concerns
1900	140	1934	90
1901	145	1935	78
1902	116	1936	71
1903	101	1937	55
1904	125	1938	58
1905	132	1939	72
1906	113	1940	64
1907	116	1941	49
1908	145	1942	36
1909	123	1943	11
1910	104	1944	6
1911	104	1945	6
1912	99	1946	7
1913	119	1947	15
1914	194	1948	23
1915	110	1949	27
1916	114	1950	32
1917	77	1951	36
1918	62	1952	37
1919	54	1953	44
1920	73	1954	57
1921	159	1955	55
1922	228	1956	53
1923	195	1957	59
1924	148	1958	55
1925	141	1959	57
1926	128	1960	72
1927	125	1961	78
1928	120	1962	82
1929	128	1963	85
1930	152	1964	98
1931	143	1965	103
1932	161	1966	93
1933	138	1967	75
		1968	67

Data includes manufacturers, wholesalers, retailers, building contractors, and certain types of commercial service including public utilities, water carriers, motor carriers and air-lines. It excludes financial enterprises, insurance and real-estate companies, railroads, terminals, amusements, and many small one-man services. Neither the professions nor farmers are included.
Source: *Research Division*, Dun & Bradstreet of Canada, Ltd., *Toronto, 1969.*

balanced experience—i.e., strength in some areas, such as sales, but weakness in others, such as finance. More than 95 percent of failures in ordinary years are characteristically laid at the door of management. About two-thirds of these are due to incompetence, less than one-twentieth are attributed to such other factors as neglect, fraud, or disaster.

Table 3–10 indicates in detail the apparent reasons and the underlying causes of Canadian business failures in 1968. Only in the case of ten con-

TABLE 3-10
Classification of Causes of Business Failures in Canada, Year 1968

ALL LINES OF BUSINESS — UNDERLYING CAUSES				ALL METHODS OF OPERATION — APPARENT CAUSES		
Number	Per Cent				Number	Per Cent
17	1.0	NEGLECT	Due to:	Bad Habits	3	0.2
				Poor Health	9	0.5
				Marital Difficulties	1	0.1
				Other	4	0.2
9	0.5	FRAUD	On the part of the principals, reflected by:	Misleading Name	—	—
				False Financial Statement	1	0.1
				Premeditated Overbuy	2	0.1
				Irregular Disposal of Assets	4	0.2
				Other	2	0.1
157	9.2	LACK OF EXPERIENCE IN THE LINE	Evidenced by inability to avoid conditions which resulted in:	Inadequate Sales	1,044	61.5
137	8.1	LACK OF MANAGERIAL EXPERIENCE		Heavy Operating Expenses	173	10.2
222	13.1	UNBALANCED EXPERIENCE*		Receivables Difficulties	161	9.5
1,132	66.7	INCOMPETENCE		Inventory Difficulties	62	3.7
				Excessive Fixed Assets	53	3.1
				Poor Location	23	1.4
				Competitive Weakness	183	10.8
				Other	21	1.2
13	0.8	DISASTER	Some of these occurrences, could have been provided against through insurance.	Fire	7	0.4
				Flood	—	—
				Burglary	1	0.1
				Employees' Fraud	3	0.1
				Strike	1	0.1
				Other	1	0.1
10	0.6	REASON UNKNOWN		Because some failures are attributed to a combination of apparent causes, the totals of these columns exceed the totals of the corresponding columns on the left.		
1,697	100.0	TOTAL				

*Experience not well rounded in sales, finance, purchasing, and production on the part of an individual in case of a proprietorship, or of two or more partners or officers constituting a management unit.

Source: Research Division, Dun & Bradstreet of Canada Ltd., Toronto, 1969.

cerns does Dun & Bradstreet state that the cause of failure could not be determined.

Finally, it should be pointed out that more than 50 percent of all new firms fail within the first five years of operation. Among the enterprises that failed in 1968, only 2.7 percent were businesses established during the year. However, firms set up in 1967 accounted for 13.2 percent of all failures, those of 1966 for 16.5 percent, those of 1965 for 12.2 percent and those of 1964 for 8.7 percent. Only 8.6 percent of all the failures in 1968 involved companies established prior to 1950. In short, the first few years is the testing period of the ability, stamina and management instinct of the entrepreneur.

One general remark should be made in concluding this section. Considering the advances in technology and communications that have occurred of late, it is clear that today's businessman requires considerably more factual knowledge and knowhow, as well as a larger initial capital investment, than did his counterpart 20 years ago. This means that the high mortality rate in recent years, even more than in the past, represents a sorting out of the men from the boys, and does not have too dire a meaning for the economy as a whole.

Summary

Business firms are the economic units that engage in production; that is, in activity that moves or transforms resources to a place or form nearer to that in which they are ultimately used. The outputs of production processes further removed from the satisfying of consumer wants are called lower-order goods while those closer to the satisfying of consumer wants are higher-order goods. Business firms produce outputs at all levels, from extraction of raw materials to the placing of goods in the hands of their ultimate consumers. Profits provide the incentive for the creation and operation of business firms.

From a legal point of view there are four forms of business organization: (1) the sole proprietorship, (2) the partnership, (3) the corporation, and (4) the co-operative. Sole proprietorships are business firms owned by one person or one family. Partnerships are firms owned by two or more individuals but which are not incorporated. Corporations are businesses set up as legal entities that can operate as a sort of legal person. Co-operatives are a kind of combination of the partnership and the corporation, in the sense that they have some of the characteristics of each.

The sole proprietorship form has both advantages and disadvantages. Among the advantages are the ease with which it can be established and the freedom and flexibility it offers with respect to decision-making by its owner-manager. The distadvantages of the sole proprietorship are that funds for financing expansion and operation of the business are limited in amount and that the proprietor has unlimited liability for business debts.

We distinguish between equity financing of a business and debt financing. The former means that funds are provided the business by owners or in exchange for ownership interests. Debt financing means that the business obtains funds by borrowing or by going into debt.

Partnerships, like sole proprietorships, are easily formed. They have broader possibilities for specialization of managerial talents and for equity financing than have sole proprietorships. The disadvantages of a partnership are unlimited liability of each partner for partnership debts, the agency rule, under which any one partner can take actions binding the partnership, and limited sources of financing.

The advantages of a corporation are easy transferability of ownership interests, limited liability of owners for business debts, and much broader sources of financing than are available to the other two organizational forms. On the other side of the ledger, corporations are somewhat more complex to establish; their incomes are subjected to more onerous tax treatment than that of proprietorships and partnerships, and there is usually a separation of ownership from control of the corporation.

The co-operative enjoys certain advantages in common with the corporation, but it also possesses others which are more or less unique. Co-ops provide for a large-scale organization while preserving democratic control (one vote for each member). Dividends are based on the purchase or sales of members and not on the amounts of stock held. Management is usually local and in close contact with the members. The chief weakness of the co-operative form of organization is the difficulty in raising capital.

We find that in Canada there are approximately 430,000 farms, and more than 300,000 separate business firms in existence. Four-fifths of these are sole proprietorships, less than one-twentieth are partnerships, and about one-tenth are corporations.

With respect to types of economic activity, the sole proprietorship is predominant in agriculture in terms of number of firms, employment provided and amount of business done. It also outnumbers the other organizational forms in retail trade and in the services; however, corporations predominate in both volume of sales and number of employees. In the manufacturing and merchandising fields, incorporated companies predominate in all categories. The partnership is predominant in none, neither in number of firms nor in sales nor in employment provided.

In recent years there has been much apprehension concerning the high degree of industrial concentration, and the extent to which Canadian business is externally controlled. Perhaps the most basic problem confronting the nation is how to reap the benefits of large-scale production and foreign capital investment without harming the public interest. As yet we have not resolved this dilemma.

In Canada, as in other countries, a substantial proportion of goods and services is produced by publicly-owned business firms. While it has its place, even in a private enterprise economy, government ownership and control of corporations has a number of definite limitations. These follow from the bureaucratic nature of government operations.

In general, it would appear that approximately 50 percent of new businesses fail during the first few years of operation, and that about 95 percent of all failures are due to the shortcomings of management.

Exercises and Questions for Discussion

1. Evaluate the statement: "Separation of ownership and control is common in Canadian corporations because only in very few instances does any one stockholder control 51 percent of the voting stock".
2. Mr. Jones goes into the business of making lamp shades. What kind of business organization is implied by each of the following situations:
   a. He invests $30,000 of his own money and hires Mr. Smith along with 10 other men to work for him.
   b. He invests $30,000 of his money, borrows $20,000 from Mr. Smith, agreeing to pay it back over a five-year period at 6 percent interest, and hires Mr. Smith along with 10 other men to work for him.
   c. He, his wife, Mr. Smith, and Smith's wife apply for a provincial charter for their business. They sell 1000 shares at $50 per share. Mr. Jones manages the business while Mr. Smith and 10 other men work for him.
   d. He invests $30,000 of his money and $30,000 of Smith's, with the agreement that they will share equally in the profits of the business. Jones manages the business, and Smith along with 10 other men work for him.
3. Indicate in each of the following cases whether a business firm is using debt financing or equity financing:
   a. It sells a $10,000 long-term bond.
   b. It sells 1000 shares of stock at $10 a share.
   c. It obtains a loan of $10,000 from a chartered bank.
   d. It obtains a loan of $10,000 from a friend of the manager.
   e. It uses $10,000 out of last year's earnings.
   Explain your answer for each case.
4. Five individuals jointly form a flying club and purchase an airplane. Should they form a partnership or a corporation? Explain your answer in detail.

5. "The day of the small business is past". Do you agree with this statement?
6. What are the two opposing views often advanced in answer to the question, Is big business bad for the economy?
7. Can you give reasons for the public ownership of corporations?
8. Popular opinion has it that when a government and business are interrelated, a less efficient business enterprise generally results. Do you agree? Why?
9. Should Canada take steps to restrain the growth of foreign control over business enterprise in this country? Justify your answer.
10. Can a business be an economic failure and not a financial failure? Can it be a legal failure and not an economic failure? Do you believe the only cause of failure is managerial inaptitude? Give your reasons.

Selected Readings

Ashley, C. A., and Smyth, J. E., *Corporate Finance in Canada*. Toronto: The Macmillan Company of Canada Ltd., 1966.

Berle, A. A., and G. C. Means, *The Modern Corporation and Private Property*. New York: Commerce Clearing House, 1932.

Government of Canada, Department of Industry, Trade and Commerce, *How to Run a Business*. Ottawa: Queen's Printer, 1968.

Guthmann, H. G., and Dougall, H. E., *Corporate Financial Policy*. Englewood Cliffs: Prentice-Hall Inc., 1962.

Rosenbluth, G., "The Relation between Foreign Control and Concentration in Canadian Industry", *The Canadian Journal of Economics*, February, 1970, pp. 14-39.

Safarian, A. E., *Foreign Ownership of Canadian Industry*. Toronto: McGraw-Hill Co. of Canada, 1966.

4

Market, Demand: Supply and Prices

Prices play a stellar role in economic analysis, although this is not always apparent to us as buyers or sellers of goods and services. When we buy textbooks or clothing or entertainment, what is most apparent to us is that we would prefer lower prices. As sellers of used books, labour, services, and well-worn automobiles we seldom receive prices as high as we would like them to be. What causes prices to be what they are?

This chapter focuses on the principles that apply not only to the pricing of consumer goods and services but also to the determination of wage rates, land rents, and the returns on capital goods. The market situation that forms the framework of price determination as it is discussed in this chapter is a simplified one called *pure competition* and its main characteristics will be explained at appropriate points. In a purely competitive market setting the price of any product, service, or resource is determined by the interacting forces of demand and supply. We shall analyze demand and supply in turn and then demonstrate how they interact to determine price. The chapter concludes with an examination of the elasticity of demand.

Markets

Is a market a physical place where buyers and sellers make contact with each other and engage in exchange? It may be, but this is a marked oversimplification. Buyers and sellers need not confront each other physically as they do at an auction or in a grocery store. Many kinds of transactions can be carried out by telephone or by mail. The important point is that a market exists wherever buyers and sellers of a product or service are in touch with one another and can engage in exchange.

The areas embraced by different markets vary widely depending partly upon the nature of what is being exchanged. The markets for some items are local. People seldom travel beyond the neighbourhood, to say nothing of the city itself, to get a haircut. Other markets are regional. For milk and fresh dairy products, the possibility of spoilage precludes shipment across the continent. Some markets are national in scope. Light airplanes from all over the nation are listed in trade publications, and a prospective buyer or seller will go almost anywhere in the country for an advantageous exchange. Still other markets, like that for such well-known securities as Dominion Foundries and Steel stock, operate on an international basis.

The extent of a market will depend, too, on whether we are thinking in terms of a short or a long period of time. Over a short period—say six months—accountants in the Windsor area may not be willing to consider employment in other cities because their homes, their families, and their friends are in Windsor. For this time period the market for accountants would be local. But if business activity in the city should become permanently slack, for example, if Ford and other automobile manufacturers moved elsewhere, better long-term earning possibilities in Hamilton or Toronto might very well entice accountants away from Windsor. The extent of the market is correspondingly broader, but a time period of several years may be required to make it so.

Demand

The behaviour of buyers in the market for a specific good or service is summed up in the term *demand*. We often speak of demand for a product as being some quantity of it that people need, but we shall find that the quantity demanded or needed is not invariate. Rather, it is determined by several factors that will be explored in some detail in this section.

Demand Schedules and Demand Curves

The determinants of demand are best explained in terms of a *demand schedule* or a *demand curve*. Suppppose we ask ourselves how much margarine per year will be purchased in a given market. An immediate and important observation comes to mind—the quantity that will be taken depends upon its price. From everyday experience with many goods and services we know that at higher prices less will be taken than at lower prices. This *law of demand* is usually illustrated with a demand schedule or a demand curve showing the quantities that will be purchased at all alternative prices, other things being equal. Such a demand schedule is presented in Table 4–1.

The demand schedule must be read correctly. Note that in the table the quantity column shows the *rates* at which buyers are willing to purchase the product; that is, it shows the quantities per month they are willing to purchase. Unless we specify the time period during which the quantities will be taken, the figures in this column have no real meaning. For example, at a price of 70 cents the schedule states that buyers are willing to take 4000 pounds. If the time period were not specified, we could infer 4000 pounds per month or per year or per day, and the information would be meaningless. However, the quantity column states that the product will be purchased by buyers at a rate of 4000 pounds per month and this is information that makes sense.

TABLE 4–1
Hypothetical Demand Schedule for Margarine

PRICE OF MARGARINE (CENTS PER LB.)	QUANTITY OF MARGARINE (LBS. PER MONTH)
100	1,000
90	2,000
80	3,000
70	4,000
60	5,000
50	6,000
40	7,000
30	8,000
20	9,000
10	10,000

The quantity column shows rates of purchase at *alternative* possible prices. Thus if the price were 70 cents per pound, purchasers would be willing to take only 4000 pounds per month; but if the price were 60 cents per pound, they would be willing to take 5000 pounds per month. Each price–quantity combination must be thought of as a separate and distinct alternative showing the total amount that buyers will take per time period at the indicated price.

A *demand curve* conveys the same information as a demand schedule, but it shows the information graphically instead of arithmetically. The demand schedule of Table 4–1 is plotted as a demand curve in Figure 4–1. Price per pound is measured along the vertical axis and pounds per month that would be purchased are measured along the horizontal axis.

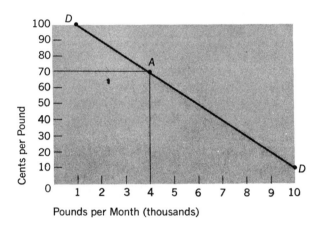

Figure 4-1
A demand curve for margarine.

Any point on the demand curve shows the quantity that would be taken at a particular price, or, alternatively, the price that consumers would be willing to pay for a particular quantity. For example, point *A* shows that at a price of 70 cents per pound, purchasers would be willing to take as much as 4000 pounds per month. It also indicates that for a total of 4000 pounds per month purchasers would be willing to pay as much as 70 cents per pound.

The Law of Demand

The law of demand, which states that more of a product will be purchased at lower prices than at higher prices, is not startlingly new to any of us, but the proposition is an important one in economic analysis. One of its most important implications is that for any given product, price can go high enough to induce purchasers voluntarily to limit their total purchases to the quantity available. This rationing function of price will be discussed in more detail later. Why do purchasers buy less at higher prices than at lower prices? In a way this seems a little like asking why water runs downhill, but our understanding of demand will be more complete if we look at the forces that are operative.

As higher prices of a product are considered by prospective purchasers, a *substitution effect* is at work. The higher the price of steak relative to that of pork chops, the less satisfaction a given expenditure on steak will yield relative to the same expenditure on pork chops—or the more satisfaction the expenditure will yield relatively when spent on pork chops instead of on steak. Thus as the price of steak rises, pork chops are substituted for steak and the total quantity of steak purchased decreases.

Additionally, there is usually an *income effect* at work. An increase in product prices when the dollars that purchasers have to spend is fixed reduces the quantities that can be purchased. A rise in the price of steak reduces the purchasing power of consumers, causing them to buy less steak as well as less of many other goods and services. The income effect ordinarily reinforces the substitution effect, making quantities purchased of any good or service vary inversely with the price.

Changes in Demand

The concept of a demand curve must be sharpened in order to avoid confusion over terminology. Suppose that DD in Figure 4–2 is the demand curve for fluid milk in the Montreal area. Price is initially P_1 and the corresponding quantity purchased by consumers is X_1 gallons. Now suppose that price falls to P_2 and quantity takes increases to X_2. Has demand for fluid milk changed? Alternatively, suppose that a new calcium diet catches on in the area, increasing the intensity of consumer preferences for milk, so that at price P_1 consumers now want X_2 rather than X_1 gallons. Has demand for fluid milk changed?

If we refer to both of the foregoing circumstances as a change in demand, we invite analytical chaos. They are quite different situations. At the outset, then, we shall assign specific terminology to each situation and adhere to it throughout the book. We shall call the first case a *movement along a given demand curve*, or *a change in quantity demanded* because of a price change, and the second case a *change in demand*.

We should think of the term demand as referring to an entire demand curve. It expresses the functional relationship between the price of a product and the quantity of the product that buyers in the market are willing to take, other things being equal or constant. Thus a movement from A to B in Figure 4–2 is not a change in demand according to our terminology.

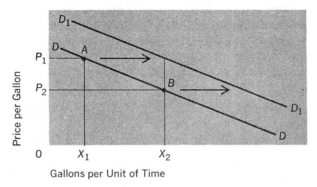

Figure 4–2
A change in demand.

A change in demand means a change in the position or slope of a demand curve. In Figure 4–2 if the demand curve moves from DD to D_1D_1, an *increase in demand* has occurred. This increase may result from such factors as an increase in consumer incomes, anticipation of an imminent increase in the price of the product, an increase in the price of powdered milk, or a decrease in the price of cereals. Conversely, a movement of the demand curve from D_1D_1 to DD represents a *decrease in demand*. The causes of a decrease will be the opposite of those that bring about an increase in demand. It is worth noting that when we define demand for a product, stipulating that "other things" remain constant, we are in no sense leaving the possibility of changes in the "other things" out of consideration. We are setting up an analytical apparatus that permits us to take explicit account of such changes.

"Other Things Being Equal"

We have just noted that the price of a product is not the only factor that affects the quantity of it that consumers in the market are willing to purchase. Several other forces are operative, the most important ones being consumer preferences, consumer incomes, consumer expectations, and the prices of related goods. A change in any one of these will change the quantity of the product that consumers are willing to purchase even if there is no change in the product price. Consequently, to establish how differences in the price alone of a product affect the quantities that consumers will take, we must rule out changes in these "other things." Only if the other things are held constant can we establish a demand curve showing a unique set of quantities that consumers are willing to take at alternative prices.

Consumer preferences refer to the intensities of consumers' desires for products. The preferences of consumers for some items change rather slowly over time. Housing and staple food items are examples. For other items preferences may change rather rapidly, for example, styles of women's clothes. Changes in preference change the demand curve for products. A given demand curve for one product can be established only on the assumption that preferences are constant at the time the curve is established.

Consumer incomes are thought of in demand analysis as the entire amount of money available for the group of consumers in the market to spend per time period. They consist of earnings plus whatever credit sources are available. Obviously, in order to establish a unique set of quantities demanded at alternative prices of a product, the total dollar purchasing power of the group of consumers must not change. If incomes change either up or down, the demand curve itself will move to the right or to the left.

Consumer expectations also affect the quantities of a product that consumers will take at alternative prices. Suppose that consumers develop an expectation that the price of the product in question will rise sharply in the near future. They are likely to increase their rate of purchase at the present price over what it would have been had the change in expectations not occurred; that is, the demand curve shifts to the right. The state of consumer expectations must be assumed constant for a given demand curve to be established for a product.

The effect of changes in the *prices of related goods* on the quantities taken of a given good at alternative prices depends upon the nature of the relationship. Related goods may be complements or substitutes. *Complementary goods* are those that must be consumed together, such as tennis rackets and tennis balls. *Substitute products* are those such as beef and pork that can be consumed in lieu of one another.

Suppose that we are trying to establish a demand curve for tennis balls. We have determined that at a price of 50 cents per ball the market will take 1000 balls per month. But now the price of rackets suddenly doubles. Tennis players cut down on their rates of purchases of rackets and on their tennis activity. The quantity of balls that consumers will take at 50 cents each drops to some figure such as 700 per month. Thus a rise in the price of one of two complementary goods will decrease demand for the other, so in defining the demand curve for one the price of the other must be held at a constant level.

Substitute products affect each other the other way around. A rise in the price of pork will cause people to increase their consumption of beef if beef prices remain unchanged. Consequently, the price of pork must be assumed to remain constant when we establish the demand curve for beef.

Supply

We use the concept of *supply* to analyze the sellers' side of a market, and many of the points developed in demand analysis can be carried over to the supply side. We first examine supply schedules and supply curves and then identify the "other things being equal." Finally, we differentiate between movements along a supply curve and changes in supply.

Supply Schedules and Supply Curves

What determines the quantities of margarine that sellers will place on sale in a given market? Obviously price will be an important determinant, but additional factors are also operative. In order to handle all of them analytically we define supply of a product as *the quantities that all sellers are willing to place on the market at alternative prices, other things being equal.* A hypothetical supply schedule for margarine is given in Table 4–2 and is plotted as a supply curve in Figure 4–3.

TABLE 4–2
Hypothetical Supply Schedule for Margarine

PRICE OF MARGARINE (CENTS PER LB.)	QUANTITY OF MARGARINE (LBS. PER MONTH)
10	2,000
20	3,000
30	4,000
40	5,000
50	6,000
60	7,000
70	8,000
80	9,000
90	10,000
100	11,000

Whereas demand curves generally slope downward to the right, supply curves ordinarily are upward sloping. The reasons for this are not hard to find. First, at higher prices it becomes more attractive to sellers to place goods on the market rather than to hold them in inventory. Second, at

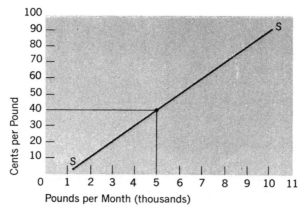

Figure 4-3
A supply curve for margarine.

higher prices the most profitable sales levels for existing producers are ordinarily greater than they are at lower prices. Third, higher profit possibilities attract new sellers into the field, expanding still more the total quantities made available for sale at higher prices.

Changes in Supply

The same considerations apply to supply as apply to demand in differentiating between a movement along a supply curve and a change in supply. We shall use the term supply to mean an entire supply curve. Accordingly, a movement from C to D in Figure 4–4 is not a change in supply but a change in *quantity supplied* as a result of a change in the product price. The supply curve has not moved.

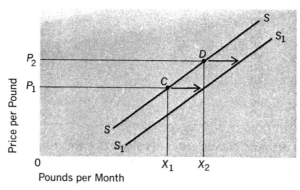

Figure 4-4
A change in supply.

A *change in supply* is represented by a change in the position or shape of the supply curve, such as that from *SS* to S_1S_1 in Figure 4–4. An *increase in supply* is a movement or shift of the supply curve to the right, while a *decrease in supply* is represented by a shift to the left. These shifts are caused by changes in the "other things."

"Other Things Being Equal"

As with demand, in order to establish a unique functional relationship between the price of a product and the quantity of it that sellers will place on the market, there are "other things" that must be held constant. These are, of course, the factors other than price that influence the quantities that sellers want to sell. The most important are (1) resource prices, (2) the range of production techniques available to producers of the product, and (3) producer expectations. Changes in any or all of these factors will affect the quantities per time period that sellers will place on the market at any given price.

Consider first the effects of different *resource price levels* on supply. Suppose that at current resource prices the sellers of Figure 4–3 are willing to place 5000 pounds of margarine per month on the market at a price of 40 cents per pound. Now suppose that prices of the resources used in making and marketing the product fall by 10 percent. Sellers can now place the 5000 pounds on the market at a lower price, or at the same price they can place a larger quantity on the market. Either alternative should be interpreted as a move off the supply curve *SS*. Thus in defining a given state of supply or a given supply curve resource prices must be held constant.

Similarly, if *production techniques* become more efficient, production of any particular quantity of a product per month becomes less expensive for producers. This amounts to saying that at any given price such as 40 cents per pound, sellers can place more than 5000 pounds per month on the market. It is clear then that in establishing a specific supply curve the state of production techniques must be held constant.

Changes in *producer expectations* operate in much the same way as do changes in consumer expectations. Suppose again in Figure 4–3 that initially at some such price as 40 cents per pound producers, expecting no price changes, would place 5000 pounds of margarine on the market. Now suppose that a decrease in the price of butter is believed to be just around the corner. Large quantities of margarine will be thrown on the market at 40 cents and a movement to the right of supply curve *SS* occurs. In order to stake out a given supply curve, then, producer expectations must remain constant.

Determination of Market Price and Quantity Exchanged

Buyers and sellers interact in markets to determine product prices. Demand curves bring together the forces motivating buyers, while supply curves accomplish the same thing with respect to sellers. In this initial discussion of price determination the market is assumed to be one of pure competition, a market form less complex than others to be discussed later. We shall explain first the concept of pure competition. Next, we shall see how the price and the quantity exchanged of a product are determined under given conditions of demand and supply. Finally, we consider the impacts of changes in demand and supply on market price and quantity exchanged.

Pure Competition

There are three essential conditions that must be met in a market if it is to be one of pure competition: (1) there must be many buyers and many sellers of whatever is being bought and sold in the market; (2) there must be no collusion among buyers or sellers; and (3) there must be no price fixing.

The condition that there be many buyers and many sellers in the market means that there must be enough of each so that any one buyer or any one seller is insignificant relative to the market as a whole. What does insignificance mean in this context? On the buying side it means simply that no single buyer takes enough of the product to influence product price. How important are your purchases of bread at the neighborhood supermarket? Are they important enough for the store to sell to you at a penny less than the posted price rather than to lose you as a bread customer? Similarly, insignificance on the selling side means that an individual seller cannot by himself influence price. Suppose you are a cotton farmer. You can sell only at the going market price—or below. If you try to charge more per bale than the market price, no one will buy from you, since cotton is available from others at the market price.

The absence of collusion is largely a self-evident concept. It means that buyers do not "gang up" on sellers to force them to sell at lower prices and that sellers do not "gang up" on buyers to force them to buy at higher prices.

The absence of price fixing is closely related to the foregoing points. Prices in purely competitive markets are free to move up and down. They are not set by guidelines, minimum wage or price laws, price ceiling laws, or by such private organizations as sellers' associations or labour unions. They are responsive to changes in demand and supply.

Equilibrium Price and Quantity

Suppose we bring the buyers and sellers of margarine together to see how the price and quantity exchanged are determined in a given market. The demand schedule of Table 4–1 appears as columns (1) and (2) of Table 4–3, while the supply schedule of Table 4–2 is shown as columns (2) and (3) of Table 4–3. The meaning of column (4) will become clear shortly.

What will happen if the price of margarine is initially toward the upper end of the range of alternative possible prices—say at 70 cents per pound? The demand schedule shows the reactions of the buyers as a group. They are willing to take only 4000 pounds per month. However, according to the supply schedule, sellers will place 8000 pounds per month on the market at that price, and a surplus of 4000 pounds per mouth, shown in column (4), will come into existence.

Surpluses in the hands of individual sellers set in motion forces that drive the price down. One seller believes that if he lowers his price to slightly less than 70 cents, buyers will favour him and he can unload his surplus. But each of the other sellers thinks the same. In the absence of collusion, they undercut each other. The price drops to 60 cents per pound but surpluses still occur. The undercutting process continues and the price drops to 50 cents per pound. At that price buyers want to buy and sellers want to sell 6000 pounds per month. Because surpluses are no longer being brought into existence, the incentive to undercut no longer exists. Sellers can sell all they want to bring to market at that price.

What happens if the market opens at 30 cents per pound? Buyers want 8000 pounds but sellers are willing to place only 4000 pounds per month on the market. Altogether consumers are 4000 pounds short of what they would like to buy each month at that price. Any individual consumer, unable to get as much as he wants at the going price, will reason that if he offers sellers slightly more than 30 cents per pound they will prefer to sell to him and his personal shortage will be alleviated. Other buyers reason the same way and the price is bid up to 40 cents per pound. The higher price then causes consumers to reappraise their positions and to cut the total amount they are willing to take to 7000 pounds. Sellers, finding the 40 cent price more profitable than the 30 cent price, expand the total monthly amount that they place on the market to 5000 pounds. However, since consumers are still 2000 pounds short of what they would like to have each month, an incentive exists for them to bid the price even higher.

TABLE 4-3

Hypothetical Demand, Supply, and Market Price of Margarine

(1) QUANTITY DEMANDED (LBS. PER MONTH)	(2) PRICE (CENTS PER LB.)	(3) QUANTITY SUPPLIED (LBS. PER MONTH)	(4) SURPLUS (+) OR SHORTAGE (−) (LBS. PER MONTH)
1,000	100	11,000	(+) 10,000
2,000	90	10,000	(+) 8,000
3,000	80	9,000	(+) 6,000
4,000	70	8,000	(+) 4,000
5,000	60	7,000	(+) 2,000
6,000	50	6,000	Neither
7,000	40	5,000	(−) 2,000
8,000	30	4,000	(−) 4,000
9,000	20	3,000	(−) 6,000
10,000	10	2,000	(−) 8,000

At 50 cents per pound, buyers cut the amount they are willing to take per month to 6000 pounds, and sellers expand the quantity they are willing to place on the market to the same amount. The incentive to bid the price higher has been eliminated.

This price and this quantity exchanged—50 cents and 6000 pounds per month—are called, respectively, *the equilibrium price and quantity*. At any other price forces are set in motion that tend to drive the price back to the equilibrium level. This is the level toward which the price will gravitate and settle as long as demand and supply remain as shown by Table 4–3.

This analysis can be presented easily and quickly by means of a demand curve and a supply curve drawn in the same diagram. In Figure 4–5

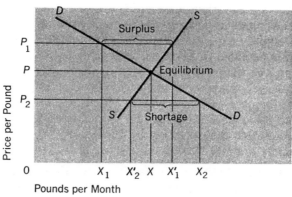

Figure 4–5
Equilibrium price and quantity.

note that at price level P_1, consumers take quantity X_1 per month, while sellers place quantity X'_1 on the market. Thus sellers find themselves accumulating surpluses at a rate of X'_1 minus X_1 per month. This situation induces individual sellers to undercut each other, thus forcing the price down. As the price falls, sellers bring smaller and smaller quantities per month to market while at the same time buyers purchase larger and larger quantities. Finally, when price has fallen to P and quantity exchanged is at X, there is no incentive for buyers or sellers to make further changes in the price and the quantity exchanged.

If the price were initially at P_2 rather than at P_1, buyers would want to buy quantity X_2. Sellers bring to market X'_2, and a shortage of X_2 minus X'_2 per month occurs. This provides an incentive for individual consumers to bid up the price. As the price rises, sellers are induced to place larger quantities per month on the market, whereas buyers are induced to ration themselves to smaller and smaller quantities. When the price level reaches P and the quantity exchanged is at X, the incentives for change no longer exist.

Changes in Demand

In the dynamic world in which we live we do not expect demand for any specific good or service to remain permanently fixed. Consumer preferences change; incomes increase; price changes in some goods cause demand changes for related goods; expectations change; and so on.

Suppose we look at the impact of a change in consumer preferences away from chicken and toward beef. In Figure 4–6(a) the initial demand for and supply of beef are D_bD_b and S_bS_b, so that P_b and B are the equilibrium price and quantity exchanged. The initial demand for and supply of chicken are D_cD_c and S_cS_c in Figure 4–6(b), making P_c and C the equilibrium price and quantity exchanged.

The shift in preferences increases the demand for beef to $D_{b_1}D_{b_1}$, creating a shortage of BB' at the original price P_b. Consumers bid against each other for the available supply, driving the price up. As the price rises, consumers restrict or ration their purchases more and more while sellers place larger and larger quantities per month on the market. When the price reaches the P_{b_1} level, the quantity that buyers want to buy will be the same as the quantity that sellers want to sell. Thus P_{b_1} and B_1 are the new equilibrium price and quantity exchanged. We can draw from this analysis the general principle that *an increase in demand ordinarily will increase both the price and the quantity exchanged of a product or service.*

In Figure 4–6(b) the demand for chicken decreases from D_cD_c to $D_{c1}D_{c1}$, resulting in a surplus of $C'C$ pounds per month at the initial price P_c. Sellers undercut each other to get rid of their individual surpluses. As the price falls, consumers increase the quantities they are willing to buy. Sellers curtail their sales levels as the production and sale of chicken becomes less profitable. At the price level P_{c1} and the quantity exchanged C_1 equilibrium under the new demand conditions is established. The

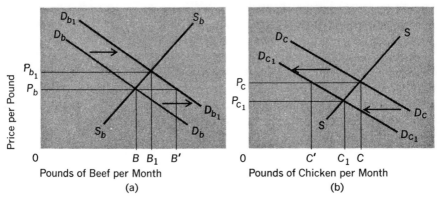

Figure 4–6
(a) Effects of an increase in demand.   (b) Effects of a decrease in demand.

general principle illustrated here is that *a decrease in demand ordinarily will decrease both the price and the quantity exchanged of a product or service.*

Changes in Supply

Changes in the conditions of supply of specific goods and services take place constantly in the economy. New resources are being discovered and existing ones are being improved. New products are developed and resources are diverted from other products toward the production of the new ones. New techniques of production are developed. Resource prices change as conditions of demand for and supply of them change.

We shall look first at an increase in supply. In Figure 4–7, D_rD_r and S_rS_r are the initial demand and supply curves for colour television receivers and P_r and R are the equilibrium price and quantity. Now suppose that as manufacturers become more familiar with production processes, cost-saving technology is developed. The supply curve will shift to the right, to some position such as $S_{r1}S_{r1}$. At the initial price P_r surpluses of

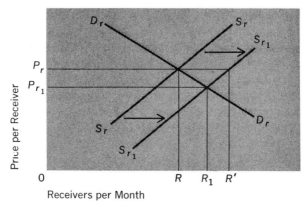

Figure 4-7
Effects of an increase in supply.

RR' per month will accumulate. The surpluses trigger undercutting by sellers and the price falls, increasing the quantities that consumers are willing to buy and decreasing the quantities that sellers will produce and place on the market. At price P_{r1} and quantity R_1, equilibrium is reached. The appropriate principle to draw from the example is that *an increase in supply ordinarily will decrease the price and increase the quantity exchanged of a product or service.*

Turning now to the impact of a decrease in supply, let us suppose that in Figure 4–8 we initially have the demand curve and the supply curve for apple pickers' services at D_aD_a and S_aS_a. The initial equilibrium price or wage rate is P_a and the quantity of labour exchanged is A man hours per week. A significant part of the apple picker supply is assumed to come from outside the country, with the foreign workers being given special work permits during the apple harvest season. Now suppose that legislation is enacted prohibiting the use of foreign apple pickers. This is equivalent to raising the prices that must be paid to domestic apple pickers in order to induce the same quantities of labour as before to seek this kind of employment. Or, from another angle, it decreases the quantities of apple picker labour available at each of the alternative possible wage rates. From either view supply decreases to some position $S_{a1}S_{a1}$, and at the price P_a there will be a shortage. Employers, faced with labour shortages, will bid against each other for the available supply. As wage rates rise more man hours of (domestic) apple picker labour are made available and apple growers want to hire smaller quantities. Wage rates will rise to the new equilibrium level of P_{a1} and quantity exchanged will be A_1. The principle here is that *a decrease in supply ordinarily will raise the price of a product or service and decrease the quantity exchanged.*

Changes in Both Demand and Supply

From the analysis of changes in demand and supply we can easily add four corollaries to the principles already deduced. (1) If both demand and supply increase, the quantity exchanged will increase but the price may increase, decrease, or remain the same. (2) Conversely, if both demand and supply decrease, the quantity exchanged will decrease and again the price may increase, decrease, or remain the same. (3) An increase in demand accompanied by a decrease in supply will increase the

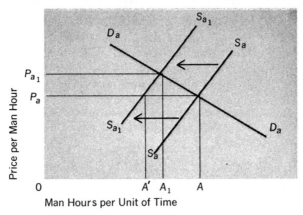

Figure 4–8
Effects of a decrease in supply.

price but the quantity exchanged may increase, decrease, or remain the same. (4) A decrease in demand accompanied by an increase in supply will decrease the price, and again the effects on quantity exchanged depend upon the circumstances of the specific case. It may be useful for the student to draw graphs for these four cases and to experiment with them. The important point to keep in mind is that for any given pair of demand and supply curves there is an equilibrium price and quantity exchanged. A change in demand or supply or both generally leads to a new equilibrium price and quantity combination.

Elasticity

We know that given the demand curve a change in the price of a product usually brings about a change in the quantity demanded even though there is no change in demand. Also we know that given the supply curve a price change usually brings about a change in quantity supplied even though there is no change in supply. But in both cases the door is left open for wide variations in the quantity response to a change in price. To sellers and buyers, as well as to economic analysts, the matter of responsiveness and quantity demanded or quantity supplied to price changes is a significant one. The measure of responsiveness is called *elasticity.* The concept of demand elasticity is more useful in economic analysis than that of supply elasticity, so we shall discuss the former in greater detail.

Elasticity of Demand

An analysis of elasticity of demand falls logically into three parts. First, how is the *responsiveness* of the quantity demanded to changes in the price of a product measured? Second, how do the *effects* of price changes on total spending on a commodity differ for different degrees of responsiveness? Third, what are the *forces that affect the responsiveness of* quantity taken to changes in the price of a product?

Measurement of Elasticity

The degree of responsiveness of quantity demanded to price changes, or the *measure of elasticity of demand*, is found by dividing the percentage change in quantity by the percentage change in price for small price changes. The number resulting from this computation is called the

TABLE 4–4
Elasticity of Demand for Hamburgers

(1) PRICE (CENTS PER HAMBURGER)	(2) QUANTITY (HAMBURGERS PER DAY)	(3) ELASTICITY
100	100	(−) 9
90	200	(−) 4
80	300	(−) $2\frac{1}{3}$
70	400	(−) $1\frac{1}{2}$
60	500	(−) 1
50	600	(−) $\frac{2}{3}$
40	700	(−) $\frac{3}{7}$
30	800	(−) $\frac{1}{4}$
20	900	(−) $\frac{1}{9}$
10	1000	

elasticity coefficient, or, more simply, *elasticity of demand.* It can be easily determined given the demand schedule or demand curve for the product being considered. Suppose that the market demand schedule for hamburgers in a small town is that of columns (1) and (2) in Table 4–4. If the price were to fall from 80 cents to 70 cents, the quantity demanded would rise from 300 to 400 per day. The percentage change in quantity is a negative 33⅓ percent, found by dividing the 100-hamburger change by the original quantity of 300. Similarly, the percentage change in price is a positive 12½ percent. Dividing the negative 33⅓ percent by the positive 12½ percent, we find the elasticity coefficient to be a negative 2.67.

All of this is more conveniently done with algebra. Let the Greek letter delta ($\triangle$) mean "the change in." The change in quantity is thus referred to as $\triangle X$. The original quantity is X. The percentage change in quantity is thus $\triangle X / X$. Similarily, if $\triangle P$ is the change in price and P is the original price, the percentage change in price is $\triangle P / P$. If we let the Greek epsilon (ε) represent the elasticity coefficient, then

$$\varepsilon = -\frac{\triangle X / X}{\triangle P / P}$$

Why the minus sign? Since the quantity demanded varies inversely with the price, either $\triangle X$ or $\triangle P$ must be negative in sign. They cannot both be positive or both be negative at the same time. Plugging the values of the preceding paragraph into the formula, we find

$$\varepsilon = -\frac{100/300}{10/80} = -\frac{100}{300} \cdot \frac{80}{10} = -2\tfrac{2}{3}$$

for the decrease in price from 80 to 70 cents.

Suppose the movement of price is from 70 to 80 cents rather than from 80 to 70 cents. The original price is 70 cents and the original quantity is 400 hamburgers. Thus

$$\varepsilon = -\frac{100/400}{10/70} = -\frac{100}{400} \cdot \frac{70}{10} = -1\tfrac{3}{4}$$

We obtain two different elasticity figures depending upon which way we move between the two price–quantity combinations.

Actually, the discrepancy appears because of the relatively large size of the price change. If the percentage price change had been extremely small, say less than 1 percent, it would have been negligible. Elasticity computations for price changes of 5 percent or larger are subject to considerable error. The smaller the relative price change for which elasticity is computed, the smaller the error will be.

Problems arise, however, in which elasticity must be computed for relative price changes large enough to result in discrepancies like that of the example. In these cases we can find and use an average elasticity coefficient that falls between the two computed above. Economists use two or three different methods of computing such an average, but an easy and convenient one is to use the lower of the two quantities to compute the percentage change in quantity and the lower of the two prices to compute the percentage change in price. In terms of algebra, the elasticity formula becomes

$$\varepsilon = -\frac{\triangle X/X_0}{\triangle P/P_1}$$

in which X_0 is the lower of the two quantities and P_1 is the lower of the two prices.

Using this formula to compute the elasticity of demand for hamburgers, we obtain an elasticity coefficient lying between the negative $2\frac{2}{3}$ and the negative $1\frac{3}{4}$. The percentage change in quantity is $33\frac{1}{3}$, the quotient of 100 hamburgers divided by 300 hamburgers. The percentage change in price is a negative $14\frac{2}{7}$. Thus the elasticity coefficient is a negative $2\frac{1}{3}$, and is more representative of elasticity for the price range of 80 to 70 cents than either of the two previously computed. The elasticities in column (3) of Table 4–4 are all computed in this way.

Turning now to Figure 4–9, we can visualize the formula for elasticity measurement in terms of the demand curve. Starting at an initial price of P_0 and a quantity demanded of X_0, let the price fall to P_1. Quantity demanded increases by $\triangle X$ to X_1. Using the lower of the two quantities as the divisor, we find that the percentage change in quantity is $\triangle X/X_0$. Using the lower of the two prices as the divisor, we find that the percentage change in price is a negative $\triangle P/P_1$. Thus between prices P_0 and P_1.

$$\varepsilon = -\frac{\triangle X/X_0}{\triangle P/P_1}$$

For most demand curves elasticity is high toward the upper end, low toward the lower end, and decreases as price decreases. This situation can be most easily illustrated with a linear or straight line demand curve like that of Figure 4–9. Suppose that for the price change from P_0 to P_1, $\triangle P$ and $\triangle X$ are the same as they are for a price change from P_2 to P_3. When price changes from P_0 to P_1 the percentage change in quantity is great because X_0 is relatively small. The percentage change in price is small because P_1 is relatively large. Consequently, elasticity is relatively high. But for a price change from P_2 to P_3, the percentage change in quantity is much smaller because X_2 is much larger than was X_0. The percentage change in price is much larger because P_3 is much smaller than was P_1. In this second case the percentage change in quantity is smaller, the percentage change in price is larger, and the elasticity coefficient is smaller than in the first case. Obviously, for price changes moving down the demand curve to the right, elasticity will be decreasing.[1] These observations are verified by the elasticity computations in Table 4–4.

Elasticity coefficients can be classified usefully into three groups. When they are numerically greater than one ($\varepsilon > 1$), ignoring the sign, we say that demand is *elastic*. When coefficients are numerically equal to 1 ($\varepsilon = 1$), we say that demand has *unitary elasticity*. And when coefficients are numerically less than 1 ($\varepsilon < 1$), we say that demand is *inelastic*. For example, the demand schedule of Table 4–4 and the demand curve of Figure 4–9 are elastic in the upper regions and inelastic in the lower re-

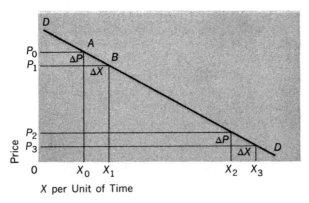

Figure 4–9
Demand elasticity computations.

gions. Between the prices of 60 and 50 cents on the demand schedule, elasticity of demand is unitary. For a linear demand curve such as that of Figure 4–9, unitary elasticity is found at the midpoint; however, this is not necessarily the case for demand curves that are nonlinear.

Effects of Price Changes on Business Receipts

When economists, legislators, sellers, and others consider the market demand for a product they are interested in what will happen to total

[1] *This will be so for demand curves with less curvature than that of a rectangular hyperbola. If the demand curve has the shape of a rectangular hyperbola, for every change in price the percentage change in quantity taken will equal the percentage change in price and the elasticity coefficient will be* —1.

business receipts (equal to total consumer expenditures) for the product when the price is changed. The demand for wheat is a case in point. A most important question for farm policy decisions is what will happen to the total receipts of wheat farmers as a group if a farm program curtailing the supply of wheat is put into effect. Given the demand for the product, the effects of supply changes and the consequent price changes on total receipts of sellers depend upon the elasticity of demand.

Consider the demand schedule for wheat together with the total receipts column in Table 4–5. Note that price decreases for which elasticity is greater than 1 increase total receipts of wheat sellers. Note also that price decreases for which elasticity is less than 1 cause total receipts to decrease. For price increases in both cases the effects on total receipts are just the opposite. When elasticity for a price change is unitary, total receipts will not be affected by a price change.[2]

TABLE 4–5
Demand, Elasticity, and Total Receipts for Wheat

ELASTICITY OF DEMAND	PRICE OF WHEAT ($s PER BU.)	QUANTITY (BU. PER WEEK)	TOTAL RECEIPTS ($s)
	1.00	1,000	1,000.00
$\varepsilon > 1$	.90	2,000	1,800.00
	.80	3,000	2,400.00
	.70	4,000	2,800.00
$\varepsilon = 1$	.60	5,000	3,000.00
	.50	6,000	3,000.00
	.40	7,000	2,800.00
$\varepsilon < 1$	.30	8,000	2,400.00
	.20	9,000	1,800.00
	.10	10,000	1,000.00

Suppose that we look at the same problem with reference to Figure 4–10. The quantity scales of Figure 4–10(a) and (b) are assumed to be identical. The vertical scale of the bottom diagram measures product price while that of the upper diagram measures total receipts of sellers. The curves *TR* and *DD* are, respectively, the total receipts curve for sellers of wheat and the demand curve for wheat. For decreases in price in the region of the demand curve where elasticity is greater than 1 total receipts

[2]*Why is this so? Consider the elasticity formula—the percentage change in quantity divided by the percentage change in price. This means that if demand is elastic, a 1 percent increase (decrease) in price generates a greater than 1 percent decrease (increase) in quantity demanded. The quantity change is thus in the* opposite *direction from and has a greater impact on total receipts than the price change. Can you apply this same line of reasoning to the case in which $\varepsilon < 1$? $\varepsilon = 1$?*

rise. For deceases in price where elasticity is less than 1 total receipts fall.

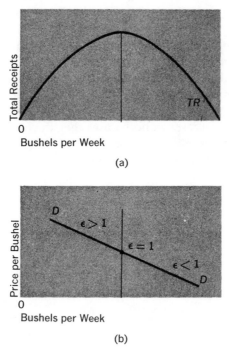

(a)

(b)

Figure 4–10
Price changes, demand elasticity, and total receipts.

If we ask ourselves now what the effects on total receipts of wheat farmers will be of a governmental farm program that decreases the supply of wheat, or if a farm organization withholds supply from the market, we know that the answer turns on the elasticity of demand. In Figure 4–11 suppose that S_1S_1 is the uncontrolled wheat supply curve and that the government succeeds in reducing it to $S'_1S'_1$. Total receipts of wheat farmers will *rise* because the elasticity of demand for the price increase is less than 1. On the other hand, suppose that S_2S_2 is the uncontrolled supply curve and that the government is able to reduce it to $S'_2S'_2$. In this case the receipts of wheat farmers will decrease, since elasticity of demand for the price increase is greater than 1. A farm program designed to increase the total receipts of wheat farmers by reducing the supply of wheat will work only if the elasticity of demand for wheat is less than 1.

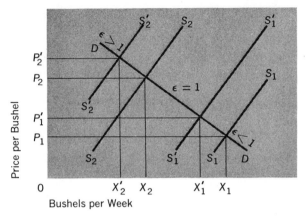

Figure 4–11
Effects of supply decreases under different elasticity conditions.

Determinants of Elasticity

What are the main factors determining whether elasticity of demand for a product is large or small? One of the most important is the *availability of substitutes* for the product to consumers. If several good substitutes for brand X of cigarettes are available, a slight rise in the price of brand X will cause a large switch by consumers to the substitute brands. If the substitute brands are not available, a slight rise in price may cause smokers to smoke somewhat less, but the decrease in quantity taken obviously would be much smaller.

The *importance of a product in consumer budgets* has some influence on elasticity of demand. This factor is most applicable to products occupying positions of insignificance. Pepper provides an example. If the price of pepper were to double, what would happen to the quantity taken off the market? The decrease would not be large because, at double the present price, expenditures for the amount now purchased would still not be large enough for consumers to give it great consideration.

Elasticity of Supply

Not much beyond definition of elasticity of supply is necessary for our purposes. Like the demand elasticity coefficient, that for supply is found by dividing the percentage change in quantity by the percentage change

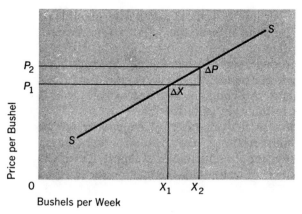

Figure 4–12
Supply elasticity computations.

in price for a small change in price along a given supply curve. In Figure 4–12 supply elasticity for an increase in price from P_1 to P_2 is usually written in the following form:

$$\eta = \frac{\triangle X/X_1}{\triangle P/P_1}$$

The more responsive quantity supplied is to changes in the price of the product, the larger the elasticity coefficient will be. We may note also that the supply elasticity coefficient will be positive in sign for an upward-sloping supply curve, since $\triangle P$ and $\triangle X$ represent changes in the same direction. They are either both positive or both negative, and thus in either case η must be positive.

Summary

This chapter explains the bedrock fundamentals of economic analysis, which include the concept of a market, the nature of demand and supply, the determination of the price of a product or service in purely competitive markets, and the concept of elasticity.

A market for a product or a service exists when buyers and sellers make contact with each other and engage in exchange. The market area varies from local to global, depending upon the nature of what is being exchanged and/or upon the time period under consideration.

Demand for an item refers to the quantities of it that consumers are willing to buy per unit of time at alternative possible prices, other things being equal. Demand information can be summarized in the form of a demand schedule or a demand curve. In identifying a specific demand curve for a product, such "other things" as consumer preferences, consumer incomes, consumer expectations, and the prices of related goods must not change. A change in any one of these will cause the demand curve to shift to the right or to the left.

Supply refers to the quantities of a good or service that sellers will place on the market at alternative prices, other things being equal. It is represented by a supply schedule or a supply curve. Changes in resource prices, in the level of technology, and in producer expectations will cause increases or decreases in supply.

The interaction of buyers and sellers in the market determines the equilibrium price and quantity exchanged of a product in purely competitive conditions. If price is below an equilibrium level, shortages will occur and buyers will bid up the price. If price is above equilibrium, surpluses will cause sellers to undercut each other. Changes in demand or supply or both will cause changes in the equilibrium price and quantity exchanged.

Elasticity of demand refers to the responsiveness of quantity demanded to changes in the price of a product. It is measured by dividing the percentage change in quantity demanded by the percentage change in price for any small price change. Demand may be elastic, of unitary elasticity, or inelastic, and the magnitude of elasticity will determine what happens to total receipts of sellers for price increases or for price decreases. Factors important in determining the elasticity of demand for a product are (1) the availability of substitutes and (2) the importance of a product in consumers' budgets.

Elasticity of supply is a less useful concept than elasticity of demand. It refers to the responsiveness of quantity placed on the market to changes in the price of a product and is measured in the same way as is elasticity of demand.

Exercises and Questions for Discussion

1. Of the following conditions, which would increase a student's demand for hamburgers?
   a. An increase in the price of hot dogs.
   b. An increase in his monthly allowance.
   c. A fall in the price of hamburgers.
   d. A note from the family lawyer that he has inherited $10,000.
   e. A bad piece of pork at a university cafeteria.

f. A vow to stop smoking.
2. Would you expect the elasticity of demand for the following items to be large or small?
   a. Insulin for diabetics.
   b. Carrots.
   c. Matches.
   d. Automobiles.
   e. Sparkly toothpaste.
   f. Toothpaste.
3. Evaluate the following statements:
   a. If demand for a good decreases and supply remains constant, price will rise and quantity taken will decrease.
   b. If supply decreases and demand remains constant, price will rise and quantity taken will decrease.
   c. If supply decreases and demand decreases, price will fall and quantity demanded will fall.
   d. If demand increases and supply decreases, price will fall but one cannot be sure of the direction of change of quantity.

Selected Readings

Boulding, Kenneth E., *Economic Analysis*, 4th ed., Vol. I. New York: Harper & Row, Publishers, Inc., 1966, Chaps. 7 and 8.

Radford, R. A., "The Economic Organization of a P.O.W. Camp," *Economica*, Vol. XII (November 1945), pp. 189–201.

Smith, Adam, *The Wealth of Nations*, Edwin Cannan, ed. New York: Random House Modern Library edition, 1937, Chaps. VI and VII.

Part 2

Markets for Goods and Services

In this part of the book we begin a detailed examination of the several faces of economic theory. We shall cover the markets for goods and services—the upper half of the circular flow model pictured in Figure 2–1. Since our subject matter will be individual consumers, individual firms, and specific industries or product groups, it properly belongs to the area of microeconomics. But it is only a part of the complete area; the remainder—markets for resources—is developed in Part III.

The objective in Part II is to shed light on the mechanisms in a free enterprise economy that determine what is to be produced and that organize production. We shall be concerned with the economic analysis of how it works and, toward the end of Part II, with economic policy measures enacted by the government, presumably to make it work better. The chapters on consumer demand focus on the forces underlying the demand concept introduced in Chapter 4, while those on the principles of production and the costs of production are intended to do the same thing for the supply concept.[1]

---

[1]*This will not be completely evident until we get into Chapter 9. In Chapters 9, 10, and 11, the determinants of prices and, consequently, of outputs of goods and services are examined much more thoroughly and under a much wider variety of circumstances than in Chapter 4. Chapters 12, 13, and 14 evaluate the effectiveness of the mechanisms as well as current major policy measures.*

5

Consumer Behaviour and Demand, I

What is it that determines how an individual allocates his available purchasing power among a number of different goods and services? And why is it that he will take more of a given product at a lower price than he will at a higher price? You have probably not given much thought to these questions, and raising them is almost like asking why an apple falls down instead of up. But pursuit of the latter question paid off handsomely in terms of fame if not fortune for Sir Isaac Newton. Similarly, for a beginning economist there are important principles to be derived from an examination of such questions.

In the late 1800s economists developed what has come to be known as the utility theory of demand, and the analysis in this chapter follows the lines that they staked out. The indifference curve analysis of the next chapter provides an alternative (or perhaps a supplementary) explanation that is generally preferred today. Yet various aspects of utility theory are used broadly in both economic analysis and economic policy-making, so that it seems worthwhile to see what the theory has to offer.

The Concept of Utility

Suppose we call the satisfaction a consumer obtains from consuming a good or service its *utility* to him. An increase or a decrease in his weekly rate of consumption of any one product, say his food intake, will increase or decrease his utility. If we pursue this causal relationship, we can distinguish between the *total amount of utility* or satisfaction received from whatever quantity he consumes per week and any *changes in utility* that may occur when he changes his rate of consumption from one level to another. We shall examine each of these more closely.

Total Utility

What can we say about the way in which the consumer's total utility from the consumption of a product or a service varies as his consumption level of the product is changed? Suppose we conduct a hypothetical experiment on a consumer who has been placed under our control. The product to be tested is beef, measured in pounds. The environment in which we keep the consumer is maintained as constant as possible: we hold his consumption of other products at constant levels; we have a psychiatrist whose sole function is to prevent changes from occurring in his mental attitudes; we have a social director who sees to it that his social contacts from week to week will not influence his beef consumption; and his level of physical activity over time is not changed.

Now, over a series of weeks we change the consumer's weekly level of beef consumption and we record the resulting levels of total utility from the product.[1] Table 5–1 shows a set of results conforming to what we would expect ordinarily. As the number of pounds of beef consumed per week increases, total utility yielded the consumer by it will increase too—up to a point. At some quantity—11 pounds per week in the example—the consumer is receiving as much utility as he is capable of receiving from this product. He is saturated with it, and we call that quantity his *saturation point*. The information contained in Table 5–1 is plotted graphically in Figure 5–1(a).

---

[1]*We are confronted immediately with a rather messy problem that has created considerable discussion among economists over time and that has never been satisfactorily dispensed with. Is utility measurable in the* cardinal *sense; that is, in such a way that we can say definitely that four units of utility represent twice as much as two? Or can we speak of utility magnitudes in an* ordinal *sense only; that is, in such a way that numbers assigned to them indicate which are greater and which are smaller without conveying any information about how much? For pedagogical purposes, we shall act as though it were cardinal, leaving the controversy for more advanced study, and assume that the consumer can inform us for each quantity of beef the number of units of utility it yields him.*

TABLE 5-1

Total and Marginal Utility Schedules for Beef

	(1)	(2)	(3)
	QUANTITY OF BEEF (LBS. PER WEEK)	TOTAL UTILITY	MARGINAL UTILITY
	1	10	10
	2	19	9
	3	27	8
	4	34	7
	5	40	6
	6	45	5
	7	49	4
	8	52	3
	9	54	2
	10	55	1
Saturation Point	11	55	0
	12	54	(—)1

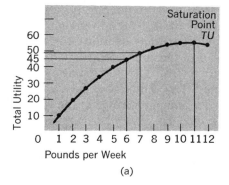

(a)

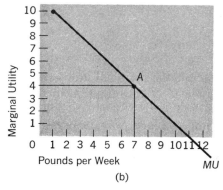

(b)

Figure 5-1

The utility from beef consumption.

Marginal Utility

The change in the total utility a consumer receives from a product when his consumption level of it is increased or decreased by a small amount is called *marginal utility*. This is the first of the many marginal concepts that we shall use throughout the book. All of them are the same mathematically and a thorough understanding of the one at hand will remove a good many bumps from the road ahead. Mathematically we can think of marginal utility as the *rate of change* of total utility as the consumer changes his consumption level by small increments.

The marginal utility of beef to our beef-eating consumer can be computed readily from the total utility schedule of Table 5–1. Consider the six-pound level of consumption. From column (2) of the table we note that a change from the six-pound level to the seven-pound level increases total utility from 45 to 49 units of utility. Or, if we start at the seven-pound level and move back to the six-pound level, total utility decreases from 49 to 45 units. In either case the change in total utility is four units for the one-pound change. This is the marginal utility of the seventh pound and is so recorded in column (3) of the table. Marginal utilities of beef to the consumer at other consumption levels are found in the same manner and round out the column.

What we can do with the table we can do also with its graphic counterpart. Consider the six-pound-per-week consumption level in Figures 5–1(a). The *TU* curve shows the consumer's total utility as 45 units. If the consumption level were raised to seven pounds, it shows that the consumer's total utility will rise to 49 units. The upward movement with reference to the total utility axis—four units of utility—is the marginal utility of a seventh pound of beef to the consumer.

Now consider Figure 5–1(b). The horizontal or quantity axis is identical to that of Figure 5–1(a), but along the vertical axis we measure *changes* in total utility per one-unit change in the consumption level; that is, we show *marginal utility*. To locate the marginal utility curve we first find the numerical magnitude of marginal utility at each consumption level and then we plot the coordinates. For example, by plotting marginal utility at the seven-pound-per-week consumption level we get point *A*. (Determine for yourself that the other points tracing out *MU* are computed and plotted correctly.)

Diminishing Marginal Utility

In the foregoing example the marginal utility of beef to the consumer decreases as his weekly level of consumption increases. Is it reasonable to expect that this will be the case for most goods and services to most consumers? It will be impossible to provide an unequivocal answer here; we can only appeal to our every day experience. What about shoes? If you have only one pair of shoes per year to consume, will you get a large increase in satisfaction from an additional pair? How would your answer differ if you had five pairs per year available to you initially? In all probability a sixth pair would add less to your total utility than a second pair, and if you think through the list of items you purchase regularly, diminishing marginal utility will prevail for most. It seems to be common enough for us to speak of the existence of the *principle of diminishing marginal utility*. In Figure 5–1(a) the principle is evidenced in the concave-downward shape of the *TU* curve. In Figure 5–1(b) the downward slope to the right of the *MU* curve is the graphic representation of it.

Some goods or services may be perverse, however. Suppose you are an avid golfer. One game per year is too little to keep in practice and two are not much better. But as you increase the yearly number of games you play, each one-game increase may add more to the total utility you receive from golf than the preceding one did; that is, marginal utility may be increasing. Still, even for golf games, there must be a saturation point. If this is so as the consumption level approaches it, marginal utility must be decreasing even though for lower levels of consumption it is increasing. (Study Figure 5–1(a) and see if you can redraw it to reflect this situation. At the saturation point what is the magnitude of marginal utility?)

Consumer Preferences

If we had the patience and if the consumer on whom we are experimenting would hold still long enough, presumably we could obtain total utility curves and the corresponding marginal utility curves for all of the things he is interested in consuming. All together these would provide us with a set of graphs rather staggering in number picturing the consumer's pattern of preferences. Suppose we simplify the matter conceptually by looking at only two of his marginal utility curves, those illustrated in Figue 5–2 for product *X* and product *Y*.

What do these two diagrams tell us? The consumer is easily saturated with product *X*. Its marginal utility (but not its total utility) falls to zero at a low level of consumption. Suppose that *X* is strychnine used for medicinal purposes and the consumer is a heart patient. Small consumption levels may yield very high marginal utilities, but the additions to satisfaction fall off very rapidly as the dosage is increased. Product *Y*, on the other hand, is an item with which the consumer is not easily saturated.

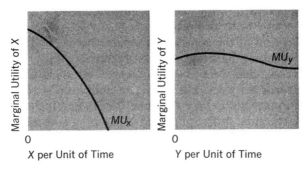

Figure 5-2
A consumer's marginal utility curves.

As the consumption level is increased, the additions to total utility decrease very slowly. The consumer is obviously a woman and product Y is clothing.

Principles of Income Allocation

In your role as a consumer what do you consider to be your major problem? Undoubtedly it is one of inadequate income to purchase as much as you would like of different goods and services. Or, to put the problem in a slightly different way, given your income you want to spend it on items available to you so as to secure as much satisfaction as possible from your purchases. This is the premise underlying the theory of consumer behaviour; that is, the objective of the typical consumer is to allocate his income among different goods and services in such a way that he maximizes his satisfaction from the consumption of all of them. The given data of the problem are the individual consumer's income, his preference pattern, and the prices of whatever is available to be purchased.

Again we shall impose on an unnamed consumer, using him as a subject for experimentation and observation. His preferences (his utility schedules or curves) are given and remain constant, that is, they do not shift, while the experiment is in progress. These are presented in schedule form in Table 5-2. His income or purchasing power per week is nine dollars and does not change. To simplify matters we shall let the consumer live in a two-commodity world in which only food and clothing are available. The price of food is two dollars per bushel and the price of clothing is one dollar per yard. Both food and clothing can be purchased in half units if this seems to be desirable.

What allocation of the consumer's income between food and clothing will maximize his satisfaction, or his aggregate utility, from the two? Suppose the consumer were to spend everything on clothing, thereby obtaining nine yards per week. His aggregate utility is 63 utility units, found by adding marginal utilities for the quantities to and including nine yards of clothing.[2] Marginal utility of a yard of clothing is three at this level of consumption. The consumer is likely to be warm but hungry and to contemplate the food supply. If he were to give up a dollar's worth of clothing, his utility would fall by three units—the marginal utility of the ninth yard. If that dollar were spent on food, he would obtain 7½ units of utility— the marginal utility of the first half bushel of food. Consequently, he would experience a net gain of 4½ units by transferring a dollar from clothing to food.

Further gains can be obtained from further transfers. By giving up the eighth yard of clothing the consumer sacrifices four units of utility, but as the dollar withdrawn from this use is spent on the remaining one half of the first bushel of food, he picks up 7½ units of utility for a net gain of 3½. Similarly, the transfer of another dollar from the seventh yard of clothing to the first half of the second bushel of food yields a net gain of two utility units. Then, if the sixth yard of clothing is given up in return for the rest of the second bushel of food, still another net gain of one utility unit occurs.

No further gains in aggregate utility or satisfaction are possible. The exchange of the fifth yard of clothing for one half of the third bushel of food would cause a one-half unit net loss in aggregate utility. Similarly, if one half of the second bushel of food were given up for the sixth yard of clothing, a net utility loss of one unit would occur. The satisfaction-maximizing allocation of the consumer's income between food and clothing is four dollars for two bushels of food and five dollars for five yards of clothing. At this point the marginal utility of a dollar's worth of food and the marginal utility of a dollar's worth of clothing are each seven units of utility.

We have uncovered the principle underlying maximization of satisfaction by an individual consumer—he must allocate his income among the different goods and services available to him in such a way that the marginal utility per dollar's worth on one is equal to the marginal utility

---

[2] *If you do not understand why the total utility of any specific quantity is found by adding marginal utilities for all units to and including that quantity, look again at Table 5–1 and Figure 5–1 and reread the textual explanation of both the total and marginal utility concepts.*

TABLE 5-2
Marginal Utility Schedules for Food and Clothing

Food		Clothing	
QUANTITY (BU. PER WEEK)	MARGINAL UTILITY (MU_f)	QUANTITY (YDS. PER WEEK)	MARGINAL UTILITY (MU_c)
1	15	1	11
2	14	2	10
3	13	3	9
4	12	4	8
5	11	5	7
6	9	6	6
7	7	7	5
8	5	8	4
9	3	9	3
10	0	10	0

per dollar's worth of every other one. We can state these conditions in the form of simple equations for our two-commodity world. First,

$$\frac{MU_f}{P_f} = \frac{MU_c}{P_c}$$

in which MU_f is the marginal utility per bushel of food at his current consumption level; P_f is the price per bushel; MU_c is the marginal utility per yard of clothing at his current consumption level; and P_c is the price per yard. Note that in the example the marginal utility per dollar's worth of each is seven units of utility. Second, the income limitation of the consumer is expressed as

$$f \cdot P_f + c \cdot P_c = I$$

in which f and c are the consumption levels, respectively, of food in bushels and clothing in yards and I is the consumer's available purchasing power. These statements are not restricted to the two-commodity world but can be extended to as many goods and services as a consumer may desire. All we need to do is add terms to the equations.

The principle of diminishing marginal utility was probably obscured by the mechanics of the foregoing analysis. Nevertheless, it was there; look at Table 5–2. If the principle were not operative, the conditions we have listed as determining maximum satisfaction for the consumer might not hold. Look again at the consumer's *equilibrium position*—his satisfaction-maximizing position—in Table 5–2. Suppose now that the marginal utility of food and clothing were increasing as shown in Table 5–3 instead of decreasing. The consumer could make net additions to his aggregate utility either by transferring dollars from food to clothing or by transferring dollars from clothing to food; and, depending upon which way he begins to transfer, he will end up spending his entire income on one product.

Consumers are not always successful in making the precise satisfaction-maximizing adjustments reached in the example. Sometimes they are not sure whether the marginal utility of a dollar in a proposed use would be greater or less than that in a present use. Experience in consuming a product may not live up to what the consumer anticipated when he decided to buy it. Tradition and habit may inhibit transfers of dollars. Sometimes consumers are ill informed as to what is available or misinformed as to the satisfaction that some goods can be expected to yield. Still, it seems reasonable to believe that most consumers most of the time are trying to place their dollars where they will contribute the most to satisfaction. (If you had an extra five dollars to spend this week what would you do with it?)

TABLE 5-3
Marginal Utility Schedules for Food and Clothing[a]

Food		Clothing	
QUANTITY (BU. PER WEEK)	MARGINAL UTILITY (MU_f)	QUANTITY (YDS. PER WEEK)	MARGINAL UTILITY (MU_c)
1	12	1	3
2	14	2	4
3	15	3	5
4	16	4	6
5	17	5	7
6	18	6	8
7	19	7	9
8	20	8	10
9	21	9	11
10	22	10	12

[a]*This table is presented solely to demonstrate the effects on the consumer's allocation of income if the principle of diminishing marginal utility were not operative. Since we assume in this chapter that the principle is operative, this table should be disregarded for all purposes except the one for which it is presented.*

Principles of Demand

The inverse relationship between the price of a product and the quantity of it that consumers will take per unit of time was introduced in Chapter 4.

Now, with the aid of the analysis developed in the preceding section, a more detailed explanation is possible. Market demand for a product is composed of the demands of individual consumers, so again we confine our attention to the consumer on whom we have been experimenting.

We are concerned with discovering what determines the demand curve of an individual consumer for any specific product and why it is expected to slope downward to the right. As we experiment with the consumer there are several conditioning factors that we want to hold constant in order to get at the unique way in which the quantity taken will vary as the price of the product changes. These are (1) the consumer's preferences—his utility schedules, (2) the consumer's income, and (3) the prices of related products. Suppose now that we limit the consumer to a two-commodity world;[3] his preferences to those of Table 5–2; his income to nine dollars per week; and the price of clothing to one dollar

TABLE 5–4
Demand Schedule for Food

P_f ($s PER BU.)	f (BU.)
2	2
1	6

per yard. All that remains is to confront the consumer with different prices of food and record the quantity he takes at each price when he is allocating his income between the two products in such a way that he is maximizing satisfaction or aggregate utility.

Repeating an earlier experiment, suppose we confront the consumer initially with a food price of two dollars per bushel. He maximizes satisfaction by taking two bushels of food and five yards of clothing, the marginal utility per dollar's worth of each being seven units of utility. We have established one point on his demand curve for food: at a price of two dollars each he will take two bushels. This is listed as the first row of the demand schedule shown by Table 5–4 and is plotted as point *A* in Figure 5–3.

Now suppose we change the price of food to one dollar per bushel. At two bushels of food and five yards of clothing the consumer is no longer maximizing aggregate utility. In the first place, he is not spending all of his purchasing power and, second, the marginal utility of a dollar's worth of food exceeds that of a dollar's worth of clothing. The former is now 14 utility units while the latter is still 7.

[3]*This limitation is not really necessary but it does greatly simplify the problem—perhaps too much.*

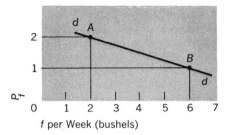

Figure 5–3
Consumer demand curve for food.

The consumer can add to his aggregate utility by spending the two extra dollars available to him on the third and fourth bushels of food. He would prefer these to the sixth and seventh yards of clothing because of their higher marginal utility per dollar's worth to him. But he is not yet maximizing satisfaction. At four bushels of food and five yards of clothing the marginal utility per dollar's worth of food is 12 units of utility while that of a dollar's worth of clothing is only 7.

Still more can be added to aggregate utility by the transfer of expenditure from clothing to food. If the fifth yard of clothing per week is given up and the dollar thus made available is spent for a fifth bushel of food per week, there is a net gain of four utility units. Further, if the fourth yard of clothing is foregone and the sixth bushel of food per week is taken in its place, a gain of one utility unit occurs. The marginal utility per dollar's worth of each is now 9.

The consumer is now maximizing satisfaction and a second point on his demand curve for food has been established. A one dollar transfer of expenditure in either direction would decrease his aggregate utility. At one dollar per bushel the consumer will take six bushels of food, giving us the second row of Table 5–4 and point *B* in Figure 5–3. We have demonstrated the principle that the consumer will take more of a product at a lower price than he will at a higher one. With more extensive marginal utility schedules in which quantities are more finely graduated, a number of points on a consumer's demand schedule could be determined in a similar manner and plotted as a demand curve.

A review of the derivation of the two points on the consumer's demand curve for food will reveal that two forces were at work causing quantity taken to rise as the price declined. On the one hand the price decline from two dollars per bushel to one dollar per bushel increased the consumer's purchasing power—his dollars spent on food go farther than they would previously. We call this an *income effect*, an increase in his *real income* or purchasing power even though his *money income* is fixed. (Have you ever thought of the fact that decreases in the prices of things that you buy constitute an increase in your real income?)

On the other hand, the decrease in the price of food relative to the price of clothing increases the marginal utility of a dollar's worth of food relative to that of a dollar's worth of clothing. Since the former now becomes greater than the latter, the consumer is induced to substitute dollars' worth of food for dollars' worth of clothing in his expenditure pattern. This is called the *substitution effect*. (What would be your reaction to a decrease in the price of steak relative to the prices of other meat, poultry, and fish dishes at your favourite cafeteria?) In the example given the entire increase in the quantity of food the consumer takes comes from a combination of the income effect and the substitution effect.

Individual Consumer Demand and Market Demand

Market demand for any good or service originates in the wants of individual consumers. Conceptually, the market demand curve that we met in Chapter 4 is built up from individual consumer demand curves for the product under consideration. The forces underlying individual consumer demand curves have just been examined.

Relation Between Market and Individual Consumer Demand

The market demand curves for particular products are built up from individual consumer or household demand curves for those products. Market demand originates in the wants of individual consumers. Each consumer of product X has his own demand curve for it. By putting together the demands of all consumers we arrive at market demand for the product.

A market demand schedule is illustrated in Table 5–5. For purposes of simplification suppose that Mr. A and Mr. B are the only consumers of product X. As the table indicates, we simply add together the quantities per unit of time that both would be willing to take at each alternative price level in order to obtain the market demand schedule. Note that at any price above eight dollars Mr. B is the entire market. A table of this kind can be readily extended to as many consumers as there are in the market for a particular product.

TABLE 5–5
Individual Consumer and Market Demand Schedules for X

Mr. A		Mr. B		Market	
P_x	X PER UNIT OF TIME	P_x	X PER UNIT OF TIME	P_x	X PER UNIT OF TIME
$10	0	$10	1	$10	1
9	0	9	2	9	2
8	2	8	3	8	5
7	4	7	4	7	8
6	6	6	5	6	11
5	8	5	6	5	14
4	10	4	7	4	17
3	13	3	8	3	21
2	17	2	9	2	26
1	22	1	10	1	32

In Figure 5–4 the construction of a market demand curve from those of individual consumers is shown graphically. At price P_2 neither Mr. A nor Mr. B would take any of the product. At price P_1 Mr. A would take none of the product but Mr. B would take quantity x'_1. Thus at price P_1 quantity X_1 for the market as a whole is the same as quantity x'_1 in Mr. B's diagram. Between price P_2 and price P_1 the market demand curve is identical to that of Mr. B, since he is the only one in the market through that price range. At price P_0 Mr. A would take quantity x_0 and Mr. B would take quantity x'_0. Together they would take quantity X_0, the sum

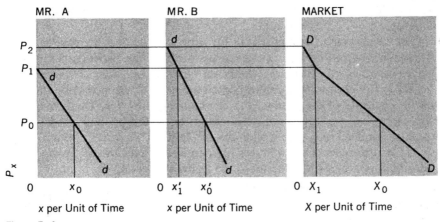

Figure 5–4
The market demand curve.

of quantity x_0 and quantity x'_0. All other points on the market demand curve are determined in the same way—by adding horizontally the amounts that both would take at each possible price level. Thus the market demand curve is found by summing horizontally the individual consumer demand curves for the product. Again the process can be extended to as many consumers as there may be in the market for the product.

Summary

The utility theory of individual consumer behaviour and demand is examined in this chapter. The preferences of a consumer are described by his total and marginal utility curves for goods and services. The total utility yielded to him by any specific commodity increases as his consumption of it per unit of time is increased up to the saturation point. Marginal utility of the product, defined as the change in total utility per unit change in the consumption level, decreases as the consumption level approaches the saturation point. This principle of diminishing marginal utility is basic to the analysis of individual consumer behaviour and demand.

A consumer tends to allocate the purchasing power available to him among different goods and services in such a way that he maximizes his aggregate utility or satisfaction from all of them. This is accomplished when (1) the marginal utility per dollar's worth of one is equal to that of every other one and (2) when his entire purchasing power is utilized. When the consumer is maximizing satisfaction he is said to be in equilibrium.

The consumer's demand curve for a product shows the quantities he will take at alternative prices, given his preferences, his income, and the prices of other goods. Under the given circumstances we specify a price for the product, let the consumer reach an equilibrium position, and read off the quantity of the product that is taken at that price. Then we change the price, let the consumer re-establish equilibrium, and read off the quantity that he will take at the new price level. A series of such price–quantity observations constitutes his demand curve for the product. Ordinarily it is downward sloping to the right. The change in quantity taken when price changes stems from a combination of an income effect and a substitution effect.

The market demand curve for a product is constructed from individual demand curves for it. At each price level the quantity point on the market demand curve is the summation of the quantity points on individual consumer demand curves.

Exercises and Questions for Discussion

1. A small boy is given \$2.25 to spend an hour at Plenti-Fun Amusement Park one evening. It is an unusual amusement park in that only two activities are offered, the roller coaster rides, which are 50 cents each, and trips through the fun house at 25 cents a trip. Given the following utility schedules, how many roller coaster rides and how many trips through the fun house will the boy take?

Marginal Utility Schedules for
Roller Coaster Rides and Trips through the Fun House

Roller Coaster Rides		Trips through Fun House	
RIDES	MU_R	TRIPS	MU_T
1	40	1	18
2	32	2	15
3	24	3	12
4	16	4	9
5	9	5	7
6	4	6	5
7	2	7	2
8	0	8	1

2. Adam Smith in *Wealth of Nations* wrote about a diamond-water paradox. He said: "Nothing is more useful than water; but it will purchase scarce anything; scarce anything can be had in exchange for it. A diamond, on the contrary, has scarce any value in use; but a very great quantity of other goods may frequently be exchanged for it." Upon reading this statement a later economist, Alexander Gray, wrote of Smith: "The wiley bird had never heard of marginal utility." Gray gave the clue to the solution to this paradox. Can you solve it?

3. Black, Thompson, and Hood are landscaping their yards and are in the market for palm trees. These three men are the only persons in the economy who want to buy palm trees and the following are their demand schedules:

Black		Thompson		Hood	
P_t	Q_t	P_t	Q_t	P_t	Q_t
\$40	1	\$40	0	\$40	0
35	2	35	0	35	0
30	3	30	1	30	1
25	4	25	3	25	2
20	5	20	5	20	3
15	6	15	7	15	4
10	7	10	9	10	5
5	8	5	11	5	6

Construct the market demand curve for palm trees.

4. Phil Parker's wife was constantly nagging him to ask his boss for a raise. One morning he screwed up his courage, asked for it, and received in return a pat on the back and a plea to be patient. On the way home at that evening as he read the *Wall Street Journal* he discovered that the general price level in the past month had dropped by 3 percent. On arriving home he burst through the front door with the announcement that he had received a raise. Was he telling the truth?

Selected Readings

Fellner, William, *Modern Economic Analysis.* New York: McGraw-Hill Book Company, Inc., 1960, Chap. 14.

Marshall, Alfred, "Value," *Readings in Economic Doctrines*, Vol. 1, H. L. Balsley, ed. Patterson, N.J.: Littlefield, Adams, and Company, 1961, pp. 119–121.

Watson, Donald S., *Price Theory and Its Uses*, 2d ed. Boston: Houghton Mifflin Company, 1968, Chap. 4.

6

Consumer Behaviour and Demand, II

In the 1930s a pair of British economists, sparked by the controversy over whether utility is measurable in a cardinal sense, came forward with an approach to the theory of individual consumer demand that avoids the concept of utility altogether.[1] Their *indifference curve approach* is widely used as an alternative to the utility approach of Chapter 5. We shall develop it here to attack again the questions of the last chapter—what determines the consumer's allocation of income among different products, and why do demand curves slope downward to the right. In so doing we shall start from scratch, completely ignoring the preceding chapter, except for the section relating individual consumer demand to market demand for a product.

Concepts of Indifference Curve Analysis

Two fundamental concepts are employed in indifference curve analysis. One of these, the *consumer's indifference map*, has to do with the consumer's preferences, or what he would like to do. The other is his *line of attainable combinations* or his *budget line*, which provides information on the restrictions he encounters in pursuing the satisfaction of his wants.

[1] *J. R. Hicks and R. G. D. Allen, "A Reconsideration of the Theory of Value,"* Economica, *February, May 1934, pp. 52-76 and 196-219, respectively.*

The Indifference Map

A consumer confronted with different combinations of mixed goods and services should be able to give us some information regarding the relative importance to him of each combination. He should be able to list the combinations he prefers, and he should also be able to indicate at any given point in his preference ranking those combinations of goods for which he has equal preference or those that he expects would yield him equivalent satisfaction.

As an example, suppose we select a consumer for observation and limit him to a two-commodity world in which only food and clothing are available. In Figure 6–1 bushels of food are measured along the horizontal axis and yards of clothing are represented by the vertical axis. Any point in the quadrant formed by the two axes represents a combination of food and clothing.

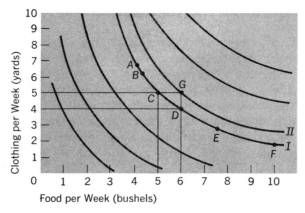

Figure 6–1
A consumer's indifference map.

Some combinations in the quadrant will be preferred by the consumer over others. Combination *C* contains five yards of clothing and five bushels of food per week. Combination *G* contains five yards of clothing and *six* bushels of food. Clearly the consumer would prefer *G* to *C*, since both contain the same amount of clothing but *G* contains a greater amount of food.[2] Other combinations preferred to *G* and still others less preferred than *C* can be located on the graph.

---

[2]*There is a possibility that at five bushels of food the consumer is saturated with it —that is, that additional units per week would add nothing to his enjoyment of food —but we shall assume for the present that the saturation point is not reached for either product.*

There must be other combinations of food and clothing that the consumer believes would yield the same satisfaction as combination *C*. Suppose he informs us that this is so for the bundle of goods represented by *D*. In comparing *D* with *C* we find that it contains one less yard of clothing and one more bushel of food per week. Apparently the consumer believes that the loss in satisfaction occasioned by the decrease in clothing consumption would be just offset by the gain in satisfaction coming from the increase in food consumption. Suppose that still other combinations equivalent to *C* are represented by *A*, *B*, *E,* and *F*. If enough such equivalent combinations were plotted, they would trace out the *indifference curve* labelled *I* in Figure 6–1. An indifference curve through point *C* is the locus of points representing all the combinations of food and clothing that the consumer considers to be the equivalent of *C*—he would be indifferent if required to make a choice among those points.

All combinations believed by the consumer to be equivalent to combination *G* are represented by points making up indifference curve *II.* Since combination *G* is preferred to combination *C*, then all combinations represented by indifference curve *II* must be preferable to all of those represented by *I*.

A graph such as Figure 6–1 contains a large number of indifference curves. The entire set is called the consumer's *indifference map* and it presents a graphic picture of his preference structure. Every preference rank is represented by an indifference curve; any curve farther from the origin than another represents a set of equivalent combinations preferred to the set of equivalent combinations of the lower curve. In drawing an indifference map we usually draw in only those indifference curves needed for the analysis at hand.

Characteristics of Indifference Curves

The indifference curves forming a consumer's indifference map have three important characteristics: (1) they slope downward to the right; (2) no two indifference curves will interesect; and (3) they are convex to the origin of the indifference curve diagram. How do we know that these characteristics prevail?

Downward Slope

If the consumer is not saturated with either of the products shown on his indifference map, it follows that an indifference curve will slope downward to the right. Suppose a student consuming both football games and dances has one football game per season taken away from him. The new combination of the two, containing the same number of dances but one less football game, would be less preferred than the old. However, since the student is not saturated with dances, additional dances could be added until a third combination just equivalent to the original one is discovered; that is, it is possible to add enough dances to his recreation schedule to just compensate for the loss of a football game. This is what the downward slope of an indifference curve means.

Look again at combination *C* in Figure 6–1. If a yard of clothing is taken away from the consumer, a bushel of food must be added to avoid moving the consumer to a less-preferred combination. This brings the consumer to combination *D*, which is equivalent to combination *C* and must necessarily lie below and to the right of *C*.

Nonintersection

Two indifference curves on the same indifference map of a consumer cannot intersect. The combinations of goods shown by one indifference curve—the one farthest from the origin—are preferable to those of the other, otherwise both could not exist. Now consider the combinations shown by the less preferable curve, say indifference curve *I* in Figure 6–1. Any preferred combination must contain at least as much of one product and more of the other than some one of the combinations on the less preferable curve. This condition in itself rules out the possibility of intersection. We cannot infer from this that two indifference curves are everywhere the same distance apart. They may approach each other without intersecting.

Convexity to the Origin

The more a person consumes of any one product relative to another the less important a unit of it will be to him relative to a unit of the other. In Figure 6–2 compare the consumer's desires at combination *A*, at which point he is consuming large amounts of clothing relative to food, with what they would be at combination *C* on the same indifference curve, at which point he is consuming small amounts of clothing relative to food. At combination *A* the consumer would surely be willing to give up more clothing—say three yards—to get an additional bushel of food than he would at point C.[3] At point C we suppose that he is willing to give up only one fourth of a yard of clothing for an additional bushel of food per week. If this is indeed the case, then as we consider combinations lying on the same indifference curve from A to C, the consumer would be willing to give up less and less clothing to obtain additional bushels of food as his weekly consumption of clothing is decreased while that of food is in-

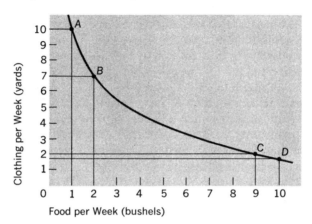

Figure 6-2
Diminishing marginal rate of substitution.

creased. This state of affairs is represented graphically by an indifference curve that is convex to the origin. A thorough study of the indifference curve in Figure 6–2 will make this point clear. What would the indifference curve look like if the consumer were willing to give up more and more clothing in exchange for each additional unit of food per week?

At any point on an indifference curve we call the amount of one product that the consumer is just willing to give up to obtain an additional unit of the other his *marginal rate of substitution* of the latter for the former. From point A to point B in Figure 6–2 the marginal rate of substitution of food for clothing, or MRS_{fc}, is 3. From C to D it is ¼. Between A and D it is decreasing as clothing is given up and as food is added to the weekly consumption pattern. This phenomenon is referred to as *the principle of the diminishing marginal rate of substitution of one product for another.*

The Line of Attainable Combinations

What are the major restrictions that you encounter as a consumer? The answer comes easily enough—your income is too small. From a slightly

---

[3]*We have not proved anything here; we are simply relying on casual observations to support the point.*

different point of view, given your income, the prices of goods and services are too high for you to purchase as much as you would like.

This problem can be expressed in a form compatible with the consumer's indifference map. Limiting the consumer to a two-commodity world, food and clothing, suppose he has 50 dollars per week to spend; the price of food is 1 dollar per bushel and the price of clothing is 2 dollars per yard. If he spends all of his income or purchasing power on clothing, he can purchase 25 yards per week. This possibility appears as point *A* in Figure 6–3(a). If the consumer were to decide that eating, too, is desirable, he could obtain 10 bushels of food by giving up 5 yards of clothing. Giving up the clothing would release 10 dollars of his purchasing power which could be spent for the 10 bushels of food. The consumer would then be at point *B*, purchasing 20 yards of clothing and 10 bushels of food each week. He can increase his consumption of food to 20 bushels by giving up another 5 yards of clothing. Substitution of food for clothing can be continued in this way until the consumer is taking no clothing and 50 bushels of food—spending his entire income on food. All possible combinations of clothing and food available to him lie on or under the straight

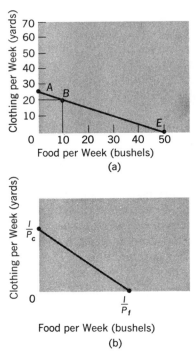

Figure 6–3
The line of attainable combinations.

line *AE*, which is called appropriately his *line of attainable combinations*, or his *budget line*.

The rate at which the consumer is able to substitute food for clothing is determined by the ratio of the price of food to the price of clothing. With the price of clothing at two dollars per yard and that of food at one dollar per bushel, the ratio is one half, meaning that one-half yard of clothing must be given up to obtain an additional bushel of food, or that two bushels of food must be given up to obtain an additional yard of clothing.

A more general representation of the consumer's line of attainable combinations is shown in Figure 6–3(b). Dividing the consumer's income, *I*, by the price of clothing, P_c, we obtain the point marked $I/(P_c)$ on the clothing axis. This represents the amount of clothing he can buy if he takes no food. Dividing his income by the price of food, P_f, we obtain $I/(P_f)$, the amount of food he could buy if he purchases no clothing. The straight line joining the two points is the line of attainable combinations. Note that its slope,[4] showing how much clothing must be given up to get an additional bushel of food, is $(P_f)/(P_c)$.

Allocation of Income Among Goods and Services

We assume that the consumer's objective is to maximize satisfaction; that is, to distribute his income among goods and services available to him in such a way that he obtains as high a level of satisfaction as possible. His indifference map and his line of attainable combinations provide the tools for uncovering the principles according to which this objective is accomplished. These are brought together in Figure 6–4. The consumer's income is fixed at I_1, while the prices of clothing and food are assumed to be P_{c1} and P_{f1}, respectively. These determine the position of his line of attainable combinations, *AF*. We have drawn only a few of the many indifference curves on his indifference map.

An Elementary Exposition

Imagine now that the consumer is at point *A* and is going to journey across his preference field along his line of attainable combinations. Any combination of clothing and food along that line or under it is available

---

[4]*The slope of the line is $[I/(P_c)]/[I/(P_f)]$, which reduces to $I/(P_c) \cdot (P_f)/I$, or $(P_f)/(P_c)$.*

to him. As he moves from *A* toward *B*, giving up clothing purchases and increasing his food purchases, what happens to his satisfaction level? He is moving to higher indifference curves—to combinations of goods more and more highly preferred—or to higher and higher levels of satisfaction. But he can do even better if upon reaching *B* he continues to and through point *C* until he reaches combination *D*. If he goes beyond *D* toward *E* and *F*, he is moving to lower indifference curves; that is, to less preferred combinations.

He maximizes his satisfaction with combination *D*, taking f_1 bushels of food and c_1 yards of clothing per week. His line of attainable combinations will not let him reach an indifference curve above *IV*. Note that on indifferent curve *IV* only combination *D* is available to him. For monetary reasons all other combinations shown by it are out of his reach. The combination at which satisfaction is maximized is that at which the line of attainable combinations is tangent to an indifference curve, that indifference curve being the highest one the consumer can reach.

An Advanced Exposition

Although the preceding section explains the consumer's allocation of income well enough for most purposes in a beginning economics course, it may be desirable to probe further into the theory of consumer behaviour. What motivates the consumer to move from *A* to *B*, from *B* to *C*, from *C* to *D*, and then to move no further down the line of attainable combinations? To be sure, the consumer seeks the most preferred of all the combinations available to him, but the explanation will be more thorough if we compare explicitly the market forces confronting the consumer with the consumer's preference patterns.

The slope of the line of attainable combinations indicates what the consumer is able to do in the markets for clothing and food. The ratio of the price of food to the price of clothing states the number of yards of clothing the consumer is required by the market to forgo in order to obtain an extra bushel of food. In Figure 6–4 if the consumer is initially at *A* and is to move from *A* to *B*, he must give up c_2A yards of clothing in order to make the move. The increase in food purchased is measured by c_2B, so the slope of the line of attainable combinations is $(c_2A)/(c_2B)$, which is, of course, equal to $(P_{f_1})/(P_{c_1})$.[5]

If we were to consider the *AH* portion of indifference curve *I* to be linear, a straight line, what information would its slope convey to us? The

---

[5]*If $P_f = \$1$ and $P_c = \$1.50$, what will be the slope of the line of attainable combinations and what does it mean?*

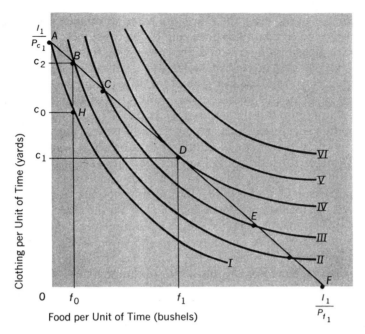

Figure 6-4
Consumer equilibrium.

slope would be measured by $(c_0A)/(c_0H)$, and, as we learned earlier, it is called the marginal rate of substitution of food for clothing—the consumer would be willing to give up c_0A yards of clothing to obtain c_0H bushels of food.

The market forces inducing the consumer to move from A to B down his line of attainable combinations now become apparent. In order to increase his food consumption by O_{f_0} ($= c_0H = c_2B$) the consumer would *be willing* to give up c_0A of clothing, according to the marginal rate of substitution. But in the market he would *have* to forgo only c_2A of clothing, according to the ratio $(P_{f_1})/(P_{c_1})$. If he behaves as the market says he must, giving up only c_2A of clothing to obtain 0_{f_0} of food, and he is willing to give up c_0A of clothing, then c_0c_2, the extra amount he was willing but was not required to give up, is pure gain to the consumer. Whatever satisfaction c_0c_2 gives him is over and above what he was obtaining at A.

Now suppose that instead of looking at the slope of a curve between discrete points we think of it at one point only on the curve. In the case of the line of attainable combinations, nothing is changed conceptually. At point B in Figure 6-4 the slope of AF is still $(P_{f_1})/(P_{c_1})$ and it indicates at that point the rate at which the market will permit the substitution of food for clothing. The slope of indifference curve II at point B is still the marginal rate of substitution of food for clothing at that point—the rate at which the consumer is willing to substitute food for clothing.

We can reason at points *B*, *C*, and all other points from *A* to *D* precisely as we did for the movement from *A* to *B*. At the point *B* intersection of the line of attainable combinations and indifference curve *II* the slope of the indifference curve is greater than the slope of the line of attainable combinations. This means the consumer *is willing* to forgo more clothing than he *has to* in the market to obtain a small increase in food; consequently, he receives a net gain in satisfaction from a trade made on market terms. At every other point between *A* and *D* the same condition prevails. At point *D* the rate at which the consumer is willing to substitute food for clothing is the same as the rate specified by the market at which he would have to do so. Thus there is no reason for further substitution to occur. Why will the consumer not move from *D* to *E*?

Symbolically the conditions that must be met if the consumer is to maximize satisfaction are:

$$MRS_{xy} = \frac{P_x}{P_y}$$

where *x* and *y* are any two products with prices P_x and P_y, and

$$xP_x + yP_y = I$$

where *x* and *y* are the quantities of *X* and *Y* taken when income *I* is all being spent. These can be readily generalized to as many goods and services a consumer takes.

Principles of Individual Consumer Demand

The hard labour has been done; the use of indifference curve techniques to show the relations between the price of a product and the quantities of it a consumer will take per time unit is almost anticlimactic. Holding constant the consumer's preferences as pictured by his indifference map, his income, and the price of one product, we shall vary the price of the other product. At each such price, when the consumer is in equilibrium or is maximizing his satisfaction, we can read off the quantity taken.

If food is the product for which the demand curve is to be derived, suppose we check the impact of changes in its price on the line of attainable combinations. In Figure 6–5 let I_1 be the consumer's income, P_{c1} the price of clothing, and P_{f1} the initial price of food. These points determine the line of attainable combinations, *EF*. Let the price of food be lowered now to P_{t2}. At the lower price, if the consumer were to spend his entire income on food, he could purchase a larger quantity, *OG*. His line of attainable combinations becomes *EG*. (Why does point *E* not change?) At a still lower price, P_{t3}, it becomes *EH*.

Each of these three lines of attainable combinations will be tangent to certain indifference curves on the consumer's indifference map. Line *EF* is tangent to indifferent curve *I* at point *A;* thus at price P_{t1} the consumer would take quantity f_1 of food. Line *EG* is tangent to indifference curve *II* at point *B*, so the quantity of food the consumer would take at price P_{t2} is f_2. At price P_{t3} for food the line of attainable combinations, *EH*, is tangent to indifference curve *III* at point *D* and the quantity of food taken is f_3.

These price–quantity relationships form a part of the consumer's demand schedule or points on his demand curve. The demand schedule

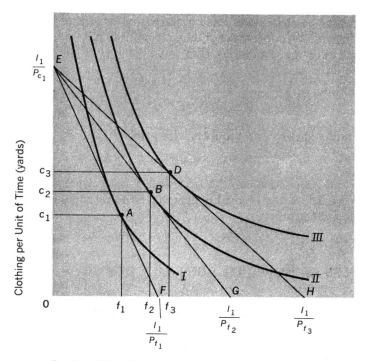

Figure 6–5
Effects of price changes.

would be that of Table 6–1, which, when plotted, would yield an individual consumer demand curve like that of Figure 6–6. The relationships are such that the demand curve slopes downward to the right; that is, the lower the price of the product, the more of it the consumer will take.

The increase in quantity of food taken in response to the decrease in its price is attributable to a combination of *income effects* and *substitution effects*. With reference to Figure 6–5, the decrease in the price of food from P_{f_1} to P_{f_2} moves the line of attainable combinations from *EF* to *EG*.

TABLE 6–1
Individual Consumer Demand Schedule for Food

Price*	Quantity**
P_{f_1}	f_1
P_{f_2}	f_2
P_{f_3}	f_3

*$P_{f_1} > P_{f_2} > P_{f_3}$.
**$f_1 < f_2 < f_3$.

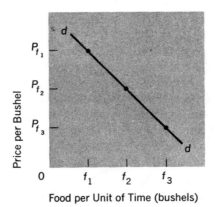

Figure 6–6
The individual consumer demand curve.

If the consumer had so desired, he could have continued to take c_1 of clothing *plus* a larger amount of food than f_1. This constitutes an increase in the consumer's *real income* or purchasing power. In the illustration only a part of this increase in the consumer's real income is spent on food; another part of it is used to increase his consumption of clothing as well.

The substitution effect is the inducement given the consumer to substitute food for clothing *because* the price of food has decreased relative to that of clothing. In Figure 6–5 note that since the slope of the line of attainable combinations is measured by $(P_t)/(P_c)$, when P_t decreases from P_{t_1} to P_{t_2} the slope is decreased also. A decrease in the slope of the line of attainable combinations causes the consumer to move around his indifference curves from a steeper point such as A on indifference curve I to a less steep point such as B on indifference curve II. The rate at which the consumer is able to substitute food for clothing in the market has been increased, thus providing a greater incentive for him to do so.

Summary

Indifference curve analysis is used in this chapter to (1) show how a consumer tends to allocate his income among different goods and services and (2) explain the demand curve of a consumer for one product.

The consumer's preferences are represented by his indifference map, which is composed of his set of indifference curves. Any one indifference curve shows combinations of two goods for which the consumer shows equal preference. Indifference curves lying farther from the origin of his indifference map show combinations preferred to those on lower indifference curves.

Graphically the slope of an indifference curve at any point indicates the rate at which the consumer is willing to substitute one product for another at the combination of goods represented by the point. This is called his marginal rate of substitution of one good for the other. As the consumer moves from combination to combination around an indifference curve his marginal rate of substitution of the product being increased for the product being decreased is decreasing, thus indifference curves are convex to the origin of the indifference map.

The consumer is restrained in what he purchases per time period by his income and the prices of the goods and services he desires. Graphically the combinations available to him are separated from those not available to him by his line of attainable combinations. The slope of the line of attainable combinations is determined by the inverse of the ratio of the prices of the two products and shows the rate at which the market will permit the consumer to trade units of one good for units of the other.

The consumer's allocation of income between the products tends to be that at which his line of attainable combinations is tangent to one of his indifference curves. This is the highest indifference curve he can reach. At this point his marginal rate of substitution of one product for another is the same as the rate at which the market will permit him to trade one for the other, and he has no incentive to move away from it.

Points forming the consumer's demand curve for one product are obtained from his indifference map as we confront him with different prices of the product. Each different price generates a different line of attainable combinations that is tangent to a different indifference curve. Because of substitution effects, generally supplemented by income effects, the lower the product price, the greater will tend to be the consumer's level of consumption.

Appendix to Chapter 6

The Basis of Exchange

Many people believe that when exchange of goods and services takes place one party is likely to gain at the expense of another. Ordinarily *both* parties to a voluntary exchange will gain; in fact, it is the expectation of gain by each party that generates the exchange in the first place. About the only way in which one party may be said to take advantage of the other is that his gains may exceed those of the other. The indifference apparatus lends itself well to a demonstration that this is the case.

Suppose in Figure 6–7 that two individuals obtain a total of *OC* yards of clothing and *OF* bushels of food per week. Mr. Smith's indifference map is rotated 180 degrees and is placed on that of Mr. Jones in such a position that Smith's food axis intersects Jones's clothing axis at point *C* and his clothing axis intersects Jones's food axis at point *F*. Further, Jones's and Smith's indifference map axes must form a rectangle so that the total amount of clothing received by both is measured by either *OC* on Jones's map or *O'F* on Smith's map. The total amount of food is measured by either *OF* on Jones's map or by *O'C* on Smith's. Any point inside the rectangle is a possible distribution of food and clothing between them. Consider point *A*, for example. If this were the distribution, it means that Jones receives *OE* yards of clothing per week and Smith receives *EC* yards. Jones receives *OG* bushels of food per week and Smith receives *GF* bushels.[1]

---

[1] *For convenience we shall use the axes of Jones's map for our measurements. If we so desired we could, of course, use those of Smith.*

If point *A* in fact represents the initial distribution, both parties can gain from exchange. For *GH* bushels of food, Jones would be willing to exchange *EJ* yards of clothing. Smith would be willing to give up *GH* bushels of food for only *EK* yards of clothing.[2] Thus for *GH* bushels of food Jones is willing to give up more clothing than Smith would require for it. Suppose they divide the difference so that Jones gives Smith *EL* yards of clothing for *GH* bushels of food. Jones is better off by whatever *JL* yards of clothing are worth to him, and Smith is better off by whatever *LK* yards of clothing are worth to him. From a slightly different viewpoint, note that after the exchange the distribution is at point *B*—on higher indifference curves of both Jones and Smith.

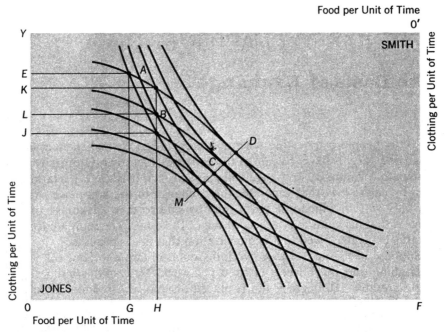

Figure 6–7
The gains from exchange.

The economic principle illustrated here is that if the marginal rate of substitution of one product for another is greater for one person than for another, both parties can gain from exchange. With reference to Jones's axes, the slope of Jones's indifference curve at point *B* is greater than that

[2]*If you have trouble understanding this point, rotate the diagram 180 degrees so that Smith's indifference map is in a familiar position.*

of Smith—Jones's marginal rate of substitution of food for clothing exceeds Smith's. Thus both can gain from further exchange, with Jones trading clothing to Smith for food.

If the distribution of food and clothing is that at point C or D or M, at which an indifference curve of Jones is tangent to an indifference curve of Smith, both parties cannot gain from exchange. The marginal rate of substitution of food for clothing is the same for both; Jones values a yard of clothing relative to a bushel of food exactly the same as Smith, so no voluntary exchange will occur.

The points of tangency between the indifference curves of Jones and those of Smith trace out a line MCD, called the *contract curve*. If the distribution of goods is represented by a point off the contract curve, both parties can gain from exchange, and any exchange that occurs will move the point toward the contract curve. Once the contract curve is reached, any further exchanges either on or away from the contract curve will make one or both of the parties worse off. Movements along the curve will make one party better off at the expense of the other; for example, exchanges that move the distribution point from M toward D will place Jones on higher and higher indifference curves while Smith is forced to lower and lower indifference curves. Movements away from the contract curve introduce the further possibility that both parties may be made worse off by the exchange.

Exercises and Questions for Discussion

1. Suppose you are at some point on the line of attainable combinations for two goods, A and B. The $MRS_{AB} = 5$ at this point. Suppose, further, that A sells for $2 per unit and B sells for $4 per unit. In which direction along the line of attainable combinations must you move in order to increase your satisfactions? What if the $MRS_{AB} = \frac{1}{8}$?

2. How do you think indifference curves for tennis rackets and tennis balls would look? for hamburgers and hot dogs?

3. Mr. Shadow enjoys spending his leisure time reading novels or watching movies. He has an "entertainment fund" of $30 a month which he uses for these purposes. Admission to a movie is $2 and the novels sell for $5 each. Draw his line of attainable combinations for these two items. Suppose the price of novels drops to $3. Draw the new line of attainable combinations on the same graph. Follow the same operation for a price of $2 per novel. Now arbitrarily draw in an indifference map for these two goods. (Be sure to make an indifference curve tangent to each of the lines of attainable combinations.) From the graph you have constructed, derive Mr. Shadow's demand curve for novels.

4. "Given a person's level of income and given that that level may not change, any

combination of two goods not located on his budget line cannot be attained by the consumer." Evaluate.

Selected Readings

Dorfman, R., *Prices and Markets*. Englewood Cliffs, N.J.: Prentice-Hall, Inc., 1967, Chap. 3.

Hicks, J.R., *Value and Capital*, 2d ed. Oxford: The Clarendon Press, 1946, Chaps. 1 and 2.

7

Principles of Production

In this chapter and the next we turn to that group of economic units falling under the heading of business firms. They will be subjected to the same detailed examination as were households as consumers in the last two chapters, and we will note that there are many parallels between the behaviour of a business firm and that of a consumer.

How does a business firm decide on the proportions in which it will use different kinds of resource inputs in producing a product? For example, in producing a product like an airstrip, why would a construction firm in India use vast quantities of workers who move earth with shovels, mix concrete in mud boxes, and carry it in baskets on their heads? Why would it not make more extensive use of earth-moving equipment and other kinds of advanced construction technology? The answer, of course, lies in the comparative costs of doing the job. It costs less in India to use relatively much of the abundant, inexpensive labour and relatively little of the scarce and very expensive capital than it does the other way around. The economics leading to the selection by a firm of the resource combinations that will minimize the costs of producing given amounts of product per unit of time are the subject matter of this chapter.

The Production Function

Schematically a firm can be thought of as a hopper into which resource inputs are poured to be stirred and mixed in special ways by special sticks

—the whole process being known as technology—and from which product output emerges. If a firm were producing shirts, the resource inputs would be machinery and tools of specific kinds, buildings to house the machinery, land on which the whole complex rests, cloth, thread, buttons, zippers, snaps, and labour representing a wide range of skills. The quantity of product output obtained per month would be related to the quantities of resource inputs. This relation is called *the production function*, the term "function" being used in the mathematical sense to indicate the dependency of the output quantity on the quantities of inputs.

Nature of the Production Function

Probably the most obvious characteristic of the production function is that if all resource inputs are increased, the firm's product output will be increased also. Almost as obvious, the firm's output will depend upon the technology available to it.

The range of production techniques available to the firm together with the resources available to it determine its production function. The firm will not necessarily use the same techniques at different output levels. For small outputs of many products not much use can be made of large, complex machines, whereas large outputs of the same products may very well be produced most efficiently with resources of these kinds. A specific production function takes into account that of the techniques available the ones selected are those most suited to the firm's level of output. New technological discoveries that will enable the firm to produce more than before at given levels of resource inputs *shift* or *change* the production function itself.

Another often overlooked characteristic of the production function is that within the function resource inputs can be substituted for one another usually to some degree and frequently to a considerable degree. Consider your own production function for washing your car. You can, if you desire, use a bucket of plain water, rags, and quite a lot of labour. You can cut down on the labour if you add detergent to the water. Labour input can be decreased still more if you use a hose rather than a bucket and a sponge to wash off the detergent before using the chamois. And the labour input can be further decreased if you increase the capital input by running the automobile through a commercial car wash. In most production processes capital can be substituted for labour; one kind of capital can be substituted for another; and one kind of labour can be substituted for another.

The possibility of substituting resources for one another in the production process opens up still another possibility. Larger quantities of one resource used with constant quantities of others should increase a firm's output up to some point. A simplified production function demonstrating this characteristic is shown in Table 7–1 and Figure 7–1. Suppose we have

Table 7-1
Total Product and Marginal Physical Product of Labour

(1) Land (Acres)	(2) Labour (Man Hours)	(3) Total Product (Bushels)	(4) Marginal Physical Product of Labour (Change in Product/ Change in Labour)
1	1	20	20
1	2	42	22
1	3	66	24
1	4	88	22
1	5	108	20
1	6	124	16
1	7	136	12
1	8	144	8
1	9	148	4
1	10	148	0

conducted a series of experiments using different quantities of labour per unit of time on an acre of land. The results of the experiment are recorded in the total product column of the table. The total product curve of labour, TP_1 is plotted from columns (2) and (3) of the table.

The Law of Diminishing Returns

Everyone has heard of the celebrated law of diminishing returns and almost everyone confuses it with the principle of diminishing marginal utility. Diminishing returns is frequently said to have set in when a boy makes himself sick eating bananas or when after 40 years of marriage a woman is ready to divorce her husband.

The term is used in economics in a much more restricted and specialized sense. It should be kept apart from the principle of diminishing marginal utility. The concepts may be parallel but they are not the same. The *law of diminishing returns* states that if in a production process the input level of one resource is increased unit by unit while those of other resources are held constant, beyond some point the resulting increases in product output will become smaller and smaller.

The law is illustrated in Table 7–1 and Figure 7–1. It becomes effective when four man hours of labour are used with a unit of land. As the quantity of labour is increased beyond that point, the increases in total product diminish. When 9 or 10 man hours per acre are used the total product obtainable from an acre is maximum and the increases in total product have decreased to zero.

Instead of referring to the law in terms of diminishing increases in total product, it is easier to view it in terms of diminishing marginal physical product of the resource being increased. *Marginal physical prod-*

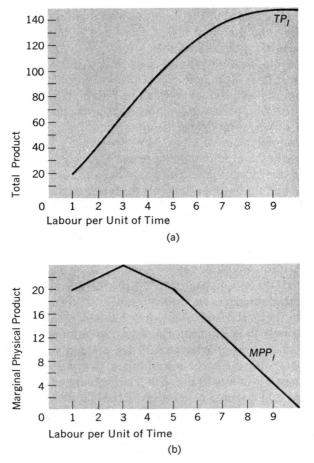

Figure 7-1
Total product and marginal physical product of a resource.

uct of a resource is defined as the change in total product resulting from a one-unit change in its level of use, the quantities of other resources remaining constant.[1] Thus when employment of labour is increased from one to two man hours the increase in total product—its marginal physical product—is 22 bushels of product. For an increase in labour from two to three man hours, the marginal physical product is 24 bushels. The rest of column (4) is derived from columns (2) and (3) in a like manner.

The marginal physical product curve for labour in Figure 7–1(b) is derived from the total product curve of Figure 7–1(a). At each level of labour employment we measure the increase in total product occurring when employment is increased to that level from a level one man hour smaller. These increases, the marginal physical product of labour at different employment levels, are plotted in Table 7–1(b).

The law of diminishing returns is operative in production processes all around us. It rests ultimately on the proposition that there is an upper limit to the amount of product that can be obtained from any given complex of resources. Suppose, for example, that a resource complex consists of 1000 acres of wheat land, specific quantities of machinery to use on it, and a given complement of labour. Now if fertilizer were applied to the complex, the wheat output would increase. The larger the amount of fertilizer applied, the larger the output would be—up to a point. This point is simply the maximum output attainable from the original complex of land, machinery, and labour, and as it is approached the marginal physical product of fertilizer must be decreasing; that is, the law of diminishing returns with respect to fertilizer must be operative. At the point at which an increase in fertilizer will not increase output, the marginal physical product of fertilizer becomes zero.

Often for relatively small quantities of a resource applied to a given complex of other resources *increasing returns* will result from the first few increments in its level of use. This may happen because the resource is used too sparingly to be efficient. Consider, for example, a large steel mill in which all of the resources necessary for making steel are available in large quantities with the exception of labour. One man working the plant alone will not produce much steel. But if helpers are added they can divide up some tasks and cooperate on others. Equal increments in the labour resource up to some point will bring about larger and larger increases in steel output. However, as the quantity of labour relative to the quantities of other resources is further increased, diminishing returns will set in.

Diminishing returns for specific resources represent a far more im-

---

[1]*We call it* marginal physical product *instead of simply marginal product in order to distinguish it from the concept of* marginal revenue product, *which we shall encounter later. Frequently both concepts are referred to loosely as marginal product, a usage which often results in confusion.*

portant phenomenon than increasing returns. In the production process each resource used by a firm will ordinarily be utilized in the range of diminishing returns. We mention increasing returns in passing in order to make the analysis of resource use as complete as possible.

Least Cost Combination of Resources

Hopefully, the discussion of a firm's production function puts us in a position to get at the main question raised in this chapter: What determines the proportions in which a firm utilizes different resources in the production process? We shall assume that the firm is motivated in this respect by efficiency objectives, or a desire to produce whatever output it produces at a total cost as low as possible. Stated another way, the firm strives to get as much output as possible from any given level of expenditure on resources. Suppose, for example, that the firm is a factory producing shirts and that it intends to produce 100 shirts per day. These can be produced at numerous different cost levels, depending upon the resource combinations and the techniques of production chosen by the firm. Assume that the least of these possible cost levels is 75 dollars. To say that 75 dollars is the least cost of producing 100 shirts is also to say that 100 shirts is the maximum number that can be produced for 75 dollars.

Suppose that the shirt factory makes a given cost outlay on two resources and the firm's intent is to secure the largest possible output of shirts with that cost outlay. We shall assume that the two resources are not directly related to one another; that is, that the quantity used of one does not directly affect the productivity of the other. Let the two resources be the labour of pressers and the labour of packers,[2] and that the quantities of each are represented by R and A, respectively. The marginal physical product schedules of both are listed in Table 7–2 as MPP_r and MPP_a; the cost outlay, TCO, is 16 dollars; the price or wage rate of pressers, p_r, is 2 dollars per unit; and the price or wage rate of packers, p_a, is 1 dollar per unit. Note that the law of diminishing returns becomes operative for pressers with the third unit and for packers with the fourth unit.

Suppose that initially the firm is spending the entire 16 dollar cost outlay on pressers. The quantity employed is eight and MPP_r is four shirts. Since the eighth presser costs 2 dollars, the marginal physical product per dollar's worth of this kind of labour, $(MPP_r/(p_r))$, is two shirts. A dollar's worth of pressers' labour contributes two shirts to the

TABLE 7–2
Marginal Physical Product of Pressers and Packers

	Pressers		Packers	
R	MPP_r (SHIRTS)	A	MPP_a (SHIRTS)
1	14	1	8
2	14	2	8
3	13	3	8
4	12	4	7
5	10	5	6
6	8	6	5
7	6	7	4
8	4	8	3
9	2	9	2
10	0	10	0

firm's output—take a dollar's worth away and a two-shirt decrease in output occurs.

Is this the best the firm can do with its 16 dollar cost outlay? Consider packers' labour. Employment of a packer will add eight shirts, the MPP_a of a single packer, to the firm's total output. The packer costs a dollar, so $(MPP_a)/(p_a)$, the marginal physical product of a dollar's worth of packers' labour at the one-unit level of employment, is also eight shirts. Since $(MPP_r)/(p_r)$ is only two shirts, the transfer of a dollar from pressers to packers will bring about a net increase of six shirts in the firm's output. Transfer of a second dollar from pressers to packers will bring about another six-shirt increase in output—a loss of two shirts more than offset by a gain of eight as a second packer per unit of time is employed. A third dollar removed from expenditure on pressers reduces output by three shirts, and if spent on a third packer increases output by eight for a net gain of five shirts. A fourth dollar withdrawn from pressers and spent on packers yields a net increase of four shirts. The transfers of fifth and sixth dollars in the same direction yield net output increases of two shirts and one shirt, respectively.

The firm is now maximizing the output obtainable from a 16 dollar per unit of time outlay on pressers and packers. Five pressers and six packers are employed. The marginal physical product of both a dollar's worth of pressers' labour and a dollar's worth of packers' labour is five shirts. Transfer of a dollar in either direction will decrease output.

We have arrived at the fundamental proposition that if a firm is to get the greatest possible product output attainable from a given outlay on resources, it must combine the resources in such a way that the marginal physical product per dollar's worth of any one resource used must be equal to that of any other resource available to it. For any two resources, *A* and *B*, the combination must be such that $(MPP_a)/(p_a) = (MPP_b)/(p_b)$. If the marginal physical product of a dollar's worth of *B* is greater than that of *A*, then output can be increased *with no increase in cost* by transferring dollars from *A* to *B* until the equality is established. Maximum output from a given cost outlay means the same thing as minimum cost for a given amount of product output. Economists have generally but not exclusively preferred to put the proposition in this latter form and to refer to it as the *least-cost combination* of resources rather than the *maximum-output combination*, although one statement is just as correct as the other.

Isoquants and Isocosts

Some people will prefer to use the more sophisticated isoquant-isocost approach to a firm's least-cost combination of resources, although the analysis in this book does not require it. The firm's production function is represented by an *isoquant map*, parallel in concept to a consumer's indifference map. Its cost restraints are represented by *isocost curves* that are similar mathematically to the consumer's line of attainable combinations. These are brought together to show how the firm's least-cost combination of resources is determined.

The Isoquant Map

A firm's isoquant map is composed of isoquant curves. The latter are similar to a consumer's indifference curves and any one isoquant shows the different combinations of resource inputs that will produce a given level of product output. The input combinations that will produce higher levels of output are shown by higher isoquants while those that can produce lower levels only are represented by lower isoquants.

Table 7–3 gives a typical isoquant schedule, and the corresponding isoquant curve is plotted in Figure 7–2. Suppose that the product being produced is shirts and the resource inputs are labour and capital. In Figure 7–2 units of labour are measured along the vertical axis while units of capital are shown by the horizontal axis. Both the output and the inputs are flows over time, or quantities per time period.

Let us assume that we have determined through experimentation the combinations of capital and labour that will yield a product output of 100 shirts per time period. These are combinations such as *A*, *B*, *C*, and *D*, listed in Table 7–3 and plotted in Figure 7–2. Still other combinations such as *E* and *F* could be determined also. All possible combinations of labour and capital that just yield 100 shirts trace out the curved line *AEBCFD*, which is an isoquant or equal-product curve.

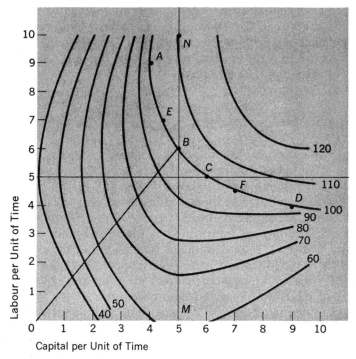

Figure 7–2
An isoquant map.

TABLE 7–3

Combinations of Labour and Capital Yielding 100 Shirts per Unit of Time

Combination	Labour	Capital
A	9	4
B	6	5
C	5	6
D	4	9

The 100-shirt isoquant is a downward-sloping curved line, convex to the origin of the diagram. Is this the shape our everyday observations lead us to expect? Initially it seems correct. The higher the proportions of labour to capital used, the less capital each worker has to work with and the less productive a man will be. Under these circumstances an additional unit of capital may substitute for or do the work of several units of labour. A movement from *A* to *B* illustrates the case. As the firm moves to smaller ratios of labour to capital, from *B* to *C* and from *C* to *D*, additional units of capital are likely to substitute for smaller and smaller amounts of labour, because labour becomes more and more productive as each man has more and more capital with which to work. Yet these statements prove nothing; rather, they indicate simply that it seems reasonable to expect that an isoquant will take on the shape illustrated.

Other isoquants can be drawn at higher and lower production levels. A number of them are shown for output intervals of 10 shirts each. If we start at the origin of Figure 7–2 and move along a straight line to point *B*, the successive points along the line show combinations containing more and more of both resource inputs. Consequently, we would expect the isoquants lying farther from the origin to show resource combinations that will yield higher levels of product output. A set of isoquants makes up the firm's *isoquant map* and provides a graphic picture of its production function.

A total product schedule for one resource like that of Table 7–1 is easily obtained from the firm's isoquant map. Suppose that the input of capital per unit of time is held constant at five units and that the firm increases its labour input unit by unit. The path followed on the isoquant map of Figure 7–2 is line *MN*.

At one unit of labour (and five units of capital) we are between the 60-shirt and the 70-shirt isoquants. The isoquant going precisely through this resource combination is not drawn, but by interpolation it appears that it would be the 67-shirt isoquant. At two units of labour (and five units of capital) the firm should be on about the 74-shirt isoquant. Continuing these observations, we construct the total product columns—(2) and (3) in Table 7–4. (Check each total poduct quantity in the table with Figure 7–2 to make sure you understand how each such quantity in the table is obtained.)

The marginal physical product of labour is computed from columns (2) and (3) of Table 7–4 and is recorded in column (4) for each level of utilization of labour. When employment of labour is increased from one to two units the increase in total product—marginal physical product—is seven shirts. The increase from two to three units of labour increases total product by eight shirts, and the other quantities in the MPP_1 column are found in the same way. The law of diminishing returns with respect to labour becomes effective with the fourth unit of labour used per time period.

TABLE 7–4
Total Product and Marginal Physical Product of Labour: Capital = 5 units

(1) Capital	(2) Labour	(3) TP_l (Shirts)	(4) MPP_l (Change in shirts/ Change in Labour)	
5	1	67	—	
5	2	74	7	
5	3	82	8	
5	4	89	7	Diminishing
5	5	95	6	returns
5	6	100	5	with
5	7	104	4	respect
5	8	107	3	to
5	9	109	2	labour
5	10	110	1	

The isoquant map provides a more general view of the firm's production function than we have been able to obtain heretofore. From it we can obtain a number of total product curves for labour. Instead of assuming that the quantity of capital used is constant at five units, we could have assumed that it was constant at three units. The total product schedule for labour would have been different; that is, it would have been lower at each level of labour input than the one of Table 7–4. Similarily, we could have assumed that the quantity of labour used is constant—say four units—and by considering larger and larger quantities of capital used with it we could have obtained a total product curve for capital. The isoquant map enables us to show the *dependency* of the productivity of labour on the quantity of capital used and the *dependency* of the productivity of capital on the quantity of labour used.

Isocosts

We turn now to the cost side of the picture. In Figure 7–3 suppose that the firm makes a cost outlay of O dollars on labour and capital. If all of it were spent on labour at a price of P_l per unit, $O/(P_l)$ units of labour could be purchased. On the other hand, if it were all spent on capital at a price of P_c per unit, $O/(P_c)$ units of capital could be purchased. Analogous to a consumer's line of attainable combinations, the straight line AB shows the combinations of labour and capital that the cost outlay O will purchase. Its slope is $(P_c)/(P_1)$, and it measures the amount of labour the firm would be required to give up if it were to purchase an additional unit of capital with no change in the cost outlay.[3] We call this line an *isocost curve*, meaning that all along its path the cost outlay of the firm is the same.

The Least-Cost Combination

If we put the firm's isoquant map on the same diagram with the isocost curve, we can readily determine the least-cost or maximum-product combination of labour and capital. The isoquant identified as X shows the combinations of labour and capital that will produce X units of product output, and the one marked X_1 shows those that will produce an output of X_1. Isoquants lying farther from the origin are for higher quantities of output than are the closer ones. In Figure 7–3, then, the least-cost or maximum-product combination of resources is that at which the isocost curve just touches or is tangent to an isoquant—combination E containing L_1 units of labour and C_1 units of capital. Quantity X_1 is the largest output that a cost outlay of O will produce. Or, looked at the other way around, cost outlay O is the least cost of producing output X_1. These propositions hold for resource combination E, at which point the isocost curve is just tangent to an isoquant. If the firm were to purchase another combination of labour and capital—D or G, for example—the product output obtained would be below X_1. Or if the firm were to purchase combination H or K a cost outlay larger than O would be required.

Since the least-cost or maximum-output resource combination is that at which an isocost curve is tangent to an isoquant, it is apparent that the tangency condition will bear additional scrutiny. At the point of tangency, point E, the two curves have identical slopes. We know already that the slope of the isocost is $(P_c)/(P_1)$ and that it indicates the amount of labour the firm must release in order to obtain an additional unit of capital, if the cost outlay is to remain unchanged.

What does the slope of an isoquant show? Suppose in Figure 7–4 that A and B are points very close together on a given isoquant and that we have this segment of the isoquant under a magnifying glass. If A and B are close enough to each other we can think of the line segment AB as

[3]$Slope\ AB = \dfrac{O}{P_1} \dfrac{O}{P_c} = \dfrac{O}{P_1} \cdot \dfrac{P_c}{O} = \dfrac{P_c}{P_1}$

If $P_c = \$2$ and $P_1 = \$1$, then slope $AB = 2/1$, meaning that, given the cost outlay, if the firm wants an additional unit of capital (costing \$2) it must give up two units of labour (costing \$1 each).

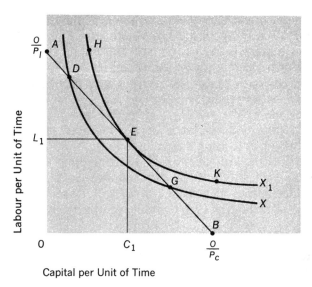

Figure 7-3
The least-cost combination.

being a straight line. So conceived, the slope of AB or of that small segment of the isoquant is $(\triangle L)/(\triangle C)$, and this ratio is referred to as the *marginal rate of technical substitution* of capital for labour, or $MRTS_{c1}$. It

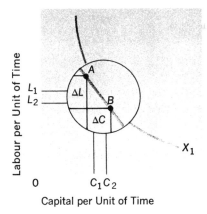

Figure 7-4
The marginal rate of technical substitution.

measures the amount of labour for which a unit of capital will just substitute with no loss in product output.

The magnitude of the $MRTS_{c1}$ between A and B depends upon the marginal physical product of labour and the marginal physical product of capital when the firm is using a combination of L_1 units of labour and C_1 units of capital. If the firm gives up $\triangle L$ units of labour, the loss in product output will be $\triangle L \cdot MPP_1$. If the firm acquires $\triangle C$ units of capital, the gain in product output will be $\triangle C \cdot MPP_c$. For such a substitution of capital for labour, if the firm is to continue producing a product output of X_1, then

$$\triangle L \cdot MPP_1 = \triangle C \cdot MPP_c$$

that is, the loss in product from giving up labour must equal the gain in product from acquiring more capital.

Restating this equality as

$$\frac{\triangle L}{\triangle C} = \frac{MPP_c}{MPP_1}$$

we see that at any given point on an isoquant

$$MRTS_{c1} = \frac{MPP_c}{MPP_1}$$

This logic is rather abstract; suppose we slip some numbers into the algebra and geometry of the marginal rate of technical substitution of capital for labour. If at point A the marginal physical product of capital is eight shirts and that of labour is four shirts, then

$$MRTS_{c1} = \frac{MPP_c}{MPP_1} = \frac{8}{4} = \frac{2}{1}$$

This means that a unit of capital will substitute for two units of labour in the firm's production function. This makes sense, since at combination A a unit of capital is twice as productive as a unit of labour.

The original purpose of this discourse was to examine the implications of tangency between an isocost curve and an isoquant. At the point of tangency—E in Figure 7–2—the slopes of the two curves are the same. The slope of the isoquant is the $MRTS_{c1}$ or $(MPP_c)/(MPP_1)$ at that point. The slope of an isocost curve is $(p_c)/(p_1)$. Therefore, at the point of tangency

$$\frac{MPP_c}{MPP_1} = \frac{p_c}{p_1}$$

or

$$\frac{MPP_c}{p_c} = \frac{MPP_1}{p_1}$$

For a resource combination to be a least-cost or maximum-output combination, the marginal rate of technical substitution of one resource for the other must be in the same ratio as their prices; or, to put it another way, the marginal physical product per dollar's worth of one resource must equal the marginal physical product per dollar's worth of any other available resource.

Summary

This chapter examines how a business firm determines the proportions in which different resources will be used in the production process. The objective of business firms is assumed to be that of producing a given amount of product at the least possible cost or of producing the maximum amount of product for a given cost outlay.

The relation between the quantities of resource inputs and the technology that a firm uses on the one hand and the quantities of product output that it obtains on the other is called its production function. In general the production function shows how product output changes when the quantities of all resources used change in the same direction, and it indicates how resources may be substituted for one another in the production process. Additionally, it shows how output will change when any one resource input is changed in quantity, the quantities of the others being held constant. This latter relation is summed up in a total product schedule or a total product curve for the resource that is varied in quantity.

Marginal physical product of a resource is defined as the change in total product per unit change in the quantity used of a resource, the inputs of other resources being held constant in quantity. Except in some cases for the first few units of the variable resource applied to fixed amounts of other resources, marginal physical product of the variable resource will decrease as larger quantities of it are used. This phenomenon is known as the law of diminishing returns.

A least-cost or maximum-product combination of resource inputs for a firm is one at which the marginal physical product of a dollar's worth of any one resource is the same for the firm as the marginal physical product of a dollar's worth of any other resource available to it. A given cost outlay so made yields the maximum possible output. Or this output can be said to be produced at the least possible cost.

Isoquant–isocost techniques provide a more sophisticated look at least-cost or maximum-product resource combinations. An isoquant is a curve showing the various resource combinations that will produce a given level of product output. A set of isoquant curves makes up the firm's *isoquant map*, showing which resource combinations will produce larger quantities of product output and which will produce less. Isoquants also show the marginal rate of technical substitution of one resource for another in the firm's production processes—that is, the amount of one resource the firm can just give up to obtain an additional unit of another, the product output remaining constant. An isocost curve shows the combination of resource inputs that a given total cost outlay on the resources will purchase for the firm.

Given the firm's isoquant map and the isocost curve for a specific cost outlay, the least-cost or maximum-product combination of resources is that at which the isocost curve is just tangent to an isoquant. At this point the slopes of the two curves are the same. Since the slope of the isocost is measured by the inverse ratio of the price of one resource to the price of the other, and since the marginal rate of technical substitution is measured by the inverse ratio of the marginal physical product of one to that of the other, for any two resources, A and B,

$$\frac{MPP_a}{MPP_b} = \frac{p_a}{p_b}$$

or,

$$\frac{MPP_a}{p_a} = \frac{MPP_b}{p_b}$$

Exercises and Questions for Discussion

1. Test your understanding of the method for finding the least-cost combination of resources by reference to the table given below. The quantities of labour and land and their respective marginal physical productivities are given. What is the least-cost combination of these two resources if the price of labour is $2, the price per unit of land is $1, and the total cost outlay is $12? Before you begin, what can you say about the relationship between the MPP_{labour} and the MPP_{land} at the least-cost combination?

Labour	MPP*labour*	Land	MPP*land*
1	9	1	14
2	10	2	12
3	9	3	10
4	8	4	8
5	7	5	6
6	6	6	4
7	5	7	2
8	4	8	0

2. Figure 7–1(a) is a production function showing both increasing and decreasing returns. Can you illustrate graphically a production function having only increasing returns? only decreasing returns? Can you give an example of each?

3. The $MRTS_{cl}$ (slope of an isoquant) shows us that the amount of labour a producer is "willing" to give up to get an additional unit of capital and still produce the same output. The slope of an isocost curve shows the amount of labour that the market tells the producer he "must" give up to get an additional unit of capital and still spend the same amount of money. Using this terminology, can you explain why a rational producer would not use combinations D or G in Figure 7–3?

4. Suppose you are at some point on an isoquant showing the different amounts of labour and capital yielding the same output of lamps. You decide to decrease your use of labour by one unit and increase your use of capital by one-fourth unit. If the MPP_l at this point is two lamps, what must the MPP_c be in order for you to remain on the same isoquant?

5. We might think of a university as being a firm that produces knowledgeable persons. Within this firm we find workers (professors) working on the raw material (students). The professors often complain that after a certain point, if they continue to add to the number of students in class, their effectiveness begins to fall off. Perhaps this is due to the fact that more students cause more distractions or that some students are farther away from the speaker or that the odds of being called on to answer a question are reduced. What important law in production theory have we illustrated?

6. What would you expect the effect to be on the total product curve for labour of the placement of a new labour-saving invention in the production process?

Selected Readings

Ferguson, C. E., *Microeconomic Theory*. Homewood, Ill.: Richard D. Irwin, Inc., 1966, Chap. 7.

Watson, Donald S., *Price Theory and Its Uses*, 2d ed. Boston: Houghton Mifflin Company, 1968, Chaps. 9 and 10.

8

Costs of Production

A steel mill has just modernized its plant and equipment. It has installed up-to-date furnaces and rolling mills and it specializes in the production of sheet steel used for making automobile bodies. But market demand for automobiles is in a slump. Orders for steel from automobile manufacturers have fallen off and the steel mill is operating at a fraction of its capacity. Among other things, management is concerned about the high costs of producing a ton of steel. Its members watch economic indicators constantly, hoping that steel orders will increase. They expect that at higher rates of utilization they can reduce substantially their production costs per ton. For plant and equipment already in place, with costs per ton high at low levels of utilization, why would they expect these costs to become lower as the level of utilization is increased? Further, is there some level of product output (plant utilization) beyond which per ton costs will increase?

A company that manufactures light aircraft has made an announcement that startles the rest of the industry. It plans to triple the plant and equipment necessary for producing the small two-place airplane at the bottom of its product line. A spokesman for the company states that lower production costs associated with the larger outputs will enable the firm to cut prices of the airplane substantially. Why is this the case? Are large plants always more efficient—that is, can they always produce at lower per unit costs than small ones? Can plants get too large to operate efficiently?

In this chapter we seek the answers to the questions just raised. The examples pose two distinct types of cost situations, the short run and the long run, that students frequently have difficulty in keeping separate. We shall examine each in detail, but first we must see what comprises costs of production.

Nature of Costs

We usually think of a firm's costs of production as being the money obligations incurred in producing its output; yet costs involve more than these. To be sure, whatever the firm must pay for the resources it uses is a cost outlay or a cost obligation. But there are frequently some costs that a firm does not pay directly. Further, what determines the magnitude of a firm's costs?

The Alternative-Cost Principle

Where there are a number of alternative uses to which units of a given resource, say machinists' labour, can be put, any one firm must pay for a unit of it whatever that unit is worth to any alternative user. An aircraft manufacturer will pay for a man hour of machinists' labour whatever it is worth to him in the production of aircraft. An automobile manufacturer, desiring to hold his force of machinists intact or desiring to hire more, must pay at least as much as the aircraft manufacturer or machinists will work for the latter instead of for him. Generalizing from this, we see that the cost of a unit of any resource used by a firm is its value in its best alternative use. This principle is known sometimes as the *alternative-cost principle* and sometimes as the *opportunity-cost principle*.

The principle operates for society as a whole as well as for any single firm. Resource units used to produce one item cannot be used to produce another. Suppose that wood and nylon strings of certain types can be used to produce either guitars or violins. An increase in the production of guitars means a sacrifice in the production of violins, so the cost of a guitar to society is the value of violins sacrificed by using the materials to produce a guitar instead.

Implicit and Explicit Costs

Some of a firm's costs are obvious ones. The owner-operator of the corner grocery store must pay his rent, his utility bills, and the cost of his stocks of goods. These obvious outlays for resources bought or hired, and which any accountant would record as costs, are called *explicit ones*.

There are, however, other resources used in the production process for which the cost obligations are not so obvious. What about the labour that the owner-operator puts into his business? What about the furniture, fixtures, and equipment owned by him and used in the business? Frequently resources such as these are left out of account in determining a firm's costs. But the self-owned, self-employed resources of a business go into its production hopper and contribute to the firm's output just as do those that are bought and hired. These costs are called *implicit costs*, and to the economist, concerned with the costs of *all* resources used in production, they are just as important as the explicit costs.

How can the implicit money costs of self-owned, self-employed resources be determined if they are not currently bought or hired in resource markets? The alternative-cost principle provides the appropriate guide. An owner-operator's labour should be appraised at what he could earn if he were to work for someone else in his best earning capacity. For other such resources we determine what similar resources are worth hired out in their best alternative use.

The Short Run and the Long Run

The short run and the long run are not really calendar concepts at all. In planning their outputs and in estimating their costs, firms generally proceed along two lines. On the one hand, they consider the different outputs per time period that can be produced with their present complement of plant and equipment. This is called *short-run* planning. On the other hand, they consider the possibilities of changing the complement of plant and equipment or *scale of plant* that they use. They consider a wider range of outputs than any one scale of plant can produce. This is called *long-run* planning.

The Short Run

For economic analysis of short-run planning it is convenient to divide resources into two classifications, fixed and variable. *Fixed resources* are the ones that comprise the firm's scale of plant, and in short-run planning changes in the quantities used of these are not considered. We think of them as being fixed in quantity and as setting an upper limit to the amount of output per time period that the firm can produce. Stated another way, the short-run planning period is one in which changes in the firm's scale of plant are not possible. Some of the resources classified in the fixed category in the short run are the firm's land site, its buildings and heavy machinery, and its key management personnel.

The short-run *variable resources* are those that we think of as being run through the plant to produce product output. The greater the quantities of variable resources used, the larger the output will be—up to the limits imposed by the firm's current scale of plant. Typical variable resources for short-run planning purposes are labour (except for top management), raw and semi-finished materials, power, and transportation services.

The Long Run

In long-run planning there are no fixed resources. The quantities of all resources used by the firm are thought of as subject to variation. The time horizon extends far enough to permit the incorporation into the firm's plans of depreciation and sale of existing plant and equipment. Similarly, the acquisition or construction of new plant facilities are possibilities open to the firm. Expansion, contraction, and reorganization of top management may occur. Thus, from the point of view of production possibilities, there are no significant limits to the range of outputs per unit of time that the firm may consider.

Short-Run Costs

The short-run costs of a firm consist of its obligations for all resources used, fixed and variable. Quantities of resources used differ at different output levels; consequently, costs will differ also, depending upon the firm's output level. First, suppose we look at the manner in which the firm's total costs vary with its output. We can then derive its per units costs for the range of outputs open to it. But as we do so there are two important conditions that we assume to be fixed for any given set of cost schedules or curves. These are (1) the prices of the resources used by the firm and (2) the technological possibilities for the scale of plant used. If either of these change, the entire set of schedules or curves will change also.

Total Costs

Since in the short run we classify resources into fixed and variable categories, we break up the firm's total costs of production in the same way. The costs of fixed resources are *total fixed costs* and those of variable resources are *total variable costs*.

Total Fixed Costs

The magnitude of a firm's total fixed costs depends upon its scale of plant and not upon the level of output produced with that scale of plant. The firm's scale of plant is defined in terms of given quantities of fixed resources, so the costs of these will not vary as output is varied. In the steel mill example the amortization costs of the furnaces and the other heavy equipment, the costs of the land site, and the salaries of top manage-

TABLE 8–1
Short-Run Total Costs of a Hypothetical Firm

(1) Quantity of X per Week	(2) TFC	(3) TVC	(4) STC	(5) SMC
0	$100	$ 0	$100	$ —
1	100	15	115	15
2	100	25	125	10
3	100	46	146	21
4	100	79	179	33
5	100	124	224	45
6	100	182	282	58
7	100	254	354	72
8	100	341	441	87
9	100	444	544	103
10	100	564	664	120

ment do not depend upon what output is produced with the plant once it is in place. They depend only upon the quantities of resources that make up the plant. They will be the same whether the product output of the firm is zero or whether it is near the maximum output capacity of its given scale of plant.

The total fixed cost schedule and the total fixed cost curve, showing the typical relation of total fixed costs to the output of a hypothetical firm, are illustrated in Table 8–1, and Figure 8–1, respectively. Suppose that the firm's scale of plant—the quantities of fixed resources used—are such that it is obligated to pay 100 dollars a week for them. Whether the output is zero or 10 units per week, this obligation remains the same. The total fixed cost schedule is therefore illustrated by columns (1) and (2) of Table 8–1, and this schedule is plotted in Figure 8–1 as the *TFC* curve.

Total Variable Costs

Total variable costs show the relation between the firm's cost obligations for variable resources and its output of product. If the firm's output were zero, there would be no need to hire or buy variable resources, so at that output total variable costs are zero. But to produce product, variable resources must be run through the plant. The larger the output produced, the larger the quantities of variable resources used, and the larger total variable costs will be. This direct relation is illustrated by columns (1) and (3) of Table 8–1 and by its graphic counterpart *TVC* in Figure 8–1.

But in addition to its upward slope as the firm considers higher output levels, the *TVC* curve of Figure 8–1 exhibits a rather peculiar inverted S-shape. Is this the usual shape of a *TVC* curve or does it result from an accident of choice in setting up the example? The principles of production,

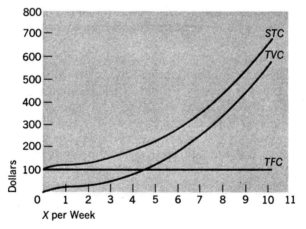

Figure 8–1
A firm's total cost curves.

covered in the preceding chapter, will help us find the determinants of its shape and its position.

First, the total variable cost curve shows the least possible cost of producing each of the outputs that the firm may consider. The least total outlay on variable resources that will yield a product output of six units per week is 182 dollars. In the terms of the last chapter, at this output variable costs can be held down to 182 dollars only if the firm uses that outlay for a least-cost combination of variable resources; that is, so the marginal physical product per dollar's worth of one variable resource used is equal to that of every other variable resource available to the firm.[1] The same reasoning is applicable to all other output levels—each one has its own least-cost combination of variable resources.

Second, the inverted S-shape of the *TVC* curve stems from the operation of both the law of increasing returns and the law of diminishing returns. Where the law of increasing returns is effective, equal increases in product output are obtainable with smaller and smaller increases in the quantities of the variable resources used.[2] Translated into costs, this means that equal increases in the product output can be obtained with smaller and smaller increases in cost outlay on the variable resources. This reasoning applies to the whole complex of variable resources used by the firm. If increasing returns are effective for the complex of variable resources used in the firm's fixed scale of plant, equal increases in product output can be obtained with smaller and smaller increases in total variable costs. Consequently, the total variable cost curve is concave downward— it increases at a decreasing rate—where increasing returns to the complex of variable resources occur.

The effects of the law of diminishing returns on the shape of the total variable cost curve are much more important for economic analysis than are those of increasing returns. For some firms there may be no increasing returns to the variable resources at all; diminishing returns may exist for all quantities of variable resources used with the firm's fixed scale of plant. In any case, as we shall see, the firm will generally be operating at an output level at which diminishing returns to variable resources occurs: the quantities of variable resources used in relation to the fixed scale of plant will be large enough for this to be the case.

The effects of diminishing returns on the total variable cost curve are precisely the reverse of those brought about by increasing returns. Where diminishing returns occur to the complex of variable resources run through the fixed scale of plant, equal increases in output require larger and larger increases in the quantities of variable resources used.[3] This means that equal increases in output require larger and larger increases in the total cost obligations for variable resources; that is, the *TVC* curve is concave

---

[1] *We can think either of 182 dollars as being the least total variable cost of producing six units of output per week or we can think of six units of output as being the maximum output attainable with a variable cost outlay of 182 dollars.*

[2] *This is the same as saying that equal increases in the quantities used will yield larger and larger increases in product output.*

[3] *Or, equal increases in the quantities of variable resources used bring about smaller and smaller increases in product output.*

upward for output levels where diminishing returns to variable resources are effective.

Short-Run Total Costs

The firm's over-all short-run total costs of production, or *STC*, are simply the summation of total fixed costs and total variable costs at each output level. Thus in Table 8–1, column (4) is the sum of columns (2) and (3). In Figure 8–1, *STC* is found by adding the *TFC* curve vertically to the *TVC* curve. The total cost curve *STC* and the total variable cost curve *TVC* look alike. This is as it should be, since the *STC* curve *is* the *TVC* curve displaced upward by the amount of *TFC*.

Per Unit Costs

Each of the total cost curves discussed above has its per unit counterpart. If we divide total fixed costs by output at the various possible output levels, we get *average fixed costs*, or *AFC*. Similarly, *average variable costs*, or *AVC*, are found by dividing total variable costs by output, and over-all short-run average costs, or *SAC*, are over-all total costs divided by output. Columns (2), (3), and (4) in Table 8–2 are thus derived from columns (1), (2), (3), and (4) of Table 8–1. These are plotted in Figure 8–2 as *AFC*, *AVC*, and *SAC*. Each of these curves has a common sense meaning important both to the economist and to the managers of the firm.

TABLE 8–2
Short-Run Per Unit Costs of a Hypothetical Firm

(1) QUANTITY OF X PER WEEK	(2) AFC (TFC/x)	(3) AVC (TVC/x)	(4) SAC (STC/x)	(5) SMC (ΔSTC)/(Δx)
0	$ —	$ —	$ —	$ —
1	100	15	115	15
2	50	$12\frac{1}{2}$	$62\frac{1}{2}$	10
3	$33\frac{1}{3}$	$15\frac{1}{3}$	$48\frac{2}{3}$	21
4	25	$19\frac{3}{4}$	$44\frac{3}{4}$	33
5	20	$24\frac{4}{5}$	$44\frac{4}{5}$	45
6	$16\frac{2}{3}$	$30\frac{1}{3}$	47	58
7	$14\frac{2}{7}$	$36\frac{2}{7}$	$50\frac{4}{7}$	72
8	$12\frac{1}{2}$	$42\frac{5}{8}$	$55\frac{1}{8}$	87
9	$11\frac{1}{9}$	$49\frac{1}{4}$	$60\frac{4}{9}$	103
10	10	$56\frac{2}{5}$	$66\frac{2}{5}$	120

Average Fixed Costs

The most obvious characteristic of the average fixed cost curve is that it decreases as the output level is increased. The greater the output, the smaller the costs of the fixed resources attributable to each unit of output. We interpret this to mean that the more output the firm can get out of its fixed scale of plant, *the more efficiently the fixed resources alone are used.*

Average Variable Costs

The average variable cost curve decreases with the increase in output, reaches a minimum, and then increases as the level of output is increased.

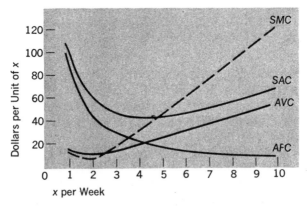

Figure 8–2
A firm's per unit cost curves.

Following the foregoing pattern of analysis, we see that this means that the efficiency of variable resources increases as output is increased up to the two unit per week level; then it decreases as the level of output is raised beyond that level.[4]

Average Costs

The short-run average cost curve, plotted as *SAC* in Figure 8–2, also exhibits a dish-shape, or a *U-shape*, as it is generally referred to by economists. Since the *SAC* curve is a combination of the *AFC* curve and the

[4]*Would increasing and decreasing returns to variable resources have anything to do with these happenings? What would the AVC curve look like if increasing returns to the variable resources did not occur?*

AVC curve, this is not altogether surprising. The shape of the *SAC* curve is a reflection of the efficiency of the firm's over-all operation in the short run. As the output level is increased from zero, average fixed costs fall as the fixed resources are used more efficiently. The output increases permit greater efficiency in the use of variable resources too if the law of increasing returns is operative for them. Increasing efficiency in the use of both fixed and variable resources means increasing efficiency for the entire operation of the firm. In Table 8–2 and Figure 8–2, from an output level of two units to four units per week average fixed costs decline and average variable costs increase. But the decreases in average fixed costs (increases in the efficiency of fixed resources) more than offset the increases in average variable costs (decreases in the efficiency of the variable resources), and short-run average costs continue to decline. Beyond the four-unit output level the decreasing efficiency in the use of variable resources becomes dominant.

The four-unit level of output for the hypothetical firm is the output of most efficient operation. This is the output level at which *SAC* is minimum. We call this output level the *optimum rate of output*. However, it is not necessarily the most profitable level of output for the firm. Profits depend upon revenues as well as upon costs, and so far we have not taken the firm's revenues into consideration.

Marginal Costs

If the management of the steel mill were contemplating an increase in the output level at which its fixed scale of plant is to be used, a very relevant question to ask is, What will the increase do to short-run total costs? Another relevant question is, What will the increase do to total receipts? Posing these two questions simultaneously, and looking at the answers concurrently, is still more relevant. If the contemplated increase in output will increase short-run total costs more than it will increase revenues, it obviously will not pay to make it. It is just as obvious that profits will be increased (or losses diminished) if the output increase raises total receipts more than it raises total costs.

With respect to costs (we shall look at revenues in the next chapter), the change in total costs resulting from a one-unit change in output by a firm is called *marginal cost*. If the change in output is $\triangle x$ and the corresponding change in cost is $\triangle STC$, then marginal cost is $(\triangle STC)/(\triangle x)$. Short-run marginal costs, or *SMC* in column (5) of Table 8–1, are computed in this way for each output level.

A firm's marginal cost curve bears a unique relation to its average cost curve. Where average cost decreases as output is increased, marginal cost will be less than average cost. Where average cost increases as output is increased, marginal cost will be greater than average cost. It follows that if average cost were neither increasing nor decreasing with output changes, marginal cost and average cost would be the same. These relations are illustrated both in Table 8–2 and Figure 8–2.

The mathematical relation between marginal cost and average cost is a commonplace one that we encounter almost every day. Suppose that on an automobile trip at some point we compute our average speed. If we have covered 100 miles in two hours, our average speed is 50 miles per hour. Now we know that if we drop the rate of speed (marginal speed) below 50 miles per hour, average speed will fall, *but it will not fall to the level of our new rate of speed*. Similarly, if we increase our rate of speed to 60 miles per hour, average speed will rise *but not to the level of the new rate of speed*. If we hold our rate of speed constant at 50 miles per hour, average speed will be equal to the rate of speed and will not change.

In the same vein, suppose that we compute the average costs of production at a given output level. If output is increased by one unit and the resulting increase in total cost—marginal cost—is greater than the previous average cost, average cost is pulled to a higher level but will be less than marginal cost. If the increase in total cost is less than the previous average cost, average cost is pulled down but not to the level of marginal cost. If the amount added to total cost is equal to the previous average cost level, average cost will not change.[5]

The Steel Mill Case

The problems of the steel mill raised at the beginning of the chapter fall into proper perspective now. Total fixed costs are large. At low output levels average fixed costs are high, making over-all average costs high. Higher output levels would reduce average fixed costs and, up to an output level at which decreasing efficiency in the utilization of variable resources more than offsets increasing efficiency of the fixed resources, short-run average costs as well.

Long-Run Costs

In long-run planning a firm has more possibilities open to it than in the

---

[5] *These same relations hold for SMC and AVC for the same set of reasons: in the short run all changes in STC as output changes are really changes in TVC, since TFC cannot change.*

short run. Increases or decreases in the scale of plant, that is, in the utilization of the resources that make up the firm's scale of plant, can be considered, and this greatly expands the range of outputs that are open to the firm. In fact, long-run planning encompasses the alternative short-run possibilities of all possible scales of plant. The meaning of this point will become clear in a moment.

Long-Run Average Costs

Suppose that technology in the light aircraft industry is such that only three alternative sizes of plant are possible—a little one, a medium-sized one, and a large one. For each of these a short-run average cost curve exists. In Figure 8–3 these are SAC_1, SAC_2, and SAC_3, respectively. For

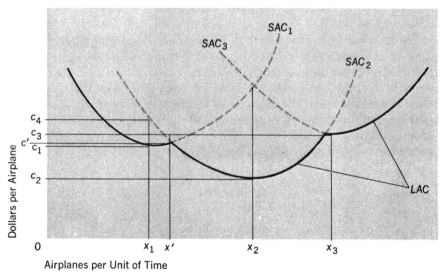

Figure 8–3
Construction of the long-run average cost curve.

long-run planning any one of the three can be built and used, and the firm can expand or contract from one scale to another. How would the firm go about choosing which one to construct and use?

The decision turns on the output to be produced. Presumably it would be desirable to produce whatever output is to be produced at an average cost as low as possible. If output were x_1, which of the three possible scales of plant would accomplish this objective? With SAC_1 average cost would be c_1 dollars per airplane, but with SAC_2 it would be c_4 dollars. The better choice would be SAC_1. Alternatively, suppose that output x' is the one to be produced. Either SAC_1 or SAC_2 could be chosen, since either will produce x_1 airplanes per unit of time at an average cost of c' dollars. Similarly, SAC_2 will produce output x_2 at the lowest possible average cost for that output, and SAC_3 is the choice for an output of x_3 airplanes.

The long-run average cost curve of a firm shows the least possible average costs at which all alternative output levels can be produced when the firm is free to make a choice among alternative scales of plant and the output ranges that can be produced with each possible scale of plant. Thus in Figure 8–3 we have already drawn the firm's long-run average cost or LAC curve. It is the solid-line portions of SAC_1, SAC_2, and SAC_3. (Can you explain why this is the case?)

Ordinarily, the long-run average cost curve of a firm would be much smoother than the one pictured in Figure 8–3. Most firms are faced with a choice among an infinite number of scales of plant rather than being restricted to three. It is almost always possible to increase or decrease the scale of plant infinitesimally, and where this is so the parts of the SAC curves that constitute portions of the LAC curve are so small that they are merely points such as A, B, and C in Figure 8–4. Thus the long-run

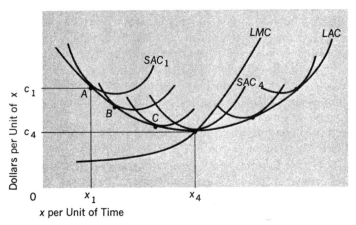

Figure 8–4
Relation of long- and short-run average costs.

average cost curve becomes the smooth LAC curve of Figure 8–4, lying tangent to the short-run average cost curves, some of which are drawn, of all possible scales of plant.

Economies and Diseconomies of Scale

We have drawn the long-run average cost curve as a U-shaped curve, first falling as output (and the scale of plant) is increased, then rising as output (and the scale of plant) is increased further beyond some certain level. Actually, there is some controversy among economists as to whether or not this is the prevailing shape of the *LAC* curve; some argue that it falls as output is increased, levels off, and does not turn up again. This controversy need not detain us here, but we shall inquire into the meaning of whatever shape the *LAC* curve takes and the forces that shape it. The U-shape provides a convenient framework for that inquiry.

If the *LAC* curve were U-shaped, as we have drawn it in Figure 8–4, what does the U-shape mean? Obviously it means that larger scales of plant up to some certain size have lower and lower *SAC* curves, and beyond that size they have higher and higher *SAC* curves. Since scale of plant with lower *SAC* curves are by definition more efficient than those with higher *SAC* curves, we must explain why efficiency increases as the scale increases and why—in some cases at least—beyond some critical size efficiency falls off.

The forces causing the long-run average cost curve to decrease as the scale of plant is increased are called *economies of scale*. Most of us are familiar with the two most important ones. First, larger scales of plant make possible the *specialization of labour* on particular parts of the production process. Greater efficiency results partly because workers can specialize on those things at which they are most adept and partly because with specialization less time is lost in moving from one task to another and from one set of tools or machines to another. Second, larger scales of plant enable the firm to use *cost-saving techniques of production* that are not possible or feasible for small scales of plant. The assembly line, automatic stamping machines, and the like can be used in the larger scales of plant, whereas their costs would be prohibitive in smaller scales of plant with low levels of output.

The forces causing long-run average costs to increase—if they increase —are called *diseconomies of scale*. These are said to consist of increasing difficulties in co-ordinating and controlling larger and larger scales of plant. Decision-making by top management becomes more complex. More co-ordination—and proliferation of red tape—among lower management officials becomes necessary. Management loses direct contact with line production workers and their problems. One thing is certain. In some industries, the automobile industry, for example, the scale of plant beyond which diseconomies occur may be extremely large.

The most efficient scale of plant of all the alternative possibilities is called the *optimum scale of plant*. It is the one lying at the bottom of the *LAC* curve—SAC_4 in Figure 8–4. It is large enough to take advantage of economies of scale but not large enough for diseconomies of scale to exert dominance over the economies. A firm will not necessarily build and use the optimum scale of plant in the long run; some other scale of plant may be more profitable. If in Figure 8–4 the market is small and the firm finds output x_1 to be the most profitable one, scale of plant SAC_1 will produce that output at a lower average cost than will any other. Scale of plant SAC_4 would be the best one to build and use only if the firm's desired output is x_4.

Long-Run Marginal Costs

For long-run as well as short-run planning purposes a firm is vitally concerned for what changes in output will do to its total costs and to its total receipts. In the long run changes in output entail changes in the quantities of scale of plant resources as well as other resources used. If the aircraft manufacturer intends to increase his output of two-place planes by 1000 per year, production facilities appropriate for the higher output must be built and put into service, and the increase in yearly costs attributable to amortization and/or depreciation of the extra facilities are a part of the extra costs of production. The increase in total costs per unit increase in output for the long run is called *long-run marginal cost*. If the 1000 unit per year increase in the production of airplanes brings about a $5 million increase in the company's yearly costs, long-run marginal cost for the increase is $5000 per airplane, although ordinarily we would compute marginal cost on a much smaller increment in output.

Long-run marginal costs bear the same relation to long-run average costs as short-run marginal costs bear to short-run average costs. Long-run marginal costs that are below long-run average costs pull the latter down. If long-run marginal costs exceed long-run average costs, they pull the latter up. At the output level at which long-run average costs are minimum—neither rising nor falling—long-run marginal costs are equal to the average. In Figure 8–4 the long-run marginal cost curve *LMC* is drawn in correct relation to the *LAC* curve.

The Aircraft Manufacturer Case

The decisions of the light aircraft manufacturing company considered at the beginning of the chapter make sense in terms of long-run planning by the firm. Apparently the firm's officials have established through engineering and cost studies that their present scale of plant is too small to effect all possible economies of scale. The present scale of plant could be represented by SAC_1 in Figure 8–4 and the output level may be x_1. Their studies indicate that if they increase the scale of plant to some such size as SAC_4 and output to some such level as x_4, per unit costs will fall[6] from c_1 to c_4. The larger scale of plant permits them to take advantage of economies of scale. A possibility exists that if the plant size is expanded far enough diseconomies of scale may become dominant.

Summary

Costs of production are the obligations incurred by a firm for the resources it uses in turning out its product output. In order to obtain or to hold resources for its own use a firm must pay for them as much as they would be worth in their best alternative uses. This principle is known as the alternative-cost principle and also as the opportunity-cost principle. Explicit costs are the costs of resources bought or hired by the firm while implicit costs are the costs of self-owned, self-employed resources.

In the analysis of a firm's costs two time viewpoints are used, the short run and the long run. The short run represents a short enough planning period that the firm does not have time to alter the quantities of resources that constitute its scale of plant. The long run is a planning period reaching far enough ahead for the firm to consider, build, use, and change its scale of plant; that is, the quantities of all resources can be changed if the firm so desires. Short-run costs relate costs to the outputs obtainable with a given scale of plant. Long-run costs relate costs to outputs obtainable with all possible alternative scales of plant.

In short-run planning those resources making up the firm's scale of plant are called fixed resources and their costs are fixed costs. Resources that can be altered in quantity are called variable resources and their costs are variable costs. Total fixed costs are constant for all levels of output that the firm can produce with its fixed scale of plant. Total variable costs vary directly with output, but increasing returns and decreasing returns to the complex of variable resources run through the plant give the total variable cost curve a sort of inverted S-shape. The short-run total cost curve is identical to the total variable cost curve, except that it is displaced upward by the amount of total fixed costs.

When short-run total fixed costs, total variable costs, and over-all total costs at various output levels are divided by those output levels, we obtain

---

[6]*There is nothing magic about these particular output levels. Nothing is said in the discussion about the size of profits made at either x_1 or x_4. All we try to demonstrate here is that if a decision were made to increase output from x_1 to x_4, long-run per unit costs would fall from c_1 to c_4.*

the average fixed costs, average variable costs, and over-all average costs of the firm. The shapes of these curves reflect the efficiency with which they are used by the firm. The average fixed cost curve decreases as output is increased. The average variable cost curve has a U-shape because of increasing and diminishing returns. The average cost curve has a U-shape also, taking its shape from those of the average fixed and average variable cost curves.

Short-run marginal cost of the firm is defined as the change in total cost (total variable cost) per unit change in the firm's output level.

In long-run planning the firm can contemplate the average costs of production for all alternative scales of plant. For any given output the firm would be expected to choose the scale of plant that would produce that output at a lower cost than the other alternatives. A long-run average cost curve, showing the least average cost of producing alternative outputs when the firm is free to choose among alternative scales of plant, is made up of very small segments of the short-run average cost curves of those scales of plant. It is generally taken to be a U-shaped curve. Economies of scale, or forces that make larger scales of plant more efficient than smaller ones, underlie the decreasing portion of it. Diseconomies of scale that cause firms to become less efficient beyond some certain size cause the curve to turn up again—if it does indeed turn up. A long-run marginal cost curve shows the changes in the firm's long-run total costs per unit change in its output, and it bears the same relation to the long-run average cost curve as does a short-run marginal cost curve to its corresponding short-run average cost curve.

Exercises and Questions for Discussion

1. The cost schedules given below are those for a firm producing refrigerators. From these derive the STC, AFC, AVC, SAC, and SMC schedules for the firm. Also draw the total cost curves on one graph and the average and marginal curves on another, using the schedules you have derived.

Short-run Total Costs of Refrigerators		
REFRIGERATORS PER WEEK	TFC	TVC
0	$200	$ 0
1	200	90
2	200	170
3	200	240
4	200	300
5	200	370
6	200	450
7	200	540
8	200	650
9	200	780
10	200	930

2. On the graphs you drew in problem 1 point out the areas of increasing and decreasing returns. What is the optimum rate of output?

3. "Anytime a producer is operating at the optimum rate of output he is also operating at the optimum scale of plant." Evaluate.

4. An aged widow suffered heavy financial losses during the bank failures of the 1930s. Since that time she has kept her savings behind a loose brick in the fireplace, content with the thought that her savings are safe and that this safety is "not costing a thing." Is this latter statement correct?

5. To prove your understanding of different time horizons, determine which of the following decisions represent short-run and which represent long-run planning problems.

   a. Metropolitan Life decides to hire two more selling agents.
   b. Beechnut decides to increase its tobacco production by adding 30 more shaving and packing machines to its assembly line.
   c. Canadian Plywood decides to increase production by extending the working day from 5 P.M. to 7 P.M.
   d. Baldridge Bakery increases its pastry production by adding to its present cake plant.
   e. Your local bank changes from manual to electronic cheque processing.

Selected Readings

Bain, Joe S., *Industrial Organization*. New York: John Wiley and Sons, Inc., 1959, pp. 145–169.

Dorfman, Robert, *Prices and Markets*. Englewood Cliffs, N.J.: Prentice-Hall, Inc., 1967, Chap. 3.

Weiss, Leonard W., *Economics and American Industry*. New York: John Wiley and Sons, Inc., 1961, pp. 347–350.

9

Competitive Pricing and Outputs

If you were about to establish, or if you were actually operating, a baby-sitting service, a computerized dating bureau, a laundry, a grocery store, an automobile manufacturing concern, or any other kind of business enterprise, you would want to make a thorough analysis of the production function of the business and of its various cost components. But the analysis would be more meaningful if you were to take an additional step —if you also analyzed the market for your product and estimated the prices and the revenues that you would receive at different possible output levels. You could compare revenues and costs at alternative output levels and determine which, if any, would make it worth your while to be in business; if there were indeed a range of profitable outputs, you could choose the most profitable one.

Thousands of business firms engage in analyses of their cost and revenue positions, and it is upon these analyses that they base their pricing and output decisions. These are the decisions that organize production in the private, as distinguished from the government, sector of the economy. Pricing patterns are established and the composition of output is determined. In this and the following two chapters we shall be concerned with the organization of production at three levels of operation: (1) that of the individual firm, (2) that of the industry, and (3) that of the entire private sector of the economy.

Competition in Selling Markets

Sellers of goods and services encounter a wide range of competitive conditions depending upon what they sell and where they sell it. The seller of wheat finds that there are *many firms selling a product identical to what he has to place on the market*—so many, in fact, that by himself he cannot affect the price of wheat. If there were no effective governmental price supports for wheat, *its price would rise or fall in response to changes in total demand of consumers and in total supply that sellers bring to market.* The seller of wheat is *free to sell wherever he desires to sell,* and this will usually be where he can receive the highest price. Any product market which sellers face in which the italicized conditions are present is said to be one of *pure competition.*

At the other end of the spectrum we find *pure monopoly.* In this market situation there is only *one seller of the product and no good substitute products exist.* Examples are provided by the seller of telephone services in a given region and by most other public utilities.

Between the extremes of pure competition and pure monopoly there are differing degrees of competitiveness. The whole in-between range of conditions is called *imperfect competition.* Sometimes in a specific market there is only a handful of sellers of a product, as is the case for automobiles. We call this situation *oligopoly,* meaning *few sellers.* Again there may be *many sellers* in a market, but the *product sold by each differs in some way from that sold by each of the others.* These are markets of *monopolistic competition.* Both oligopoly and monopolistic competition are subclassifications of imperfect competition.

Although most sellers of goods and services operate in markets of imperfect competition, situations of pure competition provide a convenient launching pad for the analysis of pricing and output. Purely competitive market models occupy about the same place in economic analysis as does frictionless mechanics in the study of physics. They provide us with rather simple cause and effect relationships that, appropriately modified, furnish much insight into the more complex conditions of monopoly and imperfect competition. Then, too, there are enough market situations reasonably close to pure competition to make purely competitive principles as such valuable tools of analysis. In this chapter we concentrate on purely competitive markets.

Very Short-Run Pricing

Suppose that there is a certain supply available of a product and that the time period during which the product must be sold is too short to permit additional quantities of it to be produced. For example, clothing stores have stocks of spring suits on hand that, because of style factors and costs of storage, cannot be carried over to next spring. Grocers have stocks of fresh fruits and vegetables that will spoil if kept on the shelves.

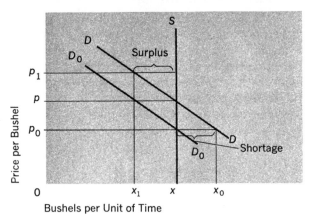

Figure 9-1
Very short-run price determination.

Following wheat harvest no more wheat can be grown until the next season. The planning period for sellers in this type of situation is called the *very short-run*—a planning period that limits opportunities open to sellers even more than the short-run period.

The main characteristic of the very short run for the sellers of any given product is the *fixed supply of the product*. The length of time for which this condition exists differs from product to product, being so short for some that it is of no importance at all. For other products, it may however, be a month, six months, a year, or even longer. Where it is a significant length of time, how does an economy determine how the fixed supply of the product is to be divided up or rationed?

The price system provides a rationing mechanism. Suppose that the year's apple harvest has been completed and that quantity x of apples in Figure 9-1 is the total supply available until the next harvest. The quantity cannot be increased no matter what price is offered to the sellers, so the supply curve is the vertical line xS. The demand curve, DD, shows the quantities per year that consumers are willing to take at alternative price levels. If the price were p_0 per bushel, there would be a shortage of apples amounting to xx_0 and consumers would bid against each other, driving the price up to p. At this price consumers would voluntarily ration themselves to the total supply available. On the other hand, if the price were p_1 per bushel, there would be a surplus of x_1x bushels that would induce sellers to undercut each other, driving price down to p. At this price consumers would be willing to take the entire supply off the market.[1]

In very short-run pricing situations costs of production play no part whatsoever in price determination. Once a given quantity of a product is in existence, the only important question with regard to price determination is how much buyers are willing to pay for that quantity. Buyers simply are not interested in what it cost at some past date to produce the item. If in Figure 9–1 demand were to decrease to D_0D_0, price would fall to p_0 and the quantity exchanged would remain at x. The moral of this story is that when you want to sell your house you might as well forget what it cost to build it. Sunken costs are sunken costs; you can get only what buyers are willing to pay.

Short Run Pricing And Output

If we extend the time horizon to the planning periods defined in the last chapter as the short run and the long run, costs of production play an important role in price determination. As we shall see, unless variable costs of production are covered in the short run and unless all costs are covered in the long run, a product will not be produced. In this section we shall be concerned with short-run pricing and output. We look at the operations of an individual firm first, and we then extend the analysis to the entire industry of which the firm is a part.

The Firm

Why are business firms established in the first place? What are the objectives of those who own and operate them? There are many reasons, of course. Someone has invented the wheel and wants to make the fruits of his knowledge available to the sliding, skidding, walking population of the world. Another sees himself becoming a captain of industry, the guid-

[1]*Do you see any resemblance between this situation and the end of season sales of clothing stores or to the low prices placed by bakers on day-old bread or pastries?*

ing genius of an industrial empire. Others find themselves in control of an already existing firm and seek to maintain its identity and position in its industry. But in all probability the most important objective is that of making money or profits. For most firms most of the time this objective is strong enough to provide the rationale for their economic activities, and we shall so accept it here.

The Firm's Profit

In economic analysis *profit* is the difference between a firm's total receipts and its total costs. It is not the same thing as the accounting "profits" of a firm that appear on its profit and loss statement. In accounting procedures all economic costs are not deducted from the firm's revenues in computing its "profits"; in particular, there are certain implicit costs that are not deducted. A corporation, for example, pays dividends to its stockholders out of its "profits" and does not classify those dividends as costs. But what are dividends from the point of view of economic analysis? Stockholders of a corporation are the owners of its capital and they let the corporation use that capital. In return, stockholders expect to receive dividends at least equal to what they could earn if they invested elsewhere in the economy. These are payments for the use of stockholders' resources, and to the economist they are costs.[2] Total costs, as the term has been defined already and as it is used throughout this book, include an average rate of return to investors on what they have invested in the business as well as all other implicit costs.

The Firm's Revenue

The costs of production of a firm were examined in detail in the last chapter, but we have said little up to this point about its revenues. The revenue side of the picture is a much simpler set of concepts and its description will require much less time and space.

Suppose there are 100 sellers of transistor radios and that all of these firms are of approximately equal size. Suppose, further, that there is no appreciable difference among the radios sold by the different firms. The

[2]*This is not to say that economists are "right" and accountants are "wrong." One of the purposes of accounting procedures is to determine what part of the firm's revenues are available to its owners. Economists seek something different. They want to know what is left after all costs, including payments for the use of the self-owned, self-employed resources, have been deducted.*

TABLE 9–1

Revenues, Cost, and Profits of a Firm Selling Transistor Radios

(1) Quantity of Radios per Day (x)	(2) Price per Radio [(TR)/x]	(3) Total Revenue (TR)	(4) Marginal Revenue [(ΔTR)/(Δx)]	(5) Total Costs (STC)	(6) Average Costs [(STC)/x]	(7) Marginal Costs [(ΔSTC)/(Δx)]	(8) Profits (TR − STC)
0	$103	$ 0	$ —	$200	$ —	$ —	$ (−) 200
1	103	103	103	215	215	15	(−) 112
2	103	206	103	225	$112\frac{1}{2}$	10	(−) 19
3	103	309	103	240	80	15	69
4	103	412	103	261	$65\frac{1}{4}$	21	151
5	103	515	103	292	$58\frac{2}{5}$	31	223
6	103	618	103	340	$56\frac{2}{3}$	48	278
7	103	721	103	410	$58\frac{4}{7}$	70	311
8	103	824	103	513	$64\frac{1}{8}$	103	311
9	103	927	103	656	$72\frac{8}{9}$	143	271
10	103	1030	103	856	$85\frac{3}{5}$	200	174

market is one of pure competition—no one seller by himself can influence the product price. The market price of the product is 103 dollars per radio. What can we deduce about one firm's revenues?

Columns (1) and (2) of Table 9–1 represent demand as it looks to the firm. *Demand* to the firm means what the firm can sell at alternative possible prices. At a price above 103 dollars it can sell no radios at all. Buyers would turn to other sellers who are selling at the market price of 103 dollars. On the other hand, one firm in a purely competitive market sells such a small proportion of the total for the industry that its sales will not significantly affect price. It can sell all it desires to sell at the going market price, so there is no need to sell for less. The demand schedule, plotted as a demand curve, is shown as *dd* in Figure 9–3. Note that it is perfectly elastic.

The total revenue of a single firm at alternative output levels is shown in column (3) of Table 9–1. For whatever output the firm sells, a price of 103 dollars per radio is received. Consequently, at each output level, *total revenue* is simply price times quantity. The higher the sales level, the

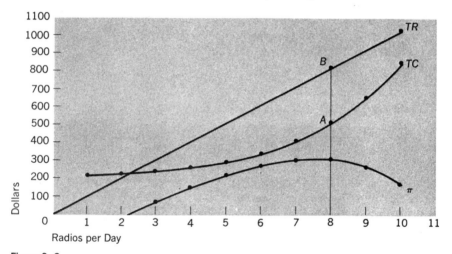

Figure 9–2
Profit maximization: total curves.

higher will be total revenue. The corresponding total revenue curve is shown as *TR* in Figure 9–2.

The change in the firm's total revenue per unit change in its sales level is called *marginal revenue*. Since the price of the product is 103 dollars per unit no matter how many units are sold, a one-unit change in the sales level will bring about a 103 dollar change in total revenue. For the purely competitive seller of product marginal revenue will always be the same

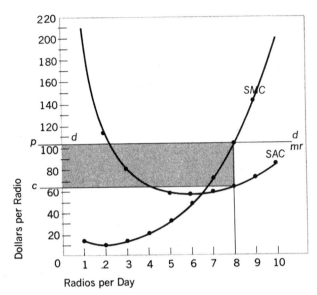

Figure 9–3
Profit maximization: per unit curves.

as the market price of the product. Marginal revenue, computed from columns (1) and (3), is shown in column (4) of Table 9–1 and as *mr* in Figure 9–3. The *mr* curve coincides with the *dd* curve.

Profit Maximization

If the costs to the firm of selling transistor radios are those of columns (5), (6), and (7) of Table 9–1, its profit-maximizing output is easily determined. Subtracting the total costs of column (5) from the total receipts of column (3), we obtain column (8), which shows the profits available at each alternative output and sales level. In Figure 9–2 we accomplish the same thing by subtracting the *TC* curve from the *TR* curve at each output and sales level. The differences are plotted as the π, or profits curve. The maximum profit obtainable occurs at either seven or eight radios per day and is 311 dollars.

The per unit cost and revenue curves also provide the information necessary for determining the firm's profit-maximizing output. The key concepts are marginal cost and marginal revenue. Since marginal cost and marginal revenue are the change in total cost and the change in total revenue, respectively, for a one-unit change in output, a comparison of the two for any change in output shows the effect of the change on profits. For example, in Table 9–1 and Figure 9–3 we note that for an increase in output from three to four radios per day the marginal cost is 21 dollars and the marginal revenue is 103 dollars, the former being the increase in total cost and the latter the increase in total revenue. Therefore, profits are increased by 82 dollars per day by the output increase. A glance at column (8) of Table 9–1 and a quick computation will verify this result.

Further increases in output will increase profits still more. If output is increased to five radios, marginal cost becomes 31 dollars and marginal revenue is 103 dollars. Profits are increased by 72 dollars. At an output level of six radios, marginal cost is 48 dollars, marginal revenue is 103 dollars, and profits are increased by 55 dollars by this one-unit addition to output. Similarly, an increase in output to seven radios will raise profits an additional 33 dollars.

For an increase from seven to eight radios marginal cost and marginal revenue are the same—103 dollars—and nothing is added to the firm's profits. But neither is anything lost. Marginal revenue is less than marginal cost for an increase from eight to nine radios as well as for an increase from nine to ten. These increments in sales levels would bring about decreases in profits.

We have uncovered an important set of principles with regard to profit maximization by a firm. Output increases for which marginal revenue is greater than marginal cost will increase the firm's profits while those for which marginal revenue is less than marginal cost will decrease profits. It follows then that *profits are maximum at the output level at which marginal cost equals marginal revenue.*[3]

The marginal cost equals marginal revenue relation shows the output level at which profits are maximum but tells us nothing about the magnitude of total profits. The per unit information from which total profits can be determined is average cost and average revenue or price at the profit-maximizing output. Consider Table 9–1 and Figure 9–3. At the eight-unit output level, price, p, is 103 dollars and average cost, c, is $64\frac{1}{8}$ dollars. The firm's profit per unit is $38\frac{7}{8}$ dollars, the difference between the two. Total profit for the entire eight-unit output level is $38\frac{7}{8}$ dollars multiplied by 8, or 311 dollars. This result checks with the computation of profit at that level of output in Table 9–1.

The Firm's Short-Run Supply Curve

Every firm selling in a purely competitive market has a *short-run supply*

---

[3]*Profits are also maximum at an output level one unit less than that for which marginal revenue equals marginal cost. However, it is convenient—and still correct—to state the profit-maximizing conditions as we have in the text.*

curve showing the amounts of the product that it is willing to place on the market at alternative price levels, other things being equal. The "other things being equal" are the fixed conditions underlying a given set of short-run cost curves—the prices of the resources used and the technological possibilities open with the firm's fixed scale of plant.

In Figure 9–4 we show the cost curves of a soft coal mine. If the price of coal were p_3 dollars per ton, what output would the firm produce? If its objective is profit maximization, and we assume it is, its output would be

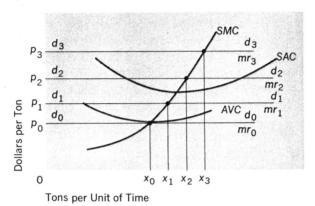

Figure 9–4
A firm's short-run supply curve.

x_3. If the price is p_3, both the demand curve facing the firm and its marginal revenue curve are horizontal at the level. Output x_3 is the one at which marginal cost and marginal revenue are the same. (Can you determine the level of average cost and show geometrically what the firm's total profits are at this price and output level?) If price were p_2, profits would be maximized by an output of x_2.

If the price of coal were p_1, the firm would incur losses, since there is no output at which that price exceeds average costs. If the firm were to reduce its output to zero, its losses would be its total fixed costs, or those that are incurred in the short run whether or not the firm produces and regardless of the output it produces. However, if it produces an output of x_1, its total receipts will be greater than its total variable costs (since the price exceeds average variable costs at that output). The excess of total receipts over total variable costs covers a part of the fixed costs, thus making the firm's losses less than total fixed cost. At price p_1 it pays to produce rather than shut down the plant; losses are minimized by producing output x_1, that at which marginal cost equals marginal revenue.

If the price of coal is p_0 in Figure 9–4 and output is x_0, total receipts and total variable costs are the same; total receipts cover total variable costs but not total fixed costs. Whether the firm produces x_0 or nothing is unimportant, since in either case losses are equal to total fixed costs.

If the market price is so low that total variable costs are not covered by total receipts (price is less than average variable costs), the firm keeps its losses at a minimum by producing no output. If price is less than p_0 and the firm does produce, a part of the variable costs are not covered nor are any of the fixed costs, so losses exceed total fixed costs. Losses are lower, therefore, if output is zero.

The firm's *short-run supply curve* is that part of its short-run marginal cost curve lying above its average variable cost curve. At any price below minimum average variable costs the firm will produce nothing. At any price above minimum average variable costs it minimizes losses or maximizes profits, as the case may be, by producing the output at which short-run marginal cost equals marginal revenue or price of the product.

The Market or the Industry

We have explained how the output of a single firm is determined when the market price of the product it produces is known. But what determines the market price? It is not determined by any one single firm; in a purely competitive selling market no one firm by itself has any influence on price. Rather, it is determined by the interaction of sellers with buyers in the market for the product. This interaction, described in Chapter 4, is examined here in more detail.

The Market Supply Curve

The market supply curve for a product is built up from the supply curves of individual firms that produce the product. Suppose that in Figure 9–5 we look at the short-run marginal cost curves, SMC_1 and SMC_2, of two coal-mining firms. We are concerned with and we show only the parts lying above the respective average variable cost curves of the firms. If product price were p_0, firm 1 would maximize profits by producing output x_0. Firm 2 would produce output x'_0. Together they would produce an output of X_0 ($= x_0 + x'_0$) at that price. If price were p_1, firm 1 would produce x_1; firm 2 would produce x'_1; and together they would produce X_1 ($= x_1 + x'_1$). The curve SS is located in this manner and shows the combined outputs of the two firms for alternative price levels; it is the combined supply curve of the two firms. By extending this sort of *horizontal summation* of individual-firm short-run marginal cost curves to all of the firms producing and selling in this soft-coal market we obtain the *short-run market supply curve* for the product.

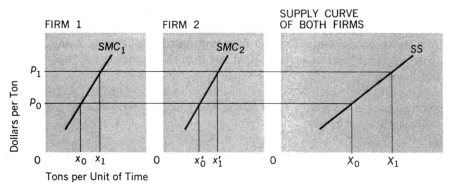

Figure 9–5
The market supply curve.

Price and Output

Both the market demand and the market supply curves for soft coal are pictured in Figure 9–6, together with the short-run average cost and the marginal cost curves of one of the many firms in the industry. The market demand curve, *DD*, is the horizontal summation of the demand curves of consumers of the product, and the supply curve, *SS*, is the horizontal summation of the marginal cost curves of all sellers. The vertical scales of the two diagrams are identical, but the horizontal scale of the

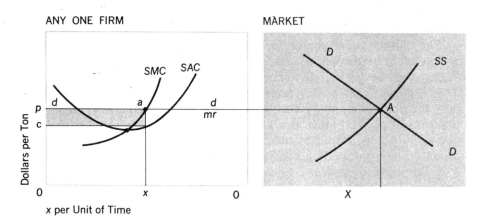

Figure 9–6
Market price, individual firm output, and market output determination.

market diagram is greatly compressed as compared with that of the firm.

The equilibrium, or market, price of coal will be p dollars per ton—determined by the interactions of *all* buyers and sellers. Consequently, the demand curve facing any one firm will be dd, and its marginal revenue, mr, will be the same. To maximize profits the firm shown, and every other firm in the industry, will produce an output at which marginal cost equals that marginal revenue. For the firm pictured the output is x and for all firms together the output level is X, the sum of the outputs of the individual firms.

The firm for which we show cost curves is making profits. At output x average cost is c. Profit per ton of coal is cp, and total profits are cp dollars multiplied by x tons.

Effects of Demand Changes

Suppose that the price of fuel oil goes up and that consumers switch to coal for heating purposes. What are the short-run effects of the change in demand for coal? The analytical apparatus that we have just put together is useful in sorting out these effects.

With reference to Figure 9–7, the increase in the price of fuel oil causes an increase in market demand for coal from DD to D_1D_1. When demand was at DD the market price was p; the market output was X; the individual firm output was x; the average cost for the firm was c; and the profits

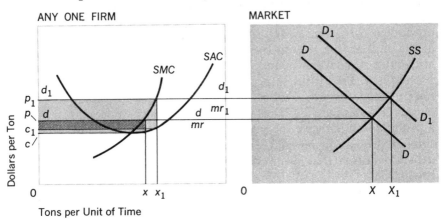

Figure 9–7
Effects of a change in demand.

for the firm were cp times x. With the increase in demand to D_1D_1, the market price rises to p_1, shifting the demand curve facing the firm and the marginal revenue curve to d_1d_1 and mr_1, respectively. To maximize profits the single firm increases its output to x_1, at which marginal cost is equal to the higher level of marginal revenue. Profits increase to c_1p_1 times x_1. Since all firms in the industry do the same thing, market output expands to X_1. Thus, in the short run, an increase in demand for a product increases the price as well as the quantity of the product that is produced and sold. Profits provide an incentive for individual firms to work their given scales of plant more intensively. A decrease in demand brings about the opposite results.

Changes in Costs

The effects of a change in costs are as easily handled as are those of a change in demand. In Figure 9–8 suppose that in the market for soft coal the initial demand is *DD*. The cost curves of any one firm are *SAC* and *SMC*. Individual firm output is x and market output is X. Profits of the firm are cp times x.

Suppose now that the United Mine Workers obtain a substantial pay

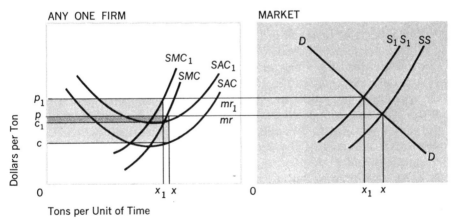

Figure 9–8
Effects of a change in costs.

increase across the board. The cost curves of each firm will be shifted upward to SAC_1 and SMC_1. An upward shift in a firm's *SMC* curve is also a shift to the left, so the market supply curve, obtained from the horizontal summation of individual-firm *SMC* curves, is shifted to the left to S_1S_1. Price rises to p_1. Individual firm output falls to x_1, where SMC_1 is equal to mr_1. Profits for the firm are now c_1p_1 times x_1. Market output and sales are X_1. Thus forces causing short-run cost increases for a product will increase the market price of the product and reduce the amount produced and sold. Individual-firm output and profits will be reduced. Forces that decrease short-run costs will have the opposite effects.

Long-Run Pricing and Output

In the long run there is much greater flexibility in the possible quantities of a product that can be put on the market than in the short run. In the short run the productive capacity of an industry is fixed by the plant size of individual firms and by the number of firms in the industry; however, this fixed over-all capacity can be operated at alternative levels of output within the limits that existing plant facilities impose. In the long run there are no fixed capacity limits to production for the industry as a whole. Individual firms can increase or decrease their investments in plant and equipment. It is also possible for new firms to enter the industry and for existing firms to leave if they so desire.

Individual-Firm Scale of Plant Adjustments

The principles involved in long-run profit maximization are no different from those established for the short run, except that the long-run average cost and the long-run marginal cost curves are the relevant ones rather than the short-run average cost and the short-run marginal cost curves. Long-run profit maximization is illustrated in Figure 9–9. The firm's long-run average cost curve is LAC and its long-run marginal cost curve is LMC. Initially we will suppose that the market price of coal is p_1 per ton. Consequently, the demand curve facing the firm and the firm's marginal revenue curve are d_1d_1 and mr_1, respectively. Long-run profits will be maximum at output level x_1 at which long-run marginal cost equals marginal revenue.

The scale of plant that will minimize cost for output x_1 is the one represented by the short-run average cost curve SAC_1. If either a larger or a smaller scale of plant, say SAC_0 or SAC_2, were used, average cost for that output level would be greater than c_1. Only scale of plant SAC can produce output x_1 at a cost per ton as low as c_1.

Entry or Exit of Firms

The firm in Figure 9–9 is making profits of c_1p_1 times x_1. Profit has been defined previously as total revenues of the firm minus *all* costs, both implicit and explicit. We include as a part of costs returns to investors in the industry equal to what they could have earned on the average elsewhere in the economy. Thus when profits occur, this means that the owners of the business earn a higher than average return on their investment in the business. Even if a firm makes no profit, as we define and use the term, it is doing all right. The owners of all resources used in making the product are receiving as much for their resources as they would had they placed them elsewhere in the economy.

The industry of which the firm in Figure 9–9 is a part is a good one in which to invest. Investors receive returns higher than they can make on

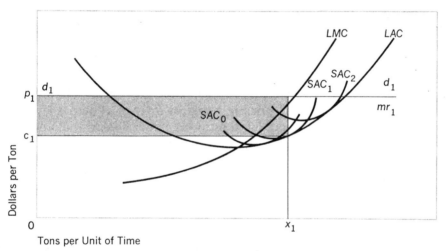

Figure 9–9
Long-run profit maximization.

the average elsewhere in the economy, as evidenced by the firm's profits. Investors go where opportunities exist, so new firms would be established in the industry.

What is the impact of the entry of new firms? One thing is certain: the market supply of the product will increase, and this will force down the price per ton of coal. As the market price falls both the demand and the marginal revenue curves facing the firm shift downward. The individual firm output level at which marginal cost equals marginal revenue becomes

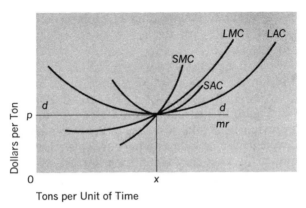

Figure 9–10
The conditions of long-run equilibrium.

smaller and smaller. However, as long as profits are made there still exists an incentive for new firms to enter the industry.

Eventually the entry of new firms will force the price down to p per ton, the level of minimum long-run average costs as illustrated in Figure 9–10. Long-run marginal cost equals marginal revenue at output x. Profits are zero, since price and long-run average cost at output level x are the same.

When enough firms have entered the profit-making industry to reduce profits to zero, the industry is in long-run equilibrium. Whenever the price is above p there is a range of outputs in the neighbourhood of x at which profits can be made. New firms are attracted in, forcing the price back to p. Whenever the price is below p there is no output level at which the firm can avoid losses. Firms begin to leave the industry, reducing supply and causing the price to rise toward p. At price p neither profits nor losses are made. Investors in the industry earn an average return on investment. There is no incentive for new firms to enter or for existing firms to leave.

Individual firms are also in long-run equilibrium. At the market price p long-run marginal cost is equal to marginal revenue at output level x. This is the firm's best output level, for at any other losses would occur. The firm builds and uses scale of plant SAC in order to hold its costs for output x as low as possible. Once the firm is at that output with a scale of plant such as SAC, it has no incentive to change either the scale of plant or its output.

Note carefully a unique characteristic of long-run equilibrium under conditions of pure competition. The individual firm is induced to build an optimum scale of plant. Only with an optimum scale of plant can the firm avoid losses. Any scale of plant other than *SAC* cannot produce at an average cost as low as *p*. Further, the optimum scale of plant *SAC* must be operated at its optimum rate of output. Any output level other than *x* will raise average costs above *p*. To put it another way, the firm is induced to build and use the most efficient scale of plant and to use it at its most efficient output level.

Changes in Demand

If an industry were initially in long-run equilibrium, what sort of chain of events would be set off by a change in demand for the product? What would be the short-run effects on the price and the output of the product and on costs of production? Then, in the long run, what further adjustments in price, output, and costs would occur? The nature of the short-run effects of a change in demand were examined earlier and will be passed over quickly here. The long-run effects depend upon whether the industry is one of increasing costs, constant costs, or decreasing costs. These different types of cost conditions are described in the following sections.

Increasing-Cost Case

Suppose that the wheat-growing industry is initially in long-run equilibrium. In Figure 9–11 the market demand curve is *DD*. For any one firm long-run average costs are shown by *LAC*. The scale of plant currently in

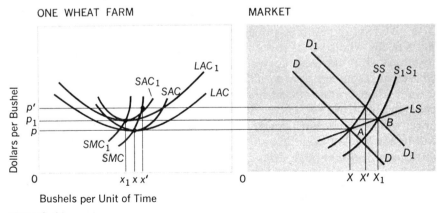

Figure 9–11
Effects of a change in demand: increasing-cost case.

operation is SAC, and the short-run marginal cost curve is SMC. The horizontal summation of the SMC curves of all firms in the industry establishes the market short-run supply curve, SS. Market price of the product is p, individual firm output is x, and market output is X. Product price and average cost are equal, so no profits are made nor are losses incurred.[4]

Suppose now that television commercials cause the tastes of children—young and old—to shift toward wheat products, moving the demand curve to D_1D_1. We use SAC and SMC to trace out the short-run effects of the demand change. Market price will rise to p'. Individual-firm output will rise to x', the level at which short-run marginal cost equals marginal revenue and at which profits are maximized after the increase in demand. Short-run profits are made by the individual firm and will be equal to the difference between price and short-run average cost at output x' multiplied by that output. Industry output will be X'. This is the extent of the short-run effects.

The long-run effects of the demand change are more complex. In the long run the profits made by individual firms in the industry provide an incentive for new firms to enter. Land formerly used for growing other crops is converted into wheat farms, and some land that might not have been cultivated at all may be brought into production. The entrance of new firms moves the market short-run supply curve to the right, since there are more and more individual-firm SMC curves to add together horizontally. Consequently, market price declines, and as this occurs the demand and marginal revenue curves facing the individual firm shift downward.

In industries of increasing costs the cost curves of individual firms are shifted upward by the entry of new firms into the industry. This situation will occur where an industry uses substantial parts of the total supplies available of the resources necessary for making its product. The entry of new firms into the industry increases demand for those resources, which in turn causes resource prices to rise. In the example at hand we would expect land prices and the prices of machinery used in producing wheat to rise along with the prices of fertilizer and labour. Since the position of a given set of cost curves for a firm, LAC, SAC, and SMC, is determined by a given set of resource prices, changes in those resource prices cause shifts in the whole set of cost curves. Therefore, increases in the prices of resources shift the cost curves upward. It follows, of course, that de-

---

[4]*The firm's long-run marginal cost curve is not needed for the analysis at hand, and in the interests of keeping an already cluttered diagram as clear as possible it is omitted from Figure 9–11. If it were drawn in, it would intersect the marginal revenue curve of the firm at output* x.

creases in resource prices would shift the cost curves downward.

Individual-firm profits decline as new firms enter. The more firms that enter the industry, the greater will be the supply of the product and the lower will be the product price. Also, the more firms that enter, the higher will be the level of each firm's costs. Profits are squeezed from above and from below until enough firms have entered to reduce profits to zero. As long as profits are positive, new firms enter. When enough firms have entered to reduce profits to zero, entrance into the industry will cease and long-run equilibrium will be re-established.

The new long-run equilibrium position of a single firm and of the industry is also illustrated in Figure 9–11. The entrance of new firms increases the short-run supply curve to S_1S_1, driving price down from p' to p_1. The firm's long-run average cost curve shifts upward to LAC_1. It uses the optimum scale of plant, SAC_1, which has the short-run marginal cost curve SMC_1. Individual-firm output will be x_1.[5]

The preceding analysis provide information for tracing out the long-run supply curve for the product. The *long-run supply curve* shows the alternative quantities of the product that would be placed on the market by all firms together at all possible prices, assuming that ample time is allowed at each possible price for long-run equilibrium to be reached. It joins such points as A and B in the market diagram. Point A shows the quantity of wheat that would be placed on the market by all firms together at price p when long-run equilibrium prevails for the industry at that price. Point B shows the same thing at price p_1. The long-run supply curve is more elastic than either of the short-run supply curves shown. Both of the latter show the quantity response of the industry to different possible prices when the number of firms and the productive capacity of the industry is fixed. The long-run supply curve allows for the entrance or exit of firms to or from the industry; that is, for variability in the productive capacity of the industry.

Constant-Cost Case

The short-run analysis of the constant-cost case is the same as that of the increasing-cost case. Suppose that the industry under consideration manufactures pins. In Figure 9–12 the initial demand is DD, and that the firm's cost curves are LAC, SAC, and SMC. The industry is in long-

---

[5]*The new individual-firm output may be equal to, greater than, or less than the output it was producing before the change in demand occurred, depending upon whether the cost curves shift straight up, upward to the right, or upward to the left. Any one of these possibilities may occur.*

run equilibrium at price p, individual firm output is x, and industry output is X. If an increase in the birth rate increases the demand for pins to D_1D_1, the market price will rise to p', the firm's output will increase to x', and industry output will increase to X'. The firm will be making short-run profits. (Can you measure them in Figure 9–12? The profit rectangle has *not* been drawn on the diagram.)

The profits will attract new firms into the industry, and it is at this point that the constant-cost case exhibits its unique characteristics. For an industry to be one of constant costs there must be no upward or downward shifts in the cost curves of its firms as new firms enter the industry

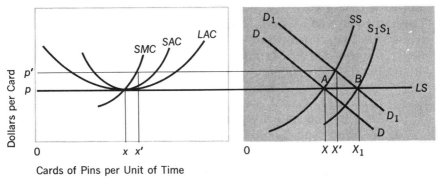

Cards of Pins per Unit of Time

Figure 9–12
Effects of a change in demand: constant-cost case.

or as existing firms leave. All firms together must take such insignificant proportions of the total supplies of the resources used in the industry that increases or decreases in the amounts they use have no effect on the prices. For example, it is hardly conceivable that increases or decreases in the manufacture of pins could affect total demand for steel enough to cause changes in the price of this resource.

Thus as new firms enter the short-run supply curve is pushed to the right and product price declines from the high short-run level of p'. But as long as market price exceeds minimum possible average costs for the firm (found at output level x), it is possible for profits to be made and firms will continue to enter. Eventually enough firms will enter the industry to increase short-run supply to S_1S_1. The price will be forced back to p, the individual firm's output will be reduced again to x, and industry output will be at X_1.

In the constant-cost case the industry's long-run supply curve, LS, joins such long-run equilibrium price–output combinations as A and B. It shows how much of the product all firms together would place on the market at various possible prices when there is ample time for all desired long-run adjustments to be made. But price *p*, at the level of minimum possible long-run average costs, is the only long-run equilibrium price level. The quantity placed on the market will be adjusted to whatever quantity is demanded at that price; that is, the long-run supply curve is perfectly elastic. Demand governs the quantity placed on the market.

Decreasing-Cost Case

Some industries may experience decreasing costs in the long run during periods of substantial industry growth. For this to be so the cost curves of individual firms in the industry must shift downward as new firms enter, a situation that seems to fly in the face of common sense. It appears that when new firms enter an industry the consequent increase in demand for resources used in producing the product will ordinarily increase the prices of those resources, giving rise to the increasing-cost case. It would seem that the constant-cost case would be the very least that one could expect, the entry of new firms having an insignificant effect on resource prices. Are there circumstances in which increases in the number of firms in an industry and consequent increases in demand for resources cause resource prices to fall?

Suppose that an industry takes root in a geographic area where large supplies of some of the essential resources used in producing the product are found but that demand for the product is not great. Now suppose that demand increases and it becomes highly profitable to produce the product. New firms enter the industry, locating in the area. Heretofore it has not been worthwhile for a branch-line railroad or an airport to be built, but with the increasing economic activity in the area transportation facilities are improved. Firms in other industries that utilize by-products of the original industry begin to locate in the area. Still other firms that are suppliers of resources to the original industry also move nearby. Warehousing facilities come into existence. An industrial complex far larger than that of the original industry is developed that provides the latter with cost-reduction opportunities. Thus decreasing costs may be possible for an industry during a period of expansion. However, the case does not appear to be reversible. Once the industry has taken advantage of the cost reductions it will become one of constant or increasing costs.

The decreasing-cost case is shown diagrammatically in Figure 9–13. Using the short- and long-run patterns of analysis developed for the increasing- and constant-cost cases, can you trace through the effects of the increase in demand on the price, individual firm output, and market output of the product?

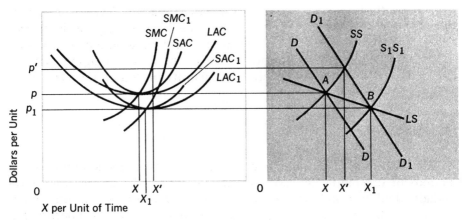

Figure 9–13
Effects of a change in demand: decreasing-cost case.

Comparison of the Quantity Responses

How do the increasing-cost, constant-cost, and decreasing-cost cases compare with one another with respect to the long-run quantity response to an increase in demand? These various situations are summarized in Figure 9–14, in which the initial equilibrium price for all three cases is

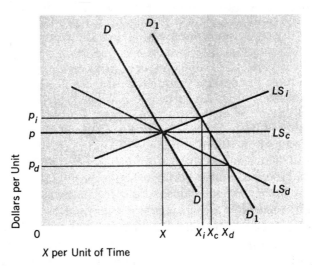

Figure 9–14
Comparison of output effects of an increase in demand.

assumed to be p and the initial equilibrium output is assumed to be X. The long-run supply curves are LS_i, LS_c, and LS_d for the increasing-cost, decreasing-cost, and constant-cost cases, respectively. The comparative effects of the increase in demand to D_1D_1 are clear. In the increasing-cost case the quantity response to X_d exceeds the demand increase, the decrease siphoned off by an increase in price. In the constant-cost case the quantity increase to X_c absorbs the entire demand increase. In the decreasing-cost case the quantity response to X_d exceeds the demand increase, the decrease in costs furnishing an impetus for an increase in output beyond that provided by the increase in demand.

Summary

The forces that determine the prices and the outputs of products produced by sellers in purely competitive selling markets are examined in this chapter. Pure competition in selling is a situation in which (1) there are enough sellers of a product that no one seller by himself can appreciably affect product price; (2) the product sold by one of the many sellers is identical to that sold by the rest; (3) prices are free to move in response to changes in demand and supply; and (4) sellers are free to sell wherever they desire to sell.

The very short run in the market for any specific product is a planning period so short that the quantity of the product available for sale cannot be changed. The price system performs the function of rationing the available supply among consumers and of clearing the market of the supply on hand. Costs of production play no part in determining the price of the product.

The short run in the market for a product is a time period too short for firms to have time to increase or decrease their scales of plant, but long enough for them to be able to increase or decrease the outputs they produce with their given scales of plant. The objective of the firm in the short run is to produce the output level that will maximize its profits, with profits defined as the difference between the firm's total revenues and its total costs.

The firm can choose its output level but not its price when selling in a purely competitive market. It accepts the market price as given and adjusts output to the profit-maximizing level. Marginal revenue, defined as the change in total revenue per unit change in output, under these circumstances is constant at all levels of output and sales and is equal to the market price of the product. Profits are maximized at the output level at which the firm's marginal cost equals the marginal revenue from its sales.

Market price of the product is determined by the interactions of all buyers and all sellers of the product. These activities are summed up in the market demand and market supply curves for the product. The short-run market supply curve is found by summing horizontally those parts of individual firm short-run marginal cost curves that lie above the firms' respective average variable cost curves and it shows the amounts that all firms together, with their given scales of plant, will place on the market at different possible product price levels. Changes in demand or changes in costs of production will change both the short-run output and the short-run price of the product.

The long run in a product market is a time period long enough for individual firms to increase or decrease their scales of plant to any desired size, as well as for new firms to enter or for existing firms to leave the industry. To maximize profits in the long run a firm selects the output at which its long-run marginal cost is equal to its marginal revenue. But if profits can be made, new firms are attracted into the industry, increasing supply and decreasing the product price until the profit level is zero. When the industry is in long-run equilibrium, with firms at a zero profit level, each firm is induced to build an optimum scale of plant and use it at the optimum rate of output.

Purely competitive industries are classified as increasing-cost, constant-cost, or decreasing-cost cases, depending upon their long-run cost responses to changes in demand. Following an increase in demand and profits, in the increasing-cost case the entry of new firms into the industry increases the prices of resources used in producing the product, thus shifting the cost curves of all firms upward. In the constant-cost case the cost curves of individual firms do not shift because the entry of new firms does not perceptibly increase resource prices. In the decreasing-cost case the entry of new firms, the expansion of the industry, the expansion of complementary industries, and better organization of resource markets cause the cost curves of individual firms to shift downward. The quantity response to an increase in demand is the greatest in the decreasing-cost case, next greatest in the constant-cost case, and least in the increasing-cost case.

Exercises and Questions for Discussion

1. A prerequisite for pure competition is that there must be many sellers of the product. Since no one seller is actually aware of what another is doing, this would seem to imply a lack of competition rather than an abundance of it. Discuss.
2. Explain and show how a purely competitive firm determines the output it will produce and the price it will charge in the short run. What assumptions have you made? Why are these assumptions necessary?

3. List several firms in your area that you think approximate purely competitive ones. From the information you can gather, is the industry of each firm an increasing-, decreasing-, or constant-cost industry? After you have established this, discuss the firm's effect on pricing and output decisions in each industry.

4. "In pricing a product a firm considers the costs incurred in producing a unit of that product and then adds a margin of profit above those costs. If this amount is not covered, a firm will not produce." Evaluate this statement.

5. "Costs of production play no part whatsoever in price determination." Under what circumstances is this so? not so?

6. A firm maximizes profits at the output level for which total revenue is the farthest above total cost. Yet the economist says that the firm maximizes profits at the output level for which marginal revenue equals marginal cost. Can both of these statements be correct at the same time? Explain.

Selected Readings

Bilas, R. A., *Microeconomic Theory: A Graphical Analysis*. New York: McGraw-Hill Book Company, Inc., 1967, pp. 159–173.

Colberg, M., D. R. Forbush, and G. R. Whitaker, Jr., *Business Economics*, 3d ed. Homewood, Ill.: Richard D. Irwin, Inc., 1964, Chap. 5 and Cases 5–1, 5–2, and 5–3.

Ferguson, C. E., *Microeconomic Theory*. Homewood, Ill.: Richard D. Irwin, Inc., 1966, Chap. 9.

Robinson, J., *The Economics of Imperfect Competition*. London: Macmillan and Company, Ltd., 1948, Chap. 17.

Stigler, G. *The Theory of Price*, 3d ed. New York: Crowell-Collier and Macmillan, Inc., 1966, Chap. 10.

10

Pricing and Output
Under Pure Monopoly

Pure monopoly, at the other end of the spectrum, is a market situation in which there is only one seller of a product for which there are no good substitutes. The monopolist has no competitors; he has the market all to himself.

Monopoly is common in public utilities. Your local telephone company is an example. There are no good substitutes for telephone service nor are there competing companies that supply the same service in your community. This is a market that does not lend itself well to competition. Imagine what it would be like if there were a half dozen competing exchanges, each operating independently of the others. How would you establish telephone contact with people having phones on exchanges other than your own? Other utilities that usually operate as monopolies are power and light companies, gas companies, and public transportation companies.

Outside the public utility field pure monopoly is harder to find, although historically this market situation has been approached in several industries. For example, between the 1840's and the 1940's the Canada Cement Company is said to have accounted for some 95 percent of the total output of the cement industry; until the late 1940's the Eddy Match Company is said to have controlled virtually the entire national supply of wooden matches; and in 1948 the International Nickel Company of Canada allegedly produced about 94 percent of the nation's nickel.[1] These have been among the more notable near-monopoly cases.

Even though firms that represent pure monopoly do not embrace a very large proportion of the productive capacity of Canada, the principles governing their economic behaviour form an invaluable part of the general body of economic theory. They are, of course, essential for analyzing cases where pure monopoly, or situations approaching it, exist. Equally important, these principles help us to analyze and understand cases of oligopoly and, in addition, serve to deepen our understanding of competitive markets.

Revenue Differences in Pure Monopoly

As we consider how the prices and outputs of products are determined in selling markets of pure monopoly we shall find that some of the principles established for the purely competitive case can be carried over intact. A monopolist's profit-maximizing output is that at which marginal cost is equal to marginal revenue. Too, the costs of a monopolistic firm have the same characteristics as those of a purely competitive one. Further, in the short run, if the total receipts of the monopolist are not sufficient to cover total variable costs, losses will be minimized by producing nothing. But the revenue concepts look different to the pure monopolist than to the pure competitor.

The Demand Curve Facing the Firm

Since the monopolist is the only seller of the product or service in which he deals, the market demand curve for the product is the demand curve that he faces. He *is* the industry on the selling side of the market; consequently, the quantities of his product that he can sell at alternative possible prices are precisely those that buyers in the market are willing to take at those prices. Instead of seeing demand as a prevailing market price at which he can sell all he wants to place on the market, the monopolist recognizes—or soon discovers—that there are limits to the quantities he can sell. In order to increase his sales volume he must lower the price

[1]*This latter figure is drawn from Table 5 in* Industrial Concentration *prepared for the Royal Commission on Canada's Economic Prospects, June 1956.*

that he charges. If he raises the price, sales will fall as the product becomes too expensive to fit into the expenditure patterns of some consumers and as other consumers reduce the quantities they purchase. He simply faces the market demand curve that we have discussed previously in some detail and that in most cases slopes downward to the right.

The Revenue Concepts

A nineteenth-century French economist provided a classic example of what it means to a monopolist to face a demand curve sloping downward to the right.[2] Suppose that an individual has discovered on his property a mineral spring with remarkable curing properties. Suppose further that the costs of selling pints of the water are negligible. If there are no costs, the monopolist's problem in maximizing profits is greatly simplified: maximization of total receipts also amounts to maximization of profits.[3] Suppose that the market demand schedule for pints of mineral water is that of columns (1) and (2) in Table 10–1. The corresponding demand curve is *DD* in Figure 10–1 (a).

TABLE 10-1

Hypothetical Demand and Revenue Schedules for Mineral Water

(1) PRICE PER PINT (p)	(2) QUANTITY PER DAY (x)	(3) TOTAL REVENUE (px)	(4) MARGINAL REVENUE $[(\Delta px)/(\Delta x)]$
$122	1	$122	$122
117	2	234	112
112	3	336	102
107	4	428	92
102	5	510	82
97	6	582	72
92	7	644	62
87	8	696	52
82	9	738	42
77	10	770	32
72	11	792	22
67	12	804	12
62	13	806	2
57	14	798	(−) 8
52	15	780	(−) 18

[2] See *Augustine Cournot,* Mathematical Principles of the Theory of Wealth. *New York: The Macmillan Company, 1897 , pp. 56 ff.*

[3] *A warning note is in order here. Only if the monopolist has no variable costs will profit maximization and revenue maximization occur at the same output level. If variable costs are associated with production and sales, as they usually are, the output of profit maximization will be smaller than the output of revenue maximization.*

Total Revenue

The relation of the monopolist's total revenue to his sales level differs from that of the pure competitor. For the latter the larger the output level, the greater the total revenue. Further, the total revenue curve for the pure competitor is a straight line from the origin sloping upward to the right. Note in column (3) of Table 10–1 what happens to the monopolist's total

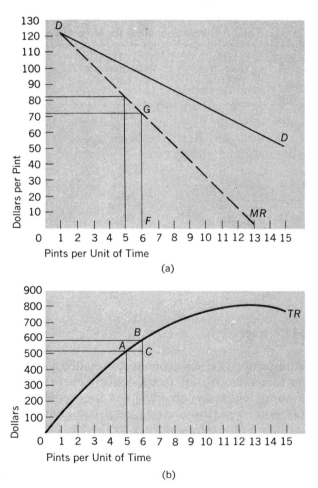

Figure 10-1
A monopolist's total and marginal revenue.

revenue as the sales level is increased: it increases to a maximum of 806 dollars at a sales level of 13 pints and then decreases for higher sales levels. This situation is also illustrated by the *TR* curve in Figure 10–1(b). The concave downward shape of the curve reflects the fact that higher sales levels, given the demand for the product, can be achieved only by lowering the asking price for the product. Beyond some point—13 pints in the illustration—the effects of lower prices more than offset the effects of higher sales levels.

Marginal Revenue

When we look at marginal revenue for the monopolist at different sales levels we discover that it is not equal to product price, as it was for the purely competitive firm. To be sure, marginal revenue for the monopolist is defined just as it was for the pure competitor: it is the change in total revenue per unit change in the level of sales $[(\triangle TR)/(\triangle x)$ or $(\triangle px/\triangle x)]$. But when we compute marginal revenue in Table 10–1, listing the results of the computations in column (4), and when we plot the relation of marginal revenue to the sales level in Figure 10–1(a), at each sales level above 1 it is less than the corresponding price of the product.[4]

Actually, it should come as no surprise to find that when a firm faces a downward-sloping demand curve marginal revenue is less than price. The demand curve is the firm's *average revenue curve*—price is revenue per unit of sales at any given sales level. Consequently, we should expect the relation between marginal revenue and average revenue (price) to be the same as that between any average curve and marginal curve derived from the same *total* curve, for example, average cost and marginal cost.[5]

To demonstrate arithmetically why the difference occurs, suppose that the firm is selling four pints of water per day at 107 dollars per pint. Sales are now expanded to five pints per day, a decrease in price to 102 dollars per pint being required in order to induce customers to make the increase in their purchases. The extra pint of sales per day by itself yields 102 dollars in revenue; but whereas the original volume of four pints formerly sold for 107 dollars each, they now sell for only 102 dollars each, a decrease in the revenue yield from them of 5 dollars each, or a total of 20 dollars. The net increase in total revenue from the one-unit increase in the

---

[4]*In Figure 10–1(a) the* DD *curve and the* MR *curve are the same at the one-unit sales level and spread apart at higher sales levels. Ordinarily, on representative diagrams, they are shown starting from a common intercept on the price axis. This apparent discrepancy comes from our use of a relatively large distance along the quantity axis to represent one unit of product. If in the diagram we had used the distance measuring 10 pints of water to measure 100 pints of water, the one-unit level would be so close to zero that we could hardly distinguish it from zero. So, for most purposes, it is quite in order to show both curves originating at a common point on the price axis.*

[5]*See pp. 152-153.*

sales level is thus 102 dollars minus 20 dollars, or 82 dollars, as is indicated in Table 10–1 and Figure 10–1(a).

The transition from diagrams such as Figure 10–1, on which the axes are actually scaled numerically, to representative diagrams on which numerical scales are not shown will be easier if we look at Figure 10–1 from both points of view. In Figure 10–1(b) consider an increase in the sales level from five to six pints per day. Total revenue rises from 510 dollars, or by 72 dollars—the marginal revenue of the sixth unit of sales. In representative terms marginal revenue is the vertical distance *CB* in Figure 10–1(b). Moving up to Figure 10–1(a), we see that marginal revenue at a sales level of six points is plotted as 72 dollars. In representative terms *FG* is marginal revenue at that sales level.

Maximization of Revenue

Have you ever heard it said that a monopolist will charge the highest price he can get? The example of the mineral spring monopolist indicates that this is not likely to be so. The highest price the monopolist can get in this example is 122 dollars per pint, the price at which he sells only one pint per day. Similarly, the highest prices that can be charged by any monopolist for his product will be that at which the sales level is only one unit.

The seller of mineral water can increase his total revenue by increasing his sales beyond one pint per day, and if revenue maximization is his aim, he will sell 13 pints. The price that he can obtain at this volume is 62 dollars per pint. An increase or a decrease in the sales volume will lower his total revenue.

Revenue is maximized at the sales level at which marginal revenue is zero, or is as close to zero as it can be for discreet sales intervals. If marginal revenue is positive, increases in the volume of sales must increase total revenue. In Table 10–1 and Figure 10–1 this is the case for sales levels up to and through 13 pints per day. Beyond that point marginal revenue is negative, meaning that increases in the sales level will decrease total revenue.

The Short Run

Suppose now that the water sold by the mineral spring monopolist is not a free good, for costs are incurred in bottling and selling. For short-

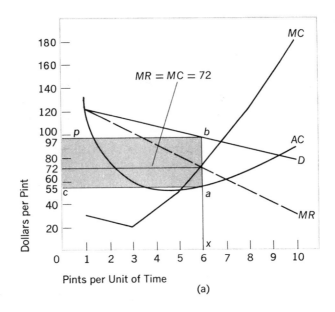

(a)

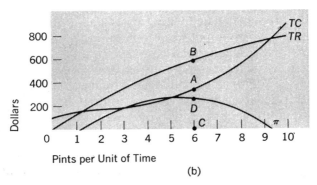

(b)

Figure 10–2
Profit maximization by a monopolist.

TABLE 10–2
Hypothetical Total Cost, Revenue, and Profit Schedules for Mineral Water

(1) Quantity per Day	(2) Total Fixed Costs	(3) Total Variable Costs	(4) Total Costs	(5) Total Revenue	(6) Profits
1	$100	$ 30	$130	$122	$(−) 12
2	100	55	155	234	79
3	100	75	175	336	161
4	100	110	210	428	218
5	100	160	260	510	250
6	100	232	332	582	250
7	100	328	428	644	216
8	100	450	550	696	146
9	100	600	700	738	38
10	100	780	880	770	(−)110

run decision-making the monopolist operates with his existing scale of plant and contemplates the alternative outputs possible with that scale of plant. He will have both fixed and variable costs, with the former independent of the output level and the latter dependent upon how much he bottles and sells.

Profit Maximization: Total Costs and Total Revenues

Hypothetical cost data for the monopolist are presented in Table 10–2. Total fixed costs are assumed to be 100 dollars per day. Total variable costs increase with the output level. Over-all total costs are the sum of the two at each possible output level. The total cost curve is plotted as *TC* in Figure 10–2(b).

Revenues of the monopolist are assumed to be the same as they were in the preceding section. Total revenue at the different levels of output is repeated in column (5) of Table 10–2 and is plotted as *TR* in Figure 10–2(b).

Profit at each level of output is the difference between total revenue and total cost. These levels are listed in column (6) of Table 10–2 and are plotted as π in Figure 10–2(b). The greatest vertical spread between the *TR* and the *TC* curve is at either five or six units of sales, and total profit is 250 dollars per day. This is measured geometrically by *AB* in Figure 10–2(b). The distance *CD* in the figure is, of course, also equal to 250 dollars, or the distance *AB*.

Profit Maximization: Per Unit Curves

Table 10–3 and Figure 10–2(a) illustrate the profit-maximization principles that apply to the monopolist in terms of per unit costs and revenues. For output levels below six pints per day, marginal revenue is greater than marginal cost, meaning that additions to output will add more to total receipts than to total costs and will therefore increase profits. An increase in output from four to five pints per day increases total receipts by 82 dollars, total costs by 50 dollars, and profits by 32 dollars. A further increase in output from five pints to six pints per day generates equal additions to both total revenue and total cost, neither adding to nor reducing profits. At this output level, where marginal revenue is equal to marginal cost, profits are maximum.[6] For further increases in output,

---

[6]*Profits are also maximum at one unit less than that at which MC equals MR; but this is because we are using discrete number intervals to measure output.*

TABLE 10-3

Hypothetical per Unit Cost, Revenue, and Profit Schedules for Mineral Water

(1) QUANTITY PER DAY	(2) AVERAGE COSTS	(3) MARGINAL COSTS	(4) MARGINAL REVENUE	(5) PRICE PER PINT	(6) ADDITIONS TO PROFITS
1	$130	$ 30	$122	$122	$ 92
2	77¼	25	112	117	87
3	58⅓	20	102	112	82
4	52¼	35	92	107	57
5	52	50	82	102	32
6	55⅓	72	72	97	0
7	61¼	96	62	92	(−) 38
8	68¾	120	52	87	(−) 68
9	77⅘	150	42	82	(−)108
10	88	180	32	77	(−)148

marginal revenue is less than marginal cost, and if these increases are made total profits will be reduced.

In Figure 10–2(a) we use the demand curve facing the firm and the average cost curve to complete profits. At the profit-maximizing output of six pints per day the monopolist can charge 97 dollars per pint for the mineral water. At that output average cost is 55⅓ dollars. Profit per unit is 41⅔ dollars. Multiplying the latter by six we find that total profit is 250 dollars.

Geometrically, profit is the shaded rectangle in Figure 10–2(a). Price at output $0x$ is measured by xb (or $0p$) and average cost is xa (or $0c$). Profit per unit is ab (or cp), and total profit is ab times $0x$ (or cp times $0x$), the area of rectangle $cpba$. (Can you find the rectangles measuring total receipts and total costs at output x?)

Effects of Monopoly on Price and Output

Monopoly is thought by many champions of the free enterprise system to constitute economic sin. The sinful acts are restrictions of outputs and increases in prices as compared with what outputs and prices would be under competitive conditions. We shall look first at why such restrictions may occur and then at whether they are always disadvantageous to the public.

Suppose that Figure 10–3 illustrates an industry of pure competition. The market demand curve is *DD* and the market short-run supply curve

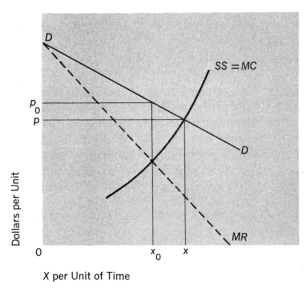

Figure 10–3
Monopolistic restriction of output.

is *SS*—the horizontal summation of individual-firm short-run marginal cost curves. Market price is p and market output is x. The short-run supply curve is the industry marginal cost curve, and industry output is that at which the industry marginal cost curve cuts the industry demand curve.

Now suppose that one firm buys up all the others and the industry becomes one of pure monopoly. The plant capacity of each of the former firms is unchanged and is used as a branch plant of the monopolist. To present the monopolist in the best possible light, suppose that no economies or diseconomies of scale are involved in the process of monopolization. What was the short-run supply curve of the purely competitive industry is now the marginal cost curve of the monopolist.

Profit maximization for the monopolist occurs at output x_0 sold at price p_0. Output is smaller and price is higher than it was for the purely competitive market. Why does this restriction occur? Individual-firm diagrams for the purely competitive case are not drawn in Figure 10–3; however, we learned in the previous chapter that each firm faces a horizontal demand curve at the level of market price. Marginal revenue for the purely competitive firm is the same as price; consequently, each firm maximizes profits at an output at which marginal cost is equal to marginal revenue *and to price*. But when an industry is monopolized the monopolist faces a downward-sloping market demand curve, and at each possible sales level marginal revenue is *less than price*. Thus, since he maximizes profits at the output at which his marginal cost equals his marginal revenue, he stops short of that output at which the marginal cost curve cuts the demand curve, or at which marginal cost is equal to price.

This illustration is not intended as an argument that all markets should be purely competitive; rather, it is meant to demonstrate the restrictive characteristics inherent in monopoly. Even though the markets facing Canadian producers are substantial, in a large proportion of these markets pure competition is not possible. For pure competition to be possible in an industry the product market must be large enough and the optimum scale of plant for any one firm must be small enough so that there can be many firms—each with an optimum scale of plant—producing and selling the product. By *many firms* is meant enough so that no one firm acting by itself can increase or decrease market supply sufficiently to influence price perceptibly. Industries where this is so represent a small proportion of the total productive capacity of the economy.

The Long Run

For long-run planning purposes the monopolist is not married to any particular scale of plant. Like the pure competitor, he has ample time to increase or decrease his scale of plant to whatever size he desires. And, as in the competitive case, there is time for the monopolist to withdraw from the market and time for new firms to enter. We shall consider these possibilities in turn.

Scale of Plant Adjustments

Suppose that a monopolist in the field of electric power generation presently operates the scale of plant SAC_0 in Figure 10–4. Demand for electricity has settled at DD and the marginal revenue curve corresponding to that demand curve[7] is MR. The short-run profit-maximizing output

[7]*The demand curves thus far have been drawn as straight lines because their corresponding marginal revenue curves are then easier to draw. The marginal revenue curve for a straight line demand curve lies halfway between the demand curve and the price axis, while that for a nonlinear curve does not. If the demand curve is convex to the origin, the marginal revenue curve will lie to the left of a line drawn midway between the demand curve and the price axis. If it is concave to the origin, the marginal revenue curve will lie to the right of such a line. See Joan Robinson,* The Economics of Imperfect Competition. *New York: The Macmillan Company, 1933, Chap. 2.*

is x_0, since this is the price at which short-run marginal cost equals marginal revenue. The price is p_0 and the short-run profits are $c_0 p_0$ times x_0.

But as a long-run proposition the monopolist can improve his profit position. At output x_0 marginal revenue exceeds long-run marginal cost. An increase in output through an increase in the scale of plant will add more to total receipts than to total costs and, therefore, will increase profits. This will be so up to output level x, at which long-run marginal cost is equal to marginal revenue. At output x long-run profits are maximized.

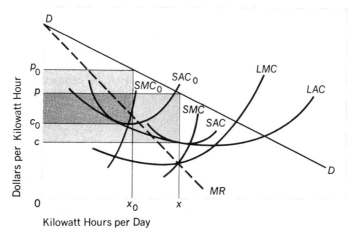

Figure 10–4
Long-run equilibrium.

The scale of plant that minimizes cost for output x is SAC, the scale of plant for which the short-run average cost curve is tangent to, or forms a part of, the long-run average cost curve at that output. With either a larger or a smaller scale of plant, average costs at output x would be higher than c. Price is p and profits are cp times x. The monopolist is in long-run equilibrium, since he has no further incentive to change either his scale of plant or his output.

Entry Possibilities[8]

Now what about the possibilities of new firms entering a monopolized industry in which profits are made? One thing is certain: it is difficult to keep firms from entering any profitable line of endeavour. This is un-

---

[8]*This section is equally applicable to long-run conditions in oligopolistic markets and we shall return to it in our study of oligopoly.*

doubtedly why monopoly is rarely found outside the area of public utilities. *If a profit-making monopoly is to remain a monopoly in the long run it must be able to block potential entrants from the field.* This is attempted in several different ways.

Probably the most effective barrier to the entrance of firms into a profit-making area is *governmental decree and legislation.* Exclusive franchises granted by governmental units protect most public utilities from competition. These may be extended to such quasi-public utilities as taxicab companies. Patents have served to block potential entrants in some cases, although in many instances they have not been completely effective. Tariffs and import prohibitions may protect a domestic firm from foreign competition. There are a number of governmental obstacles to entry, though many of these impede and limit entry rather than blocking it completely.

Firms already in an industry may block the entry of potential newcomers by *securing and maintaining control of resources* needed to produce the product. At one time, for example, a group in Chile had an almost complete monopoly of nitrate fertilizers, because the only important natural deposits were in that country. Again, prior to World War II, the Aluminum Company of America owned virtually all of the world's known bauxite supplies. Similarly, the International Nickel Company of Canada controls most of the non-communist world's nickel deposits. The concentration of resources, say of ore deposits, greatly facilitates the use of barriers of this type. On the other hand, where such resources as ore deposits or petroleum reserves are scattered throughout the world it is difficult for any one company to secure control of them.

Entry into a monopolized market may be blocked in some instances by the *size of the product market relative to the amount of output that a firm can produce* when it is using a scale of plant large enough to take advantage of economies of scale. In some cases the total market for the product may be large enough for one or two such firms to make profits, but if another firm were to enter the consequent increase in output and decrease in price might be great enough to cause all to incur losses. A potential entrant recognizing this possibility would have little incentive to move in.

Output Restriction

The output restriction stemming from the difference between price and marginal revenue for a monopolist is compounded by blocked entry in the long run. Under conditions of open entry into an industry the appearance of profits attracts firms into the profit-making areas, increasing supplies and driving prices down (and costs up in some instances) until prices are equal to average costs and the profits disappear. In the absence of profits consumers are paying for goods and services what it costs to produce them. Profits, where they occur, indicate that consumers value resources used in producing the profitable products relatively more than they value them used in producing other products; the evidence of this is that they are willing to pay more for resources so used than the resources cost, that is, more than they are worth in their other uses. But blocked entry prevents resources from moving out of the less valuable uses where no profits occur and into the more valuable uses where profits are made.

A dilemma may arise here with respect to whether governmental action against monopoly is appropriate, and, if so, what directions it should take. We often hear it said that a specific monopoly should be broken up into a number of smaller firms. The advocate of this line of action thinks that if there are a number of firms, the market situation is closer to pure competition. This, however, is not necessarily so. Consider the entry barrier case in which the monopolist has a scale of plant somewhere in the neighbourhood of optimum size and the market is not large enough to support two firms of this size. Breaking a monopoly up into several firms with smaller scales of plant may very well mean that each firm now must have a less than optimum scale of plant; that is, none is large enough to take advantage of significant economies of scale. The short-run average cost curves of all of the firms may lie at considerably higher levels than did that of the monopolist, and in order to cover costs

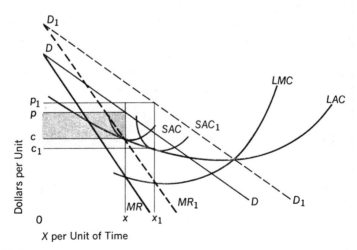

Figure 10–5
Effects of a change in demand.

they may produce even less than did the monopolist and charge an even higher price for the product.[9]

A more positive line of action may be to attack barriers to entry. Government-supported entry barriers, particularly, may need careful scrutiny to determine which ones can and should be eliminated. Where profits are made, incentives to enter are strong and monopoly positions in the absence of governmental support are difficult to maintain. Some economists go so far as to argue that in the absence of governmental support these incentives will prevent monopoly from seriously disrupting the organization of the economy's productive capacity.

Changes in Demand

What will be the effects of an increase in demand on the long-run price and output of a monopolistic firm? In Figure 10–5 the monopolist's long-run cost curves are LAC and LMC. Suppose he is confronted initially with the demand DD and its marginal revenue curve MR. The profit-maximizing output is x and the price is p. Scale of plant SAC is appropriate for producing that output. Profits are cp times x.

If consumer preferences shift toward product X, the demand curve shifts to the right to some position such as D_1D_1. Marginal revenue is now shown by MR_1 and at output x exceeds long-run marginal cost. An expansion of output to x_1, at which marginal cost is equal to marginal revenue, is necessary if profits are to be maximized. The scale of plant will be increased to SAC_1. Product price increases to p_1 and average cost becomes c_1. Profits increase to c_1p_1 times x_1.

The increase in demand does indeed bring about some expansion in the monopolist's productive capacity and output. However, the more striking effect is the increase in profits. With the entry of additional firms blocked, the only increase in the industry's productive capacity that can occur is the increase in the scale of plant of the monopolist alone.

Changes in Costs

What effects on product price and output can we expect from a change in a monopolist's costs? Again, the response to such a change is internal, that is, within the monopolistic firm itself, since there can be no entry of firms into the market if the monopolist is to remain a monopolist. Sup-

[9] *And what would prevent one of these pseudocompetitive firms from enlarging its scale of plant, undercutting the prices of the others, and securing all of the market for itself?*

pose that the monopolist's costs are *LAC* and *LMC* in Figure 10–6 and that demand and marginal revenue are *DD* and *MR*, respectively. The level of maximum profits is cp times x at output x and price p.

If the change that occurs is a technological breakthrough of some kind, the cost curves will shift downward to positions such as LAC_1 and LMC_1. The profit-maximizing output becomes x_1 and price decreases to p_1 because of the increase in output. Profits increase to c_1p_1 times x_1.

The output response of the monopolist is limited. To be sure, output rises and price declines, but only the output of the single firm is changed. Other firms cannot enter to expand output still more and erode away the extra profits arising from the change in costs. The difference between closed- and open-entry cases is simply that in the open-entry case any change that increases profits for the firm provides an incentive for new firms to enter, increasing output and decreasing price, until the profits disappear; in the closed-entry case, however, any change that increases profits induces the firm already in the industry to increase output just

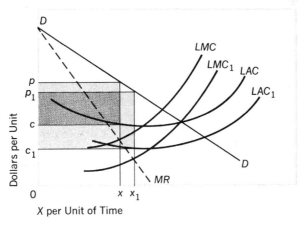

Figure 10–6
Effects of a change in costs.

enough to maximize those profits. Instead of the change being mostly absorbed by an output response, a part of it is siphoned off in increased profits.

Summary

Pure monopoly is a market situation in which there is only one seller of a product for which there are no good substitutes. It is rarely encountered in Canada outside the public utility field, but as a limiting case, at the opposite extreme from pure competition in the selling market spectrum, it provides principles useful in analyzing all selling market situations.

Monopoly differs from pure competition in that the monopolistic firm faces the market demand curve for the product. This means that the firm sees the demand curve as sloping downward to the right rather than as a horizontal, perfectly elastic curve. Consequently, total revenue for the monopolist does not increase indefinitely as sales increase, but reaches a maximum at some sales level and then decreases as sales are increased still more. For the monopolist marginal revenue at different sales levels is not equal to product price but is less than the price at which any given amount of product can be sold.

Short-run profit maximization by a monopolist occurs at the output at which his marginal cost is equal to his marginal revenue. This point will be short of the output at which marginal cost is equal to product price, since the marginal revenue curve lies below the demand curve. Thus a monopolist, because of this difference, restricts output below and raises price above what would prevail if the industry were competitive.

In the long run an additional difference between pure monopoly and pure competition is evidenced. In a profitable industry operated by a monopolistic firm, the firm must have entry into the industry blocked in order to maintain its monopolist position. Increases in the productive capacity of the industry via the entry of new firms—such as that which occurs in a profitable purely competitive industry—is not possible. Adjustments in the monopolized industry's productive capacity are limited to the changes in scale of plant that the monopolist is able and willing to make. Changes in demand for a monopolist's product tend to have greater effects on profits and less effects on productive capacity than would be the case for a product produced and sold under conditions of pure competition. The same may be said for the effects of changes in cost conditions.

Monopolists may block entry of new firms in one or more of several ways. They may be able to enlist the aid of governmental units; they may own or control sources of essential raw materials; or, in some cases, technological conditions may require that for efficient operation a firm be large enough to supply the entire market for the product.

Exercises and Questions for Discussion

1. A monopolist restricts output in order to raise the price of his product and thereby increase his profits. Evaluate this statement.

2. What would be the effects of patent laws on the operation of a purely competitive economy?
3. According to recent periodicals, profits in 1966 soared to record highs. Does this indicate that Canada is becoming characterized by more firms with monopoly power? Why or why not?
4. Some large corporations in Canada have acquired other corporations producing different lines of products. How might this situation affect the extent of monopolization by the original firm?
5. Would a monopolist ever operate in the inelastic portion of his demand curve? if so, when? if not, why not?

Selected Readings

Bladen, V. W., *Introduction to Political Economy*. Toronto: University of Toronto Press, 1956, Chapters 6 and 8.

Canada, *Report of the Commissioner, Combines Investigation Act, on Matches*. Ottawa: King's Printer, 1949.

Ferguson, C. E., *Microeconomic Theory*. Homewood, Ill.: Richard D. Irwin, Inc., 1966, Chapter 10.

Main, O. W., *The Canadian Nickel Industry*. Toronto: University of Toronto Press, 1955.

Robinson, Joan, *The Economics of Imperfect Competition*. London: Macmillan and Company, Ltd., 1948. Chapters 3, 4 and 5.

11

Imperfect Competition

Most markets are not the white or black of pure competition or pure monopoly but fall into the grey area of *imperfect competition*. In this market classification we usually find that more than one firm is engaged in selling a product or service; in most cases, however, there will not be enough such firms to make the market one of pure competition. Even in markets where are are many sellers, what any one firm sells is likely to differ in some respects from that sold by the others; that is, the product units sold by different firms in an industry will not be homogeneous. Nevertheless, the principles developed for markets of pure competition and pure monopoly—the least complex of all selling market structures—will prove helpful in the analysis of markets of imperfect competition. Markets of imperfect competition are ordinarily classified in two categories, oligopoly and monopolistic competition.

Oligopoly

Oligopoly embraces a wide range of selling market situations rather than the single type of situation of the pure competition or the pure monopoly classification. Consequently, unlike for pure competition or pure monopoly, we cannot construct for it a neat precise theory of pricing and output; there are a number of overlapping theories and many of these are imprecise. We shall initially discuss what oligopoly is and what it is not, and we shall consider demand as it looks to an oligopolistic seller. Next we shall examine pricing and output in the short run and in the long run, and finally, we shall turn to one of the most distinctive features of oligopolistic behaviour—nonprice competition.

Nature of Oligopoly

Oligopolistic markets are more easily described than defined. "Oligopoly" comes from the Greek words meaning "few sellers", and this is the essential characteristic of this market situation. If more than one seller and less than many sellers of a product or a service are operating in a given market, the market is one of oligopoly.[1] In Chapter 9 we define many sellers as a situation in which no one seller acting alone can exert an influence on the market as a whole. Few sellers, then, implies that the number is small enough for one seller acting alone to be able to affect the market for the product. What are the implications of this for the behaviour of oligopolistic firms?

The fact that there are few sellers in a given product market makes the sellers interdependent or rivalrous. If what one seller does, for example, if he advertises or increases his output or changes the quality of his product, can affect the market price or prices of the product, then what he does also affects what the other sellers are able to do; and the market behaviour of any one of the others will also affect what the first seller is able to do. Consequently, in taking any specific action that affects the market, an oligopolist tries to assess the impact of his actions on other sellers and in turn the effects of their reactions on him. Frequently this cannot be done with a high degree of accuracy, since it is difficult to predict how rivals will react to the behaviour of any one firm. We call this *oligopolistic uncertainty.*

In a given oligopolistic industry different firms may or may not sell homogeneous products. Where different firms sell identical products, the situation is one of *pure oligopoly.* The basic steel industry comes very close to product homogeneity. The different forms in which basic steel is produced conform to certain specifications and a particular form produced by one company will be the same as that produced by another.

Many industries fall into the category of *differentiated oligopoly.* In

[1]*See Fritz Machlup,* The Economics of Sellers' Competition. *Baltimore, Md.: The John Hopkins Press, 1952, pp. 79–125. This book contains excellent discussions of the different types of markets.*

this situation the product sold by the different firms will differ in some respects, although not in any basic way. Sunbeam toasters are slightly different from Westinghouse toasters; Firestone and Goodrich tires have different tread designs. The outstanding example of differentiated oligopoly, however, is the automobile industry. Certainly most of us believe that Fords differ from Chevrolets and that both differ from Chryslers. Where product differentiation occurs, consumers tend to become attached in some degree to favourite brands.

The fact that a firm sells its product as an oligopolist has nothing to do with its costs of production. Oligopoly, like pure monopoly and pure competition, refers to the situation the firm finds itself in as a seller. The firm's cost curves are of the same nature as those described in Chapters 8, 9, and 10.

Demand

The Demand Curve Facing the Firm

Oligopolistic behaviour differs from that in the other types of selling market because of differences in demand as individual sellers see it. The demand concepts to oligopolistic firms are less precise than in other market situations and hence the demand curve facing the firm cannot be located with as much precision as it can in pure competition or pure monopoly. The problem stems from the interdependence of the sellers in any given oligopolistic industry.

The demand curve facing any one firm depends upon the behaviour of the other firms in the industry, that is, how they react to changes on the part of the one. Suppose, for example, that a firm selling 14 cubic foot refrigerators is attempting to locate the demand curve it faces. If it is able to sell currently 3000 units monthly at a price of 400 dollars each, point *A* in Figure 11–1 is on its demand curve. If the firm cuts its price to 375 dollars, how much can it expect to sell at the lower price? This depends on whether and how rival firms react to the price cut. If rival firms react by holding their prices constant, the one firm can expect to pick up sales not only because the market for refrigerators is larger at the lower price but also because it cuts into the sales of its rivals. Sales will increase to some such figure as 5000 refrigerators monthly and point *B* on its demand curve is established. Apparently the demand curve follows a path such as *AB*.[2]

---

[2]*We do not know for certain that AB would be a straight line. To determine its shape with greater precision the firm must test the market at a number of price levels between 400 and 375 dollars.*

How will the demand curve look to the firm if rival firms react to the price cut by reducing their prices by a matching amount? Total sales for all firms increase, and the one gets only a roughly proportionate share of the increase. It does not encroach on the sales of rivals. Quantity sold increases to some such figure as 4000 refrigerators monthly, and the resulting demand curve *AC* is less elastic for the price change than is *AB*.

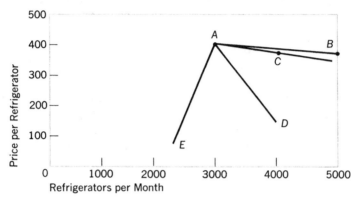

Figure 11–1
Alternative demand curves facing an oligopolist.

Rivals may do more than match the price cuts of the one firm. They may decide to teach the price cutter a lesson by undercutting the price of 375 dollars. In this case the original price cutter does not even retain the share of the market that he has been getting, since the prices quoted by his rivals are relatively more attractive to customers after the price cuts than they were before. The firm faces a demand curve such as *AD* or, perhaps, even *AE* in Figure 11–1. It is possible that rivals may undercut the original firm to the extent that the original firm actually *loses* sales.

The accuracy with which an oligopolistic firm can locate the demand curve that it faces varies directly with the degree of certainty with which the firm can predict how rivals will react to its price changes. If the firm cannot accurately predict the reactions of rivals, neither can it locate the position and shape of its demand curve. Complete ignorance of the probable reactions of rivals will not ordinarily be the case, and at least reasonable estimates can be made of the neighbourhood in which the demand curve lies. There are, however, many possible variations in the position and shape of the curve.

Most oligopolists would expect to face demand curves that slope downward to the right even though there is uncertainty regarding their exact positions and shapes. A firm will expect that a price cut will lead to an increase in its sales volume. It will also anticipate that an increase in its sales volume will cause the product price to fall. The open questions are, how stable and how elastic is the demand curve that the firm faces?

Market Demand

Under conditions of differentiated oligopoly it may be difficult or impossible to locate and draw the market demand curve because the production units sold by one firm are not the same as those sold by others. A 14-ounce box of powdered detergent differs from a 14-ounce bottle of liquid detergent. Similarly, in the automobile industry a Cadillac does not represent the same unit as a Volkswagen. What do we measure on the quantity scales for market demand curves in these cases? The indicated difficulties do not rule out the use of the concept of market demand, although they inform us that the market demand curve for a differentiated oligopolistic industry is often a fuzzy and imprecise concept and one that it is easier to discuss than to use with mathematical precision.

Short-Run Pricing and Output

In oligopolistic selling situations firms face two opposed sets of incentives. One consists of incentives among the firms of an industry to act jointly or collusively in the market while the other consists of incentives for an individual firm to act independently of the other firms in its industry. To obtain some feel for the wide range of oligopolistic policies and practices that are followed, suppose we consider several typical situations.

Cartel Arrangements

To illustrate the incentive to collude we shall consider a *cartel*. Cartel arrangements represent the most complete form of collusion possible among the firms of an industry. In an arrangement of this type the firms jointly establish a central organization to make price and output decisions, to establish production quotas for each firm, and to supervise the market activities of the firms in the industry. Firms seek to collude in this manner for two reasons. First, through joint market activities they eliminate the uncertainty that surrounds each when each operates independently. Second, through collusion and restraints of competition among the firms monopoly gains can accrue to the firms as a group.

A case of cartel pricing and output is illustrated in Figure 11–2.

Suppose that light bulbs are produced and sold by only a few firms. The market demand curve is *DD* and the short-run average and marginal cost curves of one of the firms are *SAC* and *SMC*, respectively. The price scales of the firm and the market diagrams are the same; however, the quantity scale of the market diagram is compressed as compared with that of the firm.

The primary objective of the cartel is assumed to be profit maximization. The profit-maximizing principles applicable to the cartel are the same as those that apply to purely competitive or purely monopolistic

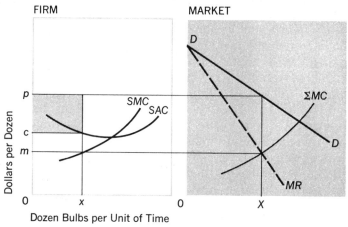

Figure 11–2
Cartel price, output, and quota allocation.

firms. The output for the market as a whole should be that at which market marginal revenue equals market marginal cost. How can market marginal revenue and market marginal cost be determined?

Since the cartel is making price and output decisions for all firms of the industry, the demand curve that it faces is the market demand curve. Individual-firm demand curves are irrelevant, since they have delegated price-making authority to the central agency of the cartel. The marginal revenue curve for the cartel, then, will be that derived from the market demand curve *DD* and is shown in Figure 11–2 as *MR*. It will bear the same relation to *DD* as any marginal curve bears to its companion average curve. For a decreasing average curve, the marginal curve lies below the average curve.

The industry marginal cost curve is constructed from individual-firm marginal cost curves. If we add the short-run marginal cost curves together horizontally we obtain a market curve similar to the industry short-run supply curve of a purely competitive industry. This curve, shown as ΣMC in Figure 11–2, is the industry marginal cost curve. It shows what the level of marginal cost will be for each firm at alternative industry output levels if the central agency always allocates quotas to the firms so that the level of marginal cost for each of the firms is the same,[3] and it also shows the level of marginal cost for the entire industry at each of those outputs.

The central cartel agency will maximize industry profits by setting the output of the industry at X—the output at which industry marginal revenue is equal to industry marginal cost. The cartel can obtain a price of p per dozen light bulbs at that output. The level of industry marginal cost (and marginal revenue) is m, so each firm will be allocated a production quota sufficient to bring its marginal cost up to that level—output x for the firm in Figure 11–2. The total of such quotas will just be equal to the industry output X. From Figure 11–2 we can also determine how much profit one firm contributes to total industry profits. For the firm pictured, average cost at output x is c per dozen light bulbs. Since the bulbs are sold at p per dozen, the profit contributed by the one firm is cp times x. If the other firms were included in the diagram, their profits could be computed in the same way.

Cartels as formal private organizations are generally illegal in Canada. The core of current Canadian anti-monopoly legislation is the Combines Investigation Act of 1923 and its amendments which forbid *restrictive* and *unfair* trade practices. Canadian competition policy and government regulation of business are the subject matter of Chapter 13.

Price Leadership

Since most formal collusive price-fixing arrangements are indictable offences in Canada, firms in some oligopolistic industries use other means of acting jointly. A favourite device is *price leadership*, with one firm setting product price and the others following its lead. The arrangement is usually an informal one and is not illegal as such as long as no explicit collusion can be proved.

The price leader is typically one of the larger firms in the industry.[4] As such it is likely to be more active in market research and to have a greater knowledge of the industry and its potentialities than its smaller

[3]*If the central agency allocates any given output among the firms so that marginal cost for any one firm is equal to that of any other firm, the industry cost for that output will be minimized. Can you explain why this is so?*

[4]*Following the lead of the largest unit is commonly supposed to be the practice of the oil companies in Canada. In the United States, the U.S. Steel Corporation has been a price leader in the steel industry since World War II.*

competitors. It may also be in a lower cost position because of economies of scale. The smaller firms frequently find the arrangement advantageous. They are spared the costs of extensive marketing research and, equally important, they are sheltered from the effects of competition among one another—competition which would surely make their profits smaller and which might very well lead to price wars.

The Incentive for Independent Action

Although the firms of an oligopolistic industry feel the incentives of monopoly gains and reduction of uncertainty in pricing pulling them toward some kind of collusive activity, another incentive pulls them in the other direction toward independent action by the single firm. A single firm of the industry, if it can break away from the others, might find that it can increase its profits by doing so, *provided the other firms continue to operate collusively and ignore what the one firm is doing.* The incentive is illustrated in Figure 11–3.

Suppose initially that we have a cartel operating in the automobile tire industry. Following the principles advanced above, the central agency of the cartel maximizes industry profits by establishing a market output of X tires, selling them at price p per tire. The quota of the one firm would be x, the quantity at which its marginal cost is equal to industry marginal revenue. The dd and mr curves for the firm are irrelevant at this point and should be ignored for the moment. Individual firm profits are cp times x.

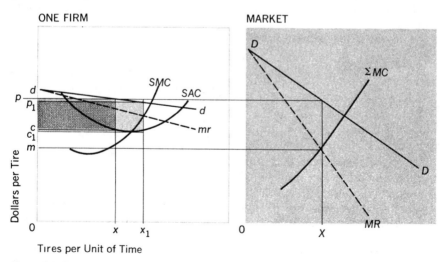

Figure 11–3
The incentive for independent action: oligopoly.

Now suppose that the one firm contemplates breaking away from the others. By charging a slightly lower price for tires it can expand it sales considerably *if no other firm does the same thing and if the cartel price is held at p.* Many consumers will switch from the other sellers to the price-cutting firm because of the latter's lower price; the price-cutting firm thus takes over a part of the other firms' markets. The resulting demand curve facing the firm, represented by *dd*, will be highly elastic, more elastic than the market demand curve for the product at price *p*. (Why is this the case?) Because the elasticity of demand for the sales of the one firm is greater than that of the market demand curve, marginal revenue for the one firm at price *p* is greater than is marginal revenue for the industry as a whole.[5] Consequently, for the firm acting independently, marginal revenue at output level *x* is greater than its marginal cost. Additions to its output will add more to total receipts than to total costs and will therefore increase profits. Under these circumstances the firm would maximize its profits by producing an output of x_1, selling it at a price of p_1. Profits would be c_1p_1 times x_1, greater than they would have been had the firm stayed in the cartel.

If all firms producing tires cut their prices simultaneously, the gains just mentioned would not be available to any of them. Each firm tends to hold only its own share of the market. It does not cut into the markets of others because they have also reduced their prices. In this case the firm does not face a demand curve more elastic than that for the market as a whole and has nothing to gain from price reductions. In fact, all firms will find their profits reduced by simultaneous price-cutting, output-increasing activities, since industry profits are maximum at price *p* and output level *X*.

The constant temptation to individual firms to act independently makes collusive arrangements hard to maintain over time. Successful collusion usually requires policing efforts by the colluding firms to prevent individual firms from breaking away from the group. Frequently they turn to the government to do their policing for them, securing the passage of such legislation as resale price maintenance, the requirement that retailers maintain minimum resale prices.

The Results of Independent Action

It should not be inferred from the preceding discussion that collusion is characteristic of most oligopolistic market behaviour. It may or it may not

---

[5]*The more elastic the demand curve at each of different alternative prices, the closer to the demand curve the marginal revenue curve will be. Consider the perfectly elastic demand curve facing a purely competitive seller. Where does the marginal revenue curve lie?*

be. There is not enough evidence available to determine conclusively the extent of collusive activity or the extent to which oligopolistic firms make independent price and/or output decisions. Certainly there must be a large number of oligopolistic firms that make their own market decisions.

An oligopolistic firm that makes its own market strategy decisions estimates as best it can how rivals will react to its market behaviour and what effects those reactions will have on its own actions. In effect, the firm attempts to determine the demand curve that it faces—or at least the neighbourhood in which it lies. Once the firm has done this, short-run pricing and output to maximize profits is a matter of determining the output at which marginal cost and marginal revenue are equal. The principle is as applicable here as it is in any other market situation.

Independent action by the sellers in an industry sometimes results in *price wars* in which firms undercut each other as they vie for market shares or as they seek to unload what they consider to be excess inventories. One seller lowers his price in order to attract more customers and to increase his sales. But this takes sales away from rival sellers. One or more of the latter may undercut the first firm in order to regain sales volume and to teach the original price cutter a lesson. Undercutting may spread rapidly through the market—to the delight of customers and to the distress of sellers. Among the best-known examples of price wars are those occurring in the retail gasoline trade.

Price was are more frequently potentialities rather than realities, but in the absence of collusive activity the possibility that they may occur is difficult to ignore. For this reason oligopolists may be rather slow to make downward price changes in response to decreases in demand or to reductions in costs. The extent to which price decreases can be postponed or avoided when demand has fallen depends, in part at least, on how easy it is to reduce the quantities brought to market. Where a few large firms dominate a selling market decreases in demand are more easily (and safely) met by reductions in quantity produced and sold. Where the number of firms is larger, however, and each believes that its own output is not of great significance in the market as a whole, price cutting rather than quantity reductions may well be the response on the part of sellers to a decrease in demand or a reduction in costs.

Price increases in response to increased demand or increased costs are much less dangerous for an individual oligopolist than are the price decreases discussed above, since a price increase by one firm does no damage to a rival firm. Nevertheless, an oligopolist that raises the price of his product will find that his customers tend to give their business to rival firms that do not raise their prices. In addition, as we have witnessed in recent years, oligopolistic firms that raise prices may find themselves subjected to strong governmental pressure to avoid such action.

Long-Run Pricing and Output

The long run for oligopolistic sellers is defined in the same way as for sellers in other types of markets. It is a planning period long enough for the firm to execute any changes it desires in its scale of plant and also long enough for new firms to enter the industry, if they are permitted to do so.

Scale of Plant Adjustments

What questions confront the firm in the long run from the point of view of production? Assuming that the firm has made its conjectures about how rival firms will react to its output and pricing policies and that it has decided on its long-run rate of output, it would be expected to produce that output at the least possible cost. This means that it chooses from among the scales of plant available to it the one that forms that small part of its long-run average cost curve at the selected output level. In Figure 11–4, for example, if the firm's long-run output were to be x_0 units per month, scale of plant SAC_0 would produce it at the least cost per unit. If the output were to be x_1, then SAC_1 would be the appropriate scale of plant. But if it were to be x_2, the firm should build and use scale of plant SAC_2.

How the long-run output is determined is an important and interesting question. It is also one that an oligopolist finds difficult to answer with any degree of precision. If the firm can make a reasonably good estimate of its demand curve, it can maximize profits at the output at which its estimated marginal revenue equals its marginal cost. If it cannot estimate the position and shape of its demand curve, the long-run output may be one that is simply at a "satisfactory" level. If the firm belongs to a cartel

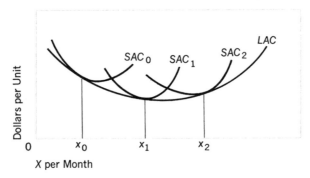

Figure 11–4
Long-run scale of plant adjustments: oligopoly.

or some other kind of colluding group, the output may be determined for it by the group.

Entry into the Industry

If profits can be made in an oligopolistic industry, new firms will have an inducement to enter. Consider the colour television field in 1964 and 1965. Very few firms had access to the patents and the know-how for making receivers. But their processes were good enough and a sufficient number of programs were being broadcast in colour to make them extremely profitable. By the end of 1966 a number of additional firms had entered the field, substantially increasing the productive capacity and the output of the industry.

Entry into some oligopolistic industries may be completely open; for others it may be completely blocked; and for still others it may be somewhere between the two extremes. If there were no barriers to entry and profits were being made, new firms would be attracted in. Individual firms and groups of firms already in the industry would find the demand curves they face shifting to the left or downward as the new firms encroached upon their shares of the market. Cost curves would remain constant or shift upward or downward, depending upon whether the industry were one of constant, increasing, or decreasing costs. Entry would continue until profit possibilities were squeezed out. Long-run profits are not possible where there are no barriers to the entry of new firms.

Long-run profits become a possibility when entry into an industry is partially or completely blocked. If entry is completely blocked the "in" group of firms may be in a position similar to that of a pure monopolist. This situation sometimes results from collusion among the "in" group to control particular patents, to control sources of raw materials, to freeze out potential entrants, and so on. Complete control over entry is difficult to maintain over time, however. Patents expire or similar products and processes are developed and new or substitute sources of raw materials are found. Innumerable, and in many cases ingenious, ways are found to enter potentially profitable fields of production.

Nonprice Competition

Individual firms in an oligopolistic industry are rivalrous and, in most cases, each firm seeks a larger share of the market for its output than it currently enjoys. An obvious way to attempt to gain a larger market share is to cut the product price below that charged by other firms. This is a dangerous tactic, however, for it often starts a price war. Other firms can meet price cuts immediately and what was originally a satisfactory situation for most firms may become a very unsatisfactory one.

What alternatives are open to the firm to increase its market share? It can launch an advertising campaign or it can change the design or quality of its product. Through these methods, either singly or together, the firm may succeed in enlarging its share of the market. A successful advertising campaign may be hard to duplicate, and the same may be true of an innovation in product quality or design, particularly if it is patented. A firm that increases its profits by these means may find that it can hold its advantage for some time.

Advertising

When an individual firm advertises it expects that the demand curve that it faces will shift to the right. It hopes also that it will make the demand curve less elastic by convincing consumers that there is a gap between the desirability of its brand and that produced by competitors. If the advertising campaign is successful, the firm will be able to increase its output, its price, and its profits. (But what is likely to happen to the other firms in the industry or even to other firms in the economy as consumers shift more of their purchasing power toward the advertised brand?)

How much should an oligopolist spend on advertising? The economic criteria are the familiar ones. Advertising is expected to generate additional revenue, and the change in revenue per dollar change in advertising is the *marginal revenue* from advertising. Similarly, each one dollar change in advertising outlay is a one dollar change in cost; that is, the marginal cost of a dollar's worth of advertising is one dollar and is constant for all levels of outlay. It pays to expand advertising outlays as long as the marginal revenue from it exceeds its marginal cost. But this is easier said than done. It is very difficult to determine in advance what the public reaction to and, consequently, the marginal revenue from, advertising will be.

A firm does not always expect that advertising will *expand* its particular share of the market, since frequently it must advertise merely to *hold* its market share. Suppose, for example, that the total market for cigarettes can be increased very little by the advertising of the different tobacco companies. Does this mean that advertising on the part of a single firm should cease? Any company that stops sponsoring television shows and running ads in the various news media will likely *lose* some of its market share. All sellers are forced to advertise because no one can quit with impunity. This situation is good for advertising agencies but costly to the general public, since product prices must be higher than they would otherwise be in order to cover the advertising expense. Advertising of this kind that increases the costs of all firms without increasing the market share of any and that does not expand the total market for the product[6] is called *competitive advertising.*

Not all of the resources used in competitive advertising are lost to the economy as a whole. Whether or not the "art work" of billboards contributes to consumer well-being is questionable. However, news media are heavily subsidized by advertising and as consumers we enjoy "free" radio and television programs. Actually, consumers as a group pay the full costs of all these benefits in the form of higher prices for the advertised goods, yet the functions of determining the kinds and quantities of newspapers, magazines, and radio and television shows that will be produced is taken away from consumers and placed in the hands of the advertisers. In addition, the consumers who pay for particular programs through their purchases of the advertised products may not be the ones who listen to or watch them. Thus the "free" goods and services furnished the consumer in this way are not "free" at all. The system is simply an inefficient way of choosing what entertainment and how much entertainment the economy's resources will be used to provide.

The advertising picture is not completely black, however. Some advertising is of an informative nature, letting consumers know what products are available, what their qualities are, and where they can be obtained. Advertising of this kind can help consumers make intelligent choices among the goods available to them. In any case, be it good, bad, or indifferent, there is much economic activity generated by, and dependent upon, the advertising outlays of oligopolists.

Product Design and Quality

Changes in product design are well illustrated by the annual model changes in automobiles, television receivers, and a host of other products. Such changes may or may not be accompanied by changes in the quality of the product. If from one year to the next only the design of the grill and the placement of chrome strips are changed, the quality of the automobile may very well be unaffected. On the other hand, the introduction of the self-starter and of individual front wheel suspension undoubtedly represented improvements in quality as well as changes in design.

---

[6]*And even if it does, the expansion may very well be at the expense of some other producing sector of the economy.*

The firm that implements changes in the design and quality of its product expects to increase the size of the market that it serves; that is, to shift the demand curve facing it to the right. The firm that accomplishes this objective does so at the expense of other firms in the industry and/or of other firms in the economy. Additional expenditures by consumers on the product in question represent a diversion of purchasing power from the products sold by others. These changes are not effected without cost, although changes in design may be relatively inexpensive to make. From the firm's point of view whenever such changes add more to total receipts than to total costs, or whenever marginal revenue as a result of the changes is greater than the marginal cost of making them, profits will be increased.

It is difficult to assess with accuracy the impact of design and quality changes on the level of consumer want satisfaction over time. Few people would question that over time, in the aggregate, such changes have made tremendous contributions to consumer well-being. Technological progress consists of making alterations in the design and quality of the product together with introducing new or modified production processes and new goods and services. But what are the prime movers of invention and innovation? Certainly a large incentive is the prospect of obtaining a profit advantage over rival firms; yet this is not the whole story. Such factors as the quest for knowledge, creativity, and even accident play important roles too, and how does one determine how much progress is attributable to each?

Whether or not design changes alone contribute to consumer well-being is ofen questionable. A design change can, of course, make a product more appealing esthetically, and the importance of this for consumer satisfaction should not be overlooked. However, where the introduction of a new model serves only to make the old model obsolete and to bring about a switch in demand from the old style to the new, there may be no net gain in consumer satisfaction levels.

Monopolistic Competition

There is not much to distinguish *monopolistic competition* as the term is now used from pure competition.[7] It refers to a market situation in which

[7]*Monopolistic competition was introduced into the discipline of economics in Edward H. Chamberlin,* The Theory of Monopolistic Competition. *Cambridge, Mass.: Harvard University Press, 1933. The term as used by Chamberlin included oligopoly as well as what is here called monopolistic competition. The case of few sellers was later put into a separate category called oligopoly, while the case of many sellers selling differentiated products retained the designation monopolistic competition.*

there are many sellers of a product, and, although all sell the same general type of product, that of each seller is in some way differentiated from that of the others. The basic distinction between monopolistic competition and pure competition is that in the former the products of the various sellers in an industry are differentiated, while in the latter they are homogeneous.

The retail and service industries in medium-sized and large cities probably offer the best examples of monopolistic competition. In these areas there are many grocery stores selling many brands of each of a wide variety of products. Each store has its group of steady customers who like its convenience, its special kinds of service, its credit arrangements, or other features. Each one also has a fringe group of customers just on the verge of trading elsewhere. Because of the number of stores in the city, however, most are not affected if one store goes out of business or if a new store is established. The same general situation is true of restaurants and bars, dry cleaners and laundries, medical service establishments, and others.

To illustrate the slight differences and the great similarities between monopolistic competition and pure competition we shall look first at demand, then at short-run pricing and output, and finally at long-run pricing and output in markets characterized by monopolistic competition.

Demand

Market Demand

Market demand curves for a firm characterized by monopolistic competition, like those for differentiated oligopoly, cannot be drawn neatly and precisely. Where products of different sellers belong generically to the

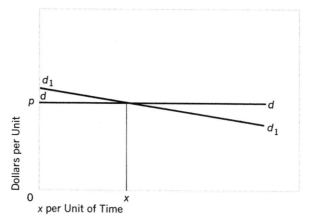

Figure 11–5
Demand curve facing the firm: monopolistic competition.

same industry but are differentiated, common units in which to measure quantities along the quantity axis may not exist. What kinds of quantity units can we use to combine fluid milk from some sellers and powdered milk from others on the same quantity axis? A further complication is that firms selling in the same market may be charging different prices for units of product that are very similar, for example, aspirin. All is not lost, however, if we are willing to think of market demand in a somewhat less precise way than we have thus far. We can think of a cluster of prices existing at any given time and a corresponding cluster of product quantities at those prices. Certainly we would expect that the quantities demanded would vary inversely with the prices. Graphic precision is lost, but the concept of market demand is still available for us to use.

The Demand Curve Facing the Firm

How does the demand curve facing a single firm in monopolistic competition look? A convenient starting point is the demand curve facing a purely competitive firm. Since the primary difference between the two types of markets is product differentiation, our main task is to examine the effects of this factor. Toward this end suppose we start in Figure 11–5 with dd, a hypothetical demand curve facing a purely competitive firm. Now consider the impact of product differentiation on it.

Where product differentiation occurs, different consumers tend to become attached to or develop preferences for the kind or brand of product sold by particular sellers. Some consumers have a stronger preference than others for a particular seller's product or service. Still, in an industry of monopolistic competition, the products sold by the different sellers are good substitutes for one another—and there are many of these—and at any given time any seller will have fringe customers just on the verge of turning to other sellers. Small relative price changes will tip the scales.

How does this affect the demand curve dd in Figure 11–5? Suppose a firm is selling quantity x at price p and that product differentiation exists between what is sold by this firm and what is sold by other firms in the industry. If the price is increased slightly, fringe customers find the products sold by other firms in the industry more attractive because of their now relatively lower prices. They desert the firm and sales fall off rapidly. Some of the more loyal customers hang on, but with so many good substitutes available it will not take a very large relative price rise for the firm to price itself completely out of the market. If the firm decreases rather than increases its price, it will pick up fringe customers of many other sellers and its sales will expand rapidly. The price decrease necessary to attract all the customers it can handle will not be large. Product differentiation, with its different degrees of consumer loyalties in individual sellers, tips the demand curve from the horizontal dd of Figure 11–5 to the downward-sloping but highly elastic d_1d_1. What factor is at work that makes d_1d_1 highly elastic?

Short-Run Pricing and Output

The analysis of short-run pricing and output of the products sold by individual firms in an industry of monopolistic competition requires the use of no new principles at all. Since the firm faces a downward-sloping demand curve—dd in Figure 11–6—the marginal revenue curve, mr, will be below dd rather than coinciding with it. The firm's cost curves are of the same type as those we have discussed previously. If SAC and SMC are the short-run average and marginal cost curves, respectively, the firm maximizes profits at output lexel x, where SMC is equal to mr. Average costs at that output are c, profits per unit of product are cp, and total profits per unit of time are cp times x.

For an industry characterized by monopolistic competition the short-run productive capacity, like that of the other types of markets, is fixed. Individual firms do not have time to change their scales of plant. Neither is there time for new firms to enter or for existing firms to leave the industry. Individual-firm outputs, as well as that of the indutsry, can be changed, of course, by utilizing the existing plant capacity to a greater or lesser degree.

Product prices will not be the same for all sellers in the industry because of product differentiation. But price differentials are not likely to be great. The single price of the purely competitive market is replaced with a cluster of prices for the differentiated items of the monopolistically competitive industry. The small price differentials reflect differences in consumer evaluations of what the different sellers of the industry place on the market.

Long-Run Pricing and Output

The long-run adjustment mechanisms are basiclly the same in monopolistic competition as they are in pure competition. The individual firm seeks the scale of plant that will minimize its costs at its estimated long-run profit-maximizing output. If profits occur in an industry, new firms have an incentive to enter, and if losses are incurred firms are pressured into leaving.

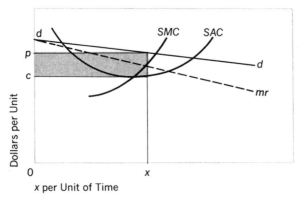

Figure 11-6
Short-run price and output: monopolistic competition.

Scale of Plant Adjustments

In Figure 11–7 if a single firm is confronted with demand curve *dd* and marginal revenue curve *mr* for its product, and if its long-run average and margin cost curves are *LAC* and *LMC*, respectively, what should be its scale of plant? Maximum profits are made at output level *x*, where *LMC* is equal to *mr*. The appropriate scale of plant for producing output *x* is *SAC*, which forms the miniscule part of the *LAC* curve for that output level. The selling price is *p* and profits are *cp* times *x*.

Entry or Exit of Firms

The entry of new firms or the exit of existing firms in response to profit or loss incentives is not usually difficult in an industry of monopolistic

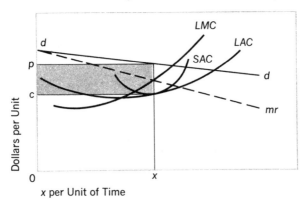

Figure 11-7
Incentives for entry: monopolistic competition.

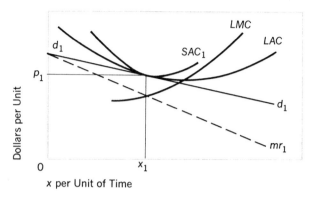

Figure 11-8
Long-run equilibrium: monopolistic competition.

competition in the long run. In a situation like that of Figure 11–7, profits can be made at any output level at which *dd* lies above *LAC*—although they are maximum at *x*. At this level new firms would enter as investors seek higher than average returns on what they invest.

The entry of new firms puts pressure on profits. The productive capacity and the total output of the industry are expanding; consequently, the demand curve facing the individual firms are shifting downward or to the left as the market share of each is reduced. The cost curves, too, may be shifting as new firms enter, the nature of the shifts depending upon whether the industry is one of increasing, constant, or decreasing costs.[8] If the firms of the industry ever reach a position like that of Figure 11–8, long-run equilibrium for the industry will exist. Note that the *LAC* curve nowhere lies below the $d_1 d_1$ curve, but at output level x_1 the two curve are tangent. At this output level and at price p_1 all costs of production are covered but no profits are made. At any other output losses would be incurred.[9]

The entry of new firms will surely make further scale of plant adjustments necessary for the individual firm. Suppose a representative firm of the industry is initially using such a scale of plant as *SAC* in Figure 11–7 and is making profits. The entry of new firms causes the demand curve facing the firm and the marginal revenue curve to shift to the left. This provides the firm with an inducement to reduce its long-run output and its scale of plant until, in the long-run equilibrium situation of Figure 11–8, the scale of plant is reduced to SAC_1.

[8]*See pp. 179-185.*
[9]*At output x_1, long-run marginal cost and marginal revenue are equal. Why is this so? The tangency of* LAC *and* $d_1 d_1$ *at output x_1 means that they coincide or are the same curve at that output. Since both are average curves, their corresponding marginal curves must be equal at that output level.*

Again there is no reason to expect that all firms in the industry will charge identical prices. Product differentiation almost provides assurance that they will not. Differences in what consumers think about comparative qualities of the products or services sold by the different firms will be reflected in price differentials.

Summary

This chapter examines the selling market situations lying between the limiting cases of pure competition and pure monopoly. These are markets of oligopoly and of monopolistic competition. An oligopolistic industry is one in which there are few enough sellers of a product or service that the behaviour of one firm affects what the others are able to do. If the product units sold by the different sellers are homogeneous, we call the situation pure oligopoly. But if consumers think that each seller in the industry sells a product that is different from those sold by every other seller, we have what is called differentiated oligopoly. An industry of monopolistic competition is one in which there are many sellers who sell differentiated products.

The analysis of oligopolistic pricing and output tends to be imprecise because it is frequently difficult to locate accurately the demand curve facing any one firm. This situation, in turn, stems from the interdependence of the sellers in the industry: what one seller does affects what others are able to do and their reactions then affect the first firm. In different oligopolistic industries there will be differing degrees of uncertainty for any one firm with respect to how this interdependence will affect it.

Oligopolists in an industry are subjected to two opposing sets of incentives. First, they have an incentive to collude or to act in concert to reduce uncertainties stemming from interpedendence and to reap monopoly gains from their selling market. Second, any one firm has an incentive to break away from a collusive arrangement provided other firms in the industry do not do so and, further, do not retaliate. The most rigorous form of collusion is that of a cartel arrangement, in which the firms of the industry surrender certain managerial functions, particularly pricing and output decisions, to a central cartel board acting for the industry. The illegality of many cartel arrangements induces firms to resort to other, lesser means of collusion such as price leadership, in which a dominant or a low-cost firm establishes a price for the product, initiates changes, and is followed by other firms in the industry.

In many oligopolistic industries firms pursue independent pricing and output policies. In some cases they expect to do better alone than they could in concert. In others a pattern of concerted action has never been initiated or built up. In still other industries fear of government anti-monopoly action discourages collusion. Independent action may touch off price wars or rivalrous price undercutting among the firms of an industry.

Short-run pricing and output analysis for oligopolistic industries centres around profit-maximizing objectives. Any firm, in order to maximize profits, attempts to produce the output at which its short-run marginal cost is equal to marginal revenue—if it can determine where the demand curve it faces and its marginal revenue curve lie.

In the long run the productive capacity of an oligopolistic industry can be altered by scale of plant adjustments of individual firms and by the entry or exit of firms. Once a firm has determined what its long-run output is to be, it minimizes costs by constructing and using that scale of plant for which the *SAC* curve is tangent to the *LAC* curve at that output. Profits or losses provide the incentives for entry or exit of firms.

Entry conditions into oligopolistic industries may vary from completely open to completely closed. Under open-entry conditions new firms will be attracted in by profits until the output levels are sufficiently increased and prices are sufficiently reduced to eliminate the profits. Under closed or partially blocked entry conditions long-run profits are a possibility.

The possibility that price changes to gain a greater share of the market will be followed by others, together with the persistent possibility of touching off price wars, induce oligopolists to engage in non-price competition or rivalry on a basis other than price. Nonprice competition takes the forms of (1) advertising and/or (2) changes in product design and/or quality. To maximize profits a firm should make such changes to the point at which the marginal revenue resulting from them is equal to the marginal cost of implementing them. Some advertising is informative and assists consumers in making choices among alternative spending possibilities. Competitive advertising, on the other hand, or the kind that firms must engage in to hold their respective places in the market, adds unnecessarily to costs of production. Some design and quality changes are of dubious value to consumers; but others are the essence of technological progress.

Monopolistic competition differs from pure competition in a minor way: it is a many-seller case with product differentiation. Product differentiation and some attachment of consumers to specific sellers' products or services make the demand curve facing the firm slope downward to the right to some small extent. In the short run a monopolistically competitive firm maximizes profits at the output at which its marginal costs equal its marginal revenue. In the long run, if profits are made, new firms may enter until the profits are squeezed out.

Exercises and Questions for Discussion

1. List a few of the advertisements you have heard and/or seen lately. Under what type of market structure would you classify each of the firms producing the advertised products? Why do you think each was advertising?
2. Why is rivalry among firms peculiar to oligopoly? What effects has this fact had on oligopolistic pricing and output policies?
3. Cite as many examples as you can of price leadership. Why is one firm able to set prices? How would it determine what price to charge?
4. If a monopolistic competitor advertises, he may influence fringe buyers and increase the demand for his product. However, with an increase in demand, price will rise and he may lose more customers than he gained by advertising. Evaluate this statement.
5. Could long-run profits ever exist in a market of monopolistic competition? Why or why not?
6. Under what circumstances is advertising beneficial to the consumer? When is it not?

Selected Readings

Bain, J. S., *Industrial Organization*. New York: John Wiley and Sons, Inc., 1959, Chap. 7.

Chamberlin, E. H., *The Theory of Monopolistic Competition*, 8th ed. Cambridge, Mass.: Harvard University Press, 1962, Chaps. 3, 4, and 5.

Colberg, M. R., D. R. Forbush, and G. R. Whitaker, Jr., *Business Economics*, 3rd ed. Homewood, Ill.: Richard D. Irwin, Inc., 1964, Ch. 6.

Jones, J. C. H., "Mergers and Competition: The Brewing Case," *Canadian Journal of Economics and Political Science*, November, 1967, pp. 551–68.

Kilbourn, W., *The Elements Combined: A History of the Steel Company of Canada*. Toronto: Clark Irwin, 1960.

Mason, E. S., *Economic Concentration and the Monopoly Problem*. Cambridge, Mass., Harvard University Press, 1957.

Phillips, W. G., *The Agricultural Implement Industry in Canada: A Study of Competition*. Toronto: University of Toronto Press, 1955.

Restrictive Trade Practices Commission, *Report on an Inquiry into the Distribution and Sale of Automotive Oils, Greases, Anti-Freeze, Additives, Tires, Batteries, Accessories, and Related Products*. Ottawa: Queen's Printer, 1962.

12

Market Structures and the Operation of the Economic System

Why classify selling markets as we have in the preceding three chapters? Elegant though it may be, the classification is of no particular value in and of itself. Rather, its merits lies in the fact that it can aid us in assessing how well the economy operates and in determining what government policy measures should be implemented to make it work better. Our goal in this chapter is to piece together the relation between market structure and economic performance.

How do we measure the performance of an economic system? What do we expect it to do for us? As we noted earlier, we look to our economic system to provide us with high and rising standards of living. Additionally we expect our economic system to help us achieve the following subgoals (1) efficiency in production, so that our resources and our existing state of technology are used in ways that contribute a maximum value of goods and services to the economy; and (2) innovation and economic progress in the sense of continual development of new products and modifications of old ones to fulfil more accurately consumer desires, and in the sense of continual discovery of new resources, resource modifications, and new technologies to permit continual expansion of output; (3) responsiveness of the productive capacity of the economy to an ever-changing structure of consumer demand and cost conditions; and (4) the availability of a broad range of choices in the quality and style of specific products and services. What are the implications of the different market classifications with respect to the degree to which these goals are attained?

Efficiency

The market classifications provide clues to the efficiency with which the firm comprising an industry operate. *Efficiency* refers to the value of output produced in relation to the value of resource inputs used to produce that output. The greater the value of output obtained per dollar of cost, the greater the efficiency of the productive process used. To put it the other way around, the smaller the cost per dollar's worth of product output, the more efficient the productive process used.

Efficiency Criteria

Some rough notions of the comparative efficiency of firms in the different market classifications can be obtained by examining their cost curves. For example, of the scales of plant available to the firm in the long run, which are most efficient? An optimum scale of plant is the logical choice, since the firm's short-run average cost curve lies at the lowest possible level—at the bottom of the long-run average cost curve. Further, of the possible output levels that can be produced with an optimum scale of plant, the optimum rate of output is produced more efficiently than the others, or at the lowest per unit cost for that scale of plant. A firm achieves maximum efficiency in production, then, when it uses an optimum scale of plant at the optimum rate of output.

We must ask ourselves, too, whether resources are more likely to be used wastefully in some selling markets than in others. For example, is there rivalry among firms that leads to wasteful advertising in some kinds of markets but not in others? Does rivalry lead to wasteful changes in product quality and design in some but not in others?

Cost Comparisons

Suppose we compare firms operating in the different market classifications on the basis of the scale of plant they would tend to build and operate in the long run. It should be emphasized that we can speak only of *tendencies*. We cannot compare with complete validity long-run equilibrium *positions* under pure competition, pure monopoly, oligopoly, and monopolistic competition because these are situations that are seldom if ever reached in the real world. Firms *tend* to move toward long-run equilibrium positions, but before they reach that point changes occur in demand or in costs, thus altering long-run equilibrium positions. They chase, but never catch, long-run equilibrium. These qualifications should be kept in mind as the comparisons are made.

The scale of plant of a pure monopolist will be of optimum size only by accident or chance. Three possibilities exist for such a firm, all illustrated in Figure 12–1, and which of the three we find in any given monopolized market depends upon the cost possibilities faced by the firm together with the size of the market (the position of the demand curve) for the product being sold. In Figure 12–1 (a) the technology available to the monopolist is such that his cost curves lie well to the right as compared with demand for the product. His long-run profit-maximizing output is x_a sold at price p_a, and the scale of plant that will minimize cost for that output is SAC_a—

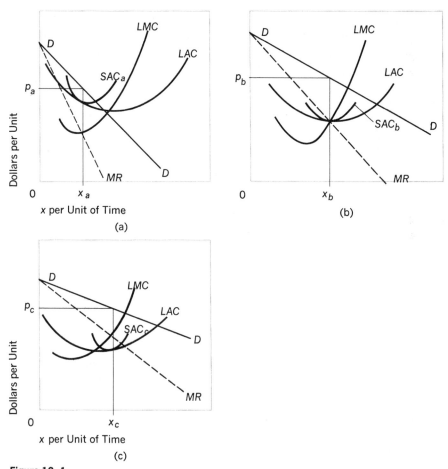

Figure 12–1
Alternative scales of plant for a monopolist in long-run equilibrium.

a less than optimum scale of plant operated at less than the optimum rate of output. In Figure 12–1(b) the monopolist finds the conditions of cost and demand that he faces such that his profit-maximizing output is x_b sold at price p_b. Scale of plant SAC_b—the optimum scale of plant—is the appropriate one for him to use, and he will use it at its optimum rate of output. The monopolist will push toward a larger than optimum scale of plant operated at more than the optimum rate of output if the situation of Figure 12–1(c) prevails. Profits are maximized at output x_c sold at price p_c, and scale of plant SAC_c minimizes costs at that outuput.

In contrast, as a purely competitive industry moves toward long-run equilibrium, the individual firm is *forced* to move toward the use of an optimum scale of plant. Consider Figure 12–2. If the firm uses any scale of plant other than SAC, its average cost will exceed the price of the product and losses will occur. If the price of the product is high enough for some part of the (horizontal) demand curve facing the firm to lie above some part of the LAC curve, profits can be made. New firms are attracted into the industry until profits are squeezed out; that is, until the LAC curve for each firm is tangent to the dd curve faced by it. Since the demand curve facing the firm is horizontal, it can only be tangent to the LAC curve at the minimum point of the latter, or when the firm is using an optimum scale of plant at the optimum rate of output. Thus in the long run the purely competitive firm is forced toward an optimum scale of plant used at the optimum rate of output by the horizontal position of the demand curve that it faces and by the entry of new firms into the industry whenever profit possibilities exist.

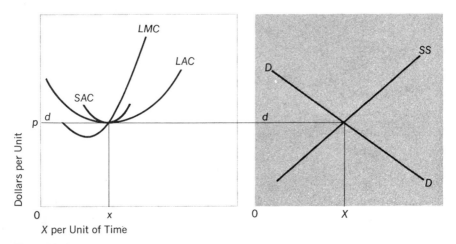

Figure 12–2
Scale of plant for a purely competitive firm in long-run equilibrium for the industry.

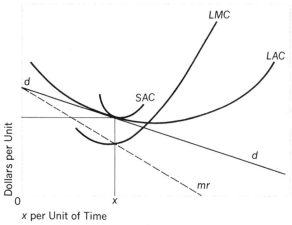

Figure 12-3
Scale of plant for a monopolistic competitor in long-run equilibrium for the industry.

Monopolistic competition is not much different from pure monopoly in this respect. The individual firm under full long-run equilibrium conditions for the industry would be somewhat less efficient than a purely competitive firm under the same conditions. Where profits occur new firms enter until the demand curve faced by each firm is tangent to its long-run average cost curve. Since under monopolistic competition the demand curve facing the firm slopes slightly downward to the right, this tangency must occur to the *left* of the minimum point of the *LAC* curve, as Figure 12-3 demonstrates. Therefore, the firm is forced toward a less than optimum scale of plant operated at less than the optimum rate of output.[1] The more elastic the demand curve facing the firm, the less will be the deviation of the scale of plant used from that which is optimum. Since monopolistically competitive firms face highly elastic demand curves, and since full long-run equilibrium conditions are seldom achieved, the decrease in efficiency attributable to this type of market structure is not likely to be large.

With respect to the efficiency of its plant over the long run, the oligopolistic firm is closer to the purely monopolistic firm than to the competitive one. If entry into an oligopolistic industry is open, individual firms are forced toward a situation in which the demand curves they face are tangent to their long-run average cost curves. This situation leads toward a less than optimum scale of plant similar to that of monopolistic competition: the less elastic the demand curve, the greater will be the deviation from the

[1] *On this basis economists frequently argue that industries characterized by monopolistic competition will have excess productive capacity; that is, that individual firms are not induced to make full use of their plants.*

optimum scale. If entry into the industry is blocked or obstructed, so that firms are not forced into a no-profit situation, the scale of plant that firms tend to use may be optimum, less than optimum, or greater than optimum, depending upon the characteristics of the firms' cost curves and on the output they expect to produce over the long run. We would expect that whatever outputs they choose to produce in the long run, they will build and use those scales of plants that will minimize costs for those outputs.

Evaluation of Comparative Productive Efficiencies

The preceding discussion seems to imply that on grounds of productive efficiency pure competition and monopolistic competition are the superior types of selling markets, with oligopoly and pure monopoly bringing up the rear. Yet these surface manifestations are somewhat misleading; the more important implications of each of these market situations are more subtle.

In the private sector of the economy what conditions must be present for an industry to be one of pure competition? By definition there must be many firms producing a homogeneous product. This situation can exist only if the market for the product is large enough to support many firms *each operating an optimum scale of plant*. If the market for the product is not large enough to support many firms, each with an optimum scale of plant, then the first firm or firms to enlarge their plants to optimum size will have cost advantages over other firms. They will fill the market for the product at prices equal to or above their average costs, and either oligopoly or, in the most extreme case, monopoly must prevail.

When we consider how large the optimum scale of plant must be in many leading industries, it becomes apparent that pure and monopolistic competition cannot be the predominant types of selling markets. As extensive as the North American market for automobiles is, it cannot support a large number of firms each with an optimum scale of plant. In this industry modern technology and the requirements of product distribution and servicing make the optimum scale of plant for a firm such that pure or monopolistic competition is out of the question. An optimum scale of plant in the auto industry seems to be one on the order of that of General Motors or of Ford.[2]

Let us examine the problem from another angle. Suppose that the

[2] *It is possible, of course, that the scales of plant of General Motors or Ford are larger than optimum. Still, the fragmentary evidence available indicates that the average costs of these firms lie at lower levels than those of Chrysler or American Motors.*

government were to break up the automobile industry into many firms. Each firm would likely be too small to take advantage of certain significant economies of scale, and each would probably have a scale of plant like *SAC* in Figure 12–4. The resulting higher cost levels—higher than those

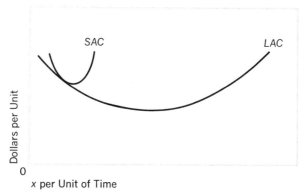

Figure 12–4
Possible effects on costs of breaking up a large firm.

that would prevail with fewer firms, each with a larger scale of plant—could well lead to higher prices and lower outputs than those possible in the current oligopolistic market structure.

The market structure postulated above is frequently thought to be one of enforced pure or monopolistic competition. Yet this is erroneous thinking, since in this case we would have a situation of *pseudo* pure or monopolistic competition. The scale of plant of each of the many firms in an industry must be of almost optimum size if the market is to be one of *real* pure or monopolistic competition.

From the point of view of market realism there is no avoiding oligopolistic market structures in many segments of the economy and monopoly in most of the public utility industries. But if entry into oligopolistic industries is kept open, the resulting scales of plant may not be significantly far from optimum, especially if there are enough firms in the industry and if there is sufficient absence of collusion for the demand curves facing individual firms to be highly elastic.[3]

---

[3]*It would be worthwhile to diagram this case. Show an oligopolistic firm with a highly elastic demand curve making economic profits. Now let new firms enter until the profits disappear; that is, the demand curve shifts to the left (or downward) until it is tangent to the firm's LAC curve. Is the scale of plant at the point of tangency significantly far from an optimum scale?*

Wastes from Nonprice Competition

Whenever resources are employed in such a way as to contribute nothing to consumer well-being or to contribute less than they would in alternative uses, the economic system is operating at a lower level of efficiency than it is possible to achieve. What do we learn from theories of market structure about the possibilities of waste in the use of resources? Consider the likelihood of competitive or rivalrous advertising and/or of changes in product design and quality in the different kinds of selling markets.

Waste of this kind is most likely to occur under differentiated oligopoly. At first glance it appears that monopolistic competition, too, could be responsible for the same thing, the culprit here being product differentiation. However, there is an important difference between differentiated oligopoly and monopolistic competition; namely, the numbers of sellers in the industry. In monopolistic competition the fact that there are many sellers precludes rivalrous nonprice competition among the firms, since no single firm believes that the activities of any other firm will affect it nor that its activities will affect others. Only in industries of *few* firms will the kind of rivalry exist that may lead to significant wasteful nonprice competition.

We must at this point sound a warning whistle. Non-price competition is a major avenue for innovation and economic progress. Therefore, how can we minimize its wastes while at the same time we take advantage of its merits?

Innovation

Nature of Innovation

The term "innovation" covers at least five basic kinds of contributions to economic progress. First, it means the discovery and the development of new kinds of resources. Second, it refers to modifications of existing resources. Third, and closely related to the first two, the development of new technologies is a type of innovating activity. All three of these forms of innovation must be cost reducing in nature if they are to contribute to economic progress or to consumer well-being. The other two kinds of innovation are, fourth, modifications of existing products and, fifth, the development of new products. Again for the latter two to represent economic progress they must enable the resources used in carrying them on to satisfy wants more fully than if the innovations had not been made.

What are the circumstances under which innovations are most likely to occur? The well-known U.S. economist J. M. Clark distinguishes among (1) underlying conditions, (2) enabling conditions, and (3) incentives or inducements to innovate.[4] *Underlying conditions* conducive to innovation are those in which people are not tradition or culture bound but are willing to depart from the usual ways of doing things; that is, they are cultural conditions that foster a spirit of innovation. *Enabling conditions* refer to the institutional arrangements of the society within which innovation takes place. Are firms of sufficient size financially to be able to put substantial funds into research? Are there agencies apart from private firms that either accomplish or facilitate research? *Incentives* or *inducements* are the financial rewards for innovation—that is, whether innovating firms can expect innovating activity to be profitable.

Impact of Market Structures on Innovation

So far research has yielded no clear-cut answers concerning the relation between market structure and the amount of innovating activity that is carried on in a free enterprise economy. An examination of the effects of different market structures on the conditions conducive to innovation may indicate why definite answers have not been forthcoming.

Enterprises that operate in oligopolistic markets are usually thought to provide superior enabling conditions and superior incentives for innovation. It is argued that on the average such firms are larger than those in purely competitive and monopolistically competitive markets and, therefore, can afford to devote larger amounts of resources to research. It is pointed out further that oligopolistic rivalries spur individual firms to seek ways and means of reducing costs and of expanding their individual product markets. Under pure competition, and usually under monopolistic competition, it is argued that profits made in this manner are soon eroded away by the entrance of new firms, whereas in an oligopolistic industry the fact that new firms are blocked or impeded from entering makes it possible for a firm to enjoy the profits from its innovations for a longer period of time, the length of the period depending upon how strong the entry barriers are.

Many people believe that monopolies provide excellent enabling conditions for innovation. Size is the important ingredient here, and American

[4]*John M. Clark*, Competition as a Dynamic Process. *Washington, D.C.: The Brookings Institution, 1961, pp. 195–211.*

Telephone and Telegraph Company is the classic example. On the other hand, monopolists are not subjected to the rivalry that exists in oligopolistic industries and may lack incentives to innovate; that is, they may not be forced to innovate to hold their market share or their profits. Further, many monopolies, public utilities in small and medium-sized towns, for example, are not gigantic enterprises at all but can be classified as small businesses.

Markets of pure and monopolistic competition are generally populated by small firms among whom there is no rivalry. There may be a spirit of freedom and initiative associated with these market structures— although not necessarily greater than under monopoly and oligopoly—that provides the underlying conditions for innovation. But a problem of incentives may occur. Easy entry of new firms would be expected to erode away the profits resulting from innovating activity.

Responsiveness

The responsiveness of the productive capacity of an economy to changes in both consumer demand and cost conditions is, of course, a part of the general issue of economic efficiency. To be efficient over time an economy must have flexibility—it must be able to take in stride changes in consumer preferences as well as the discovery and development of new resources, new products, and new technology, for these are integral aspects of economic progress.

Profits and losses are the signals provided by the price mechanism to show that shifts in productive capacity from some goods and services to others are in order. Profits made by the firms in any one industry indicate that consumers place a higher value on what the resources can produce in that industry than on other products that the same resources could have been used to produce. The alternative or opportunity cost principle is the basis of this observation. The cost of producing any product is the value (to consumers) of the resources used in their best alternative uses. Similarly, where a product is produced at a loss, it is evident that consumers prefer alternative products which the resources could be used to produce.

It seems clear enough that monopoly provides serious obstructions to the responsiveness of the productive capacity of the economy to dynamic change. Contraction of productive capacity in the long run where losses are incurred is not really a problem: a monopolist who is incurring losses will go out of business as readily as a pure competitor. The problem lies in the amount of expansion of productive capacity that will occur in a monopolized industry when profits are made. The monopolist can be expected to expand his productive capacity, or his scale of plant, only to the extent necessary to maximize his profits. Further expansion of the industry's productive capacity through the entry of new firms seeking profits is ruled out. The monopolist has entry blocked.

What can we say about the responsiveness of productive capacity in oligopolistic markets? The answer depends on the conditions of entry into the industries and will differ from one oligopolistic industry to another. Where entry is relatively unrestricted, for example, in the case of filling stations in a small city, profits attract new firms and new capacity grows readily. Where entry is blocked or highly restricted, as in commercial air transport, profits may persist over a long period of time, indicating that consumers get less of the product than they would like to have relative to other goods and services that are produced.

Responsiveness would be expected to be optimum under conditions of pure and monopolistic competition. Any single firm in one of these markets tends to adjust its productive capacity to maximize its profits, as does a monopolist or an oligopolist. But where profits are made new firms are attracted in, further expanding productive capacity until profits disappear. Examples are provided in the retail grocery field, in the textile industries, and in the manufacture of men's and women's clothing. The large part of the economy's output comes from oligopolistic industries. Modern technology precludes the existence of an economic system composed entirely of purely and mopolistically competitive industries. What then can we advocate in the way of economic policy to insure that the economy's productive capacity will respond readily to dynamic change?

We are not likely to achieve perfection. Yet in the absence of perfection there seem to be two possible avenues that policy-makers can follow in the interests of making productive capacity as responsive as market and technological circumstances will permit. The first is the establishment of price ceilings or maximum prices for the limited number of goods and services produced under conditions of monopoly or near-monopoly. Rate regulation in public utilities provides an example. This possibility is explored in some detail in the following chapter. The other is a systematic elimination of barriers to entry into oligopolistic and into some monopolized industries. As we noted earlier, many such barriers are government made and government enforced and as such can be reduced or eliminated.

Generally speaking, the economy of Canada seems to be surprisingly responsive to dynamic change, providing testimony that in the long run monopoly and strong oligopoly positions are difficult to maintain. Where profits are made and there are incentives for new firms to enter, enter they will in one way or another. If direct entry through the front door with a competing brand of the same product is closed, entry through the back door with a reasonably good substitute for the product is likely to take place.[5]

Range of Choices Among Qualities and Styles

How do you react to a housing development where all of the dwelling units on a given block are identical in style and design? What would you think of an economy that produced only Volkswagens in the automotive field? Would you prefer that neckties came in brown only and that all shirts have button-down collars?

Consumers are widely diverse in their tastes. Some prefer elaborate houses and yards while others are primarily interested in keeping out the cold and the rain and in minimizing their yard work. To some people an automobile is a prized possession and the more elegant it is the better it satisfies their desires. For other people an automobile simply represents a means of getting from here to there. Since people differ for a variety of reasons, an economy that produces many styles and qualities is likely to provide higher levels of consumer well-being than one that does not. For example, for one whose tastes run to Cadillacs, a dollar's worth of Datsun will yield less satisfaction than will a dollar's worth of Cadillac. For one interested in economy of operation and ease of handling in traffic, the Datsun may well yield greater satisfaction per dollar's worth than the Cadillac.

In providing a wide range of choices in product quality and style oligopolistic market structures receive a high score. As such firms jockey for market shares they make available a broad array of variations through product differentiation. In purchasing a washing machine one has a choice between agitator types and tumbler types, among several different wash and rinse cycles, and among a number of other features, the presence or absence of which makes the machine more or less expensive and even more or less useful. The consumer can choose the make and model that best suits his desires and his pocketbook. The automotive field offers an even better example. No longer are consumers given a choice of "any colour they want as long as it is black," as Henry Ford was credited with saying about his famous Model T. There are literally hundreds of possible variations in automobiles among which consumers may choose. The Ford Mustang, for

---

[5]*See Joseph Schumpeter,* Capitalism, Socialism, and Democracy, *3rd ed. New York: Harper & Row Publishers, Inc., 1950, Chap. VIII.*

example, has well over one hundred different options available. Such examples abound in oligopolistic industries.

Monopolistic competition, like oligopoly, offers consumers a wide range of variations on any given product. It should be noted, however, that too much product differentiation may occur in some cases. Consumers may be so overwhelmed with the shapes, sizes, qualities, and packaging of clothing, detergents, floor waxes, cameras, and the like that comparison, evaluation, and choice is difficult. In some cases confusion stemming from this sort of thing may make consumers susceptible to fraud. There are, of course, certain guides available to aid in evaluating product design and quality, the best known being the testing services of the Consumers' Association of Canada and the Consumer Service and Information Branch of the Federal Bureau of Consumer Affairs.

Monopolists may or may not provide a multiplicity of design and quality in their products since they are under no competitive or rivalrous pressures to do so. A monopolist may find that he can expand his market by producing several qualities—say good, better, and best—and/or several different designs, but he will expand his costs of production, too. If an expansion in the range of qualities offered promises to add more to total receipts than to total costs, we would expect it to be made.

Purely competitive market structures may limit the consumer in his range of choices, since the firms in a purely competitive industry produce homogeneous units of product. The production of several qualities, designs, or styles is not precluded, but if the market structure is to remain one of pure competition there must be enough sellers of *each* variant of the product so that no one seller can influence the total market for it. *Incentives* for product variation—expansion of the market faced by a single firm—are missing in purely competitive markets.

Summary

We conclude in this chapter that no one of the different market structures is clearly *the* market structure in terms of economic performance. Purely competitive firms, and to a slightly lesser extent monopolistically competitive firms, tend in the long run to be pushed toward the most efficient scale of plant and rate of output, but technology, together with limited market size, will not permit either to exist in the industries that produce the bulk of the economy's output. Oligopolistic markets appear to be the type most conducive to innovation. Pure competition and monopolistic competition provide the greatest measure of responsiveness of productive capacity to dynamic changes. Oligopoly and monopolistic copetition are the structures that make possible a wide variety of choice in product design, style, and quality.

Surely we are looking for too much if we expect all monopoly to be eliminated. In most public utility fields monopoly probably performs better than the other types of market situations. But we should always ask whether monopoly is necessary as we look at any given industry, for unregulated monopoly will generally restrict the outputs of the monopolized items below what the public desires as compared with those of non-monopolized goods and services.

Apart from the public utility fields the key to satisfactory performance of the private sector of the economy seems to lie in minimizing the restrictive effects of monopoly and oligopoly. This means that in both types of markets every effort should be made to remove barriers to entry so that productive capacity can expand in response to profit signals. It also means that collusion among oligopolists—activity that makes them behave in a monopolistic fashion—must be minimized. In other words, to secure the best possible performance the economic system must be kept workably competitive. Policy measures aimed at achieving this objective are examin the next chapter.

Exercises and Questions for Discussion

1. List a few of the manufacturing concerns in your area. In what type of market structure do they participate? What kinds of product differentiation do they have? To your knowledge, what innovations have they made?
2. Under what circumstances is advertising considered to be a wasteful form of nonprice competition?
3. Monopoly is always inferior to the other types of market structures. Evaluate this statement.
4. Discuss the effects you think yearly model changes have on costs and outputs in differentiated oligopolistic and monopolistically competitive industries.
5. Is the Canadian economy "workably competitive"? Comment.

Selected Readings

Britnell, G. E., V. C. Fowke, Mabel F. Timlin and K. A. H. Buckley, "Workable Competition and Monopoly," a submission to the Royal Commission on Canada's Economic Prospects, March 1, 1956.

Clark, J. M., *Competition as a Dynamic Process*. Washington, D.C.: The Brookings Institution, 1961.

Dominion Bureau of Statistics, *Industrial Research and Development Expenditures in Canada, 1965.* Ottawa: Queen's Printer, December, 1967.

Economic Council of Canada, *Interim Report on Competition Policy.* Ottawa: Queen's Printer, July, 1969, Chapters 1, 2, 3, and 5.

Hamberg, G., "Size of Firm, Oligopoly and Research: The Evidence," and F. M. Schrier, "Size of Firm, Oligopoly and Research: A Comment," *Canadian Journal of Economics and Political Science*, February and May, 1965.

Jewkes, J., D. Sawers and R. Stillsman, *The Sources of Invention.* New York: St. Martin's Press, 1958.

Mansfield, Edwin, *Industrial Research and Technical Innovation.* New York: Norton and Company, 1958.

————, *Monopoly Power and Economic Performance.* New York: Norton and Company, 1964, Part I.

Monsen, R. Joseph, Jr., *Modern American Capitalism.* Boston: Houghton Mifflin Company, 1963, Chap. 3.

Rosenbluth, Gideon, "Concentration and Monopoly in the Canadian Economy," in M. Oliver (ed.), *Social Purpose for Canada.* Toronto: University of Toronto Press, 1961.

Schumpeter, Joseph, *Capitalism, Socialism, and Democracy.* New York: Harper & Brothers Publishers, 1947, Part II.

Weintraub, Sidney, *Intermediate Price Theory.* Philadelphia: Chilton Company, 1964, Chap. 13.

Wilson, Andrew H., *Science, Technology and Innovation.* Ottawa: Queen's Printer, 1968 (Special Study No. 8, Economic Council of Canada).

13

Government and Business

The impact of different market structures on economic performance poses a set of perplexing problems for government policy-makers. Monopolized markets are characterized by output restriction below the level at which marginal costs are equal to product prices and, where profits are made, blocked entry prevents the desired (by the public) expansion of productive capacity and output. The same effects may be found in oligopolistic industries, particularly where collusion occurs and where entry is either blocked or made difficult. Yet the large scales of plant that are made possible by our present level of technology, together with the limited sizes of the markets served, make monopoly in some industries and oligopoly in others inevitable. In view of these and other points made in the preceding chapter, what constitutes appropriate public policy?

Government policy-making in this area has been somewhat piecemeal; consequently, it has been neither uniform nor completely consistent. As it has emerged over time, three general approaches to policy-making can be discerned. Firstly, the inevitability of "natural" monopoly and oligopoly in public utility and in some transportation industries has been recognized and accepted. Thus in many instances policy-makers have sought to impose government ownership or regulation. Secondly, efforts have been made to restrain collusive and monopolizing activities in other industries, through anticombines legislation. Thirdly, in still other industries legislators have indicated that they think the public interest is best served by reducing or restraining competition.

Control of "Natural" Monopoly

In some industries cost structure and market size simply make competition not feasible. Consider, for example, the sale of electrical services in a medium-sized city. Economies of scale in the generation and distribution of electricity are so marked that if several companies were in competition in the market, costs would be substantially higher than they are with a single firm. Further, in the distribution of electricity, water and gas, consider the construction chaos that would result if several competing companies laid mains and took them up again as customers switched from one seller to another. Or consider the inconvenience of having half a dozen competing telephone companies in a given community. For each customer to be able to communicate with every other customer, a half dozen phones would be necessary; or, alternatively, the companies would have to have some sort of operating agreement among themselves and thus any advantages of competition would be lost. The inevitability of monopoly in public utility cases has been generally accepted, and in many instances government, both provincial and municipal, has attempted to control their operations.

Other industries, in which only a limited number of firms can operate, have also been subjected to government control as public utilities. These include interprovincial and international railways, highway transport, air transport, water transport, pipelines and telecommunications. These oligopolistic industries operate extra-provincially and are therefore controlled by the federal government. However, apart from radio and television broadcasting some economists question whether control in these areas is either necessary or desirable.

Governmental control, presumably to prevent natural monopolists or oligopolists from taking undue advantage of their position, takes two forms: public regulation and public ownership of industry. With regard to regulation, accounting and financial practices are frequently scrutinized by government agencies. Specifications are often set with respect to the quantity and quality of a product or service. But above all else, regulatory agencies have concerned themselves with rate regulation (i.e. price fixing).

The Theory of Price Regulation

If you were serving on a commission charged with regulating the price charged by a natural monopoly, how would you approach your task? The theory of monopoly and of oligopoly pricing should provide framework for action, but you would inevitably run into a number of serious

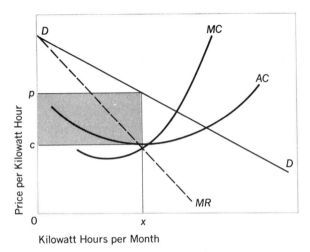

Figure 13-1
Profit maximization by a monopolist.

practical problems. From the point of view of theory, two alternative approaches to the problem suggest themselves. These are (1) a marginal cost approach and (2) an average cost approach.

The simple individual firm diagram of Figure 13–1 is basic to both approaches. Suppose that the firm produces and sells electricity. The market demand curve for its service is *DD* and the corresponding marginal revenue curve is *MR*. Its average cost and marginal cost curves are *AC* and *MC*, respectively. In the absence of regulation the profit-maximizing output is *x* kilowatt hours per month and the price is *p* per kilowatt hour. Profits are $cp \cdot x$. The problem is to improve the firm's market performance. How can the firm be induced to lower its price and increase its output; that is, how can monopolistic restriction of output be mitigated in some degree?

Marginal Cost Pricing

Suppose that a commission is empowered to set a maximum limit on what the company can charge for electricity. Suppose further that it decides to set the limit at p_1 in Figure 13–2, the level at which the marginal cost curve of the firm intersects the market demand curve. The company is permitted to charge less than p_1 but not more. Carefully compare Figures 13–1 and 13–2.

The shape of the demand curve facing the firm is changed by the ceiling price. Since the firm cannot charge more than p_1, and since at that price consumers are willing to take up to x_1 kilowatt hours, the demand

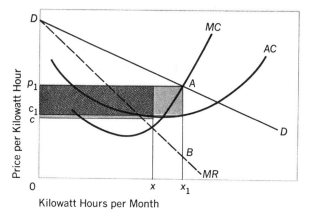

Figure 13–2
The effects of marginal-cost pricing.

curve facing the firm is horizontal at level p_1 for all sales levels between zero and x_1. Sales levels greater than x_1 can be obtained only if lower prices are charged—the demand curve facing the firm for these coincides with the market demand curve.

The marginal revenue curve, too, has a different shape. Since the firm faces the horizontal demand curve $p_1 A$ for output levels from zero to x_1, marginal revenue is equal to the product price and coincides with $p_1 A$. Beyond output level x_1, where the demand curve facing the firm is also the market demand curve, the marginal revenue curve is the same as it was before the maximum price was established. At output x_1 it is discontinuous, jumping from point A down to point B.

The profit-maximizing output of the firm under the new set of circumstances will be greater than it was before. If output were held at the previous level, x, profit would be measured by the area $cp_1 \cdot x$. But at this output marginal revenue is greater than marginal cost, that is, additions to the output level increase total receipts more than they increase total costs, and an expansion of output will increase profits. The new profit-maximizing output is x_1 kilowatt hours per month. Profit at this output level is $c_1 p_1 \cdot x_1$. Although profit still exists, it is smaller than it was before the maximum price was established, and the restrictive effects of the original monopoly position are partially offset.

Average Cost Pricing

Average costs of the power company may be easier to find than marginal costs. In Figure 13–3, suppose a maximum price of p_2 per kilowatt hour is established and is at the level at which the firm's average cost curve intersects the market demand curve. What will be the firm's response to the price ceiling?

If left to respond to the usual profit incentives, the price ceiling will induce the firm to increase its output to x_1 kilowatt hours. The firm faces a horizontal demand curve, p_2A_2, for output levels from zero to x_2 and a marginal revenue curve that coincides with it. Consequently, x_1, at which marginal cost is equal to the new marginal revenue, is the profit-maximizing output after the imposition of the ceiling price.

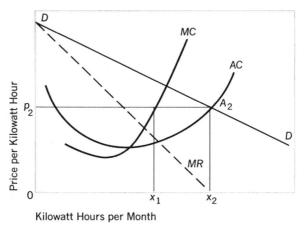

Figure 13–3
The effects of average-cost pricing.

But all is not quite as it should be. At output x_1 there is a shortage of x_1x_2. Consumers want more electricity at price p_2 than the company is inclined to produce. If a shortage is to be avoided, the commission will find it necessary to *require* that the firm produce as much as consumers demand. The firm can, of course, produce x_2 without incurring losses, but if it were permitted to reduce the output level below x_2 it could not only avoid losses but could make profits as well.

Price Regulation in Practice

Regulation of natural monopoly and oligopoly prices in the public utility field has not met with unqualified success for several reasons. One is that those who serve on regulatory agencies are often inadequately trained and usually lack the information necessary to carry out what they are supposed to do. Another is that the tasks given such bodies are for the most part ill-defined conceptually.

Regulatory Agencies

Commissions and boards empowered to regulate the rates of natural monopolies or oligopolies are appointed at the government level appropriate to the market the industry serves. Utilities with provincial and local markets are usually regulated by provincial commissions, although in some instances municipal commissions may have jurisdiction. Those with regional, national and international markets are regulated by federal commissions.

At the provincial and municipal level, personnel appointed to the regulatory agency seldom have specialized training for the task at hand, and, as in many government positions, salaries are not sufficient to attract the most capable people. Those on the commissions usually come from law or business and in some cases may have some background in the industries that are to be regulated. In their day-to-day operations commission personnel are continually subjected to the viewpoint of the utilities that they are to regulate, and it becomes difficult to maintain detached judgments on the issues coming before them. A major drawback to the effective operation of such commissions is that they seldom have access to detailed information in the businesses they regulate, or if such information is available to them they seldom have the staff necessary to analyze it. Members of federal regulatory commissions generally have been better qualified for the positions they fill than members of provincial commissions. Moreover, federal commissions have funds available for hiring professionals in key staff positions.

The most important federal agencies of this kind are the Canadian Transport Commission, the National Energy Board, and the Canadian Radio-Television Commission. *The Canadian Transport Commission* is divided into five committees for the purpose of performing its duties under the National Transportation Act (1967): (1) The Railway Transport Committee regulates certain statutory rates,[1] services, extensions, and abandonments on all railways; it also regulates express companies, telegraph and telephone companies (except those provincially or municipally controlled), and sets the tolls of international bridges and tunnels. (2) The Air Transport Committee licenses all commercial air services and fixes their rates. (3) The Water Transport Committee licenses most ships for most inland waterways, regulating their charges; it does not prescribe the tolls for bulk cargoes or license bulk carriers, except on the Mackenzie River

---

[1]*Except for certain statutory rates such as the "Crows Nest Pass" rates for grain shipments, and subject to certain powers of the Commission to deal with rates that it finds to be contrary to public interest, the railways are free to set rates as they wish. However, the Commission may prescribe maximum rates for traffic which can be shown to be captive to the railways.*

(accordingly, most shipping on the Great Lakes is outside of its juris-diction). (4) The Motor Vehicle Transport Committee is responsible for the regulation of commercial interprovincial and international motor vehicle transport. (5) The Commodity Pipeline Committee is respon-sible for the licensing of interprovincial and international (solids) pipe-lines and the regulation of pipeline tolls. *The National Energy Board* regulates the construction, operation, and tolls of all oil and gas pipelines which are under federal jurisdiction, and also the export and import of gas and the export of electric power, and the construction of the lines over which such power is transmitted. *The Canadian Radio-Television Commission* regulates and supervises all aspects of the broadcasting system. One observation is worth stressing here. It would appear that federal regulatory agencies are no longer concerned solely with rate-setting. Today, regulatory authorities attempt to serve larger national goals. This is obviously true of the new CRTC. It is also true of the National Energy Board and the Canadian Transport Commission.

Problems of Rate Regulation

Available evidence seems to indicate that most regulatory commissions follow an average cost pricing approach to rate regulation. This approach is based on the hoary principle that maximum regulated rates should allow a "fair return on a fair value." Presumably this means that in setting maximum prices, regulatory commissions should aim at permitting the regulated firms to earn a rate of return on their investment equal to the average that is earned throughout the economy. This could be accom-plished if, as in Figure 13–3, the maximum price were set at p_2 and the firm were required to serve all comers at that price; that is, place quantity x_2 on the market.[2] But there is many a slip between the cup and the lip. The rate of return on investment is computed arithmetically by dividing the yearly net income of a business by the value of investment in the business. The obvious problems are (1) what constitutes a "fair" value of investment in a business, and (2) what price and quantity of the services rendered by the business will yield a net income that provides a "fair" return on investment?

Regulatory agencies have found it difficult to compute the "fair" value of investment in a business. The data available to an agency on invest-

[2]*A prime example of a situation in which a regulated industry is required to produce more than it wants to produce is railway transport. Railroads frequently desire to abandon passenger service but are prevented from so doing by the Canadian Transport Commission. It should be added that railways are required to maintain un-profitable services only when the Commission is satisfied that reasonable alternative public transport does not exist.*

ment in a specific firm will usually be incomplete, and agency personnel, far removed from active management of the business, may not be able to evaluate accurately the data they have. Nevertheless, evaluate it they must. In so doing, at different times and in different cases, two methods of evaluation have been developed. One is known as the *original cost method* while the other is called the *replacement cost method.*

Roughly, to value investment in a business using the *original cost method,* we start with the initial costs of the firm's assets—its land, buildings, equipment, and so on. To these costs we add those of additions to assets made from time to time, in each case valuing the additions at what they cost when they were made. Depreciation must be deducted in order to arrive at a valuation figure.

If, however, there has been inflation between the time that assets were acquired and the time they are valued, does the original cost of the firm's assets accurately reflect their present value? A machine that cost $20,000 two years ago may still be worth $20,000 today simply because prices have risen, even though the firm has charged off $8,000 in depreciation for the two years. The original cost valuation would be only $12,000, so inflation causes the assets of the firm to be undervalued when this method is used. (Can you carry the effects of deflation through to their logical conclusions?)

The *replacement cost method* of determining the value of investment in a business asks, essentially, what it would cost at the present time to replace the assets of the firm. This method is in line with the type of cost reasoning generally used in economic analysis—the alternative cost principle. It does not tell us what amount of investment has been made in the business but rather what investment in the business is currently worth, based on the value of the best alternative uses of the resources that would be required to recreate the firm's assets. This method of computing the amount of investment in the business avoids the difficulties created by inflation and deflation in the original cost method. However, it may be difficult to arrive at replacement cost figures for some parts of the firm's assets.

No completely satisfactory method of determining the amount of investment in a business has been found as yet. Regulatory agencies find the mechanical simplicity of the original cost method convenient; Canadian provincial commissions prefer it, and the former Board of Transport Commissioners used this approach on railway rates. But economic analysis would point to the replacement cost method as involving fewer logical pitfalls.

The difficulties involved in regulating public utility prices do not end when the regulatory agency arrives at a valuation figure for investment in the business. The problem remains of determining a price that will yield a "fair" return on that investment. What should be considered a "fair" return on investment? Is it 6 percent, 8 percent, 10 percent, or some other figure? Some general guidelines are offered by the alternative cost doctrine. We ask what the average return on investment is over the economy as a whole. Yet this is a difficult question to answer with precision. Return on investment varies a great deal from industry to industry and from firm to firm, depending upon the length of time for which investments are made, the degree of risk associated with different investments, and the like.

Further, can a regulatory commission determine a product price that will yield the firm a net income permitting, say, a 6 percent return on investment? It seems highly unlikely that it can, for its ability to do so presupposes economic knowledge that the commission does not have—indeed, that the firm itself usually does not have. It presupposes that the demand curve for the product is known, or that the sales volume and total revenue for each of several feasible prices can be predicted accurately. It presupposes, in addition, that average costs of the firm for each of those sales volumes are known.

Besides setting prices, regulatory agencies, as noted earlier, become involved in all sorts of auxiliary activities—for example, regulating entry into the industry or specifying qualities and quantities of services—that effect the efficiency with which the firm operates. Regulation by commissions is far from a perfect answer to the problems of natural monopoly and oligopoly.

Publicly-owned Enterprises

The second type of control over "natural" monopoly is the ownership of business enterprises by governments. In such cases, the regulatory function is in effect combined with the operating function. This approach stems from the widely held but highly questionable assumption that government ownership always works to the public benefit.

In Canada, most electric companies are publicly-owned. Well known examples are Ontario Hydro, the Saskatchewan Power Corporation, and the Nova Scotia Electric Power Commission. In most Canadian cities, the transit system is also publicly-owned—usually, though not always, by the local government. Some illustrations are the Toronto Transit Commission and the Ottawa Transportation Commission. Half the railway system and more than half of the airline system and the broadcasting system in Canada are owned by the federal government. Clearly government ownership of business firms is very important in Canada—far more so than in the United States.

In general, it would appear that the main argument for government ownership of public utilities, a term reflective of the "public interest" with which they are particularly affected, is that problems of rate-setting and expansion can be taken into the parliamentary pale where their full impact on resource allocation and efficiency within the economy and upon individual welfares can be discussed. Unfortunately, the focus in this form is almost exclusively on capital and operating expenditures. In other words, questions of finance, not questions of economic efficiency and consumer satisfaction, are the relevant considerations for assessing the conduct of government enterprises. Thus government-owned activities may be just as anticompetitive and antisocial as privately-owned activities. Not surprisingly, this situation has led many people to question the propriety of public ownership.

Anticombines Legislation

Generally speaking, "the purpose of Canadian anticombines legislation is to assist in maintaining free and open competition as a prime stimulus to the achievement of maximum production, distribution and employment in a system of private enterprise."[3] To this end, the legislation seeks to eliminate certain practices in restraint of trade that serve to prevent the nation's manpower, capital and natural resources from being most effectively used for the advantage of all Canadians. Moreover, where competition is such as to promote the efficient use of economic resources, it obviates or lessens the need for other forms of control over industry such as government regulation or ownership.

Until 1960, Canadian legislation to preserve effective competition consisted of two sections of the Criminal Code, one enacted in 1889 and the other in 1935, and the Combines Investigation Act, passed in 1910 and amended extensively in 1923, 1935, 1937, 1946, 1949, 1951 and 1952. In 1960 the two legislative texts were amended and consolidated into one by inserting the provisions from the Criminal Code into the Combines Act.

The Present Combines Investigation Act

The basic provisions of the Combines Act are as follows:

Section 32, generally speaking, prohibits suppliers from making agreements to limit *unduly* the entry into any line of goods-production, to pre-

---

[3]*Director of Investigation and Research, Combines Investigation Act,* Annual Report, 1969. *Ottawa: Queen's Printer, p. 9.*

vent or lessen *unduly* competition in the production or sale of any good and of insurance, and to restrain or injure trade or commerce in relation to any article. Notwithstanding the illegality *per se* of unduly restrictive agreements, the section explicitly permits persons to participate in arrangements relating to the exchange of statistics, the defining of product standards, the exchange of credit information, cooperation in research and development, and restriction of advertising. However, such practices must not *unduly* lessen competition or they will be considered offences under the Act. This section also exempts any conspiracy, combination, agreement or arrangement from prosecution so long as it relates only to the export of articles from Canada, and so long as it does not limit entry into the export trade, harms neither other Canadian suppliers nor export volume, and does not lessen competition unduly in the domestic market. Although the word "unduly" is repeatedly used in this section, it is nowhere defined. Thus it is left to the courts to decide what constitutes a conspiracy in restraint of trade.

Sections 2 and 33 forbid mergers and the formation of monopolies that are of such a character as to have harmful effects on consumers, producers or others. *Merger* is defined as the acquisition by one or more persons of any control over or interest in the whole or part of the business of a competitor, or of control of markets or sources of supply, that has or is likely to have the effect of lessening competition to the detriment or against the interest of the public. *Monopoly* means a situation where one or more persons either substantially or completely control a particular trade or industry and have or are likely to operate against the public interest.

Sections 33A and 33B prohibit "discriminatory discounts" and "predatory price cutting". A supplier may not offer one of his competing trade customers a preferred price that is not available to the others who are willing to buy in "like quality and quantity". Similarly, when a supplier grants advertising or display allowances he must give them to all his business customers who are in competition with each other in proportion to their purchases. Likewise, a supplier may not sell his products at prices that are lower in one locality than in another, or "unreasonably low" anywhere, if the purpose or effect of his actions is to lessen competition substantially or eliminate a competitor. For obvious reasons, these sections have been used infrequently by the combines authorities.

Section 33C prohibits misleading price advertising. A supplier must not make, in his sales promotion, a "materially misleading" representation concerning the ordinary price of an article. Several prosecutions have occurred under this section.

Section 33D makes it an offence to publish an advertisement which contains a statement of fact which is, in reality, untrue, deceptive or misleading. This section is used to look after the advertising of games and contests such as those used by supermarkets and service stations. Several charges have been laid under this section recently, some against very prominent firms.

Section 34 prohibits the practice of resale price maintenance. A supplier of goods may not prescribe the prices at which they are to be resold by wholesalers or retailers nor may he cut off supplies to a merchant because of the merchant's failure or refusal to abide by such prices. This section also provides certain defences for suppliers charged with refusing to sell. A seller may refuse to sell to a dealer, and Section 34 does not apply, if "he and any one upon whose report he depended had reasonable cause to believe and did believe" that the dealer was using the goods as "loss leaders" or as bait advertising or was making a practice of misleading advertising in regard to such articles or was not providing the level of servicing that his customers might reasonably expect. Despite these qualifications, a fair number of prosecutions have occurred under this section.

Several remedies may be ordered by the courts against violators of the act. *Injunctions* may be issued against alleged violators where the activities enjoined may be of irreparable harm to the party claiming injury even though violation of the act has not been proved. *Cease and desist orders* may be issued directing companies or persons found guilty of violating the act to stop the illegal practices. The courts may even order dissolution of a company found guilty of violating the act; that is, order that the company be broken up into several firms of smaller size. The *revocation of patent and trade mark rights* may be ordered where such rights have been used to contravene the act. In addition, the courts can recommend the *reduction or removal cf customs duties*. This eventually requires executive (the Governor-in-Council) action.

Fines and *prison sentences* can be levied on those found guilty of illegal restraint of trade or monopolization. A business enterprise as such can only be fined, but individual officers who are found responsible for the illegal activities can be both fined and sentenced to jail as individuals. The maximum prison sentence is two years; the size of fines is left to the court's discretion. As yet there have been no imprisonments under the act and no fine exceeding $75,000 has been imposed.

Finally, *publicity* has always been considered to be an important deterrent to anticompetitive practices. In sponsoring the Combines Investigation Acts of 1910 and 1923, W. L. Mackenzie King implied that criminal prosecution was secondary to investigation and publicity in effective social control of combines. The sort of publicity almost always relied upon is contained in the reports of proceedings under the Combines Investigation Act, supplemented at times by brief references in the press at the time a conviction is obtained. Whether such publicity is sufficient to constitute an effective deterrent to firms and to alert buyers of products produced by those firms is very much open to question.

The Combines Investigation Act is enforced by the federal Department of Consumer and Corporate Affairs. An inquiry related to monopolistic situations or restraint of trade may be launched at the request of any six Canadian citizens or on the initiative of the Minister of Consumer and Corporate Affairs. The *Director of Investigations and Research* is responsible for investigating complaints under the Act, and the three-man *Restrictive Trade Practice Commission* is responsible for appraising the evidence submitted to it by the Director and the parties under investigation. When there are reasonable grounds for believing that a forbidden practice is engaged in, the Director submits a statement of the evidence to the Commission, which then holds hearings and receives the plea of the accused. Following this hearing, the Commission prepares and submits a report to the Minister, which ordinarily is required to be made public within thirty days. At this stage the Attorney General decides whether, on the basis of the facts contained in the Commission's report, legal proceedings are called for. If the decision is positive each person against whom an allegation is made is brought to court and charged. The guilt or innocence of the persons is then determined by normal judicial procedures.

Assessment of the Present Combines Act

We cannot assess the effects of the Combines Investigation Act and its enforcement solely on the basis of the cases that have come to court. The actual number of cases tried has been relatively limited. Many people believe that the legislation has its greatest impact as a deterrent to those who would otherwise engage in anticompetitive practices. This having been said, however, it remains a fact that the record has not been impressive. According to the Economic Council of Canada's "Interim Report on Competition Policy, July 1969",

> " . . . there appear to be few grounds for supposing that the total impact of the legislation on *economic efficiency* (italics added) has been more than modest. Certainly, the impact has been uneven. The Act has mainly been effective in restraining only three kinds of business conduct deemed to be detrimental to the public: collusive price-fixing, resale price maintenance, and misleading price advertising . . .

It is unlikely that the Act has done much to affect efficiency via changes in the structure of the Canadian economy. The main claim that might be advanced is that the banning of resale price maintenance has probably encouraged the entry into some sectors of price-cutting retailers. It is possible too that other prohibitions of conduct in the Act may have had some indirect effects on economic structure. But in respect of corporate mergers, which are one of the most important means by which changes in industrial concentration and other dimensions of economic structure take place, the Act has been all but inoperative. The only two cases brought to court under the merger provisions (the Canadian Breweries and Western Sugar Refining cases) were both lost by the Crown, and were not appealed . . .

There have been no court cases in respect of the section of the Act dealing with price discrimination. As to whether this section has exerted any important deterrent effect, opinions differ."[4]

A sound evaluation of Canadian competition policy must of course recognize the fact that the federal government is able to frame its combines legislation only in terms of criminal law, despite its powers to regulate trade and commerce under civil law. The consequences of the criminal law basis for the Combines Investigation Act have been well described as follows:

" . . . Criminal offences must be proved beyond a reasonable doubt. Charges must be expressed and proven in the categorical manner specified in the statute. The present provisions for injunctive proceedings against existing or proposed arrangements can only add limited flexibility because they must rest on the capacity of the Crown to meet the rigorous standard of criminal proof. Courts have no latitude to consider all the economic and commercial qualifications which might apply to particular cases and are compelled to adopt an 'all or nothing' approach in deciding whether offences have been committed. In addition, the classification of commercial arrangements as criminal has created a bad psychological background for administration which . . . has undoubtedly militated against wholehearted acceptance of the legislation by the business community"[5]

For these reasons, many qualified observers are of the opinion that criminal law prosecutions in this domain are both unsuitable and ineffective. In this connection, it should be pointed out that the Economic Council of Canada has recommended that the federal government should seek to place some of its competition policy on a civil law basis.

[4]*Economic Council of Canada,* Interim Report on Competition Policy. *Ottawa: Queen's Printer, July 1969, pp. 64-65.*

[5]*Gordon Blair, "Combines: The Continuing Dilemma,"* Contemporary Problems of Public Law in Canada. *O. E. Lang, ed. Toronto: University of Toronto Press, 1968, p. 159.*

Finally, it should be noted that the coverage of the Combines Investigation Act does not extend to most service industries.[6] Needless to say, most observers find it strange that goods should fall within the ambit of the Act and most services should not, especially since services amount to about 35 percent of our gross national product. Other practices not now covered by the Act include "exclusive-dealing" and "tying arrangements".[7] As might be expected, the Economic Council of Canada has suggested that the Act be extended to cover the service industries and exclusive arrangements.

As already mentioned, the last substantial revisions to Canadian anti-combines law took place in 1960. Over the intervening decade, many serious and important criticisms have been made of Canadian competition policy. In 1969 the Economic Council of Canada, after three years of research, made a number of fundamental proposals for new legislation on competition policy with the emphasis upon the improvement of economic efficiency and the avoidance of economic waste in the interests of the general consumer. Upon publication of the Council's report, the Minister of Consumer and Corporate Affairs announced that he had already initiated a complete review of the Combines Investigation Act. As yet, no action has been taken to revise the legislation.

Measures to Decrease Competition

Those who comprise the general public, sometimes in their roles as consumers but more often in their roles as producers, have not always been happy with the results of competition. Through their elected representatives they have sometimes seen fit to curb competition. Legislation restricting competition has been enacted at both the provincial and federal level. One word of caution may be needed here. Legislation restricting competition is sometimes designed to fulfill other objectives of govern-

---

[6]*Service industries include all industries other than primary resource industries, manufacturing, construction and utilities. The courts have, however, established the principle that service industries engaging in restrictive behaviour may be considered to fall within the ambit of the Act where the effect of such activities is to lessen competition in the market for particular goods.*

[7]Exclusive dealing *involves "a contractual undertaking between a supplier and a purchaser under which the purchaser agrees not to handle a product or products sold by competitors of the supplier." A* tying arrangement *(contract) involves an obligation between a supplier and a buyer that obligates the latter to buy from the supplier a product or service (tied good/tied service) in addition to the one the distributor wants to obtain (tying good/tying service). See Economic Council,* loc. cit., *pp. viii and ix.*

ment policy, such as the protection of health and safety, and that the effect on competition is incidental to the achievement of these other objectives.

Provincial Regulation of Competition

Licensing Laws

Suppose that you are a barber struggling to make a living. You try to run a clean, sanitary shop and to give good haircuts. It seems, however, that there are entirely too many people wanting to be barbers. New shops are being set up in your territory, many by inferior workmen who cut corners on sanitation. It becomes difficult for decent craftsmen like yourself to make a living.

You and others like you become concerned about your profession. You get together to discuss your problems, and your chief complaints are that (1) the unsanitary shop conditions of some of your competitors are likely to endanger the public health, and (2) the public is getting inferior service in these shops. In the interest of protecting the public you talk to your legislators and eventually you get a licensing law passed and a barbering board appointed composed of your fellow barbers. To become licensed, barbers must pass examinations given by the board, and new barbers coming into the profession must, in addition, have attended approved barber colleges. The presumption appears to be that standards in the craft would be elevated by this technique. Certainly numbers plying the trade are reduced below what they would be otherwise because it has become more costly to enter and to operate. The public will also pay a higher price for a haircut since the supply of barbering services has been reduced.

Licensing laws for a host of occupations have been established in all the provinces. The professions covered vary from province to province but common ones include medicine, dentistry, law, engineering, architecture, accountancy, real estate, electrical, plumbing, undertaking, barbering, and dry cleaning. For some of these licensing is based on public health and safety arguments while for others it must rest on a "protect the public from its own ignorance" justification. All such licensing has one feature in common: it tends to hold down the number of persons in the occupation and, consequently, the price of the service is higher than it would otherwise be.[8]

---

[8]*In this connection, it should be mentioned that municipal licensing laws may also affect the entry of new competitors into an industry. In general, however, it would appear that such licensing is perfunctory and permissive, and mainly of significance as a source of municipal revenue.*

Price Fixing

In all provinces legislators have been persuaded to take an additional step and to permit some professional licensing bodies to fix their own fees. The typical cases in point are medicine and law. As one prominent Canadian businessman has aptly observed:

" ... Lawyers can without fear or shame make legal agreements as to the prices they will charge for their services and scales of recommended charges are usually discussed, agreed, and published by the impeccably respectable provincial law societies. Judges, including those who preside over anti-combine cases, are of course an outstanding example within the legal profession of those who have successfully achieved security and eliminated all competitive influences in their personal lives."[9]

Or, to put it another way, each of the self-governing professional bodies has been given a statutory monopoly through its licensing powers.

Similarly, some quasi-professions are free to make price agreements for the sale of their services. Among such agreements are those relating to minimum commission rates on bond and share issues or purchases and to the rates charged by fire and casualty insurance companies which are members of the Canadian Underwriters' Association.

What is the economic rationale of fee-setting? If lawyers are allowed to compete, the demand curve for legal services facing any single lawyer will be highly elastic. Other lawyers provide good substitutes for the services of the one. If any single lawyer raises the price in this sort of situation above an equilibrium level, he will lose clients and find his total income falling. But the *market demand* for legal services in the neighbourhood of an equilibrium price level is likely to be inelastic. Thus all lawyers, acting together, can raise the price and *increase* the total income of the group and of individual members of the group. Needless to say, the same rationale applies in other professions.[10]

---

[9]*R. M. Fowler, "The Future of Competition in Canada—A Businessman's View,"* in J. J. Deutsch, et al., The Canadian Economy. *Toronto: Macmillan Company of Canada, 1965, p. 234.*

[10]*As might be expected, professional bodies contend that their price-fixing is in the public interest. For example, the operators of private and public insurance plans argue that agreement on fees is necessary for forecasting likely calls on their funds. The skilled professions reason that the technical nature of the services performed by their members makes it very difficult for laymen to assess the competence of the practitioner and gauge the value of the services he has received. Thus it is best to allow professional bodies to set standard rates of remuneration for their individual members. And so it goes.*

Federal Restraints of Competition

Patent Laws

Another anticompetitive measure is the federal law governing patents. One who discovers a new product or process can apply for and receive a patent on it granting him the exclusive right of the use and the sale or lease of it for a period of 17 years. The purpose of this monopoly privilege is to encourage invention, innovation and economic progress.

There is much controversy concerning whether the patent laws accomplish their objective. Some people argue that in reinforcing monopoly and near-monopoly conditions their adverse effects on the use of the economy's resources more than offset any contributions to progress that they might make. Others argue that without them innovative activity would be significantly lower. The validity of these arguments is hard to assess. How important are they in fostering the innovative process? Do they contribute markedly to the extent of monopoly in the economy? These are questions that need to be but have not been answered in determining whether or not the patent laws in and of themselves are an important economic issue.

It may be useful to add that the government has requested the Economic Council of Canada to undertake a study of patents, trademarks, copyrights and registered industrial designs. It is anticipated that the Council will report its findings in 1971.

Other Restraints

There are several other, more significant ways in which the federal government operates to diminish competition. These are so important, in fact, that we shall devote separate chapters to them at appropriate places in the book. They include policies having to do with agriculture, labour, and international trade.

Summary

Over the years government policies with respect to market structure and the economic performance of business enterprises have evolved in three general forms: (1) regulation of natural monopoly and oligopoly in public utility and transportation fields, (2) promotion of competition through anticombines legislation, and (3) reduction of competition in some areas where such reductions are thought to be in the public interest.

Regulation of public utilities and transportation generally takes the form of maximum price setting; however, regulatory commissions may also concern themselves with the qualities and quantities of services produced and sold. Two approaches to price setting that are suggested by our discussion of pricing are the marginal cost pricing approach and the average cost pricing approach, with the latter more commonly used in practice.

The objective posed by the courts for price or rate regulation is to permit a "fair return on a fair value" of investment in the business being regulated. This stated objective poses important difficulties for regulatory commissions. A "fair return" on investment is difficult to determine. Further, the net investment in a business is not easily computed. Finally, it is almost impossible to determine a price that will yield income and cost figures such that the rate of return on investment will be some specified "fair" rate. Regulation by commissions has not enjoyed unqualified success.

Canadian anticombines legislation, first introduced in 1889 and changed many times through the decades, seeks to eliminate certain practices in restraint of trade that serve to prevent the achievement of high levels of economic efficiency. The Combines Investigation Act enforces its provisions through three institutions—the Director of Investigation and Research, the Restrictive Trade Practices Commission and the courts. Penalties under the Act are injunctions, cease and desist orders, forced dissolution in the case of merger or monopoly, revocation of patents and cancellation of trade mark registrations, imposition of fines or prison sentences, publication of the reports of the Restricted Trade Practices Commission.

On the whole, the postwar record of Canadian competition policy has not been impressive. Certainly, the impact of the combines legislation has been limited and uneven. Yet, it is also true that the legislation has become a more important factor in the minds of Canadian businessmen and hence in the operation of the economy.

Federal, provincial and municipal governments have enacted legislation aimed at decreasing competition in the economy. At both the provincial and municipal level we find licensing laws and price fixing. At the federal level patent laws have been enacted, giving rise to debate over their effectiveness in stimulating innovation. Other restraints to competition that will be considered later include policies with regard to agriculture, labour, and international trade.

Exercises and Questions for Discussion

1. "If the Combines Investigation Act was strictly enforced, monopolistic situations and restraint of trade would be sufficiently curbed." What do you think about this statement? What suggestions can you make for improvement in regard to our present Act?

2. Is large firm size in itself a hindrance to competition? Discuss instances when it might and when it might not be.
3. Suppose your city is served by a privately owned, publicly regulated electric company. Discuss the merits and lack of merit as well as the possible difficulties involved in setting a maximum price per kilowatt hour that the company may charge.
4. Describe the economic effects of the following developments:
   a. The movie theater owners of your city collusively set a minimum admission price.
   b. A large chain store undercuts the price of local competitors on brand-name products.
5. Some people have recommended that the Canadian steel industry be placed under public regulation. What arguments do you think could be used both for and against this proposal?
6. Should professional bodies be placed under combines legislation? Discuss.

Selected Readings

Bain, J. S., *Barriers to New Competition.* Cambridge, Mass.: Harvard University Press, 1956.

Caves, Richard, *American Industry: Structure, Conduct, Performance*, Second Edition. Englewood Cliffs, N.J.: Prentice-Hall, 1967.

Economic Council of Canada, *Interim Report on Competition Policy.* Ottawa: Queen's Printer, 1969.

————, *Interim Report—Consumer Affairs and the Department of the Registrar General.* Ottawa: Queen's Printer, 1966.

English, H. E., "Competition and Policy to Control Restrictive Practices" and "Other Policies Affecting Competition" in Brewis *et al., Canadian Economic Policy*, revised edition. Toronto: Macmillan, 1965. Chaps. 2 and 3.

Rosenbluth, Gideon, "Concentration and Monopoly in the Canadian Economy" in Michael Oliver (ed.), *Social Purpose for Canada.* Toronto: University of Toronto Press, 1961, pp. 198-248.

Skeoch, L. A., *Restrictive Trade Practices in Canada.* Toronto: McClelland & Stewart Ltd., 1966.

————, "The Combines Investigations Act," *Canadian Journal of Economics and Political Science*, February, 1956, pp. 17-37.

Stykolt, Stefan, "Combines Policy: An Economist's Evaluation," *Canadian Journal of Economics and Political Science*, February, 1956, pp. 38-45.

Wilcox, Clair, *Public Policies Toward Business*, 3d ed. Homewood, Ill.: Richard D. Irwin, Inc., 1966, Chaps. 3, 5, 11, 12, and 19.

14

Government and Agriculture

The agricultural sector of the Canadian economy represents another major area in which there has been considerable government intervention in the operation of the price system. Much debate has centred on "the farm problem," and "solutions" to it have been advanced in the political arena and in the press. Emotions run high on this issue and, as is so often the case, they tend to obscure a great many facts. We shall attempt in this chapter (1) to determine what the major economic problems are in agriculture, (2) to indicate how the government has responded to these problems, and (3) to consider directions that long-run solutions to the problems should take.

Agricultural Problems

Two conditions in particular that have characterized economic activity in agriculture have generated concern on the part of government and the public. The first is *low average incomes or poverty*, and the second is *instability of farm prices and farm incomes over time*. The two are inter-twined—indeed, each may be partly responsible for the other—but there is an analytical advantage in treating them separately.

Poverty and instability are not problems unique to the agricultural sector. Both occur in other sectors of the economy. Yet a large number of people are affected by these conditions in the farming sector, and the people so affected in turn have had a disproportionately large representation in Parliament and in the provincial legislatures. Consequently, agricultural programs, presumably intended to alleviate the problems, have been given a high place on the legislative agenda.

The Low-Income Problem

There are a number of special problems in defining and measuring the incomes of farm families,[1] and the figures in this area are not much more than educated guesses. It would appear that, in 1966, Canadian average urban family income was $7,135; in contrast farm families averaged only $4,525, that is, nearly 37 percent less.[2] Thus the evidence, such as it is, indicates that average incomes among the farm population are appreciably lower than those in other areas of the economy.

Also deserving of mention is the fact that the agricultural labour force has declined by 55 percent since 1946. This massive net shift out of the farm labour force indicates that there must have been a substantial income differential throughout the postwar period between agricultural and alternative nonagricultural occupations even after all of the psychic and nonmonetary forms of income had been included. In describing this long-run trend, the Economic Council of Canada explained that:

" . . . By 1963 farmers' incomes were 54 percent above the 1949 level while incomes of wage and salary workers elsewhere in the economy had increased by 94 percent. Measured in constant 1949 dollars, incomes in agriculture had increased by 13 percent while incomes in nonagricultural occupations had increased by 46 percent. If an allowance for a return on capital (investment) was deducted from farmers' incomes, the increase in current dollars was 21 percent, and in constant dollars there was a decline of about 10 percent."[3]

[1]*Attempts to measure and compare farm and nonfarm incomes are difficult because of problems of pricing, income in kind, personal satisfaction (sometimes termed "psychic income"), security of income, cost of living, growth of asset values, off-farm earnings, etc.*

[2]*In 1966 Canadian net farm income (net income is the sum of cash income from the sale of farm products, income in kind and federal government supplementary payments less operating and depreciation expenses, and is adjusted for inventory changes) was $1,948 million or $4,525 per farm for the 430,522 farms identified in the census of that year. Average urban family income is based on Economic Council of Canada,* Fifth Annual Review. *Ottawa: Queen's Printer, 1968, Table 6-1, p. 107. It should be pointed out that the farm income figures mentioned here do not include off-farm earnings of farmers. As one would expect, the incidence of work off the farm is most prevalent in the small-farm sector.*

[3]*Economic Council of Canada,* First Annual Review, 1964, *Ottawa, Queen's Printer, pp. 140-41.*

To sum up, the existence of a major farm income problem in Canada is beyond question.

Distribution of Income within Agriculture

Are all farm families poor? A drive through the large wheat farms of Saskatchewan, Manitoba and Alberta or the fruit and vegetable farms of southern Ontario will reveal large modern homes, colour television sets, Cadillacs in garages, swimming pools, and the like. At the same time, a drive through parts of rural Quebec, or New Brunswick or Newfoundland will show tumbled-down shacks and poverty of the bleakest kind. Let us now look at the way families in the agricultural sector fare with respect to one another.

Some idea of how income is distributed among agricultural families can be inferred from the data presented in Table 14–1. In 1966 only 31.2 percent of farms had gross sales of $7,500 or more per year, leaving 68.8 percent of farms with gross sales of less than $7,500. Suppose we call the former group "good" farms and the latter group "poor" farms. Support for this classification is provided by the column showing net income per farm for each value of sales classification.

These data indicate that poverty is not typical of all farms. It does not reside to any significant degree with the good farms. Most of the latter are reasonably well-operated commercial enterprises and some are outstandingly successful business firms. The good farms take advantage of the

TABLE 14–1
Classification of Farm Operators by Value of Farm Products Sold, 1966

Classification by Value of Sales (Dollars)	Number of Farms	Percent of Farms	Gross Value of Farm Sales (Millions of Dollars)	Percent of Sales	Estimated Net Income from Farming[1] (Dollars)
250 or less	36,692	8.5	3	.3	25
250 — 1,199	55,271	12.8	37	1.1	500
1,200 — 2,499	60,947	14.1	110	3.3	1,200
2,500 — 3,749	47,024	10.9	145	4.3	1,900
3.750 — 4,999	37,923	8.8	164	4.9	2,500
5,000 — 7,499	58,103	13.5	357	10.7	3,200
7,500 — 9,999	38,753	9.0	335	10.0	4,400
10,000 — 14,999	44,217	10.3	536	16.0	6,000
15,000 — 24,999	31,149	7.2	586	17.5	7,200
25,000 — 34,999	9,384	2.2	273	8.2	15,200
35,000 and over	10,282	2.4	778	23.3	
All farms	430,522	100.0	3,338	100.0	

[1]*Includes income in kind and an imputed rental value of the farm house.*
Source: Based on Low Income Sector in Canadian Agriculture, *a paper prepared for the Canadian Agriculture Congress by the Federal Task Force on Agriculture, Ottawa, 1969, Tables 1 and 2.*

latest developments in farm technology—equipment, plant and animal genetics, fertilization, and soil care—with their resulting economies of scale. The farm income problem rests with the poor farms. This 68.8 percent of all farm units consists mostly of small, infertile, poorly run farms that provide little beyond subsistence for their operators.

Causes of Poverty

Why do we find so many small-scale, low-income-producing farm units in Canada? The answer turns to a large extent on what has happened over time to demand for and supply of a good many agricultural products. It also turns on the slowness of the rural population to adjust to the changing economic climate of the country as a whole.

Over time demand for agricultural products in Canada has not kept pace with the rapidly rising demand for other products. This pattern is typical in an economy that has reached a relatively high level of economic development. The demand for agricultural products—for food, feed, and fibre—is more closely geared to the physical needs of the population than is that for manufactured goods and for services. Once an economy reaches the stage at which most of the population is reasonably well fed and clothed, for further increases in per capita income the portions that are spent on agricultural products diminish while the portions spent on automobiles, houses, appliances, medical care, government services, and so on, increase. In terms of demand for its output, agriculture is a *relatively declining industry*; that is, demand for its output is increasing more slowly than demand for the output of the nonagricultural sector of the economy.

On the supply side, tremendous advances have occurred in farm technology over the last 50 years. Until the 1940s it was not at all uncommon to see plows, cultivators, grain binders, and other farm machinery pulled by horses. But beginning in the late 1920s, the horse was in the process of being replaced by the tractor. Further, more intensive use was being made of crop rotation and of fertilizers. Advances in plant and animal genetics were increasing the yields of plant and animal products. Since World War II there have been spectacular increases in the efficiency of agricultural production, and ours is indeed an era of scientific farming.

The slowly rising demand for agricultural products, coupled with the rapidly increasing supply, have caused prices of farm products to lag behind those in other areas of the economy. That is, farm prices have been decreasing relative to the prices of manufactured goods and services. These effects are illustrated in Figure 14–1, in which we let automobiles represent manufactured products and wheat represent farm products. Suppose that in 1920 the demand for automobiles was D_aD_a and the supply was S_aS_a. In the same year suppose that the demand for wheat was D_wD_w

and the supply was S_wS_w. By 1970 suppose that the demand for automobiles has increased to $D_{a_1}D_{a_1}$. Automobile supply has also increased markedly to $S_{a_1}S_{a_1}$, but the demand increase has outstripped the supply increase by enough to bring about a large relative increase in both automobile prices and the quantities sold. For the same period, suppose that the demand for wheat increased from D_wD_w to $D_{w_1}D_{w_1}$—much less, relatively, than for automobiles. Improvements in farm technology have increased wheat yields and dramatically lowered costs per bushel of producing specific quantities, increasing the supply from S_wS_w to $S_{w_1}S_{w_1}$. The much smaller increase in the demand for wheat relative to the increase in its supply brought about a much smaller relative increase in its price and in the

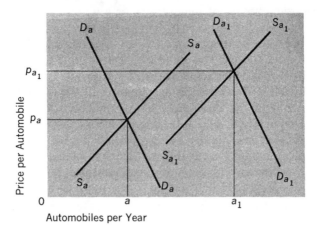

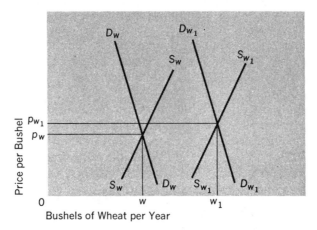

Figure 14–1
The impact of increases in demand on prices of agricultural products as compared with manufactured products.

quantity sold than was the case for automobiles. The slower increase, or the relative decrease, in farm prices as compared with nonfarm prices has been accompanied by a slower increase in the total income earned from agriculture than from other sectors of the economy. This situation, however, has not affected all farmers adversely. The more progressive ones, or those on the good farms, have adjusted very well. By taking advantage of the latest technological developments and by increasing their scales of operations they have been able to keep pace with, or even to exceed, the rate of increase of average family income in Canada. Farming for this group is no longer simply a way of life. It has become a business proposition, conducted in every respect as any other well-run business.

On the other hand, the 68.9 percent of farm units run by small, marginal operators have failed to adjust to the changing economic facts of farm life. These people are usually poorly educated and lack the business acumen that characterizes their more progressive brethren. They have not been able to compensate for lower relative farm prices by increasing their outputs and sales volumes. Cultural and social forces, together with an absence of training for other pursuits, conspire against the economic incentives that would pull them into more lucrative employments and they tend to remain on the farm. This part of the farm population constitutes the real problem area from the income point of view.

The Instability Problem

Instability of farm prices and income, the second major farm problem, arises primarily from two sources. One is such natural phenomena as the uncertainties of the weather. The other is the peculiar vulnerability of agriculture to recession, depression, and inflation.

Natural Causes of Instability

Agricultural production is more dependent on natural phenomena than is that in most other sectors of the economy. For example, the amount of rainfall in an agricultural area may vary from year to year. Droughts may occur over a wide section of the wheat belt in some years, or, as it happened in the 1930s, for a succession of years. In other years rainfall may be more than ample, resulting in flooding and washing out of crops. Too, excessive rainfall may seriously delay harvests or make grain recovery difficult. In addition, crops are subject to damage from wind and hail, and insect invasions have occasionally cut yields substantially. All of these factors may create uncertainties and instability in farm businesses, particularly where entire farms are dependent on a single crop.

External Economic Causes of Instability

Economic fluctuations are generally thought to bear more heavily on farm prices and farm incomes than on average price and income levels. Farm prices tend to fall more than do average prices during periods of recession, while in periods of prosperity and expansion farm prices tend to rise more rapidly than do prices in general. This is so because the demand for and the supply of most farm products tend to be less elastic than for most nonfarm products. These circumstances are illustrated in Figure

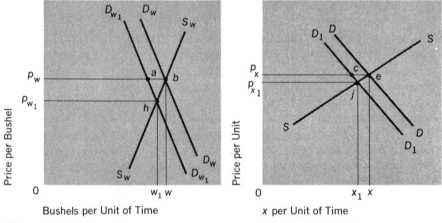

Figure 14-2
Comparative responses of agricultural and manufacturing prices and incomes to economic fluctuations.

14-2. Suppose that product X is some nonfarm product and that in the neighbourhood of the initial equilibrium price p_x, both demand and supply, DD and SS, are fairly elastic. Suppose that demand and supply of wheat, D_wD_w and S_wS_w, are much less elastic in the neighbourhood of the equilibrium price, p_w. Consider now a recession that decreases the demand for wheat and the demand for X in about the same proportion in the neighbourhood of their respective original equilibrium prices; that is, ab is to p_wb as ce is to p_xe. The decrease in the price of X is from p_x to p_{x1} only. It is cushioned by the high elasticity of both demand and supply. The decrease in the price of wheat from p_w to p_{w1} is much greater because demand and supply are much less elastic. The income from wheat sales before demand decreased is represented by the area of the rectangle Op_wbw. After the decrease in demand, it is represented by the area of rectangle $Op_{w1}hw_1$. Income from X decreases from area Op_xex to area $Op_{x1}jx_1$.

Government Responses

Our review of the agricultural sector of the Canadian economy has revealed that the core of the "farm problem" is the low level of farm incomes and the volatility of farm prices. But these problems are not new, having been with us in more or less aggravated form since the early 1920s. In the mid-1930s, however, they became so serious that the federal government initiated several programs aimed at their alleviation such as the Prairie Farm Rehabilitation Act (1935) to deal with the results of subnormal precipitation and soil drifting in the Provinces of Manitoba, Saskatchewan and Alberta; the Canadian Wheat Board Act to maintain stability in the market for wheat grown in Canada; and the Prairie Farm Assistance Act (1939) to mitigate the effects of crop failure due to drought or other causes. As the years of war, and postwar boom and recession have passed, federal action in behalf of the farmers has included the creation of agencies for these purposes: price support (Agricultural Stabilization Act and Canadian Dairy Commission); markets stabilization (The Canadian Wheat Board Act and the Agricultural Products Marketing Act); crop insurance (Crop Insurance Act); resource development (Agricultural and Rural Development Act); feed grain assistance (Livestock Feed Assistance Act) and credit facilities (Farm Improvement Loans Act, Prairie Grain Advance Payments Act, Farm Credit Act and Farm Machinery Syndicates Credit Act). Generally speaking, these measures, which are described individually below, have been initiated to improve the economic status of farm families. As we shall see later, some of these measures are often criticized because too little attention has been paid to their effects on the allocation of resources.

It should be added that the British North America Act provides for concurrent federal and provincial jurisdiction in the field of agriculture but gives the Parliament of Canada overriding authority in case of conflict. In general, it would appear that "all eleven governments co-operate with cordiality and a real degree of success in attempting to work out mutually acceptable policies and solutions."[4]

Price Supports

The Agricultural Prices Support Act, enacted in 1944, was originally designed to assist the agricultural industry in affecting a smooth, orderly transition from the economic conditions of war to those of peace. There was no mandatory list of farm products that had to be supported under this Act and there was no standard established as a guide for price support,

[4]Federal Task Force on Agriculture, Report. *Ottawa: Queen's Printer, 1970, p. 278.*

corresponding to "parity" in the United States.[5] Thus the federal government, acting through a Board, was free to decide what prices would be supported and at what level and by what method to extend assistance. Actually, comparatively few products were supported under the Act and most of these for short periods only.[6] Supports were usually provided through the purchase of surpluses. The scope of the price-support programs is indicated by the fact that the total net cost of operations under the Act, from 1946 when it came into operation, to 1958 when it was superseded, was only slightly over $100 million. Moreover, approximately $70 million of this was incurred in connection with the support of cattle and hog prices, following the outbreak of foot and mouth disease in 1952.

The Agricultural Stabilization Act, inaugurated in 1958, provided for the establishment of (1) an Agricultural Stabilization Board "to stabilize prices of agricultural commodities to assist producers in realizing fair returns for their labour and investment and to maintain a fair relationship between prices received by farmers and the costs of goods and services they buy, thus to provide them with a fair share of the national income";[7] and (2) a revolving fund of $250 million for carrying out these purposes. The Board is required to support, at not less than 80 percent of the previous ten-year average market or base price, the prices of nine "named" commodities—cattle, hogs and sheep; butter, cheese and eggs; and wheat, oats and barley grown outside the prairie areas. The Board can set the upper support level. Other products, known as "designated" commodities, may be supported at such percentages of the base price as may be approved by the federal cabinet.

The Board may support the price of a product by any one of three means. These are (1) the offer-to-purchase method, (2) the deficiency payment method, and (3) the fixed subsidy method. Let us see how each method works.

[5]*Price supports in the United States are based on the concept of a "parity price" formula. Parity prices refer to "fair" prices received by farmers for what they sell relative to the prices they must pay for nonfarm products. The parity formula was originally related directly to the base period 1910-1914, a period in which the ratio of prices received to prices paid was relatively favourable to farmers. Prices have been supported at 60 to 90 percent of parity. A new parity formula was introduced in 1948. Instead of using the ratios of prices received to prices paid during the 1910-1914 period, moving ratios over the most recent 10-year period were to be used for computations of parity prices.*

[6]*The commodities were potatoes, apples, butter, cheese, beans, honey, turkeys, fowl, eggs, dried skim milk, hogs and cattle. In most cases the programs were instituted to deal with temporary emergencies. For only two products, butter and eggs, were continuous programs administered which worked to stabilize prices over the year.*

[7]*Canada Department of Agriculture,* Federal Agricultural Legislation, *Ottawa, October 1969, p. 22.*

Offers to Purchase

The first price support operations were accomplished by an offer-to-purchase program. That is to say, the government set the support price, consumers bought as much as they wanted at the prescribed price, and the government then offered to purchase the output that the market would not take at the support price.

The economics of the offer-to-purchase approach are illustrated in Figure 14–3. In the absence of the program, the market price would be p and the quantity produced and sold would be w. Suppose now that a support price level is established at p_1. At that price consumers will take only w_1 of the product, but farmers will produce quantity w_2. The quantity w_1w_2 is a surplus that cannot be sold at that price, and therefore it is purchased by the government.

Effective price supports invariably result in product surpluses. And therein lies the rub. What does the government do with surpluses it has acquired? They cannot be sold to Canadian consumers if the support price is to be maintained. Attempts to dispose of surpluses by sales abroad at

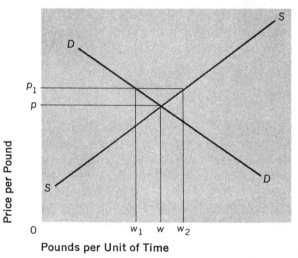

Figure 14–3

Offer-to-purchase program

low prices or even giving them away antagonizes other countries which produce the same commodities for export. Domestic "giveaways" are self-defeating in the task of reducing surpluses if they provide products to those who would otherwise obtain them through the market. Deliberately destroying foodstuffs is definitely an anti-social solution when large portions of the world's population go hungry. Surplus commodities can be stored, as has been done with many products including butter, eggs, pork and skim milk. But sooner or later these stored supplies will deteriorate and therefore, be wasted unless some use for them arises. Quite fortuitously, a series of world wide droughts in the early 1930s eased the wheat surplus disposal problem for Canada in 1936. Short supplies of wheat on world markets caused Canadian wheat prices to rise well above support levels, thus allowing the government, which had accumulated considerable stocks of wheat between 1930 and 1935, to sell all its holdings at prices which fully covered the cost of buying and storing the wheat.

We can identify at least three types of costs associated with the offer-to-purchase method of supporting prices. Firstly, consumers receive smaller quantities of the price-supported goods and pay higher prices for them whenever the price supports are effective than they would if the supports were not effective or were absent. Secondly, the handling, storing, and disposal of surplus goods is costly.[8] Resources used for these purposes could have been used to produce other goods and services. Thirdly, taxpayers must provide the funds used by the government to purchase surpluses. Apart from such direct costs as restrictions in the quantities available of supported products and the resource costs of handling, storing, and disposing of surpluses, the offer-to-purchase program transfers purchasing power from consumers and taxpayers to farmers. From a policy point of view we must ask ouselves whether or not this is desirable. We shall have more to say about this in a later section of this chapter.

Deficiency Payments

By 1959 the agricultural surplus problem was sufficient to create strong demands that something be done about it. The Minister of Agriculture proposed a "deficiency payment" system, and this method of providing price support went into effect on October 1, 1959 for eggs, and on January 11, 1960 for hogs. Under this program the market is allowed to find its own level and the producer is paid the difference between the national average market price and the established support price. All producers will receive the same deficiency payment regardless of the price each obtained for his product.

The mechanics of the deficiency plan are illustrated in Figure 14–4. Suppose that the product was sugar beets. Given demand and supply as *DD* and *SS*, the equilibrium price is *p*. But suppose a support price is set at p_1. Producers will place quantity w_2 on the market and consumers will be willing to pay p_2 for that amount. The payment per standard ton that

---

[8]*For the fiscal year 1959-60 total price support expenditures were $60 million, just about double the $30 million expended on normal tasks under the Agricultural Prices Support Act in the twelve years of its operations.*

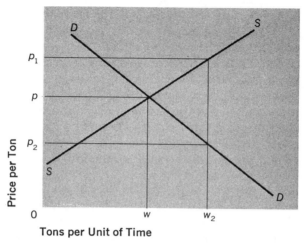

Figure 14–4
A deficiency payment program

the government must make is thus p_2p_1. The total cost to the government of the support operation is $p_2p_1w_2$.

Proponents of the deficiency payment method claim three advantages for it over the offer-to-purchase approach. Firstly, with a deficiency payment no surpluses occur, so storage and disposal costs are eliminated. Secondly, consumers get larger amounts of the product at lower prices, thus increasing what their incomes will buy. Thirdly, the deficiency payment is in the open for everyone to see. Under an offer-to-purchase program neither consumers nor producers know what the market price would be in the absence of the price support nor do they know what it would be for the quantities actually produced at the support price level. The total costs of such a program can be computed, however.

In Canada the deficiency payment method has been used to support the prices of hogs, sheep, eggs, soybeans, wool, sugar beets, honey, cattle, tobacco, and grain grown in Ontario. The programs for hogs and eggs have a unique feature: the deficiency payment is made only *on a limited amount of product per producer.* The annual limit for eggs is set between 1,000 dozen and 10,000 dozen Grade A Extra Large, Grade A Large, and Grade A Medium eggs per farmer. For hogs, the limit is set at 100 hogs per producer (of index 100 and up). This feature, which permits the Stabilization Board to limit support to a certain volume of output, keeps the cost of the price support program down by encouraging production curtailment; but it also discriminates against the larger more specialized commercial farms in favour of the smaller family ones.

Fixed Subsidies

The third method to put a support price on an agricultural product into effect is a fixed payment or subsidy to the producer. As a rule, this method is used where much of the designated crop is grown under contract. If the contract price is less than the prescribed or support price, the government makes up the difference and pays it directly to the producer. This method has been employed to support the prices of whole milk for manufacturing, milk and cream for butter manufacturing, and dried casein.

The Canadian Wheat Board

The Wheat Board was created by the federal government in 1935 as an emergency marketing measure and is still operative. Its present functions are: (1) to administer a *guaranteed minimum floor price* for wheat, oats, and barley (produced on the prairies and in northern British Columbia and entering interprovincial and international trade) through the payment of initial prices on these grains; (2) to negotiate country elevator charges; (3) to ration elevator space through a system of delivery quotas and to control the movement of grain to terminal points or other destinations; (4) to establish the selling price for the various grades of wheat; (5) to engage in the sale of wheat for export itself and through exporting agents, and to carry on a sales promotion program; (6) to control the quantities, grades, shipping period and export positions for all export sales of wheat; (7) to return to the producers all funds received less only operating costs.

When a grain farmer delivers his crop to the local grain elevator, he receives the "initial payment price", net of handling and transportation charges, which has been set earlier in the year by Parliament on the basis of its estimates of the future selling price of grain, and of farmers' needs. This price provides a guaranteed floor price in that if the Board, in selling the grain, does not realize this price and the necessary marketing costs, the deficit is borne by the federal government. But this is seldom necessary. After the end of the crop year the producer may receive a further interim payment, and after the Board has sold all of a year's output he gets a final payment. In the end the western farmer has received the price for his grain that the Board received, minus its operating costs. To put it differently, the Canadian scheme involves neither a price supplement nor an income supplement tied to wheat. In this respect it is very unlike the "storage and loan" program associated with the grain trade in the United States.[9]

[9]*Under the U.S. storage and loan program, the Commodity Credit Corporation stands ready to make loans to farmers (who comply with acreage allotments set by the Department of Agriculture), secured by grain crops that are placed in approved*

It may be useful to add that the general level of prices received by the Canadian Wheat Board is determined by competitive conditions in world markets. In 1947, the major wheat exporting and importing countries drew up a pact to provide price and quantity controls in the world wheat market. The first International Wheat Agreement became effective in 1949-1950 and provided for export and import controls to assure producers and consumers of minimum sales and purchases according to agreed-upon quotas, and set minimum prices (depending on grades and location) at which importing countries guaranteed to purchase certain amounts and also maximum prices at which exporting countries guaranteed to sell stated quantities. The I.W.A. was revised periodically and the last agreement ended on July 31, 1967, with only the administrative provisions extending until July 1, 1968, when the International Grains Arrangement came into force. Like its predecessor, the I.G.A. also provided a schedule of maximum and minimum prices for most major classes and/or grades of wheat moving in world trade. The new agreement, however, lacked any overall purchase commitments by importing countries and, in view of the huge pile-up of exporters' surplus stocks, the minimum prices came under severe pressure almost from the start and, in fact, were soon breached. In these circumstances, the Canadian government announced, in March 1969, that it would sell grain below I.G.A. minimums in order to retain its competitive position with other exporting nations. As countries continued to undercut one another through the summer months, the Canadian government guaranteed the Prairie grain producers a floor price (i.e. $1.95½ per bushel for No. 1 Northern in store at the Lakehead) for wheat consumed in the domestic market. This arrangement covers about 60 million bushels or around 15 percent of the recent total annual disposal of wheat. Clearly, if heavy supply conditions persist, the possibility exists that the Canadian Wheat Board, which is basically a marketing agency, could end up supporting wheat prices. As evidence of this danger, the government is likely to have to cover a loss of about $50 million on sales of 1968-1969 prairie wheat.

storage facilities. For example, a wheat farmer could obtain a loan at harvest time amounting to the announced support price (wheat is now supported at three different levels) multiplied by the number of bushels of wheat he has placed in approved storage bins. Such loans are called nonrecourse loans, meaning that if during the year the market price of the product goes far enough above the support price to more than pay storage costs, the farmer may sell the crop and pay off the loan and storage costs. Any excess of receipts over the loan and storage costs is his. On the other hand, if the market price is not high enough to make it worthwhile for the farmer to sell the product, he simply keeps the loan and lets the government have the crop. Thus the market price stays near the support level. In effect the government buys any quantities of the crop that the market will not take at support price levels.

Two other comments are worth making here. First, under the *Temporary Wheat Reserves Act*, which came into force in 1956, the federal government pays storage and interest cost of stocks of wheat held by the Wheat Board in excess of 178 million bushels at the beginning of a crop year. This subsidy, which averages about $35 million per year, assists producers in paying costs of storing large stocks accumulating from bumper crops. Second, the *Prairie Grain Advance Payments Act*, which came into operation in 1957, provides for interest-free advance payments to producers for threshed grain in storage other than in a commercial elevator under a unit quota. Advance payments of $1.00 per bushel of wheat, 70 cents per bushel of barley and 40 cents per bushel of oats are made, subject to certain restrictions as to quota and acreage. Maximum advances per application is $6,000.

Supply Restrictions

An important feature of national agricultural policy in the United States, but not in Canada, has been the restriction of supplies of basic farm products; that is, attempts to move the supply curves of certain products to the left. The Agricultural Adjustment Act of 1933, which became a cornerstone of American agricultural policy, was based on this philosophy. The subsequent pegging of U.S. support prices above equilibrium levels, the introduction of nonrecourse loans to farmers, secured by crops placed in storage, and the resulting surpluses accumulating in U.S. government hands led to supply restriction features as integral parts of farm legislation in order to hold down or to reduce those surpluses.

Supply Restriction, Prices, and Receipts

Will supply restriction for a specific product in and of itself raise the receipts of the producers of that product? We know that a decrease in supply, given the demand for the product, will raise the price. It will also decrease the quantity exchanged. What are the effects on the producers' receipts? In Figure 14–5 suppose DD and SS are the demand and supply curves, respectively, for tobacco. The price is p_c and the quantity sold is c. The total receipts of tobacco producers are $c \cdot p_c$ or the area of the rectangle $op_c ec$.

If the government now enacts measures that succeed in moving the supply curve to the left to $S_1 S_1$, the price will rise to p_{c_1} and the quantity sold will fall to c_1. Consumers are moved up and to the left on DD to position f. What happens to consumer expenditures, or, what amounts to the same thing, to producers, receipts? A review of demand analysis indicates that the answer turns on the elasticity of demand for tobacco.

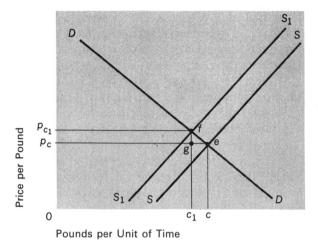

Figure 14–5
A supply restriction program.

If demand for tobacco is inelastic for the increase in price, as it is in Figure 14–5, the total receipts of tobacco farmers will increase. The area of the rectangle $op_{c_1} fc_1$ represents total receipts after the change in supply, and by inspection we can determine that it is larger than that of $op_c ec$[10]. However, if the elasticity of demand were unitary for the price increase, there would be no change in the total receipts of tobacco farmers. If demand were elastic, total receipts would actually decrease. Supply restriction by itself, then, can always raise the price of a product, but it can increase the total receipts of sellers *only if demand for the product is inelastic*.

Supply Restriction and Surpluses

As the U.S. agricultural program has developed since 1933, supply restrictions have not really been used directly for the purpose of increasing receipts of sellers, except for a short period in 1933. Rather, they have been aimed at reducing yearly surpluses and at holding down the total costs of price-support operations. In Figure 14–6, given the demand curve *DD* and the supply curve *SS*, if the price of wheat were to be supported by the storage and loan method (or the offer-to-purchase method) at p_1, surpluses of $w_1 w_1'$ per time period would accrue. These would build up a surplus stock of the product that would present problems with respect to storage costs and what to do with it.

If supply could be decreased toward $S_1 S_1$, the periodic additions to

[10]*The reduction in supply chops* $c_1 gec$ *off the original total receipts rectangle and adds* $p_c p_{c_1} fg$ *to it.*

the stockpile of the product would be smaller. If it could be decreased even more to S_2S_2, the stockpile could be diminished by an amount w_2w_1 per time period. Restriction of supply to S_1S_1 would make it unnecessary for farmers to seek government loans and this very substantial cost of the program would be eliminated. The only remaining costs would be those of storing and disposing of any existing stock that has been accumulated in past years.

Methods of Restricting Supply

The U.S. government has employed two primary methods to reduce supplies of price-supported products. Farm legislation has included *acreage allotments* for reducing acres planted for some crops. In some instances the "stick" technique has been used to secure compliance with acreage allotments—that is, penalties have been placed on noncomplying farmers. In other cases the government has used the "carrot," or payments to farmers for placing land in a soil bank; that is, for diverting land to soil-building uses or for leaving it idle altogether. For other crops it has used *marketing quotas* specifying the amounts that individual farmers can market at support prices. For still others acreage allotments and marketing quotas have both been employed.

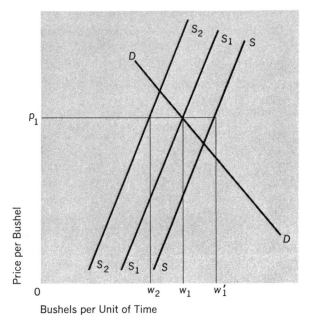

Figure 14–6
A combination of price support and supply restriction.

Marketing quotas are generally more effective than acreage controls in reducing supplies. The effectiveness of acreage allotments is reduced by at least two reactions on the part of farmers. Firstly, farmers withdraw their most infertile acres from cultivation. Secondly, they tend to farm more intensively those acres left in cultivation by working the ground better and using better fertilizing techniques. Consequently, the reductions in the total outputs of a farmer are likely to be proportionally much less than the reduction in the acreage that he plants.

The Canadian Experience

As already indicated, the Canadian Wheat Board does not control acreage planted to wheat. By the beginning of 1970, however, it was abundantly clear that a serious wheat surplus situation was rapidly building up. Thus, on February 27, 1970, the federal government proposed a wheat acreage reduction program for 1970. When announcing Operation Lift —Lower Inventory for Tomorrow—the Minister of Agriculture said that, apart from the immediate benefit of approximately halving the 950 million-bushel stockpile, the Canadian plan would add impetus to international efforts to stabilize the world grain economy.

Under the federal program, which applies only to the 1970-1971 crop year, producers who reduce wheat acreage below 1969 levels and increase perennial forage or summer-fallow land will receive compensation payments of $6 per acre for additions to summer-fallow or $10 per acre for additions to perennial forage. Allowances will be available to a maximum of 20 million acres of additional summer-fallow and 2 million acres of additional perennial forage. A maximum of 1,000 acres for any individual farmer will be eligible. Thus the maximum payout to a single producer is $10,000 if he transfers 1,000 acres out of wheat production into perennial forage crops such as hay.

As a supporting incentive, the wheat delivery quotas for the 1970-1971 crop year will be based not on wheat acreage planted but on a formula involving forage and summer-fallow land. Basically, the more such land a farmer has, the more of his farm-stored wheat surplus he can deliver to the local grain elevator.

The cost of this scheme to the government will vary with the number of acres that producers actually take out of wheat. While the government estimates the cost at $100 million, the bill could run to $140 million. To the individual farmer there is, of course, the cost of cultivating the land to keep it free of weeds and an additional cost for seed in the case of converting to perennial forage.

In sum, it would appear that the government's program will inject much needed cash into the Prairie economy, induce farmers to take some of their wheat land out of production temporarily, help reduce Canadian wheat stocks, and provide a short breathing space for longer-term production and marketing policies to be formulated.

Canadian Dairy Commission

The Canadian Dairy Commission, which came into operation on April 1, 1967, is authorized to purchase, sell, export or import any dairy product, and to make payments for the benefit of producers of milk and cream for the purpose of stabilizing the price of such products. The Commission operates offer-to-purchase programs for creamery butter, dry skim milk, and the two top grades of cheddar cheese;[11] it provides fixed subsidies on industrial milk and cream. In this latter connection, it should be emphasized that each milk and cream producer is assigned a quota for the amount for which he is eligible for subsidy. Notwithstanding these quotas, dairy surpluses in calendar 1969 were created as follows: 28.2 million pounds of butter, 203 million pounds of dry skim milk and 32 million pounds of butter. Total support payments to the Canadian dairy industry in the 1969-1970 dairy year were $131 million.

To alleviate the surplus disposal problem, the government recently announced a $1.25 a hundredweight penalty for industrial producers of milk and cream who deliver above their quota. In addition, it has decided to reduce the dairy support payments by $10 million in fiscal 1970-1971. Even so, dairy price-support expenditures will remain the largest single governmental payment in Canadian agriculture.

Other Agricultural Assistance Programs

The Prairie Farm Rehabilitation Act, passed in 1935, provides for the development of water supplies and for land use adjustment in the agricultural areas of Manitoba, Saskatchewan and Alberta. Since the inception of the program up to March 31, 1967, PFRA assisted in the construction of 97,121 farm projects and more than 1,000 small community projects.

The *Prairie Farm Assistance Act*, which came into operation in 1939, provides for direct financial assistance by the federal government on an acreage-and-yield basis to farmers in areas of low crop yield in the Prairie Provinces and in the Peace River area of British Columbia. Its purpose is to assist in dealing with a relief problem caused by drought or other uncontrollable happenings which the provinces and municipalities could not manage alone and to enable farmers to put in a crop the following year.

---

[11]*Cheese is currently supported at 46½ and 47 cents a pound for the top two grades, butter at 65 cents a pound and milk powder at 20 cents a pound.*

Contributory payments are made by participating farmers in the form of a levy of 1 percent on the value of all their sales of wheat, oats, barley, rye, flaxseed and rapeseed. As of July 31, 1969, $378.2 million had been paid out in benefits and $201.9 million collected from the levy. Farmers who have crop insurance under a provincial plan are not eligible for benefits.

Parliament enacted crop insurance legislation in 1959 to help remove from the shoulders of the Canadian farmer some of the risks inherent in agriculture. The *Crop Insurance Act* permits the federal government to assist provinces in providing insurance but the initiative for establishing programs to meet their own specific requirements rests with the provinces. Insurance schemes may be based on particular crops or areas within provinces. Federal assistance may run to 50 percent of the administrative costs incurred by a province in the operation of an insurance scheme and 25 percent of the amount of premiums charged by a province in any one year. In addition, the federal government may also lend money to a province under certain limitations when indemnities paid exceed premium receipts. As an alternative to such loans, the federal government may reinsure a major portion of the provincial risk in a program administered under the Crop Insurance Act. In the 1968-1969 crop year, insurance schemes were in effect in Prince Edward Island, Quebec, Ontario, Manitoba, Saskatchewan, Alberta and British Columbia involving 64,376 farmers and providing $188,192,000 insurance coverage. The federal share of costs paid under federal provincial crop insurance agreements was $4.8 million.

The federal government is involved in seven different farm credit programs each having different loan limits, terms and various government administrations. Of these, the Farm Credit Act, the Farm Improvement Loans Act and the Farm Machinery Syndicates Credit Act are the most important. *The Farm Credit Act*, passed in 1959, set up the Farm Credit Corporation as successor to the Canadian Farm Loan Board established in 1929. Its primary purpose is to provide long-term mortgage credit under suitable terms and conditions to assist farmers to organize viable family farm businesses. The need for intermediate term and short credit to finance the purchase of agricultural implements and a wide range of farm improvement projects was met with the enactment of the *Farm Improvement Loans Act* in 1944. It authorized the federal government to guarantee chartered banks against loss on loans made to farmers for such purposes and under certain limitations. In 1968 a new loan purpose was added to the Act to enable farmers to purchase land where such land is an addition to the existing farm and is to be used for farming. Since inception of this legislation, 1,460,578 loans were made by the banks for a total of $2,270 million to June 30, 1969. The *Farm Syndicates Credit Act* (originally entitled the Farm Machinery Syndicates Credit Act) provides the Farm Credit Corporation with authority to make loans to groups or "syndicates" of farmers organized to share in the purchase and use of farm machinery buildings and installed equipment. From the inception of this program in 1965 up to March 31, 1969, the Corporation had approved 577 loans totalling $4.6 million.

The *Livestock Feed Assistance Act*, proclaimed in 1966, replaced a 1941 statute under which the federal government contributed to the cost of moving feed grains from the Prairies to British Columbia and to Eastern Canada. The Board provided for by the Act is required to carry out the administration of the freight and storage assistance programs, to ensure the availability of feed grain stocks and storage to meet the needs of livestock feeders, and to ensure reasonable stability and a fair equalization in feed grain prices in Eastern Canada and British Columbia. During the year ended March 31, 1969, $17,997,461 was spent on the freight assistance program, aiding in the transport of 2,154,471 tons of feed grain and grain products into Eastern Canada and British Columbia.

Before leaving transportation subsidies, it should be pointed out that the *Crow's Nest Pass Agreement*, which remains in force, has prevented an increase in railway freight rates over the rates of 1898 on grain and flour moving from the Prairie areas into export channels. Under the National Transportation Act, 1967, the railways now receive a federal grant to compensate them for their losses on these shipments.

The Agricultural Rehabilitation and Development Act, proclaimed in 1961 and amended in 1966 as the *Agricultural and Rural Development Act* (ARDA) and its companion legislation, the *Fund for Rural Economic Development Act* (FRED) of 1966, were initiated to help rural people adjust to economic, social and technological changes. They provided for shared-cost programs involving alternate land use, soil and water conservation, development of rural income and employment opportunities, and for research necessary to these purposes. There have been two federal-provincial ARDA agreements to date: the first was in force from June 22, 1961 to March 31, 1965; the second commenced on April 1, 1965 and terminated on March 31, 1970. Recently the federal government entered into new ARDA agreements with the Provinces of Ontario and British Columbia. Under the first agreement, which stressed rehabilitation and improvement in agriculture, ARDA approved projects involving a federal share totalling $34.5 million of which $26.9 million was expended up to March 31, 1970. In addition, $2.7 million has been spent on research. The 1965-1970 ARDA agreement placed its emphasis on the social and economic needs of the people of rural areas, and on developing various resources to meet these requirements. It provided for project expenditures of $125 million during that period. Up to March 31, 1970 the federal government had spent $76.3 million on approved ARDA projects plus another $21 million on research. The Fund for Rural Economic Development Act provided for an additional $300 million during the five-year period to finance major projects in special rural development areas. Comprehensive regional rural development programs were set up in Prince Edward Island, New Brunswick, Eastern Quebec and the Interlakes region of Manitoba. Federal expenditures under FRED totalled $39.4 million up to March 31, 1970, at which time the Act lapsed. Of course, federal commitments made earlier will be honoured, but henceforth aid to rural areas will be extended under other federal legislation.

Marketing Boards

No account of government involvement in agriculture would be complete without mention of marketing boards. The control of fluid milk marketing was first undertaken in Manitoba during the 1930s. By 1940, most provinces had enacted such legislation. The control bodies established set minimum prices that distributors may pay for milk sold for fluid consumption and most of them also set either minimum or fixed wholesale and retail prices for fluid milk. The federal Canadian Dairy Commission complements provincial legislation by regulating the marketing and pricing of milk and milk products that move in interprovincial or international trade.

In contrast to milk control boards, which are government agencies, there are about 120 provincial farmer-controlled marketing boards. It is estimated that 45.6 percent of the 1968 Canadian farm cash income was received from sales made under provincial marketing board programs, including the following commodities: hogs, certain dairy products, poultry, wool, tobacco, wheat, soybeans, sugar beets, potatoes, other vegetables, fruits, seed corn, white beans, honey, maple products, mushrooms, oysters, and pulpwood.

Producer marketing boards are established under provincial law after a favourable vote of those farmers who produce the commodity to be marketed by a board. Though the provincial marketing laws vary in detail, the same basic powers are given to producers in all provinces. These powers include authority for a producer board to control the marketing of 100 percent of a specified commodity produced within the province or within specified areas of the province. Some boards may control production; for example, the Ontario Tobacco Growers Marketing Board sets maximum production quotas for its members. Some, such as the Ontario Vegetable Growers Marketing Board, may control the marketing of several related commodities. Some have received an extension of powers for purposes of interprovincial and export trade from the federal government under the Agricultural Products Marketing Act of 1949.

The primary purpose of a marketing board is to raise farm incomes by raising farm prices. The method is the same as that illustrated in Figure 14–6. That is, marketing boards attempt to move the supply curves of products under their jurisdiction to the left. Some boards use marketing quotas. Most hold some of the crop off the market, storing it or consigning it to a low-price use.

An Appraisal of the Farm Program

What can we say about the effectiveness of the federal farm program in alleviating agriculture's twin problems of instability and relatively low incomes? Now that we have some grasp of the nature of farm legislation, we should be able to make a tentative appraisal of what it has accomplished in these areas.

The Impact on Instability

To begin with, we can ask ourselves how a price-support program, particularly an offer-to-purchase program, might be expected to contribute toward stability of farm incomes. Many proponents of this sort of plan argue that accumulated stocks of farm commodities act as a buffer against the exaggerated effects of fluctuations in economic activity, in general on farm prices and farm incomes, as well as against irregularities in supply caused by natural phenomena. The argument runs to the effect that in periods of recession and depression the government should support prices above their equilibrium levels and thus accumulate surpluses. This would serve to hold farm incomes above what they would be if equilibrium or free market prices were to prevail. During periods of boom and inflation, the government's stocks of goods should be placed on the market, depressing prices below the equilibrium or free market levels that would otherwise prevail. This would curb the disproportionately large rise in farm incomes that ordinarily occurs in times such as these. The average level of farm incomes would be neither increased nor decreased by the government's purchase and sale operations. It would simply be leveled out over the range of business fluctuations.

The main fly in the ointment in the practice of offer-to-purchase operations has been that in periods of prosperity and inflation the government has not been willing to depress domestic prices of farm products enough to sell off its surpluses. Support prices since World War II have, with some exceptions, been above equilibrium levels and the surpluses discussed in the preceding section were accumulated. Only by disposing of these—often at substantial losses—to other countries has the Agricultural Stabilization Board been able to relieve itself of serious surplus problems. To put all of this another way, stabilization of farm incomes over the course of economic fluctuations has been subordinated to the goal of supporting farm prices.

The Impact on Poverty

The farm program has undoubtedly served to increase average farm income, but there is considerable room for doubting that it has decreased farm poverty. The fact that net income[12] of farm operators from farming operations rose from $317 million in 1935-1939 to $1,797 million in 1968 provides supporting evidence for the first part of this seeming paradox, while Table 14–1 furnishes us material for the doubting expressed in the second part.

The methods used for distributing funds to farmers simply have not been geared to alleviating poverty. In fact, they have tended to increase the differences between the incomes of large and small farmers. Price supports reward farmers in direct proportion to the amounts they produce. Similarly, much of the benefit of marketing boards (including the Canadian Wheat Board) goes to farmers with the largest delivery quotas. Likewise, compensation payments under the recently announced wheat acreage reduction program for 1970 will be greater for those owning large amounts of wheat land (up to a 1000 acres) than for those owning smaller amounts or none at all. Again, farm credit is normally tied to the assets farmers already have—their land, buildings, machinery and livestock. Too little credit is available to the really small farmers, who have little in the way of collateral. Even ARDA programs are more resource-oriented (especially land) than people-centred. In short, those farmers who need government assistance the least are precisely those who receive the largest amounts of it. These are the operators of the large, efficient farm businesses. The poor farmers, the small, inefficient operators, who should receive relief if relief is to be based on any kind of an income test, receive very small amounts of help. What kind of a welfare program is this?

---

[12]*Net income is the sum of farm cash receipts from the sales of farm products, income in kind and federal government supplementary payments, less operating expenses and depreciation charges.*

Some Modest Proposals

Destructive criticism is easier to offer than constructive recommenda-tions. We have been critical of farm legislation as it has developed in Canada. What can we say of a positive nature? If the farm problems were tossed in our laps, how would we go about trying to alleviate them?

Toward Stability

The problem of inherent instability of farm incomes during fluctuations in economic activity is only one piece of the larger problem of instability of the economy as a whole. If economic fluctuations for the entire economy can be controlled, then we will have gone far toward achieving stability in farm incomes. The last half of this book is largely devoted to the causes and consequences of economic instability and to its control.

Instability of farm incomes stemming from natural phenomena is a less serious problem and is being attacked in a number of ways. The present crop insurance program goes far toward providing protection from hail, drought, frost, flood, and insect invasion. Much research done under the auspices of the federal Department of Agriculture is aimed toward pest and insect control. In many areas irrigation techniques have been developed that materially decreases farmers' dependence on uncertain rainfall. Thus, much is being done to mitigate instability of this kind.

Toward Alleviating Poverty

We have already discussed the causes of farm poverty. The relatively slow increase in demand for agricultural products, together with the rapid rise in agricultural technology, has caused the proportion of the economy's resources used in the production of agricultural products to become too large compared with that used for nonagricultural goods and services. Further, on a large number of farms, resources are used inefficiently. The great many small farms, producing under $7,500 worth of product per year, are too small to take advantage of some very important economies of scale.

In terms of cold, hard logic, there appear to be two key elements neces-sary for alleviating farm poverty. One is the movement of resources, particularly human resources, out of agriculture and into nonagricultural uses. The fact that consumers are willing to pay less for what those resources can produce in agriculture than for what they could produce in other sectors of the economy[13] points toward this sort of movement as

---

[13]*This, in turn, is evidenced by the lower earnings of resources used in agricultural pursuits.*

a solution. The other is the consolidation of small, inefficient farm units into larger, businesslike operations.

Changes of both types are occurring. From 1931 to 1966 the farm population decreased from 3.2 million to 1.9 million persons, and the exodus from the farm continues. Average acreage per farm in Canada increased from 244 acres in 1931 to 404 acres in 1966.[14] These data reflect a decreasing number of small farms, or those under 500 acres, and an increasing number of large farms. But these changes have not yet progressed rapidly enough nor gone far enough to solve the low income problem.

Agricultral legislation appears to have done little or nothing toward eliminating the causes of poverty. Rather, it has been directed at the symptoms of the problem—relatively declining agricultural prices. To some extent, by rewarding large-scale farmers more handsomely than small-scale farmers, it may have accelerated the trend toward larger numbers of large farms and smaller numbers of small farms. But on the other hand, in paying extra amounts per unit of product produced, such legislation has made farming in general relatively more attractive than it would otherwise be, and thus to some extent it impedes the flow of resources out of agriculture.

Government agricultural policies should facilitate the structural readjustment now going on. The requisite background is a stable prosperous economy with low levels of unemployment. Instead of paying out large sums of money to the already prosperous segments of the farm population, large sums of money could be paid to the poor segments, retraining them for nonfarm occupations and subsidizing their migration out of agriculture. To some extent these objectives are being accomplished through the "Just Society" legislation of the late 1960's. Further, government and quasi-government programs designed to encourage young people to enter agriculture should receive less emphasis. This is not to say that those who want to be farmers should not be trained to be efficient farmers. But young people, particularly in rural areas, should be made aware of alternative occupational and earning opportunities.

Federal Task Force on Agriculture

In September 1967 the federal government appointed a Task Force to assess the agricultural industry and recommend policies and programs for improvement. In its 475 page report published in May 1970, the five-man Task Force made serious criticisms of the existing involvement of

[14]*Canada Department of Agriculture,* Selected Statistical Information on Agriculture in Canada, *October, 1969, p. 28.*

the federal government in Canadian agriculture and proposed some fundamental changes.

The 132 recommendations contained in the report may be summarized as follows:

—Farm surpluses must be controlled and reduced by drastically cutting production, by shifting agricultural land to other uses or by taking it out of production altogether.

—The federal and provincial governments should provide temporary, limited programs for crop switching and land retirement while, at the same time, emphasizing programs to expand demand, particularly on world markets.

—Price supports and subsidies that are not effective in achieving high-priority objectives should be eliminated.

—Younger nonviable farmers—nonviable, that is, in the sense that they cannot produce a reasonably good standard of living for themselves from farming operations alone—should be retrained or provided with jobs in other sectors of the economy and older farmers should be given assistance to ensure that they have a satisfactory level of living.

—Funds should be made available by governments for management training, provision of information processing systems, market and price forecasts and other management tools.

—Decision-making by objectives (in contrast to expediency); program planning and budgeting, cost-benefit analysis and other modern management techniques should be adopted by both government and the private sector.

—Basic differences among the five principal economic regions of Canada—the Maritimes, Quebec, Ontario, the Prairies and British Columbia—make national farm policies almost impossible, the report states.[15]

On July 8, 1970 the federal Minister of Agriculture announced that a national Agricultural Conference would be held in Ottawa on November 25-27 to "provide a forum of discussion of the ramifications of recommendations in the Task Force report in the hope that a degree of consensus might be established on the general direction of agricultural policy for the years ahead".

[15]*See Canadian Press Release, "End to Subsidies For Farmers Urged,"* **Ottawa** Journal, *May 20, p. 1.*

Summary

The economic problems in agriculture that have evoked wholesale government intervention in that sector of the economy are (1) low average incomes and (2) instability of prices and incomes.

Not all farmers are poor. The largest part of farm product output and farm sales—over 75 percent of the latter—is generated by less than one-third of all farm units. Most of these are well-run business enterprises. The poverty problem occurs in the other two thirds of the total number of farm units that generate less than 25 percent of total farm sales.

Farm poverty comes about because a large sector of the farm population has not been willing or able to adapt to changing conditions of demand for and supply of agricultural products. Over time, demand for these has increased at a slower pace than it has for industrial products and for services. At the same time, farm technology has advanced rapidly, creating relatively large increases in supply. Thus farm prices have risen more slowly than prices in general. These circumstances call for a shift of population out of agriculture—a shift that has been taking place at a pace too slow to solve the income problem. They also call for an increase in the acreage size of farms in order that advantage can be taken of economies of scale.

Instability of farm prices and incomes stems from two sources. One is the peculiar dependence of agriculture on the forces of nature. The other is the sensitivity of agriculture to instability in the economy as a whole.

The main response of government to agricultural problems has centred on maintaining farm prices above what they would be in a free market. Price supports for certain key farm commodities have been instituted through three programs: an offer-to-purchase program, a deficiency payment program, and fixed subsidies.

Under an offer-to-purchase program farmers sell what they can at support prices and the government buys and stores the remainder. When price supports are above equilibrium price levels, surpluses accumulate.

Deficiency payments permit farmers to sell their entire supplies at whatever the market will pay, with the government making up the difference between the support price and the market price. Such payments have the virtue of avoiding surplus and of being easily and directly seen for what they are. Similar comments apply to fixed subsidy payments to producers.

Surpluses are troublesome as well as costly and have induced the government to search for as many outlets for disposal as possible. To date, disposal of surplus products in foreign countries at low prices or giving them away have had the most success in keeping surplus stocks manageable.

Price support is only one of several government policies of assistance to agriculture. Others include: production and market stabilization, crop insurance, feed grain assistance, credit facilities, and resource development.

The Canadian farm program has not been an unqualified success in attacking the problems of instability and poverty. The former has been subordinated to the latter to some extent, but in any case, stability of farm incomes is to a large extent dependent on stability of the economy as a whole. Undoubtedly, the price-support program has increased average farm incomes, but it has done so by giving much more to larger, higher-income farmers than to smaller, lower-income farmers. It is a sort of topsy-turvy relief program.

From the point of view of economic analysis, the alleviation of farm poverty calls for two things: (1) the movement of resources, human resources in particular, out of agriculture and into other sectors of the economy and (2) a movement toward more and more large farms together with fewer and fewer small farms. Both of these shifts are taking place. It would appear desirable that newly contemplated farm programs be geared to facilitating them.

Exercises And Questions For Discussion

1. What would be the consequences if the present price-support programs were suddenly eliminated?
2. "Agricultural incomes are low because the farmer is paid less than a 'fair' price for his produce." Evaluate this statement.
3. If you were in a position to make decisions regarding the current "farm problem", how would you modify the present approach?
4. Under what type of market structure would you classify the agricultural industry? Is there a need for government intervention? Give reasons.
5. Why might foreign countries complain about the Canadian government selling its surplus in their market? How might this affect Canadian private producers' exports of agricultural products?

Selected Readings

Bank of Montreal, "The Canadian Wheat Situation", *Business Review*, March 25, 1970, p. 4.

Canadian Agricultural Congress, *Low Income Sector in Canadian Agriculture.* (a position paper prepared by the Federal Task Force), Ottawa, March, 1969.

Campbell, D. R., "The Farm Problem" in Officer and Smith (ed) *Canadian Economic Problems and Policies.* Toronto: McGraw-Hill Company 1970, pp. 194-209.

Dominion Bureau of Statistics, *Canada: One Hundred Years 1867-1967*. Ottawa: Queen's Printer, 1966, pp. 104-121.

————, *Canada Year Book*. Ottawa: Queen's Printer, 1968, pp. 418-487 and pp. 918-923.

Drummond, W. M., "The Role of Agricultural Marketing Boards" in J. J. Deutsch, et al (ed), *The Canadian Economy*. Toronto: Macmillan Company, 1965, pp. 246-256.

Morgan, L. I., "Price Supports and Farm Surpluses" in Watkins and Forster, *Economics: Canada*. Toronto: McGraw-Hill Company, 1963, pp. 47-55.

Federal Task Force on Agriculture, *Canadian Agriculture in the Seventies*. Ottawa: Queen's Printer, 1970.

Part 3

Markets for Resources

In Part 3 we turn the microscope from the upper half of the circular flow model of Figure 2–1 to the lower half. We shall examine in detail the markets for resources—the ingredients used by business firms to produce the goods and services they sell. The participants in resource markets are the business firms that use them on the demand side and the resource owners who place them in employment on the supply side.

Since we earn our incomes by selling or hiring out the resources we own, it is small wonder that we evidence great individual and collective interest in the operations of resource markets. We worry about the opportunities for the employment of our resources—and rightly so. The Great Depression of the 1930s, with its massive unemployment of both labour and capital, must rank among the major economic disasters of modern times. In more recent times—in the late 1950s and early 1960s—many economists thought that unemployment rates of from 4 to 7 percent of the labour force were unduly high and policy measures were enacted by the federal government to reduce them.

Many people believe that incomes in Canada are not distributed equitably. They think that some — usually the other fellows — make too much, while others—usually themselves—make too little. Thus we have legislation that superimposes redistribution schemes on the market mechanism. The best examples are the progressive income tax, social welfare legislation, including War on Poverty measures and Medicare, minimum wage laws, and agricultural legislation. Additionally, we have labour unions dedicated to income redistribution among other things.

The debates that turn on these issues in the newspapers, in periodicals, on television, and from soap boxes are generally marked by a lack of understanding of elementary economic principles. What are the relations between resource prices and their levels of employment? How do resource prices affect their allocations among different employments? Does it matter whether the firms that use resources sell their outputs in competitive or in monopolized markets? What do resource prices have to do with the distribution of income and of the economy's output? How do unions affect all this? These are the kinds of questions that Part III should help us to answer.

15

Resource Pricing and Employment in Competitive Markets

A competitive model provides the simplified framework for establishing the principles of resource pricing and employment. Using such a framework in this chapter, we shall review first the nature and objectives of competitive firms. Next, we shall examine the conditions of demand for and of supply of specific resources. The determination of prices and quantities exchanged follows. Finally, we shall take another look at a subject we met in Chapter 7—least-cost combinations of resources for a single firm.

Competitive Firms

Competition in Resource Purchases

Competition in the sale of products has already been explored, but we have not said much about competition in purchasing. We noted that the essential ingredient for competition among sellers is that no one seller of a product can place a large enough proportion of the total supply of the product on the market to influence its price. The seller faces a horizontal demand curve for his output at whatever the going market price happens to be. He cannot, by himself, influence market price of the product.

Competition in purchasing is very similar. *Pure competition* in the purchasing of an item or a service can occur only if each purchaser demands such a small part of the total amount demanded that by himself he cannot influence the market price. Any single purchaser can take as much or as little as he desires at the going price. As we shall see, this makes the supply curve of whatever he is purchasing appear to him to be at a constant level, or horizontal at the going market price. This, together with pure competition in the selling of products, is the kind of situation that we assume exists in the analysis presented in this chapter.

Objectives in Resource Purchases

Business firms are usually established to make money, and the people who operate them are usually interested in making more money rather than less. Technically, we say the objective is to make profits. Generally we suppose that, given the economic climate within which business firms must operate, they attempt to maximize profits. We have already discussed the behaviour of firms as product sellers, based on the postulate of profit maximization. Firms tend to produce at the output levels at which their marginal costs equal their marginal revenues.

Consider now a profit-maximizing firm contemplating the quantities of variable resources that it ought to use per unit of time. Since by itself the firm has no control over the prices of the resources it buys, it can adjust only the quantities employed. Consider specifically such a resource as common labour. How much of it should the firm employ? The answer is found by increasing or decreasing slightly the quantity employed and by observing the resulting effects on the firm's total revenues and total costs. If a one-unit increase in the level of employment increases the firm's total receipts by more than it increases its total costs, then the increase in the employment level brings about a *net addition* to the firm's profits. It pays to make the increase. If a one-unit decrease in the employment of labour decreases total receipts by less than it decreases total costs, then profits are increased by the decrease in the employment level.

No new principles were introduced in the preceding paragraph; we simply placed familiar principles in a new setting. Instead of looking at marginal cost and marginal revenue in terms of one-unit increases or decreases in the firm's *output*, we view the same concepts in terms of one-unit increases or decreases in the firm's *resource inputs*. In this latter context the fundamental principles still hold. If the marginal revenue of a resource input exceeds its marginal cost, it pays to increase its employment. If its marginal revenue is less than its marginal cost, its employment should be contracted. Profits are maximized at the employment level at which the marginal revenue of the input is equal to its marginal cost. This concept will be examined in detail in the following sections.

Demand for a Resource

Do you believe that the quantity demanded of a resource varies inversely with its price? Do you expect that farmers will purchase less fertilizer per year at higher prices than at lower prices? Do you believe that higher beef prices will induce your student union or dormitory cafeteria to put less meat in the stew? If wage rates rise, will the amount of labour employed in the supermarket decrease? Most of us intuitively would answer these questions in the affirmative, yet in our everyday discussions with others we frequently deny their validity. Suppose we look into the nature of demand for a resource. The first step is to get a firm grasp of a concept called *marginal revenue product* of a resource. This will enable us to define and construct an individual firm's demand curve for the resource. We shall then consider the forces that cause changes in demand and, finally, how individual firm demand curves are put together to form the market demand curve.

Marginal Revenue Product

The *marginal revenue product* of a resource is defined as the change in a firm's total receipts resulting from a one-unit change in the quantity of the resource employed. How is it computed and how does it behave as the firm increases or decreases the employment level of the resource? The answers to these questions are constructed from the analytical framework established in Chapters 7 and 9. In Chapter 7 we observed how changes occur in a firm's product output for one-unit changes in the quantities of its resource inputs. We related this *marginal physical product* of a resource to the quantity of it employed and we noted that, because of the law of diminishing returns, it declines as the quantity of the resource employed is increased. In Chapter 9 we found that a firm selling its output under conditions of pure competition sells as much or as little as it desires at a constant price—the market price—per unit, and that marginal revenue from a one-unit increase or decrease in sales is equal to that price. Putting these together, we see that a one-unit change in the employment level of a resource changes the firm's output by some certain amount—the marginal physical product of a resource. This change in the firm's output multiplied by the change in its total receipts per unit change in output—the marginal revenue—is the marginal revenue product of the resource. If we compute the marginal revenue product for each possible level of employment, we obtain a marginal revenue product schedule that slopes downward to the right.

Table 15–1 presents a marginal revenue product schedule for common labour in a hypothetical brick factory. The total daily outputs of bricks at different employment levels are given in columns (1) and (2). Marginal physical product of labour at different employment levels in column (3) is computed from the total product schedule. The price of bricks is assumed to be given at 25 cents each, so marginal revenue from the firm's sales will also be 25 cents. This is shown in column (4). The marginal revenue product schedule is found by multiplying the marginal physical product of labour at each level of employment by marginal revenue from the sale of bricks. For example, when the employment level is increased from three to four workers, marginal physical product is 110 bricks. Since each brick sells for 25 cents, the increase in the employment level increases the firm's total receipts by 110 times 25 cents, or by $27.50. Similarly, a further increase in the employment level to five workers would increase total receipts by another $25. When this is done for all levels of employment, we obtain the marginal revenue product schedule of column (5), which indicates at each level of employment how much a one-unit change in employment will change the firm's total receipts. The schedule is plotted as marginal revenue product curve MRP_1 in Figure 15–1.

Demand Schedules and Demand Curves

The firm's marginal revenue product schedule or curve for a resource is really its demand schedule or curve for the resource, although this may not be readily apparent. The demand schedule should show quantities of the resource that the firm will take at alternative prices, other things being equal. When the firm is a purely competitive purchaser of the resource, the marginal revenue product schedule shows just that.

What about the impact of changes in the employment level on costs? Suppose the price per unit of labour for the brick factory is $15. Since it purchases labour under conditions of pure competition, it can get all it wants at that price, so a one-unit change in the quantity of labour employed changes the firm's total costs by $15, an amount equal to the price. We call the change in total cost per unit change in the employment level the *marginal resource cost* of whatever resource we are considering. Thus the marginal resource cost of labour is $15 at all employment levels, as indicated in column (6) in Table 15–1.

We now have all the information we need to determine the firm's profit-maximizing level of employment. Referring to Table 15–1, we see that the employment of one unit rather than none increases total receipts by $35 ($MRP_1$) while it increases total costs by $15 ($MRC_1$). Thus $20 is added to the firm's profits by this move. We call the change in profit per unit change in the employment level the *marginal profit* from employment of the resource. A further increase in employment to two units per day yields a $17.50 increase in profits. Third, fourth, fifth, and sixth units per day also yield profit increases. But now, consider a move to the seven-unit

TABLE 15-1

Profit Maximization with Respect to Common Labour
in a Hypothetical Brick Factory[a]
(outputs and inputs are rates per day)

(1) QUANTITY OF LABOUR (L)	(2) TOTAL PRODUCT (X)	(3) MARGINAL PHYSICAL PRODUCT $\left(\frac{\Delta X}{\Delta L} = MPP_l\right)$	(4) MARGINAL REVENUE $\left(\frac{\Delta TR}{\Delta X} = MR_x\right)$	(5) MARGINAL REVENUE PRODUCT $(MPP_l \cdot MR_x = MRP_l)$	(6) MARGINAL RESOURCE COST $\left(\frac{\Delta TC}{\Delta L} = MRC_l\right)$	(7) MARGINAL PROFIT $\left(\frac{\Delta \pi}{\Delta L}\right)$
1	140	140	$0.25	$35.00	$15.00	$20.00
2	270	130	0.25	32.50	15.00	17.50
3	390	120	0.25	30.00	15.00	15.00
4	500	110	0.25	27.50	15.00	12.50
5	600	100	0.25	25.00	15.00	10.00
6	680	80	0.25	20.00	15.00	5.00
7	740	60	0.25	15.00	15.00	0.00
8	780	40	0.25	10.00	15.00	(−) 5.00
9	800	20	0.25	5.00	15.00	(−) 10.00
10	800	0	0.25	0.00	15.00	(−) 15.00

[a]Let X represent quantities of bricks and L quantities of common labour.

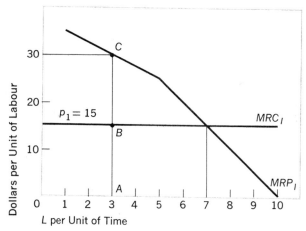

Figure 15-1
The profit-maximizing level of employment of a resource.

level of employment. It adds $15 to total receipts and the same amount
to total costs; therefore, it adds nothing to profits. Neither does it decrease them. However, pressing the employment level to eight units
causes profits to fall by $5. If profits increase up to the seven-unit level of
employment and fall with the eight-unit level, they must be maximum at
seven units, or where the *marginal revenue product of labour* (MRP_1) is

equal to the *marginal resource cost of labour* (MRC_1). Thus if the price of labour were $15, the brick factory would be in equilibrium—that is, would be maximizing its profits with respect to labour—by taking seven units of labour.[1] This price–quantity combination is one point on the firm's demand curve for labour.

The marginal revenue product column, column (5) in Table 15–1, also indicates the other quantities that the firm would take at alternative possible prices of labour. If the price (and marginal resource cost) were $30, the firm would employ three units per day. If it were $10, the firm would take eight units per day. Whatever the price of labour happens to be, profits are maximized with respect to it by adjusting the quantity employed to a point at which MRP_1 is equal to MRC_1. In other words, the marginal revenue product schedule is the firm's demand schedule for the resource.

All of the data for the preceding analysis can be presented graphically. In Figure 15–1, the MRP_1 curve is simply column (5) of Table 15–1 plotted against column (1). The MRC_1 line represents column (6). If the employment level were lest than seven units—say three units—marginal resource cost is AB, or $15; and the marginal profit of labour is BC, or $15. At the seven-unit employment level MRP_1 is equal to MRC_1 and marginal profit is zero; that is, profits have reached their maximum. At higher employment levels marginal profit is negative and total profit could be increased by decreasing the level of employment.

If we step back now and look at the firm's demand curve for a resource —that is, the marginal revenue product curve—we note that it slopes downward to the right because of the law of diminishing returns. Marginal revenue product is composed of two elements: (1) the marginal physical product of the resource and (2) the marginal revenue of the product being produced and sold. Letting MPP_a be the marginal physical product of resource A and MR_x be the marginal revenue from the sale of product X, we can define the marginal revenue product of A as

$$MRP_a = MPP_a \times MR_x.$$

The law of diminishing returns assures us that as the employment of A is increased, MPP_a will decline, causing MRP_a to decline also. (What happens to MR_x as the purely competitive seller of X increases its sales?) The downward slope of the resource demand curve indicates, too, that an increase in the price of a resource, other things being equal, will reduce the firm's level of employment of it.

[1]*Actually, with the discrete—as opposed to a continuous—set of quantity numbers used in Table 15–1, profits are maximum at the six- as well as at the seven-unit level of employment. It is more convenient and not incorrect to consider the $MRP_1 = MRC_1$ quantity, or the one as close to it as one can get, as the profit-maximizing quantity.*

Changes in Demand

Changes in a firm's demand curve for a resource may occur when "other things being equal" change. The three most important of these other things are (1) the quantities of those resources used by the firm that are related to the resource under consideration, (2) the marginal revenue from the product that the resource is used to produce, and (3) the techniques of production available to the firm. Let us examine the significance of each of these factors.

Quantities of Related Resources

The resources used by a firm in making a product may be related to one another in either of two ways. Some of them may be *complementary*— the more of one such resource used, the more productive those complementary to it will be. Other resources may be *substitutes*—the more of one that is used, the less productive the substitutes will be.

Consider, for example, the production of men's suits. Labour used in the production process is, in general, complementary to the capital comprising the plant in which production takes place. Given the work space, tables, thimbles, and needles, the quantity of labour can be varied, and a marginal physical product curve such as MPP_{1_1} in Figure 15–2(a) is determined. Given the price at which men's suits are sold, the marginal physical product at each level of employment can be multiplied by the marginal revenue (equals price) per suit, and the marginal revenue product curve, MRP_{1_1}, of Figure 15–2(b) is thus established. Now suppose that the amount of capital is increased through the addition of sewing machines. At each of the alternative employment levels the marginal physical product of labour will now be greater, shifting the curve to the right to MPP_{1_2}. This in turn shifts the marginal revenue product curve in Figure 15–2(b) to the right to MRP_{1_2}—that is, *an increase in the quantity of one of two complementary resources utilized will increase the demand for the other. A decrease in the quantity of one such resource will decrease the demand for the other.*

Consider another example, one that has now become history. In the 1920s and 1930s horses and tractors were substitute sources of power for farming operations. Given the tractor power available to a wheat farm, the marginal physical product curve for alternative numbers of horses can be determined. Then, given the price per bushel of wheat, the marginal revenue product curve of horses can be computed. Suppose now that the tractor power available increases. The marginal physical product of horses at each of the possible employment levels will now be less than before, or, as we usually put it, there is "less for horses to do now."

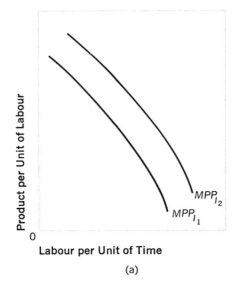

(a)

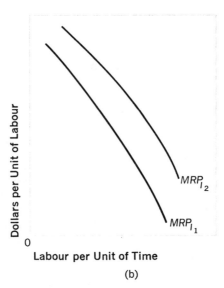

(b)

Figure 15-2
The effects on *MPP* and *MRP* of a resource of changes in quantities employed of
related resources.

The marginal revenue product curve for horses—that is, the demand
curve for them—will now have shifted to the left. (Can you show this
situation diagrammatically?) *An increase in the employment level of one of
two substitute resources will decrease the demand for the other. A decrease
in the employment level of one will increase the demand for the other.*

Changes in Marginal Revenue

Anything that changes the price or marginal revenue that a firm receives from the sale of the product it produces will change the firm's demand curve for any resource that it uses. Price and marginal revenue changes come from changes in the conditions of market supply of and demand for the product. The latter were discussed in Chapters 4 and 9.

Table 15–2 illustrates the effects of changes in the firm's marginal revenue on its demand for a resource. Suppose that columns (1) and (2) represent the marginal physical product schedule of 100-pound bags of fertilizer on a wheat farm. The price of wheat and the marginal revenue from its sale are given in column (3) as $2 per bushel. The resulting marginal revenue product schedule, or the demand schedule for fertilizer, is given in column (4). Now suppose that in the economy the demand for wheat increases, raising the price to $3 per bushel, as indicated in column (3a). The marginal revenue product schedule or the demand schedule for fertilizer becomes that of column (4a). *An increase in the marginal revenue received from the sale of its output will increase a firm's demand for the resources that it uses.* A decrease in marginal revenue will have the opposite effect.

TABLE 15–2
Effects of Alternative Marginal Revenue
Levels for Wheat on the Demand for Fertilizer[a]

(1) FERTILIZER (F IN 100-LB. SACKS) $\left(\frac{\Delta W}{\Delta F} = MPP_f\right)$	(2) MARGINAL PHYSICAL PRODUCT	(3) MARGINAL REVENUE $(MR_w = P_w)$	(4) MARGINAL REVENUE PRODUCT $(MRP_f = MPP_f \cdot MR_w)$	(3a) MARGINAL REVENUE (MR_w)	(4a) MARGINAL REVENUE PRODUCT $(MRP_f = MPP_f \cdot MR_w)$
1	15	$2.00	$30.00	$3.00	$45.00
2	14	2.00	28.00	3.00	42.00
3	13	2.00	26.00	3.00	39.00
4	12	2.00	24.00	3.00	36.00
5	11	2.00	22.00	3.00	33.00
6	9.5	2.00	19.00	3.00	28.50
7	7.5	2.00	15.00	3.00	22.50
8	5.5	2.00	11.00	3.00	16.50
9	3	2.00	6.00	3.00	9.00
10	0	2.00	0.00	3.00	0.00

[a]Let F represent quantities of fertilizer in 100-pound sacks and W quantities of wheat in bushels.

Changes in Technology

Demands for resources are affected by changes in the technology used by a firm. Technological improvements will increase the demand for some resources while for others demand will fall as new technology makes them obsolete.

Many examples exist of increased demand for resources generated by technological changes. How have improvements in automobile technology affected General Motors' demand for steel? What impact has the development of atomic energy plants had on the demand for uranium? How has the advent of computers affected the demand for keypunch machines?

Similarly, an abundance of examples can be found in which new technology has decreased the demand for certain resources. Physicians and traveling salesmen no longer demand horses and buggies. Cigar rolling machines decreased the demand for human cigar rollers (but increased the demand for machine tenders). The development of television teaching techniques may reduce the demand for instructors in economics.

Market Demand Curves

Now that we understand individual firm demand curves for a resource, how do we move on to the total market demand curve? We can learn a lesson here from Chapter 5. The construction of the market demand curve for a resource from individual firm demand curves is similar to the construction of the market demand curve for a product from those of individual consumers.

In Figure 15–3, suppose that firm I and firm II are two of the many firms using some certain resource A. At a price of p_a, firm I wants quantity a and firm II wants quantity a'. Quantities desired by other firms at that price are similarly determined, and the sum of all of these quantities will be the market quantity A. Quantity A at price p_a is one point on the market demand curve, the point labelled H in the market diagram. Similarly, at a price of p_{a_0}, firm I would take a_0; firm II would take a'_0; and other firms would also take those quantities at which their MRP_a curves are equal to p_{a_0}. Together, firms will take quantity A_0, which, when plotted against the price, locates point J in the market diagram. The quantities that will be taken by all firms at other price levels can be determined in this way and they trace out the market demand curve D_aD_a. Thus the market demand curve is found by summing at each possible price level the quantities that individual firms will take.

The firms using resource A need not at all be in the same industry, and, as a matter of fact, probably will not be. Any given resource is likely to be used in making a number of different products. Common labour, for example, is used in the making of almost all goods and services. Thus in Figure 15–3, firm I may very well be producing one product while firm II produces another. Each has its own demand curve for A, and these can be used to construct the market demand curve, or the quantities that all firms together will take at different possible price levels.

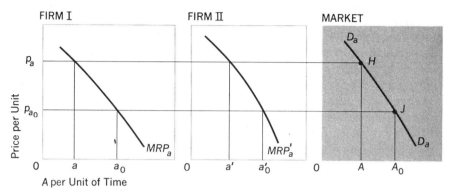

Figure 15-3
Construction of market demand for a resource.

Supply of a Resource

Turning now to the supply side of the picture, we need to discover what determines the market supply of any given resource. First, we must determine who resource owners are, and these include a wide variety of persons and institutions. Labour resources are owned and placed in employment by almost every family in the economy. Government units own some resources, or at least control the services of them; electricity sold to businesses by a municipally owned power plant is a case in point. The outputs of some firms, for example, those in the basic steel industry, are resource inputs to others. Even churches may own land and buildings that they rent out to others to be used in production processes.

Individual resource owners have their own individual supply curves for whatever it is that they own. The shape of one such curve depends upon the response that the owner would make to alternative price offers. Owners of a given kind of labour may be willing to work more hours per day at good wage rates than at lower wage rates; for example, desire for a higher salary may well induce a professor to spend nights in his office in hopes that he can improve his publication record and earn more money. At higher wage rates leisure time is made more expensive and people may thus be willing to do with less of it. Business enterprises, the outputs of which are resource inputs for other firms, are motivated by higher prices to expand the quantities they place on the market because they can make more profits by doing so.[2] In general, then, we expect the supply curves of individual suppliers of resources to slope upward to the right; that is,

[2]*See Chapters 9, 10, and 11.*

more of a resource will be placed on the market at higher prices than at lower prices.[3]

What about market supply curves? We construct them from the supply curves of individual owners in the same manner as we construct market demand curves. In Figure 15–4, if the price of resource A were p_a, owner I would place quantity a on the market; owner II would place a' on the market; other owners would do likewise, and the total quantity forthcoming at that price would be A. Point L on the market supply curve would thus be determined. By similar additions of quantities at other prices, other points tracing out the supply curve S_aS_a are found. Since supply curves of individual owners generally slope upward to the right, we expect market supply curves to do so too.

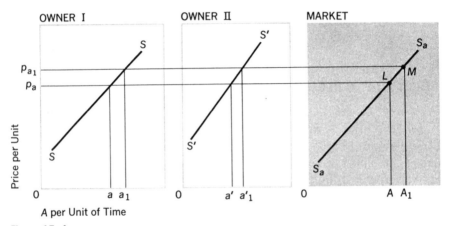

Figure 15–4
Construction of market supply of a resource.

At higher price levels more resource owners may be pulled into the market for any given resource. A workman may have talents as a carpenter, as a bricklayer, and as a plumber, and his choice of trade will depend upon the comparative earning possibilities in the three. If there are a number of workers with several such arrows for their bows, a relative increase in carpenters' wages will draw additional workers into that occupation, whereas a relative decrease will cause workers to choose one of the other occupations.

---

[3]*Sometimes the opposite seems to occur. A man may "moonlight" because his primary employment pays too little to provide the consumption level desired by him and his family.*

Resource Pricing and Employment

The remaining problem of how the price and employment levels of a resource are determined in a purely competitive market is a familiar one. When we bring market demand and market supply together, the pricing problem is identical to the one we met in Chapter 4. We shall add to it a discussion of a persistent problem that recurs in our economy—the use of minimum pricing in an attempt to secure greater equity in income distribution.

The Equilibrium Price and Employment Level

Suppose in Figure 15–5 that the market demand and supply curves for common labour are D_1D_1 and S_1S_1, respectively, and that MRP_1 is the demand curve of one of the many firms that employ this resource. Although the vertical scales of the two diagrams are identical, the quantity scale of the market diagram is greatly compressed as compared with that of the firm.

The equilibrium price or wage is p_1. It is determined by the forces of demand and supply in the same fashion as any other price is determined under conditions of pure competition. If the wage rate were above p_1, surpluses or unemployment of some units of labour would occur and, in the interest of obtaining employment, some workers would shade their asking prices, moving the wage rate downward toward p_1. If the wage rate were below p_1, the labour market would be plagued by shortages. Em-

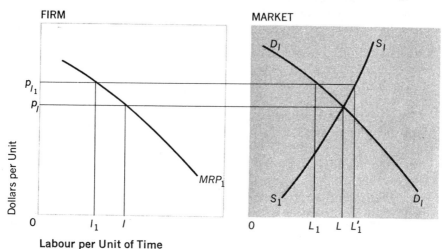

Figure 15-5
Resource pricing and employment.

ployers would bid against each other for the available supply, driving the wage rate toward p_1. The quantity of labour that employers want to employ is equal to the quantity of labour desiring employment at wage rate p_1.

The equilibrium employment level is L units of labour for the market as a whole. For any one firm using the resource, the employment level is some quantity at which the marginal revenue product of the resource is equal to its marginal resource cost; that is, the firm employs the quantity of the resource that maximizes its profits. The quantity L in the market diagram is the sum of such quantities as l for the individual firm at wage rate p_1.

Minimum Prices

Many people expect that firms will employ as much of a given resource at higher prices as they will at lower prices. Indeed, there is wide support for laws or policies that establish minimum prices for certain resources, and the advocates of such measures insist that there will be no adverse effects on employment levels. Cases in point are minimum wage laws and legislative and other government support of labour union activities in the wage-setting sphere. In certain imperfectly competitive markets, which we shall discuss in the next chapter, these advocates may be correct; but in competitive markets, a minimum price that is effective—that is, that lies above the equilibrium level—will result in unemployment.

Suppose in Figure 15–5 that a minimum wage level is set at p_{11} either through collective bargaining between unions and employers or by means of a minimum wage law. The individual firm pictured there will reduce this employment level from l to l_1 units of labour. Other firms in the market for this kind of labour will do the same thing, and altogether the market level of employment will be reduced from L to L_1. But at the higher wage level more labour units are placed on the market and unemployment is measured by $L_1 L_1'$.

That unemployment is the ordinary consequence of minimum price fixing in competitive markets should elicit no surprise. Given the price it must pay for a resource, an individual firm maximizes its profits by adjusting the quantity of the resource taken to that level at which its marginal revenue product is equal to its marginal resource cost (and price). The higher the price, the smaller the profit-maximizing quantity. In Figure 15–5, if the firm were taking quantity l at price p_{11}, it could increase its profits by reducing employment toward l_1. Each one-unit reduction in the employment level would reduce total costs more than it would reduce total receipts until employment level l_1 is reached.

Have Canadian minimum wage laws brought on large-scale unemployment of labour? The answer to this question is clearly negative. Although there may have been unemployment effects in certain low-paying areas of the economy—logging, sawmilling, the garment industry, the canning or processing of fish, and the like—the numbers involved have not been large. But this in no way negates analysis of this section. By and large minimum wages have not been effective in any significant proportion of the economy. Until the early 1960's minimum wage rates in Ontario, Nova Scotia, New Brunswick and Prince Edward Island applied only to women workers, or to industries where most of the workers were women. In Newfoundland, Alberta and British Columbia there were separate regulations for men and women and lower rates were set for women. Only Manitoba, Quebec and Saskatchewan provided the same minimum scale for both sexes. Also deserving of mention is the fact that federal "fair" wage legislation applies only to about 5 percent of Canada's paid labour force. More important, demand for labour has increased greatly since the 1930's, pressing most equilibrium wage levels well above the minima established by the various laws, thus leaving the minimum levels largely ineffective.

The Value of a Resource

A question frequently raised by resource owners concerned with whether their incomes are as high as they ought to be is what the resources they place in employment are really worth. We should push the question one step further and ask what their resources are worth *to whom*. In economic analysis we distinguish between (1) the value of a resource to the firm that employs it and (2) the value of the resource to society.

To the Firm

How can we measure the value of units of a given resource to any one firm that employs them? Actually, we have solved this problem already. A unit of a resource is worth to the firm what it adds to the firm's total receipts—its marginal revenue product. This is why the firm will expand the employment level of the resource if the marginal revenue product of the resource exceeds its marginal resource cost; that is, if the resource is worth more to the firm than it costs. This is also why the firm will contract the employment level of the resource if the marginal revenue product of the resource is less than its marginal resource cost; that is, if the resource is not worth what it costs. In order to maximize profits the firm adjusts employment to that level at which the resource is just worth its marginal resource cost, or to the level at which marginal revenue product equals marginal resource cost. Thus, in general, in competitive markets resource units are worth to the firm just about what they are paid.

To Society

Although the value of a unit of any given resource to society as a whole is the same in dollar terms as it is to the firm where resource markets are competitive, its measurement is different, conceptually. Suppose we add one unit of common labour that had previously been unemployed to a firm's level of employment of that resource. The firm *and* society gain a certain amount of product—the MPP_1. If X is the product being produced, then $MPP_1 \cdot MR_x$ represents the *marginal revenue product*, or the worth to the firm of the increase in employment. Note carefully that this is marginal physical product of the resource multiplied by the *marginal revenue* to the firm of the increment in product output and sales. The value placed by society on the extra product produced is measured by the price, p_x, that society is willing to pay for each unit of product. Thus the worth of a unit of labour to society is measured by $MPP_1 \cdot p_x$, or the marginal physical product of the resource multiplied by the *price* of the product. This measure of the value of a unit of resource to society is appropriately called the *value of marginal product of the resource*, or in this case, VMP_1. To repeat, the value of a unit of any given resource to the firm is the marginal revenue product of the resource, while its value to society is its value of marginal product.

The marginal revenue products of a resource and its value of marginal product will not always be identical. Only where the resource users sell in competitive product markets are they the same. This statement can be easily understood with the following symbolic definitions:

$$MRP_1 = MPP_1 \cdot MR_x$$
$$VMP_1 = MPP_1 \cdot p_x.$$

A one-unit change in the employment level of labour or any other resource will change product output by MPP_1, but only in purely competitive selling markets will MR_x and p_x be the same. What if the firm were selling its product under conditions of pure monopoly?

Combinations of Variable Resources

The analysis of resource pricing and employment contained in the preceding sections enables us now to round out the discussion, introduced in Chapter 7, of least-cost combinations of variable resources used by a firm. Two points can be readily demonstrated. First, when a firm using two or more variable resources is using the profit-maximizing quantity of each, it is also using them in least-cost proportions. Second, when the profit-maximizing quantity of each variable resource is employed, the firm is producing the profit-maximizing quantity of output.

Suppose that a firm uses two variable resources, A and B, to produce product X. The profit-maximizing employment level of A is that quantity at which the marginal revenue product of A is equal to its marginal resource cost. For a firm that buys resource A under conditions of pure competition, marginal resource cost and the price of the resource are the same. All of these statements are equally valid for resource B. Consequently, we can express th profit-maximizing conditions for the employment of A and B as follows:

$$MPP_a \cdot MR_x = MRC_a = P_a \qquad (15.1)$$

and

$$MPP_b \cdot MR_x = MRC_b = P_b. \qquad (15.2)$$

Least-Cost Combinations

Equations 15.1 and 15.2 look differently from the least-cost conditions expressed in Chapter 7, but appearances are sometimes deceiving. Dividing through equation 15.1 by MR_x and p_a, and dividing through equation 15.2 by MR_x and p_b, we obtain the following statements:

$$\frac{MPP_a}{p_a} = \frac{1}{MR_x} \qquad (15.3)$$

and

$$\frac{MPP_b}{p_b} = \frac{1}{MR_x}. \qquad (15.4)$$

It now becomes apparent that since both $(MPP_a)/(p_a)$ and $(MPP_b)/(p_b)$ are equal to $1/(MR_x)$, they are also equal to each other; thus we can write

$$\frac{MPP_a}{p_a} = \frac{MPP_b}{p_b} = \frac{1}{MR_x} \qquad (15.5)$$

or, for our present purposes, simply

$$\frac{MPP_a}{p_a} = \frac{MPP_b}{p_b}. \qquad (15.5a)$$

Equation 15.5a is, of course, the familiar statement of the conditions that must be met if resources are to be used in a least-cost combination. The last dollar spent on resource A must yield the same increment in the total output of the firm as the last dollar spent on resource B.

The Profit-Maximizing Product Output

We learned in Chapters 9 and 10 that a firm maximizes its profits by producing the product output at which its marginal cost is equal to its marginal revenue. We can state these conditions as

$$MC_x = MR_x. \tag{15.6}$$

Suppose now that we work with equation 15.5. If we invert each term we have

$$\frac{p_a}{MPP_a} = \frac{p_b}{MPP_b} = MR_x. \tag{15.7}$$

If we can show that $(p_a)/(MPP_a)$ and $(p_b)/(MPP_b)$ are each the same thing as MC_x—that is, the marginal cost of producing product X—we are home. We will have shown that employment of the profit-maximizing quantity of each variable resource results in the profit-maximizing product output for the firm.

Consider now a one-unit increment in the employment of resource A. It adds an amount to the total cost of the firm equal to its price, or p_a. It contributes an addition to the firm's output of MPP_a. Thus the expression $(p_a)/(MPP_a)$ means the increase in the firm's total cost per unit increase in its output of product, and this is nothing more nor less than the marginal cost, or MC_x, at whatever output level the firm is producing. Similarly, $(p_b)/(MPP_b)$ also defines MC_x. Therefore,

$$\frac{p_a}{MPP_a} = \frac{p_b}{MPP_b} = MC_x = MR_x. \tag{15.8}$$

In order to maximize its profits a purely competitive firm must employ those quantities of variable resources at which their marginal revenue products are equal to their respective prices, and this in turn means that the firm will be using a least-cost combination of resources and that the marginal cost of its output is equal to marginal revenue.

Summary

The principles governing profit maximization by a firm with respect to its purchases of resources are no different fundamentally from those we studied with respect to a firm's sales of product. If a one-unit increase in the firm's employment level of a resource adds more to total receipts than to total costs, it pays to make the increase. If a one-unit decrease in the employment level decreases total costs more than it decreases total receipts, then the move adds to profits. Profits are maximized at that employment level at which a one-unit change in the quantity of a resource used has the same effects on total costs and total receipts.

A firm's demand curve for a resource is the same thing as its marginal revenue product curve for the resource. Marginal revenue product is defined as the change in the firm's total receipts per unit change in the employment level of the resource. It is found by multiplying the marginal physical product of the resource at each possible employment level by the marginal revenue from the firm's sales of product at the corresponding output levels; that is, for a given resource A used in making product X.

$$MRP_a = MPP_a : MR_x$$

Profits are maximized with respect to resource A when the employment level is such that its marginal revenue product is equal to its marginal resource cost. Marginal resource cost is defined as the change in the firm's total costs per unit change in its employment level of the resource. For the purely competitive purchaser of the resource, marginal resource cost is the same as the resource price. Thus for profit maximization by the firm,

$$MRP_a = MRC_a = p_a.$$

Changes in the firm's demand curve for the resource occur when there are changes in one of the "other things being equal." These are (1) the quantities of related resources used, (2) the marginal revenue from the products that the resource is used to produce, and (3) the techniques of production used by the firm.

The forces of market demand and supply determine the equilibrium price of a resource under competitive conditions. Market demand is found by summing the quantities that all firms will take at alternative prices, the horizontal summation of the marginal revenue product curves. Market supply indicates what all owners of the resource are collectively willing to place on the market at each alternative price. The equilibrium price is that price at which users of the resource are willing to take the quantity that suppliers are willing to place on the market.

The normal downward slope of the demand curve for a resource means that firms are willing, generally, to employ more of the resource at lower prices than at higher prices. Consequently, if minimum prices are set above equilibrium levels, the result will be unemployment for some units of the resource. We distinguish between the value of a resource to the firm that uses it and its value to society as a whole. The value of a unit of any given resource to the firm that uses it is measured by the marginal revenue product of the resource, or marginal physical product of the resource multiplied by the marginal revenue from the sale of that product. Its value to society is measured by the value of the marginal product of the resource, or its marginal physical product multiplied by the price paid by consumers for that product. These values are the same when the firms using resources buy and sell as pure competitors; but, as we shall see in the next chapter, they differ where there is monopoly in the sale of products.

When a firm uses several variable resources to produce a product it would be expected to use the profit-maximizing quantity of each, under ordinary circumstances. This would mean that the firm would also use the least-cost combination of those resources. It means, too, that the firm will be producing the profit-maximizing level of output.

Exercises and Questions for Discussion

1. Minimum wage laws are probably the least effective of the many means available of redistributing income as we desire to have it redistributed. Discuss this statement.
2. "The coming of the computer age will cause human employment to decline rapidly as men are replaced by machines." Evaluate this statement critically.
3. In a competitive society could there be individuals who are being paid less than they are worth? Why or why not?
4. "If labour unions succeed in getting wages raised, the result will be higher incomes for those employed." Is this statement true? What additional statement could be made?
5. If a firm is using a least-cost combination of resources, is it automatically using those amounts of resources that will maximize its profits? Explain.

Selected Readings

Carter, Allan M., *Theory of Wages and Employment*. Homewood, Ill.: Richard D. Irwin, Inc., 1959, Chaps. 2-5.

Chamberlain, Neil W., *The Labor Sector*. New York: McGraw-Hill Book Company, Inc., 1965, Chaps 17 and 18.

Friedman, Milton, "Minimum Wage Rates," *Newsweek*, September 26, 1966.

Hicks, John R., *The Theory of Wages*, 2d American ed. New York: St. Martins Press, 1963, Chaps. 1 and 5.

Woods, H. D. and Sylvia Ostry, *Labour Policy and Labour Economics in Canada*. Toronto: Macmillan Company of Canada, 1962, Chaps. 14, 15, 16, and 17.

16

Resource Pricing and Employment in Monopolistic and Monopsonistic Markets

Although purely competitive markets provide a convenient base on which the principles of resource pricing and employment can be constructed, as we look around us we find that many, if not most, markets are of different types. In the sale of automobiles and television sets we know that the selling markets are oligopolistic. The telephone company sells as a monopolist. On the buying side, too, many markets are not purely competitive. For example, are there enough buyers of the services of hockey players or of professional actors so that no one buyer can influence the purchase prices? Clearly the answer is no. Just as sellers in many product markets exercise some degree of monopoly power, buyers in many resource markets also exercise some degree of monopsony power, or monopoly in buying. We must take both sets of forces into account and as we do so we must draw a clear distinction between the selling side and the buying side of markets.

The Effects of Monopoly in Selling

We use the term "monopoly" in a broader sense in this chapter than we did in Chapter 10. For present purposes it is not necessary that we distinguish pure monopoly from oligopoly and from monopolistic competition, so "monopoly" will be used to cover all three of these types of markets. The important implication of the term is that the seller of a good or service faces a downward-sloping demand curve for whatever he sells, with the result that the marginal revenue curve for his sales lies below the demand curve.

We shall continue to suppose in this section that pure competition prevails in the buying of resources; in other words, that there are enough buyers of any given resource and that each takes a small enough proportion of the total supply available to prevent one firm through its own actions from influencing the price. Pure competition in resource purchasing means exactly the same thing here as it did in Chapter 15. By proceeding in this manner we can isolate the effects of monopoly in product sales on resource pricing and employment.

Demand for a Resource

What determines the demand curve of a monopolistic seller for a resource that the firm purchases under conditions of pure competition? It seems reasonable to expect that the marginal revenue product curve for the resource is the firm's demand curve, just as it is in the case of a purely competitive seller. This is indeed so, but because of monopoly in the product market, the construction of the curve is somewhat more complex.

Marginal Revenue Product

Suppose that the Ford Motor Company wants to find its demand curve for machinists. The first step is to increase or decrease the level of employment by one-unit changes and to record the consequent changes in the firm's output. The result is a marginal physical product schedule or curve like that of Figure 16–1(b).

Given the quantities of other resources used by the firm, each employment level of machinists will correspond to a specific level of product output. Measuring product output along the X-axis in Figure 16–1(a), suppose that employment level m_1 yields an output level X_1; employment level m_2 yields an output level X_2; and so on. There will not be, of course, a one-to-one correspondence between the employment level of machinists and the output of automobiles because of the operation of the law of diminishing returns. Equal increases in the input of machinists' labour will eventually yield smaller and smaller increments in the output of automobiles.

The marginal revenue product of machinists or of any resource was defined in the last chapter as the change in the firm's total receipts per unit change in its level of employment of that resource. At any given employment level the marginal revenue product is found by multiplying the marginal physical product of the resource by the marginal revenue at the corresponding level of product output. With reference to Figure 16–1, when m_1 units of machinists are employed, the marginal physical product of machinists is E_1 automobiles.[1] At output level X_1 for automobiles, marginal revenue is R_1. Thus marginal revenue product of machinists at employment level m_1 is found by multiplying E_1 automobiles—the change in output from increasing employment from one less than m_1 to m_1—by R_1.

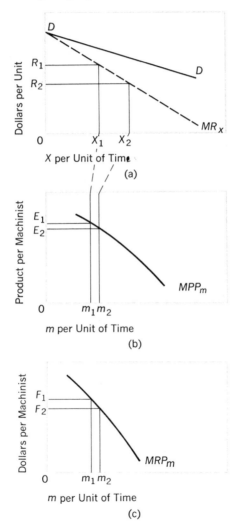

Figure 16–1
A monopolistic seller's demand curve for a resource.

[1]*This may well be only a fraction of an automobile.*

The result is recorded as F_1 in Figure 16–1 (c). Similarly, at employment level m_2, we find F_2 by multiplying E_2 by R_2.

The marginal revenue product curve for machinists is a downward-sloping curve, meaning that the greater the level of employment of machinists, given the quantities of other resources used, the smaller will be the increase in the firm's total receipts per one-unit increase in the employment level. This downward slope occurs for two reasons. First, because of the law of diminishing returns the marginal physical product of machinists decreases as the quantity employed increases. Second, as the output of automobiles increases with increases in the employment level of machinists, marginal revenue from the sale of automobiles declines.

The Firm's Demand Curve

The marginal revenue product curve is the firm's demand curve for the resource, since it shows the quantities of the resource that the firm will take at alternative possible prices. Like the purely competitive seller, the monopolistic seller will maximize profits with respect to any specific resource by employing that quantity of the resource at which its marginal revenue product is equal to its marginal resource cost. Since the monopolistic seller in this case is assumed to be a pure competitor in the pur-

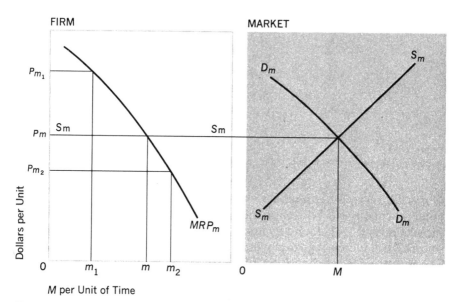

Figure 16–2
Equilibrium price and employment level of a resource.

chase of the resource, he cannot influence resource price, and marginal resource cost is therefore the same as the price. In Figure 16–2, if the wage rate or price of machinists were p_{m1}, the firm would maximize profits by employing quantity m_1. If the wage rate were p_{m2}, the profit-maximizing level of employment would be m_2.

Pricing and Employment

The determination of the equilibrium price and employment level of a resource, where its buyer exercises monopoly in *product selling* but is a pure competitor in *resource buying*, is no different from that of the thoroughgoing purely competitive case of the last chapter. In Figure 16–2, the market demand curve, D_mD_m, is found by summing horizontally the MRP_m curves of the firms that use machinists—that is, at each alternative price level the quantities taken by each of the firms are added to find the corresponding total market quantities. The market supply curve, S_mS_m indicates the quantities of machinists' labour that would be placed on the market at alternative wage or resource price levels. The equilibrium price is p_m. At this price any one firm maximizes profits at an employment level such as m. The market level of employment is M.

Monopolistic Exploitation

Monopolistic sellers of product are said to *exploit* resources that they employ, which implies that resource units are worth more than they are paid. Again we must ask, Worth more to whom? The terms *value of marginal product*, introduced in Chapter 15, and *marginal revenue product*, as we have used it in both Chapter 15 and in this one, are the key concepts for discussing the issue. It should be clear by now that the marginal revenue product of a resource is the measure of its worth to the firm that employs it and that firms operating as purely competitive buyers adjust the quantity employed so that the marginal revenue product is equal to the marginal resource cost and to the resource price. Units of the resource are paid what they are worth to the firm.[2]

The value of marginal product of the resource measures the worth of any one unit of it to society and, where firms are monopolistic sellers of the product, it will differ from the marginal revenue product. The difference is illustrated in Figure 16–3, which builds on Figure 16–1. Suppose now that the firm employs m_1 units of machinists' services and that the product output corresponding to this level of employment is X_1. Marginal

---

[2]*Note that what they are worth to the firm, marginal revenue product, is brought into line with the market price of the resource by the adjustments in the quantity employed.*

physical product is E_1. To the firm the resource is worth E_1 times R_1, or marginal revenue product F_1—that is, what it will add to the firm's total receipts. Society values the resource at E_1 times p_{x1}, or by the value of its marginal product, V_1. In general, at any specific level of employment of a given resource A used in making some product X, the marginal physical product of the resource and, consequently, any one unit of the

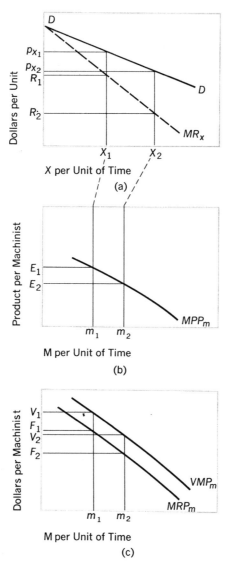

Figure 16–3
The difference between marginal revenue product and value of marginal product.

resource, is worth to the firm what it will add to the firm's total receipts; that is,

$$MRP_a = MPP_a \cdot MR_x.$$

The value of a unit of the resource to society is whatever society is willing to pay for the marginal physical product of it; that is,

$$VMP_a = MPP_a \cdot p_x.$$

Where product sellers are monopolistic, product price is greater than marginal revenue from it; therefore the value of marginal product exceeds marginal revenue product. This situation is shown at all levels of employment in Figure 16–3(c).

Monopolistic exploitation of a resource is the difference between what a unit of the resource is worth to society as a whole and its marginal resource cost when this difference results from monopoly in the sale of the product. In Figure 16–4, suppose that the equilibrium price for machinists is p_m. The profit-maximizing employment level is m; however, the value of any one unit to society is v_m. Exploitation amounts to $p_m v_m$ per unit of machinists' services. If exploitation is to be avoided, the employment level should be m', but if the firm is to increase employment from m to m', more will be added to the firm's total costs than to its total revenues and profits will fall. Exploitation is not a malicious act on the part of the firm; it is simply the natural consequence of monopoly in selling.

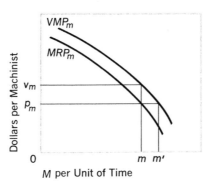

Figure 16–4
Monopolistic exploitation of a resource.

Monopolistic Restriction of Employment

Suppose now that among the many users of a specific kind of resource some sell their product outputs monopolistically and others sell competitively. The monopolistic sellers will restrict their individual levels of employment below that which is economically desirable, while at the same time the competitive sellers will employ too much.

We shall use a construction company to illustrate a monopolistic seller of product and a farm operation to illustrate a competitive seller. Both use common labour to produce their products. There are, of course, many other users of common labour, but we are concerned here only with these two. The appropriate diagrams are given in Figure 16–5. At the equilibrium price p_1 for labour, the construction firm will employ l_c workers while the farm employs l_t.

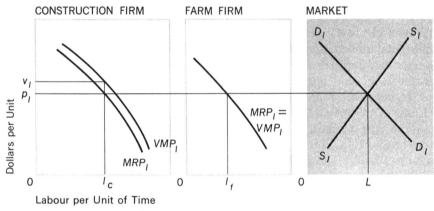

CONSTRUCTION FIRM   FARM FIRM   MARKET

Figure 16–5
Monopolistic restriction of employment.

How do we know that, from the point of view of consumers, the construction firm's employment level is too small while that of the farm is too large? How much value do consumers attach to a unit of labour employed in construction? How much worth do they ascribe to a unit of labour used on the farm? The answers are provided by the value of marginal product of labour in each of its uses. In the construction operation the value of marginal product is v_1 while on the farm it is only p_1. The greater value that society places on a unit of labour used in construction indicates the desirability to society of expanding employment in construction while contracting it in farming. The market provides no incentives for this to take place. Each firm is employing precisely the quantity of the labour resource that it desires to employ. Each is maximizing profits with respect to the employment of labour. This is what we mean when we say that monopolistic sellers of product restrict the employment of the resources that they use below that which society considers desirable.

The Effects of Monopsony in Buying

Monopsony in buying is a market situation that we have not yet met. We have assumed heretofore that pure competition among buyers exists —that no one buyer of anything takes a large enough proportion of the total supply to be able to influence the price. *Monopsony*, on the other hand, implies that an individual buyer does take a large enough part of the total supply to exercise an influence on the price. Essentially it is in buying what monopoly is in selling.

The Firm's View of Supply

Suppose that General Motors uses large quantities of a unique kind of bearing in the manufacture of its automobiles that none of the other manufacturers uses. Specifications for the bearing have been given to a number of machine shops in the Windsor area and these constitute General Motors' source of supply. How does the supply curve for bearings appear to the company? What will be the pattern of its marginal resource cost?

The Supply Curve Facing the Firm

Because it is the only purchaser of the bearings, General Motors faces the market supply curve for them. The machine shops producing and selling bearings would be willing to place more on the market at higher prices than at lower prices, so we would expect the supply curve to be upward-sloping to the right.[3] This is the distinquishing feature of monopsony in resource buying.

As an illustration of the difference between pure competition and monopsony in resource buying, consider Figure 16–2. The firm in that diagram is a purely competitive buyer of machinists' labour and as such faces the horizontal supply curve $S_m S_m$ at the going market price p_m. But now suppose that only one firm in the economy has a need for machinists. The firm would face the market supply curve $S_m S_m$ and the price that must be paid for machinists' labour would depend upon the quantity per unit of time that it desires to employ.

Marginal Resource Cost

The fact that the monopsonistic buyer faces a nonhorizontal supply curve has important implications for the marginal resource cost to the

---

[3]*The bearing supply curve is, of course, the output supply curve of all the machine shops together, and as such it is determined in the same way as any other output or product supply curve (see pp. 172, 173).*

firm of the resource so purchased. In the usual case, in which the buyer sees an upward-sloping supply curve, marginal resource cost will be greater than the resource price rather than equal to it. Why is this so?

Suppose that the supply situation for bearings purchased by General Motors is that of Table 16–1. Columns (1) and (2) comprise the supply

TABLE 16–1
Hypothetical Supply Situation for Bearings for General Motors Corporation

(1) QUANTITY (A)	(2) PRICE (p_a)	(3) TOTAL COST (TC_a)	(4) MARGINAL RESOURCE COST (MRC_a)
200	$1.00	$200.00	
201	1.00	201.00	$1.00
202	1.01	204.02	3.02
203	1.02	207.06	3.04
204	1.03	210.12	3.06

schedule. For any given quantity purchased, the total cost in column (3) is found by multiplying quantity purchased by the price necessary to obtain that quantity. Marginal resource cost, listed in column (4), is found at any given level of employment by reducing the level of employment one unit and observing the resulting change in total costs. Where higher resource prices are necessary to draw out larger quantities supplied of the resource, simple arithmetic demonstrates that marginal resource cost exceeds resource price.

This unique relation occurs because the resource supply schedule or curve is really the average cost schedule or curve of the resource to the firm. The marginal resource cost curve bears the same relation to the average resource cost curve as any marginal curve bears to its average curve.[4] If the supply schedule of Table 16–1 were plotted, it would be horizontal from 200 to 201 bearings. Note that for the increase in quantity purchased the marginal resource cost and the price of bearings are the same. But for an increase in the quantity purchased per unit of time from 201 to 202, the price must rise to $1.01 per bearing. The additional bearing costs the firm $1.01. Each of the other 201 bearings that had previously cost $1.00 each now cost $1.01, thus adding $2.01 more to the firm's total costs. The entire change in total costs to the firm from the one-unit increase in the employment level of bearings is $1.01 plus $2.01, or $3.02. Similarly, if the level of employment is raised from 202 to 203 bearings,

---

[4]*Compare the relation between average revenue and marginal revenue (see p. 192) and average cost and marginal cost (see pp. 152-154).*

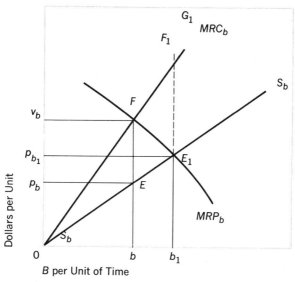

Figure 16–6
Monopsony pricing and employment of a resource.

the extra bearing by itself costs $1.02. The other 202 now cost $1.02 rather than $1.01 each, so the additional cost of all of these together is $2.02. Thus the marginal resource cost becomes $3.04. (You should be able to compute the marginal resource cost of bearings at the 204-bearing employment level.)

A representative marginal resource cost curve, MRC_b, for bearings is drawn in Figure 16–6 in proper relation to the supply curve, S_bS_b, in that diagram. If the level of purchase or employment were b, the marginal resource cost would be bF and the price would be bE. At a purchase level of b_1, the marginal resource cost would be b_1F_1 and the price would be b_1E_1.

Resource Pricing and Employment

The Profit-Maximizing Price and Employment Level

What are the effects of monopsony on the price and employment level of a resource? Suppose in Figure 16–6 that the marginal revenue product curve of this particular kind of bearings is MRP_b.[5] The profit-maximizing level of utilization by General Motors must be that at which the marginal revenue product is equal to the marginal resource cost. The appropriate

[5]*Other kinds of bearings may be substitutes for it.*

level of utilization is b, at which marginal revenue product and marginal resource cost are both at F. At a lower level of employment marginal revenue product exceeds marginal resource cost and an expansion of employment to b will increase profits. If employment is expanded beyond b, the additions to the firm's total receipts are smaller than the additions to its total costs and profits will contract. The equilibrium price of the resource is p_b even though marginal revenue product is v_b. Price p_b is all that is necessary to attract the machine shops into supplying b bearings per unit of time.

Monopsonistic Exploitation

Monopsony in the purchase of resources, like monopoly in the sale of products, causes units of the resource to be exploited. We define *monopsonistic exploitation* of a resource as the difference between what the resource is worth to the firm and what is paid for the resource when this difference is brought about by monopsony in its purchase. In Figure 16–6, when General Motors is buying b bearings per unit of time the marginal revenue product of a bearing is v_b. The price paid is p_b per bearing, so exploitation amounts to $p_b v_b$ for each one purchased.

Monopsonistic exploitation does not arise from any malicious act on the part of the monopsonist. The monopsonist, like any other business firm, including the pure competitor, is simply trying to maximize his profits and he does this at the level of purchase at which marginal revenue product is equal to marginal resource cost. It does not pay—in fact it will make him worse off—to expand employment beyond b. Yet this is what society wants. If a resource is worth more than it is paid in some certain use, this is positive proof that society desires its employment level in this use to be expanded.[6] But it is not maliciousness that is responsible for this situation; it is the mathematical fact that the supply curve facing the firm is upward sloping to the right, and, therefore, marginal resource cost exceeds the price of the resource.

Nevertheless, monopsonistic as well as monopolistic exploitation have adverse effects on the efficient use of resources. We shall explore the matter further in the next chapter, but an explicit statement of the nature of the problem is warranted here. Wherever monopoly in product selling and monopsony in resource purchasing occur, it is likely that the value

---

[6]*If marginal revenue product of the resource is greater than the price paid for the resource, then certainly value of marginal product must be also. Can you explain why this is so? Can you draw a diagram showing a resource being exploited both monopolistically and monopsonistically, indicating exactly the magnitude of each? Check the definition of monopolistic exploitation again.*

of marginal product of any one resource used by different firms will differ from one firm to another, even if units of the resource were paid the same price by each firm. This would mean that consumers place a higher value on units of the resource in some uses than in others. It also means that from the point of view of consumers too little of the resource is employed in the higher value of marginal product uses and too much is employed in lower value of marginal product uses.

Sources of Monopsony

How many employment alternatives are open to concert pianists? How many hospitals in Canada can utilize effectively the talents of a skilled brain surgeon? How many major league hockey clubs are bidding for the talents of gifted young players? How many television networks bid for the services of topflight entertainers? How many large-volume users of Bendix magnetos are there in Canada?

These questions point up one of the main sources of monopsonistic buying or hiring of resources, to the extent that it occurs. Whether the resource is labour or magnetos or bearings or something else, *if it is specialized to one user or to a small group of users* monopsony is likely to occur. The number of alternative employment opportunities are limited in number, so that any one user faces an upward-sloping supply curve for his purchases. If he wants a larger number of units or a better quality, he must pay a higher price.

A second source of monopsony is *immobility of resources among geographic areas*. The classic example of this was the one-company mining town of northern Ontario and Quebec where the town's population was dependent on the company for employment. Communications with the rest of the country were limited and the labour force was not well informed as to alternative earning opportunities elsewhere. Many youngsters growing up in the area remained as permanent residents. The town constituted a self-contained labour market and the company faced the market supply curve.

Both of the sources of monopsony discussed above are forms of immobility, but they arise from different circumstances. The first, specialization to particular uses, arises from economic activity of a dynamic, inventive, and progressive kind and as such is not likely to cause us great concern. The second, fortunately, is much less common today than it was 40 to 50 years ago. Some geographic immobility of labour undoubtedly still exists, but with modern methods of travel, mass communication, and rising educational levels its importance is diminishing.

Methods of Counteracting Monopsony

Although it is by no means certain that monopsony creates problems of significant magnitude, certain kinds of preventive types of action, like preventive medicine or preventive maintenance on an automobile may be worthwhile. Of course, the best way of avoiding monopsonistic exploitation and restriction of employment of resources in certain uses is to eliminate or control the factors responsible. Failing in this, minimum prices set out on a resource may possibly be of some benefit.

Control of the Causes

Few people would argue that there is a pressing need to prevent monopsonistic exploitation of television stars, big league hockey players, and brain surgeons. Monopsony in the purchase of highly specialized resources may very well be one of the prices we must pay for economic progress. In any case, the owners of high-paid, specialized resources are not likely to get a sympathetic ear when they complain that they are paid less than they are worth.[7] The resource owners we are concerned with are those whose incomes are low because their resources are purchased monopsonistically.[8] Ordinarily we would expect these to be workers who for some reason or another are immobile. Conceivably they can be or are being helped by government policies aimed at increasing mobility. These include the operation of a nation-wide system of federal employment exchanges, federal and provincial legislation aimed at retraining and relocating workers from poverty areas, and the upgrading and improving of educational facilities.

Employment exchanges can and should perform several important tasks. They should collect and disseminate data on the kinds of job openings available and where they are located. They should also gather and publicize information on occupational and geographic wage structures; that is, on what occupations pay the highest wages and on what geographic areas are high-wage areas. In addition, they should perform the more perfunctory job of matching those desiring employment with the job opportunities that are available. Most of these tasks are now being per-

---

[7]*On grounds of economic efficiency, however, where there is monopsonistic exploitation of high-paid resources, the argument for expanding employment of the resources in those uses is as strong as it is in the case of monopsonistic exploitation of low-paid resources.*

[8]*We are usually concerned with these people on grounds of inequities in income distribution rather than of economic inefficiencies. Nothing said here should be taken to imply that monopsony is a major cause of poverty. It may be one small contributing factor but there is no evidence available to indicate that it is of prime importance.*

formed by the Canada Manpower Division, but the information made available is by no means complete nor does it always reach those in need of it.

Most of the anti-poverty legislation is aimed at making labour more mobile among occupations and geographic areas. It is not aimed specifically at monopsony situations but at increasing the productivity, and consequently, the incomes of low-income workers, whatever the cause of their low-income situations. Nevertheless, through the retraining of workers whose skills have become obsolete or through training those who have never developed skills in the first place not only may workers be made more productive but at the same time a blow may be struck at monopsony.

There is a high correlation between the educational levels attained by individuals and their mobility. High school graduates are much less likely to remain in their home towns and follow their fathers' occupations than are grade school graduates and high school dropouts. University graduates are even less likely to remain in the environment in which they were raised. How many of your present class will return to their home towns upon graduation? Will you? Educational opportunities promote mobility upward from occupations requiring lower to those requiring higher skill levels. Adult education may enable those in declining occupations to move into other areas that show greater promise. Counseling services may do much to steer those entering the labour force toward more remunerative jobs.

Minimum Pricing

Monopsonistic exploitation of a resource can be offset by the establishment of a minimum price for it—provided the minimum is "correctly" set. Suppose in Figure 16–6 that B refers to bricklayers and that in the market under surveillance they are hired by only one large construction company. The supply curve is S_bS_b and the marginal resource cost curve is MRC_b. The marginal revenue product curve for bricklayers to the firm is MRP_b. The profit-maximizing level of employment is b and the wage rate necessary to secure that quantity is p_b. Monopsonistic exploitation amounts to p_bv_b per unit of labour.

If a minimum wage rate were fixed at p_{b_1}, how would the supply curve facing the firm appear?[9] Since the firm is not permitted to purchase labour at a price below p_{b_1}, that part of the supply curve below E_1 is no longer relevant. At p_{b_1} the firm can get any quantity of labour it desires up to b_1.

[9]*The minimum wage rate could be set by law or by collective bargaining between a bricklayers' union and the firm. The method of setting it is of no consequence at this point; all that matters is that no labour is sold at a price below that minimum.*

But if more were desired, higher wage rates would be necessary to attract the larger quantities into employment. For quantities of labour greater than b_1, that part of the market supply curve lying above E_1 is relevant.

The change in the supply curve facing the firm changes in turn the marginal resource cost curve. The horizontal part of the supply curve—the $p_{b_1}E_1$ part—is now like that facing a purely competitive firm; consequently, the marginal resource cost curve for that part coincides with the line $p_{b_1}E_1$. At employment level b_1 the marginal resource cost curve is discontinuous, jumping from point E_1 to point F_1. For employment levels greater than b_1 the marginal resource cost curve follows its original path.

Now that the marginal resource cost curve is $p_{b_1}E_1F_1G_1$, employment level b no longer maximizes the firm's profits. At employment level b marginal revenue product is v_b but marginal resource cost is p_{b_1}. Profits will be increased by an increase in the employment level to b_1. At that point marginal revenue product and marginal resource cost are equal at p_{b_1} and profits are maximum. The resource is paid p_{b_1} also, so monopsonistic exploitation has been eliminated. Note that the employment level is higher than it was before.

The correct minimum price is much easier to establish on paper than in practice. Presumably the devices used to set it would be either minimum wage laws or collective bargaining, and there is little evidence to indicate that either legislators or union leaders try consciously to offset monopsony by these means. As a matter of fact, most of them have never even heard of the term.

A general minimum wage like that set under the Canada Labour (Standards) Code of 1965 is clearly not appropriate for this purpose. The number of workers affected by it has been small (only 5 percent of all workers are under federal jurisdiction). Further, to the extent that monopsony in labour markets occurs, it is a set of different situations, each calling for a different minimum to offset exploitation, rather than a general situation embracing all labour. The single rate of the minimum wage law may accidentally be correct for some situations but certainly it will not be for all.[10]

Minimum wages set through collective bargaining could be more nearly tailored to differing monopsony situations. However, even if the two parties in collective bargaining knew the correct minimum to set, do you think they would settle on that wage level? Is it likely that business firms,

---

[10]*All provinces have enacted minimum wage legislation. All provinces except British Columbia issue general minimum wage orders, supplemented by special orders in some cases. In British Columbia the minimum-wage-fixing board authority issues a separate wage order for each industry or occupation and a general order for employees not so covered.*

purchasing labour monopsonistically, would be willing to raise wage rates up to that level? If the union were able to force it that high, would it then be content to force it no higher?

Combinations of Variable Resources

When we introduce the possibility of monopoly and monopsony into the principles of resource pricing and employment we come up with some slight modifications of the analysis of least-cost combinations and profit-maximizing levels of employment presented in the preceding chapter. Suppose a firm producing and selling product X uses two variable resources, A and B. Suppose, further, that X is sold monopolistically and A and B are purchased monopsonistically. To maximize profits with respect to these resources the employment levels must be such that the marginal revenue product of each is equal to its marginal resource cost; that is,

$$MPP_a \cdot MR_x = MRC_a \qquad (16.1)$$

and

$$MPP_b \cdot MR_x = MRC_b . \qquad (16.2)$$

Least-Cost Combinations

Equations 16.1 and 16.2 together show the conditions for a least-cost combination of resources A and B. We divide through equation 16.1 by MR_x and by MRC_a. We divide through equation 16.2 by MR_x and MRC_b. These operations yield

$$\frac{MPP_a}{MRC_a} = \frac{1}{MR_x} \qquad (16.3)$$

and

$$\frac{MPP_b}{MRC_b} = \frac{1}{MR_x} \qquad (16.4)$$

so

$$\frac{MPP_a}{MRC_a} = \frac{MPP_b}{MRC_b} = \frac{1}{MR_x} . \qquad (16.5)$$

Keeping in mind the definitions of marginal physical product and marginal resource cost of a resource, we know that $(MPP_a)/(MRC_a)$ means *the change in product per dollar change in expenditure on A*. Similarly, $(MPP_b)/(MRC_b)$ means *the change in product per dollar*

change in expenditure on B. Thus equation 16.5 means that the last dollar
spent on *A* yields the same increase in the firm's product output as the last
dollar spend on *B*. This, of course, means that equation 16.5, ignoring
$1/(MR_x)$ for the moment, states the conditions that must be met for
variable resources to be used in a least-cost combination.

Equation 16.5 also expresses the profit-maximizing conditions for the
firm with respect to its output of product *X*. If we examine $(MRC_a)/(MPP_a)$ *and* $(MRC_b)/(MPP_b)$, we find that each of these is an expression
of the marginal cost of product *X*—the change in total cost per unit
change in the level of the firm's output. Consequently, equation 16.5 can
be rewritten as

$$\frac{MPP_a}{MRC_a} = \frac{MPP_b}{MRC_b} = \frac{1}{MC_x} = \frac{1}{MR_x} \qquad (16.5a)$$

or, inverting the two equalities on the right,

$$MC_x = MR_x . \qquad (16.6)$$

If a firm employs those quantities of variable resources at which their
respective marginal revenue products are equal to respective marginal
resource costs, it will be using those resources in a least-cost combination
and will at the same time be producing the profit-maximizing quantity
of product.

Summary

In this chapter we examine the effects of monopoly in product selling
and monopsony in resource purchasing on the pricing and employment
of resources. The term "monopoly" is used broadly to mean any market
situation in which the seller faces a downward-sloping demand curve for
his product. "Monopsony" means any market situation in which a resource buyer faces an upward-sloping supply curve for the resource.

The principles of resource pricing and employment are basically the
same where firms are monopolistic sellers as they are where firms are
purely competitive sellers. The firm's demand curve for a resource is its
marginal revenue product curve for it. The market demand curve is the
sum of the quantities that individual firms will take at each price. Market
demand and market supply determine the equilibrium price and employment level. Each firm employs that quantity at which the marginal
revenue product of the resource is equal to the marginal resource cost or
price—provided the firm is a purely competitive purchaser of the resource.

Monopolistic sellers of product are said to exploit the resources they
purchase. Monopolistic exploitation of a resource means that resource

units are paid less than their value of marginal product—what they are worth to society—because of monopoly. They are paid a price equal to their marginal revenue product—what they are worth to the firm. For monopolistic sellers of product the value of marginal product of a resource exceeds the marginal revenue product because the price of the product sold exceeds the marginal revenue from its sale. Where the resource is used by both monopolistic and competitive sellers of product the monopolistic users will restrict the employment of the resource below the amounts that society desires used in the production of those products.

The monopsonist in the purchase of a resource, like any other resource purchaser, maximizes profits by employing that amount at which marginal revenue product is equal to marginal resource cost. But since the monopsonist faces a resource supply curve (average cost curve) that slopes upward to the right, the marginal resource cost curve lies above the supply curve. Consequently, at the profit-maximizing level of employment the price paid for each unit of the resource is less than either its marginal revenue product to the firm or the value of its marginal product to society.

Monopsonists also exploit resources and restrict the levels of their employment as compared with purely competitive reosurce purchasers. Monopsonistic exploitation of a given resource is measured by the difference between its marginal revenue product to the firm and the price paid for it and is the consequence of the difference between the resource supply curve facing the firm and the marginal resource cost curve. In the absence of monopsony, the resource would be employed up to the level at which its marginal revenue product is equal to the resource price.

If we are to attempt to counteract monospsony, we should understand its causes. These are (1) specialization of the resource to a particular user and (2) geographic or occupational immobility of the resource. Measures to increase resource mobility are of primary importance in controlling the impact of this factor on the economy. The alternative is minimum pricing techniques.

Where monopoly in selling products and monopsony in the purchase of resources occur, the conditions of least-cost resource combinations and profit-maximizing levels of employment of several variable resources must be modified slightly. Monopsonistic purchases of the resources requires for a least-cost combination that

$$\frac{MPP_a}{MRC_a} = \frac{MPP_b}{MRC_b} = \cdots = \frac{MPP_n}{MRC_n}$$

for as many variable resources as are so purchased. For profit maximization, we extend the conditions to

$$\frac{MPP_a}{MRC_a} = \frac{MPP_b}{MRC_b} = \cdots = \frac{MPP_n}{MRC_n} = \frac{1}{MC_x} = \frac{1}{MR_x}.$$

Exercises and Questions for Discussion

1. In the prairie farmlands the average wage of migratory workers is comparatively low. What are some possible bases of this problem? Could the organization of a labour union improve the situation? What other methods might be used?
2. Are monopoly and monopsony equally adverse in their effects on labour? Explain.
3. The American and National football leagues in the United States recently merged and will have a common draft of players. Discuss with the help of graphs what the effects of the merger are likely to be.
4. "Labour unions have perhaps done as much as the Justice Department, with their enforcement of antimonopoly laws, in curbing monopoly power." Evaluate this statement.
5. Labour unions often argue that because of the workers' increased productivity, wages should be increased. Is this a legitimate argument? Elaborate.
6. It has been said that "it is unfair to accuse an employer of monopsonistic exploitation because even if it exists he is not responsible". Discuss this statement.
7. In the absence of monopsony, is there any justification for the establishment of a minimum price for a resource? Why or why not?

Selected Readings

Bloom, G. F., and Herbert R. Northrup, *Economics of Labor Relations,* 5th ed. Homewood, Ill.: Richard D. Irwin, Inc., 1965, Chaps. 9 and 10.

Cartter, A. M., and F, R, Marshall, *Labor Economics.* Homewood, Ill.: Richard D. Irwin, Inc., 1967, Chap. 10.

Chamberlain, E. H., *The Theory of Monopolistic Competition*, 8th ed. Cambridge, Mass.: Harvard University Press, 1962, Chap. 8.

Colberg, M., D. R. Forbush, and G. R. Whitaker, Jr., *Business Economics*, 3d ed. Homewood, Ill.: Richard D. Irwin, Inc., 1964, Chap. 12, Cases 12-1, 12-2, 12-3.

Economic Council of Canada, "Labour Market Policy", *First Annual Review.* Ottawa: Queen's Printer, 1964, pp. 170-184.

Meltz, N. M. and A. Kruger (eds), *The Canadian Labour Market.* Toronto: University of Toronto Centre for Industrial Relations, 1968.

Robinson, Joan, *The Economics of Imperfect Competition*, 2nd ed. Toronto: Macmillan Company of Canada, 1969, Chaps. 25 and 26.

17

Resource Allocation

New discoveries, new inventions, and new knowledge make these years exciting ones in which to live. During your lifetime you have seen colour television come into its own as a standard item of household consumption. You have witnessed the advent of supersonic airplanes, flights into space, utilization of atomic energy, and the computer. You have seen polio and other dread diseases brought under control. Synthetic fabrics, TV dinners, and cake mixes are commonplace to you. So are tape recorders, transistor radios, and high-fidelity stereo sets. Much less obvious to most of us have been the tremendous changes accomplished in production methods for a wide variety of goods and services. New discoveries, new inventions, and new knowledge change the supplies of resources available to be used in the economy. They also bring about changes in consumer tastes and demand. If in the face of these dynamic changes the economy is to use its resources efficiently, there must be flexibility in where and how resources are to be used. Continuous reallocation of resources must occur from areas that are becoming less important to consumers to those that are increasing in importance.

In this chapter we are interested primarily in the mechanism employed in a free enterprise type of economic system to bring about the desired reallocation of resources. We can understand it best if we discuss it initially as though it worked almost perfectly. Toward this end, in the first part of the chapter we shall assume that the economy is purely competitive. Later, monopoly, monopsony, and other problems will be introduced.

Allocation Among Geographic Areas

As a vast oversimplification, think of Canada as being divided into two economic regions, the *East*, comprising the provinces of Newfoundland, Nova Scotia, New Brunswick, Prince Edward Island, and Quebec and the *West*, encompassing the provinces of Ontario, Manitoba, Saskatchewan, Alberta, and British Columbia. Over a short period of time, say one year, suppose that resources are not mobile between the two areas but that over a longer period the owners of both labour and capital are willing to migrate from one to the other to seek employment for their resources, wherever it appears to be to their advantage. To put this in technical economic language, we assume that in the short-run the East and the West are separate resource markets. In the long-run they are interconnected.

We shall make two further simplifying assumptions. First, think of all units of labour as being homogeneous. Second, assume that pure competition in the sale of products and in the purchase of resources prevails in both areas. Neither of these fits the facts of the real world. With regard to the first, there are thousands of different kinds of labour—the Canada Manpower Division lists over 10,000 different occupational classifications. On the second point, although pure competition is approached in some markets, it is by no means a universal market condition. Nevertheless, together these assumptions enable us to get at the most important principles that are at work and that often tend to be obscured in the much more complex real world.

Allocation of Labour

Suppose now that there are differences in the amounts of capital that labour has to work with in the East and in the West. It may be, for example, that machines, factory buildings, mineral deposits, transportation facilities, and other capital resources have been more abundantly developed and accumulated relative to the labour supply in the West than in the East. These are the circumstances depicted in Figure 17–1.

Evidence of Misallocation

What can we say about the demand for and the supply of labour in the West and in the East? What about the wage rates and the productivity of labour in the two areas? Do these provide any clues as to whether labour is correctly or incorrectly allocated between the West and the East?[1] Because of the larger ratio of capital to labour, the demand curve for labour in the West lies farther to the right with respect to its supply curve than does that of the East. Or, in the East, the supply curve for labour lies farther to the right with respect to the demand curve than does that of the West.

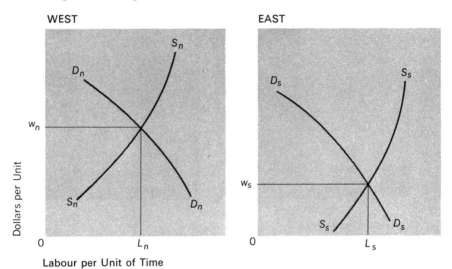

Figure 17-1
Misallocation of labour between the West and the East

Basic demand—supply analysis informs us that the price of labour, or the wage rate, will be higher in the West than in the East. The difference in the wage rate makes us suspicious that labour may not be correctly allocated. The lower wage rate in the East leads us to believe that there may be too much labour in the East as compared with the West.[2] Can we support this view with the analysis we developed in Chapter 15? Can we show that any one unit of western labour is more productive than any one unit of eastern labour?

If we compare the value of marginal product of eastern labour with that of western labour, we obtain the information required to answer the questions just raised. Because of pure competition in resource purchases

[1]*The correct allocation of a resource is that in which the resource makes its maximum contribution to the value of the economy's output, or to national income. If a resource were correctly allocated the transfer of a unit of it from one use to any other use would cause national income to fall. We shall take a closer look at the correct allocation shortly.*

[2]*Some people seem to believe that low wage rates wherever they appear are indicative of exploitation. What do you think about this?*

in the West and in the East, the marginal resource cost in each area is the same as the respective wage rates, w_n and w_s. In the West, we expect each firm to be employing that quantity of labour at which the marginal revenue product is equal to the marginal resource cost. Thus in the West the marginal revenue product of labour is also w_n. In the East we expect the same thing, so the marginal revenue product of labour in that area will be w_s. Since w_n is greater than w_s the marginal revenue product of labour used by western firms is greater than that used by eastern firms. Because of pure competition in the sale of products, the marginal revenue product of the resource in each area is equal to its value of marginal product in that area. Thus the value of marginal product of labour is greater in the West than in the East; that is, the last one-unit increase in the level of

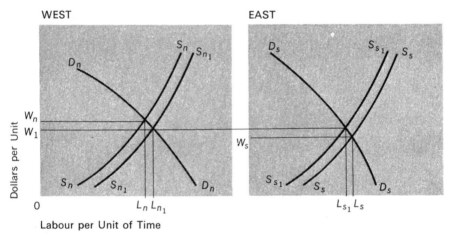

Figure 17-2
Reallocation of labour from the East to the West

employment in the West is valued more highly by consumers than is the last one-unit increase in the level of employment in the East. This difference in the value of marginal product of labour in its different uses is the evidence that labour is not correctly allocated. Consumers would like more labour used in western employments and less in eastern employments.

The Mechanism of Reallocation

The incorrect allocation of labour brings about differences in the wage rates, and these differences provide the motivating force for the desired reallocation. Given sufficient time, workers will tend to migrate from the low-wage area to the high-wage area, since the latter provides the prospect of higher incomes. This situation is illustrated in Figure 17–2. The movement of labour from the East to the West shifts the supply curve in the West to the right, toward $S_{n_1}S_{n_1}$. It shifts the supply curve in the East to the left, toward $S_{s_1}S_{s_1}$. The price of labour in the West falls toward w_1, while in the East it rises toward the same level. When enough labour has moved West so that the wage rate is w_1 in both areas, the incentive for migration is no longer present. The marginal revenue product of labour is the same in both the West and the East, and so is the value of marginal product.

Effects on National Income

What will be the effects of the reallocation of labour on national income, or the value of the economy's output? Look again at the original situation pictured by Figure 17–1. As we determined above, the value of marginal product of labour is greater in the West than in the East. Now, if a unit of labour is withdrawn from employment in the East, by how much does national income fall? It falls by w_s dollars—the value of marginal product of labour in the East. If the unit of labour goes to work in the West, by how much does national income (after the decrease just described) rise? The increase is equal to slightly less than w_n. Putting these two results together, we see that the transfer of a unit of resource from the lower value of marginal product area to the higher value of marginal product area will increase national income: the increase in national income when the unit of labour goes to work in the West is larger than the decrease in national income occasioned by its withdrawal from the East. The following is a valid general principle: *whenever units of a resource are moved from lower value of marginal product uses to higher value of marginal product uses, national income is increased.*

Suppose we restate this very important proposition numerically. Let w_s be $10, meaning that any one unit of labour employed in the East yields a value of marginal product of $10. Take away a unit of labour and the economy loses $10 worth of product or services. Let w_n represent $16. Any one unit of labour employed in the West yields a value of marginal product of $16. Take away a unit of labour and the economy would lose $16 worth of product. But if instead of taking away a unit of labour in the West one unit more than L_n is employed, the economy would gain almost $16 worth of goods and services. (Why almost $16 worth?) The transfer of a unit of labour from the East to the West under these circumstances would increase national income by almost $6 worth of goods and services.

The Correct Allocation

Homogeneous units of labour or of any other resource are correctly allocated when the value of marginal product of the resource is the same in all of the alternative uses of the resource and when there is no higher value of marginal product possibilities available to the resource. Once the resource is so allocated, any further transfers from one use to another will bring about a net decline in national income. The law of diminishing returns, which makes the value of marginal product curve of the resource slope downward to the right for any firm that uses it, assures us that this will be the case.

It is useful to look at this proposition the other way around. Units of a resource are misallocated when its value of marginal product differs in different uses. In the labour example, the first indication of misallocation between the West and the East is the difference in the wage rate between the two areas. On closer examination we find that the wage rate differences in this case are also value of marginal product differences and, hence, represent actual misallocation.

The operation of the price mechanism as it continually reallocates resources under purely competitive conditions is summed up in a few sentences. Firstly, an incorrect allocation of a resource causes different prices to be paid for it in different areas or uses. Secondly, these prices provide the incentive for reallocation in the correct direction. Thirdly, the price differences decrease as the reallocation takes place—when the resource is correctly allocated they will have disappeared. Fourthly, the reallocation increases national income.

Capital Allocation

In the East-West example, capital as well as labour may have been poorly allocated initially. If the ratio of labour to capital was lower in the West than in the East, then the ratio of capital to labour must have been higher. This opens up the possibility that, if capital in the East is not inferior to that in the West, the marginal revenue product and the price of capital may be greater in the East than in the West.[3] If this were so, then investors (resource owners) seeking the greatest possible earnings or return on their investment, would have an incentive to reduce the

---

[3]*Capital is made up of so many different items that it is difficult to conceive of a* quantity *of capital in such a way that we can compare the quantity in the West with that in the East. The best procedure probably is to think of the quantity of capital in the West (or the East) as the investment in buildings, machinery, tools, and other items measured in dollar terms. The marginal revenue product and the price of capital will then be the yield, or return, on each dollar invested.*

dollars invested in the West and to increase the dollars invested in the East. What this amounts to, of course, is a transfer of plant, equipment, and other capital resources from the West to the East.

The transfer of capital from the West to the East would decrease the demand for labour in the West and increase it in the East, thus reducing the extent to which labour should be reallocated from the East to the West. This situation is illustrated by Figures 17–1 through 17–3. Let the initial situation be that of Figure 17–1. There is relatively too much labour and relatively too little capital in the East. In the West these circumstances are reversed. Figure 17–2 indicates what we would expect to happen if reallocation of labour but not of capital were possible. Figure 17–3 completes the picture. An out migration of capital from the West reduces the demand for labour in the West toward $D_{n2}D_{n2}$. An in migration of capital to the East increases demand for labour in that area toward $D_{s2}D_{s2}$. The achievement of a correct reallocation of labour requires only that the eastern supply curve shift left to $S_{s2}S_{s2}$, while that for the West shifts to the right to $S_{n2}S_{n2}$, and these are smaller shifts than those pictured in Figure 17–2.

Any reallocation of capital that occurs will also increase national income. Under conditions of pure competition, movement of capital from the West to the East would occur only if the value of marginal product of capital were greater in the East than in the West. Thus a unit of capital leaving the West would decrease national income by less than the increase in national income brought about by its employment in the East. As is the case for any resource, units of homogeneous capital are correctly allocated when the value of marginal product is the same in all its uses.

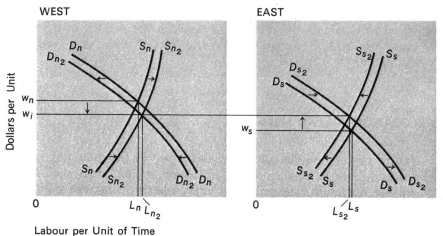

Figure 17-3
Reallocation of labour and capital

We cannot determine from Figures 17–1 though 17–3 whether the allocation of capital is correct. None of the figures shows the return per unit of capital or the value of marginal product of capital. All we can say is that if, in Figure 17–1, capital as well as labour is incorrectly allocated, the resulting economic events would be those described.

The East-West Historical Record

The historical record suggests that a pattern of resource reallocation much like that just discussed has, in fact, been taking place in Canada over the past 50 years. In the early years of the twentieth century the five eastern-most provinces specialized in the primary sectors of fishing, forestry and agriculture, while industry grew up around the population centres of the five western-most provinces. Later, as demand for industrial goods and services outstripped demand for primary products and as capital accumulated more rapidly in the West, the East found itself with too much labour and too little capital as compared with the West. This situation has been evidenced by the well-known East-West income differential. Income levels in the western region have been generally higher than the national average since 1926 while those in the eastern region of Canada have been lower.[4]

An indication of the absolute and relative income disparity among the regions of Canada since 1926 can be gained from an analysis of the data provided in Table 17–1. Perhaps the most striking impression is the large percentage difference in income levels between the richest and poorest province. The most recent data indicates that personal income per head in Ontario is about one half larger than in Prince Edward Island and more than twice that of Newfoundland. As for the other regions, personal income per capita in British Columbia is appreciably higher than the average for the country as a whole; income levels in the Prairies are very close to the national average; Quebec's per capita income is well below the average for all provinces. In the four Atlantic provinces, income levels are considerably lower than those in all other regions of the country. Moreover, while there has been some reduction in the *percentage* range of income differences since 1926, the extent of interregional income disparity in Canada has remained large and substantially permanent.

The actual East-West income differential is only partly explained by differences in the amount of capital each worker has to work with, although to be sure, this has been much smaller in the five easternmost prov-

[4]*Economic Council of Canada*, Second Annual Review. *Ottawa: Queen's Printer, December, 1965, p. 100.*

TABLE 17–1

Level of Personal Income Per Capita by Province for the Years 1926 and 1968 (in Current Dollars)

Province	1926	1968
Newfoundland	—	1,467
Prince Edward Island	241	1,682
Nova Scotia	291	2,072
New Brunswick	278	1,897
Quebec	363	2,406
Ontario	491	3,065
Manitoba	465	2,654
Saskatchewan	437	2,386
Alberta	488	2,645
British Columbia	524*	2,847
Yukon and North West Territories	—	2,326
Canada	429	2,660

Includes Yukon and North West Territories.
   Source: *D.B.S.* National Accounts, Income and Expenditure, *1968*

inces. The average eastern worker is more extractive—fishing, forestry, mining and agriculture—oriented, less skilled, and he is not as well educated as his western counterpart. For these reasons, eastern labour has been less productive and, consequently, less well paid. To a very large extent the East-West differential in income levels (and wage rates) and productivities is an urban-rural differential. Much of what has just been said about the East compared with the West could also be said in almost any rural-urban comparison.

The differential apparently has provided a continuing incentive for migration of labour to the West. This shift has been particularly in evidence since the 1930's as the means of transportation and communication have been improved. As will be seen in Table 17–2, seven provinces experienced net out migration between 1941 and 1950,[5] only the provinces of Ontario and British Columbia gained from net inflows. In the interval between 1951 and 1960, net out migration occurred in six out of ten provinces, with Quebec and Alberta joining the ranks of recipient provinces. Table 17–2 also reflects the large scale migration from rural areas and primary industries to urban centres. Clearly, without these population movements, interregional differences in income per person would be even greater than the present degree of disparity.

[5]*It should be pointed out that every province experienced some population growth over the period 1921-1961—ranging from 18 percent in Prince Edward Island to 211 percent in British Columbia. Net out migration merely requires that the number of people leaving an area be greater than the number of people coming into it from outside. If it is more than offset by an excess of births over deaths, the population of the area continues to grow.*

TABLE 17-2

Rates (per 1000 of population) of Interprovincial and Rural-Urban Migration for Intercensal Intervals, by Province, 1941-50 and 1951-60

	Interprovincial Migration		Rural Migration		Urban Migration	
	1941-1950	1951-1960	1941-1950	1951-1960	1941-1950	1951-1960
Canada	8	68	−81	−55	88	163
Newfoundland	—	−32	—	−166	—	253
Prince Edward Island	−142	−105	−179	−208	−20	148
Nova Scotia	−61	−52	−60	−54	−62	−49
New Brunswick	−83	−71	−113	−172	−19	114
Quebec	−5	43	−170	−232	96	169
Ontario	65	131	94	131	45	130
Manitoba	−87	−7	−207	−244	67	215
Saskatchewan	−234	−95	−354	−291	115	242
Alberta	18	112	−255	−228	350	386
British Columbia	229	176	253	239	206	109

Note: The figures shown are decennial crude rates, defined as the number per 1,000 of the population. The population base is the average of the population at the beginning and the end of the interval.
Source: Economic Council of Canada, Second Annual Review, Ottawa, Queen's Printer, December 1965, Table 5-5, P. 111

To sum up, the present scale of migration of labour to the West and of capital to the East is not sufficient to eliminate interregional disparities in income per person. Moreover, the gap has not narrowed substantially since the late 1940's. In this connection, it should be emphasized that the Canadian experience is in sharp contrast to that of the United States where the per capita incomes of various regions are converging on one another with the result that the difference between the average region and the poorest is being reduced. To put it differently, in the United States, unlike Canada, the poorer regions are catching up to the richer regions.

Allocation Among Uses

The theory of resource allocation developed in the preceding section is not limited in its application to broad geographic areas such as the East and the West. The principles apply wherever different markets or different uses for a resource can be distinguished—among counties, metropolitan areas, rural areas and adjacent metropolitan areas, industries, firms, and so on. The East and the West in the previous example are simply replaced by the appropriate different uses among which units of the resource can move over time. As an illustration, suppose we look at a hypothetical allocation of accountants' services between the oil industry and the construction industry.

We shall take as our starting point an equilibrium situation, although this is not strictly necessary. Assume that both the oil industry and the construction industry sell their products and services under conditions of pure competition. Initially accountants are correctly allocated between them—the value of marginal product of accountants' services used in the oil industry is the same as it is in the construction industry. Marginal revenue product will also be the same in both industries and, if pure competition prevails in the employment of accountants, the marginal resource cost and the price per unit of accountants' labour will be equal. If firms in both industries are employing profit-maximizing quantities, the marginal resource cost of accountants will be equal to their marginal revenue product in each industry. If we put all of this together symbolically—and it is extremely convenient to do so—we can state the equilibrium conditions as:

$$VMP_{ao} = VMP_{ac} = MRP_{ao} = MRP_{ac} = MRC_a = P_a \ . \qquad (17.1)$$

Be sure that you understand what each of these symbols means and why equilibrium is implied by equation 17.1.

What economic forces, bearing on accountants, would be set in motion by a shift in consumer demand away from petroleum products and toward construction services? We would expect the lower demand for petroleum products to bring about a decrease in their price level, p_o. The increase in demand for construction services would increase the per unit price, p_c, of these. Thus the value of marginal product of accountants used in the construction industry would be higher while that of accountants used in the oil industry would be lower. We can express the result symbolically as:

$$VMP_{ac} > VMP_{ao} \qquad (17.2)$$

or, breaking each of these terms down into its component parts, we can write

$$MPP_{ac} \cdot p_c > MPP_{ao} \cdot p_o \qquad (17.2a)$$

in which MPP_{ac} is the marginal physical product of accountants used in construction and MPP_{ao} is their marginal physical product in the oil industry. Equations 17.2 and 17.2a simply mean that consumers now value the services of accountants (and other resources) more highly in the construction industry than in the oil industry.

Accountants are now incorrectly allocated, but the market mechanism moves to correct the situation. Firms in the oil industry find that the value of marginal product of accountants (and other resources) is less than the price they must pay to employ them, or

$$VMP_{ao} < p_a \ . \qquad (17.3)$$

Consequently, they reduce the quantity of accountants that they employ. At the same time, firms in the construction industry find that the value of marginal product of accountants (and of other resources) is greater than the resource price, or

$$VMP_{ac} > p_a . \qquad (17.4)$$

They thus have an incentive to increase the quantity of accountants that they employ.

Accountants will have an income incentive to transfer from the oil industry to the construction industry. The reduction in the oil industry's demand for accountants will reduce the price paid for them in that industry slightly below p_a. At the same time, the increase in the construction industry's demand for them will advance the price offered to slightly more than p_a. In other words, the incorrect allocation causes a resource price differential between the two uses to develop.

The reallocation of accountants will continue until the correct allocation is achieved. As more and more accountants (and other resources) are employed in the construction industry and as its output expands, the price of construction services will fall. So, too, will the value of marginal product of accountants in that industry. The exit of accountants (and other resources) from the oil industry reduces the supply of petroleum products, causing their prices to rise. This will raise the value of marginal product of accountants in that industry. When the prices of construction services have fallen far enough—with the increase in the industry's output—and the prices of oil products have risen enough—with the contraction of the industry's output—to make the value of marginal product of accountants once more the same in both industries, the incentives for transfer will have disappeared. The appropriate adjustment to the change in consumer demand will have been made in the economy's productive capacity. The conditions of equilibrium stated in equation 17.1 will again prevail.

Thus, as changes constantly are occurring in consumer demand, technology, and resource supplies, the price mechanism operates to correct the resulting misallocation of resources. Value of marginal product and price differentials in different uses appear for the misallocated resource, providing the incentives for the resource owners to transfer what they own from the lower-paying to the higher-paying uses. Often, or probably generally, before the reallocation of such a resource is completed other changes take place, calling for a still different allocation pattern. To achieve high efficiency, the economic system must operate so that resources can make the necessary movements rapidly and smoothly.

Impediments to Correct Resource Allocation

The price mechanism does not always work as smoothly as we have just described it as it goes about the job of reallocating resources. Sand from several different sources clogs the gears. Two come to mind immediately. The economy is not one of thoroughgoing, pure competition. Monopoly in product sales and monopsony in resource purchases are troublesome. Price-fixing by the government or by private organizations as well as certain social and cultural factors may also impede movements toward correct allocations.

Monopoly

What effect does some degree of monopoly in the sale of products—such as DuPont with nylon or Xerox with copying machines—have on the allocation of resources? One effect can be deduced from the fact that entry into monopolistic and oligopolistic industries is obstructed or blocked, permitting profits to be made over a period of years. Thus even though the value of marginal product of resources used by a monopolist or an oligopolist may be higher in those industries than in others, the entry barriers prevent the movement in of additional quantities of them. As long as the entry barriers remain, the resources used by the firms that maintain the barriers are likely to remain incorrectly allocated.

For any given resource used by a monopolist, there is a more subtle reason why a correct allocation is not likely to be achieved. This is the difference that always exists between the value of marginal product and the marginal revenue product of a resource used by a firm that faces a downward-sloping demand curve for its output.[4] The difference will not be the same for different monopolists that use the resource. In Figure 17–4, for example, monopolist I and monopolist II are two of many users of resource A. The market price of the resource is p_a and, assuming that it is purchased competitively, so is its marginal resource cost. To maximize profits, each of the firms will employ that quantity of A at which its marginal revenue product is equal to its marginal resource cost. For monopolist I this is quantity a_1 and for monopolist II it is quantity a_2. Will any further reallocation of the resource occur? Is resource A correctly allocated?

The price system is through with its allocation job. The price of the resource is the same in both employments, so resource owners have no incentive to transfer resource units from one to the other. Since each firm

---

[4]*See pp. 321-323 for a review of the difference.*

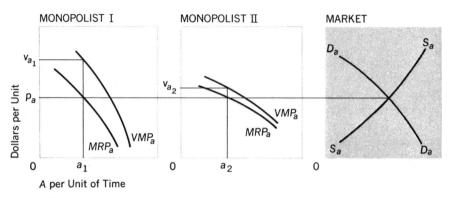

Figure 17-4
Monopolistic misallocation of a resource.

is obtaining the quantity it wants at the market price, p_a, neither has an incentive to bid for additional units nor to reduce the current employment level.

The resource is not correctly allocated even though the price system will bring about no changes in its present allocation. The value of marginal product of A is higher in the use to which monopolist I puts it than it is for monopolist II and differences of this kind would be expected to prevail among its different uses—except as among purely competitive sellers of product. Thus monopoly in product selling tends to cause distortions in the allocation of resources among different uses.

Monopsony

Distortions in the allocation of resources similar to those just discussed are caused by monopsony in resource purchases. In a situation of pure monopsony there is only one user of a given kind of resource, so no allocation problem exists. But if there are four or five buyers of the resource, each one large enough to influence its price, then each has some degree of monopsony and an allocation problem among the different users may exist. This is the situation that we analyze here.

We would expect the owners of the resource to seek employment where they can obtain the highest price. This means that units of the resource will be allocated among the monopsonists so that the resource price, p_a, is the same to all. This situation is illustrated in Figure 17–5 for two monopsonists, employing quantities a_1 and a_2, respectively. At price p_a, each monopsonist faces an upward-sloping supply curve for the resource, meaning that if either wants to employ larger amounts it must increase the offering price to obtain them. But at price p_a the supply curves facing the two firms are not likely to have the same elasticity and, consequently,

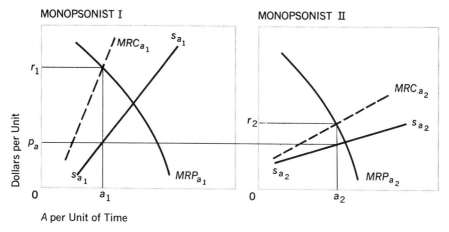

Figure 17-5
Monopsonistic misallocation of a resource.

for one—monopsonist I in this case—at price p_a the marginal resource cost will be higher than for the other. The price system has completed its job. The price of the resource is the same wherever it is used. But among the monopsonists marginal resource costs differ, and if each monopsonist is in equilibrium—maximizing profits—marginal revenue products of the resource will differ, too. With marginal revenue products of A differing for the different firms, it is highly unlikely that values of marginal product will be the same in all uses.

Price-Fixing

Incorrect allocations sometimes may be caused in whole or in part or may be maintained over time by price-fixing on the part of the government or by private organizations. There are two general classes of price-fixing cases. First, minimum prices may be placed on resources; second, prices of products may be fixed.

Resource Price-Fixing

Collective bargaining between business enterprises and labour unions provides by far the most common case of resource price-fixing. Suppose that common labour is used both in the construction industry and in agriculture. The demand and supply curves for the resource used in agriculture have become D_aD_a and S_aS_a in Figure 17–6, while in construction they have become D_cD_c and S_cS_c. Labour is not correctly allocated.[5] The

[5]*This may have come about because product demand relative to supply has risen faster in construction than in agriculture.*

incorrect allocation will cause wage rate differences to develop between the two types of employment—in agriculture it will be p_a and in construction it will be p_c. If there were no impediments to movement, labour would migrate from agriculture into construction until the wage differential is eliminated. The labour supply curve in construction will have shifted to the right to $S_{c_1}S_{c_1}$, while in agriculture it will have shifted to the left to $S_{a_1}S_{a_1}$. Wage rate p would prevail in both markets.

What would happen if before the migration of labour has time to occur a union of construction workers through collective bargaining with an association of contractors establishes a minimum wage rate for labour at level p_c in the construction industry? The minimum would prevent the desired reallocation from occurring. At wage rate p_c, employers in the construction industry will employ only L_c workers. Each firm is employing that quantity at which the marginal revenue product of the resource is equal to the wage rate. For any firm the employment of a larger quantity will decrease its profits. If workers leave agriculture, where are they to go? Who will employ them? The minimum wage rate in construction bars them from that industry. If these were the only two industries employing common labour, those in agriculture would be forced to remain in that sector. The supply curve would remain at S_aS_a and the wage rate would remain at p_a. The resource would be chronically misallocated and national income would be below its potential maximum.

Minimum wage laws are another means of establishing minimum prices for labour resources. In the foregoing example, suppose that Parliament

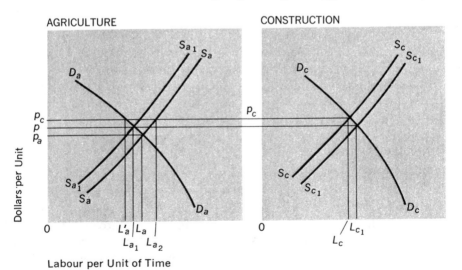

Figure 17-6
Misallocation through resource price-fixing.

decides that any wage rate below p_c is substandard and, consequently, that it is illegal for any employer to pay less. In Figure 17–6, with the original demand and supply situation, employers in agriculture would be willing to hire only L'_a workers at that wage rate. Quantity L_{a2} will be seeking employment, so there will be L'_aL_{a2} workers made unemployed by the enforcement of the minimum. These cannot be absorbed by any industry such as construction that currently pays the minimum wage rate.

An argument frequently made by proponents of minimum wage laws is that workers who lose their jobs because of the minimum—some of the agricultural workers in this case—will be forced to seek employment in higher-paying areas. In the above example, uses that currently pay more than the minimum—more than the construction industry pays—must be available if the unemployed are to be "kicked upstairs". Unemployment may well provide an incentive to workers to move. But so may a differential in the wage rate. The argument for the minimum wage rests on a value judgment that unemployment is the more effective and the more desirable incentive. An argument against the minimum wage rests on a value judgment that the more desirable—but possibly not the more effective—incentive is the wage differential.

Product Price-Fixing

Misallocation of specific resources can be caused when product prices are fixed by the government, although in some cases such price-fixing may improve the allocation rather than make it worse. Resource allocation is likely to be made worse when the price-fixing is done in competitive product markets, in which the value of marginal product and the marginal revenue products of the resource or resources in question are not far apart. A case in point is agricultural price supports.

What is likely to be the impact of a support price for wheat that is above the equilibrium wheat price level? The demand curves for resources used in the production of wheat will be shifted to the right. For any given resource, say labour, the marginal revenue product curve of a firm prior to the imposition of the support price will lie to the left of the position it will take after a support price is put into effect. In Figure 17–7, MRP_1 represents the presupport marginal revenue product curve for labour and, since a wheat farmer acts as a purely competitive seller of product, the value of marginal product curve for labour coincides with it. Since the curve shows the marginal physical product of labour at different employment levels multiplied by the price of wheat, it also shows the value that consumers attach to labour used by the firm at each of those employment levels.

The implementation of a support price for wheat shifts the marginal

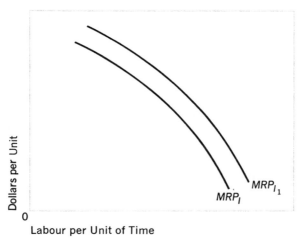

Figure 17–7
Effects of product price-fixing on *MRP* of a resource.

revenue product curve and the value of marginal product curve to the right to MRP_{l_1}. At each level of employment the marginal physical product of labour is now multiplied by the (higher) supported price of wheat. The curve no longer reflects consumers' valuation of the labour used by the firm. It reflects an arbitrary higher valuation that will attract units of labour away from other employments into this one. That which we expect for the one wheat farmer we would expect for all, thus larger quantities of resources will be attracted into wheat farming relative to other employments than consumers desire.

Other Impediments

A number of other factors may impede the price system in its task of reallocating resources in response to dynamic changes occurring in the economy. Some, in fact, may circumvent it altogether. We might characterize these as sociocultural and as educational and training factors.

In the sociocultural area we frequently find obstacles to geographic mobility of resources. Workers may be reluctant to move from one area to another even though the latter promises higher earning opportunities. There are several reasons why this may be so. Social ties to family and friends may be strong. They may be reluctant to go into a new and unknown community. The older the workers, the stronger such forces seem to operate on them. Thus we see pockets of unemployed or underemployed persons in the Atlantic provinces, Quebec, and in other areas depending on welfare payments to make ends meet.

Educational and training factors tend to block upward mobility of labour resources. The higher earnings available to more skilled workers provide the economic incentive to acquire those skills, or for upward mobility, but the opportunities for developing them are not always available to everyone. Maritimers in particular have a much lower average level of schooling than other Canadian workers. Consequently, they have not been able to respond to such incentives. To some extent the same problem may affect workers in the province of Quebec and the prairie provinces. For some occupations training facilities are not available to all who desire to enter and who have the necessary ability. Medicine provides an outstanding example.

Economic policy-making with respect to persons earning low incomes must centre around making such individuals more productive. Particularly, it should work toward removing impediments to geographic and to upward mobility. This is, of course, the aim of much recent antipoverty legislation. As impediments are removed, the price system should become more effective in performing its reallocation functions.

Summary

New inventions and new discoveries create continual changes in consumer wants, in resource supplies, and in techniques of production. These call for corresponding changes in the productive capacity of the economy, or in the allocation of resources among different uses. This chapter sets out the principles that guide resource allocation in a free enterprise economy—how the price system signals that misallocation is occurring and how it goes about correcting the misallocation.

If pure competition prevails in product selling and in resource buying, the price system will tend to correct any misallocation of a given resource. Misallocation will result in different prices being paid for the resource in its different uses. Where its marginal revenue product and value of marginal product are higher, the price or prices paid for the resource will also be higher. These are the uses in which consumers want more of the resource employed; that is, in which they value it more highly. The different prices provide the incentive to resource owners to transfer units of the resource from lower-paying, lower-value uses to higher-paying, higher-value uses. Every such transfer increases national income. As the process of reallocation takes place, the differences in prices paid for the resource become less and less, and when the malallocation has been entirely corrected—if it ever is—the price of the resource and its value of marginal product will be the same in all its uses.

Monopoly in product selling prevents the price system from allocating units of a given resource in an entirely correct way. The price system tends to allocate the resource so that its price and its marginal revenue product are everywhere the same. But monopoly causes the value of marginal product of a resource to be higher than its marginal revenue product for the monopolistic firm. For different monopolists the difference between value of marginal product and marginal revenue product will vary, causing the latter to be different even though the former are the same. Firms in which the value of marginal product is higher are using less of the resource than consumers wish to have employed in producing that product or service.

Some degree of monopsony in resource purchasing also prevents the price system from fulfilling its allocation functions completely. The price system tends to allocate a given resource so that its price is the same in all uses. However, because of differing elasticities of supply for different monopsonists, marginal resource cost will differ among them. So, too, will marginal revenue product and value of marginal product.

Price-fixing by private organizations or by government agencies may prevent resources from being correctly allocated. Collective bargaining, for example, may establish a high minimum price for labour in high value of marginal product, high-paying uses. This will preclude the transfer of labour from lower value of marginal product lower-paying uses. If the minimum is extended to the lower-paying uses, raising the wage rate above the equilibrium level, unemployment will result.

Product price-fixing may also cause resources to be allocated incorrectly. A product price support, above the equilibrium level, shifts the demand curves for resources used in producing the product to the right of where consumer desires indicate they should be. Thus larger quantities of resources will be drawn into production, leaving smaller quantities in uses other than those consumers' desire.

Sociocultural together with educational and training factors may interfere with or negate the operation of the price system in reallocating resources. Family and community ties may impede the geographic mobility of labour resources. Lack of educational and training opportunities may also impede the upward mobility of workers.

Exercises and Questions for Discussion

1. List several groups or kinds of labour in your community within which units of labour seem to be homogeneous. For each group is the wage the same in the different employments of its labour? If it is not, why do you think it is different?

2. Under what circumstances would a minimum price for a product or resource improve the allocation of resources? In what situations would it not?

3. "If all agricultural price supports were abruptly removed, many farmers would become unemployed. Since unemployment is a forceful incentive for resources to find other employment, the allocation of the economy's resources would be improved." What do you think about this statement? What might impede the correct reallocation of these resources?

4. If its marginal revenue product is higher in one employment than in another, will national income be increased if units of a resource move from the lower marginal revenue product use to the higher marginal revenue product use? What assumptions did you make? What if one industry is purely competitive and another is monopolistic in product selling (both are purely competitive in resource purchasing)?

5. Suppose that the government sets the price of a product produced by a purely competitive industry below the equilibrium level. What would be the impact of this action on the allocation of those resources of which this industry uses a part?

6. What methods are currently being used in your community to improve the mobility (horizontal or vertical) of resources? How would you modify the current program?

Selected Readings

Bloom, G. F., and H. R. Northrup, *Economics of Labor Relations*, 5th ed. Homewood, Ill.: Richard D. Irwin, Inc., 1965, pp. 417-432.

Boulding, K. E., *Economic Analysis*, Vol. I, *Microesconomic Analysis*. New York: Harper & Row, Publishers, Inc., 1966, Chap. 6.

Economic Council of Canada, *Second Annual Review*. Ottawa: Queen's Printer, 1965, Chap. 5.

Economic Council of Canada, *Fifth Annual Review*. Ottawa: Queen's Printer, 1968, Chap. 7.

Economic Council of Canada, *Sixth Annual Review*. Ottawa: Queen's Printer, 1969, Chap. 8.

Ginzberg, E., *The Development of Human Resources*. New York: McGraw-Hill Book Company, Inc., 1966, Chap. 17.

Stigler, G. J., "The Economics of Minimum Wage Legislation," *American Economic Review*, June 1946, 36:3, 358-361.

Wilson, G. W., and S. Gordon, S. Judek, *Canada: An Appraisal Of Its Needs and Resources*. Toronto: University of Toronto Press, 1965, Chap. 3.

18

Distribution of the Product

Why is it that E. P. Taylor can claim a much larger share of the economy's yearly output than can a farm worker in the Atlantic provinces or eastern Quebec? We know of course, that the distribution of the economy's output among consuming units depends primarily on how income is distributed among them. Each can obtain a share approximately in the same proportion as his income bears to total income earned in the economy per year. During any given year individuals also have the alternative either of not spending a part of their income or of spending more than their income, if they are willing to use up a part of their past accumulated wealth. Thus, basically, the distribution of the economy's output depends upon the distribution of income. To rephrase the question, why is it that E. P. Taylor has a large income while a farm worker in the Atlantic region or eastern Quebec has a small one?

The price system plays a key role in the distribution of income or product, the third major function of an economic system. It is not the only factor at work and it does not necessarily lead toward the distribution that we would consider most desirable. After we have surveyed briefly what the actual distribution of income has been, we shall turn to the principles of income distribution, with emphasis on the functions of resources prices in the accomplishment of the distribution process. Next, we shall seek out the causes of income differences, and, finally, we shall examine the possibilities of income redistribution.

The Facts of Income Distribution

Income differences among consuming units of an economy have been an age-old source of conflict. In Canada they have been a major issue in many political campaigns and they have provided much of the basis for support of socialistic and communistic activities in the less developed countries of the world. Our purpose here is to get away from the more emotion-laden aspects of income distribution and to get at some of the facts.

The Functional Distribution of Income

Unfortunately, there is available no statistical information to tell us with any accuracy how the national income is divided among the factors that contribute to the productive process. However, the Dominion Bureau of Statistics provides figures which show the distribution of income from year to year on a basis which roughly approximates the division among the factors. The breakdown of income determination used by the Dominion Bureau of Statistics is shown in Table 18–1. This table separates out most of the wages, salaries and supplements earned by labour resources, including payments to members of the Canadian forces. For convenience, we call these *compensation of employees*. It also separates out most of the income earned by capital resources in the form of *corporate profits* (excluding profits transferred to nonresidents), and *interest and miscellaneous investment income*. It contains still another classification, income of *unincorporated enterprises* (including farms), which it does not break down between labour resources and capital resources.

Table 18–1 gives an impression of the functional distribution of income for 1947, 1955, 1964, and 1967. The most pronounced characteristic of earned income that is reflected in the Table is that between 64 and 73 percent of it is compensation of employees, clearly earned by *labour resources*. The portion clearly earned by *capital resources*—corporate profits, net interest, and miscellaneous investment income—varies between 17 and 19 percent of the total. The 10–19 percent allocated as net farm income and net income from other unincorporated businesses is a combination of earnings by labour resources and capital resources.

Suppose we make a rough division of the income of unincorporated enterprises between the labour and capital resource classifications in order to get some idea of the total shares of each over time. For example, for 1968, suppose we divide the amount between labour income and capital income in the same proportion as the rest of income earned was divided

TABLE 18-1
Net National Income at Factor Cost by Source,[1] 1947, 1955, 1964, 1968

	1947		1955		1964		1968	
	Income (millions)	Percent of Total	Income (millions)	Percent of Total	Income (millions)	Percent of Total	Income (millions)	Percent of Total
Compensation for employees	6,482	63.5	13,967	66.7	25,886	69.5	39,353	73.0
Income of unincorporated enterprises[2][3]	1,961	19.2	3,411	16.3	4,360	11.7	5,372	10.0
Corporate profits before taxes	1,566	15.3	2,826	13.5	5,255	14.1	6,566	12.2
Interest and miscellaneous investment income	197	2.0	744	3.5	1,697	4.6	2,580	4.8
Total	10,206	100.0	20,948	100.0	37,198	100.0	53,871	100.0

[1] An output measure which excludes capital consumption allowances and indirect taxes and includes subsidies.
[2] Includes inventory revaluation adjustment.
[3] Includes net rental income of persons.
Source: Based on data from Dominion Bureau of Statistics, National Income and Expenditure Accounts, 1926-1968, Ottawa, Queen's Printer, 1969.

between those two classifications. The 1968 percentage figure of 10 percent would be split, allocating 1.9 percent of total income to capital and 8.1 percent to labour.[1] Total labour income for 1968, then, is 81.1 percent of total income. Total capital income is 18.9 percent of total income. These results are recorded in the 1968 column of Table 18–2. For 1955, the allocation of the income of unincorporated ventures is 3.3 percent of total income to capital and 13.0 percent to labour. The allocation of total income earned for that year is 79.7 percent earned by labour and 20.3 percent earned by capital. Using the same procedures for 1947 and 1964, we obtain the results shown in the appropriate columns of Table 18–2. Clearly, there has been relatively little change in the distribution of income during the period covered by the tables.

The functional distribution of income tells us nothing about why some income recipients are in higher income brackets and others in lower ones. It is commonly believed that the really well-to-do live mostly on income from capital while the family units clustered at the bottom of the income scale live on income from labour. This is not entirely so. According to taxation statistics for 1967, only 14.8 percent of the persons with incomes

TABLE 18-2

Distribution of Net National Income at Factor Cost by Source for Selected Years, 1947, 1955, 1964, 1968

	1947 (Percent)	1955 (Percent)	1964 (Percent)	1968 (Percent)
Labour	78.6	79.7	78.7	81.1
Capital	21.4	20.3	21.2	18.9
Total	100.0	100.0	100.0	100.0

Source: Computed from Table 18-1

[1]*Labour income (compensation of employees) exclusive of income of unincorporated enterprises is 73.0 percent of total income. Capital income (corporate profits + net interest + miscellaneous investment income) exclusive of income of unincorporated enterprises is 17 percent of the total. Income of unincorporated enterprises is 10 percent of the total and is to be divided between capital and labour in the ratio 17/73. Letting C represent the part of income of unincorporated enterprises to be allocated to capital and L the part to be allocated to labour, we have the following equations:*

$$\frac{17.0}{73.0} = \frac{C}{L} \tag{18.1}$$
$$C + L = 10.1$$

Solving these simultaneously for C and L, we obtain

$$C = 1.9 \text{ percent of total income.}$$
$$L = 8.1 \text{ percent of total income.}$$

above $25,000 derived their income mainly from interest, dividends, rents and royalties.[2] The rest were generally dependent on incomes received from the operation of a business or a professional practice or a high salary in managerial occupations. On the other hand, about one-third of the families in the lowest 20 percent of income receivers were over 65 years of age, in retirement, living on government pensions. Still others were families with no workers who were living on private pensions, government welfare payments, such as family allowances or unemployment insurance benefits, or income other than earnings from labour.

The Personal Distribution of Income

The *personal distribution of income* provides us with more useful information than the functional distribution. The term refers to how families and unrelated individuals[3] share in the total income or total value of output of the economy. It lets us know the number of "household units" in each of certain income groups, and how wide the gaps are between the lower income groups and the upper income groups. It also helps us to understand what is happening to economic well-being over time.

How does the current distribution of personal income look? How has it changed over the last 15 years or so? Tables 18–3 and 18–4 provide relevant information. Column 4 in Table 18–3 indicates that, in 1965, 25 percent of the nation's families earned less than $3,000—a level which is sometimes used to describe the poverty line. At the other end of the scale, 11.8 percent of the families earned $10,000 or over per year. Another 18.9 percent earned yearly incomes of $7,000–$10,000. Median family income (this is the middle value on the income scale) was $5,245 while the average or arithmetic mean income was $5,965.

During the period covered by Table 18–4, average incomes of nonfarm Canadian families and unrelated individuals increased very rapidly. However, with respect to changes in the percentages of aggregate income going to different income groups, it is apparent that there was little variation for the 15 years 1951 to 1965. During these years the highest one-fifth of income receivers accounted for between 41.1 and 38.4 percent of nonfarm family income. At the opposite extreme, the lowest one-fifth of income receivers accounted for between 6.1 and 6.7 of aggregate nonfarm income. In other words, though average money incomes have risen substantially in recent years, inequalities of income are still very great.

---

[2]*Department of National Revenue,* Taxation Statistics. *Ottawa: Queen's Printer, 1969 edition.*

[3]*Unrelated individuals are those living alone, unattached to any family group.*

TABLE 18-3

Distribution of Families and Unrelated Individuals by Size of Income,* Canada, 1965

Income Class	Number in this class (Thousands)	Percentage of total number in this class	Percentage of total number in this class and lower ones	Total income received in this class ($ Millions)	Percentage of total income received in this class	Percentage of total income received in this class and lower ones
(1)	(2)	(3)	(4)	(5)	(6)	(7)
Under $1,000	390	6.9	6.9	223	0.7	0.7
$1,000-1,999	499	8.9	15.8	765	2.3	3.0
$2,000-2,999	516	9.2	25.0	1,319	3.9	6.9
$3,000-3,999	700	10.7	35.7	2,122	6.4	13.3
$4,000-4,999	625	11.2	46.9	2,837	8.4	21.7
$5,000-5,999	673	11.9	58.8	3,736	11.2	32.9
$6,000-6,999	598	10.6	69.4	3,944	11.8	44.7
$7,000-7,999	426	7.6	77.0	3,225	9.6	54.3
$8,000-9,999	635	11.3	88.3	5,673	16.9	71.2
$10,000-19,999	498	8.9	97.2	5,881	17.5	88.7
$15,000-over	165	2.9	100.0	3,828	11.4	100.0
Total	5,625	100.0		33,553	100.0	

*Includes farm incomes

Source: Based on data from *Dominion Bureau of Statistics, Income Distribution by Size in Canada, 1965.*

TABLE 18-4

Percentage Distribution of Nonfarm Incomes of Canadian Families and Unrelated Individuals, Selected Years, 1951, 1961, 1965

	Distribution of Total Income Before Tax			Average Income per Family
	1951	1961	1965	1965
Lowest income fifth of families	6.1	6.6	6.7	$ 2,263
Second fifth	12.9	13.4	13.4	$ 4,542
Third fifth	17.4	18.2	18.0	$ 6,102
Fourth fifth	22.5	23.4	23.5	$ 7,942
Top fifth	41.1	38.4	38.4	$13,016
All families	100.0	100.0	100.0	$ 6,669

Source: *Economic Council of Canada* Fifth Annual Review, Ottawa, *Queen's Printer,* September, *1968, Table 6-1, p. 107*

Causes of Income Differences

We return now to the fundamental question of *why* some people are rich while others are poor. We shall look first at the determinants of individual or family income. Then we shall examine the specific causes in income differences—differences in labour resources owned, in capital resources owned, and in prices received in different employments of the same resource.

Income Determination

The principles governing income determination are relatively simple and will not detain us long. They follow directly from those that govern resource pricing and employment. The income of an individual or a family depends upon two factors: (1) the quantities of resources owned and (2) the prices received for them.

Quantities of Resources Owned

Some families own labour resources only, but most own both labour and capital. Given the prices of different kinds of labour and different kinds of capital, the more the family is able to place on the market, the larger its income will be. Consider the resources owned by a university professor. His full-time work—teaching, research, and counseling students —may be all that he cares to do, and his university salary may represent the entire family income. It is quite possible, however, that he has the energy and the desire to do additional work, so he spends evenings, weekends, and holidays writing a textbook. Hopefully, he receives additional income from its sale. If he still has energy to burn he can take on consulting work for business or for government and earn still more from his labour resources.

The professor seeks investment possibilities for that part of his income that he saves, so he begins to accumulate capital resources. He may invest in real estate—buying apartment houses, farm land, or other kinds of real property. He may invest in stocks and bonds; that is, acquire titles or claims to capital resources used by corporations in producing goods and services. As he acquires larger quantities of capital resources, his income becomes correspondingly higher.

Resource Prices

The forces that determine the market price of a resource were examined in Chapters 15 and 16 and need not be repeated here in any detail. When a resource is purchased competitively its market price is determined by the demand for and the supply of it. A firm will employ that quantity of the resource at which the marginal revenue product of the resource is equal to its market price. Thus any unit of the resource is paid a price approximately equal to what it is worth to its employer—its marginal revenue product. Yet even though units of the resource are paid what they are worth to the employer, they may or may not be paid what they are worth to society. If the firm is a purely competitive seller of product, the value of marginal product of the resource will tend to be the same as the price paid for it, but if the firm is a monopolist, the value of marginal product of the resource will exceed its price. Only under conditions of monopsony will the value of a resource to its employer be greater than its price.

Differences in Labour Resources Owned

There are large differences in the earnings received from labour resources among different individuals. Why is this so? The labour resource classification does not really contain one unique kind of resource. There are a great many different resources within the classification. Suppose we subclassify these, differentiating among different *skill levels*. We obtain *vertical* groupings ranging from the lowest type of unskilled labour to the highest skill levels in existence. Garbage collectors are in one resource group. Ordinary carpenters are in another. Ordinary economics professors are in still a different group. Further, suppose that at each skill level we differentiate among occupations, obtaining a number of *horizontal* groupings. At any one level—say a professional level—we place lawyers in one group, physicians in another, university professors in another, and so on. These classifications are useful in explaining income differences stemming from differences in labour resources owned.

Vertical Differences

Most of the large differences in individual incomes earned from labour resources spring from differences in skill levels. Unskilled workers—common labourers—usually receive comparatively low wages. Highly skilled workers—entertainers, physicians, business executives—usually command high fees or salaries for the labour services they perform. The technical reason for this pattern is not hard to find. The demand for the services in the higher-skill occupations is greater relative to the supply available than is the case in the lower-skill occupations.

As we move upward from the lower- to the higher-skill occupational categories, we find that to a considerable extent each occupation constitutes a separate labour market. Hockey players operate in one market. Television and movie actors operate in another. Business executives are in another. Mathematics professors are in still another. Machinists, carpenters, and plumbers each have their own markets, and so does common labour. These separate groups of workers are sometimes referred to as *noncompeting* groups, but this is probably putting it too strongly. Interrelationships occur among groups at any given skill level and among groups at adjacent skill levels. Elvis Presley moved from truck driving into the entertainment field. Albert Schweitzer was a musician and a theologian before becoming a physician. Plumbers and carpenters can learn to be machinists. Common labourers can develop higher skills.

On the demand side, highly skilled workers, per man hour exerted, generally produce goods or services more urgently desired than those produced by workers with lesser skills. To put it another way, the value of marginal product curves for workers with high skill levels ordinarily is higher than that for unskilled workers. Compare, for example, the value of marginal product of a heart surgeon with that of a bricklayer, measuring man hours of labour on the horizontal axis and value of marginal product on the vertical axis.

On the supply side, the higher the skill level, the smaller the supply of labour seems to be. The number of persons eligible for top-management jobs in Bell Canada, Imperial Oil, or Alcan Aluminium is rather limited. There is a scarcity of dentists. Topflight history professors can be rather easily counted. Several factors contribute to this pattern.

The higher the skill level required for an occupation, the fewer persons there will be with the physical and mental characteristics necessary to qualify for it. There are more mediocre minds than there are outstanding ones. And for the number of people with the physical dexterity necessary for accomplishing certain complex processes varies inversely with the level of physical skill required. These differing capacities of individuals to attain specific skill levels result from myriad possible combinations of mental and physical characteristics. They have nothing to do with merit but are accidents of birth or inheritance.

Even if individuals have the physical and mental capacities to move up to high skill levels, there is no assurance that they can do so. The opportunities for developing inherited characteristics differ widely for different individuals. *Social obstacles* may block higher education—or even secondary education—for individuals who are inherently capable. The attitudes of family, friends, and community have much to do with an individual's desire to develop his capabilities. For verification of the point one needs only to look at the slum areas of Toronto, Montreal, or Halifax. Some people may find that training facilities are not open to them because of *racial and cultural* obstacles. Certainly this has been the case in the past in many Canadian communities; however, it appears that such discrimination is rapidly decreasing. *Financial obstacles* also tend to limit the supplies of high-level manpower. The tuition at law schools, medical schools, and engineering schools is high. These are more easily available to persons with wealthy parents than to the children of the poor.

Obstacles notwithstanding, many individuals from underprivileged backgrounds have been able to move into high-skill occupations. It has been no easy task, but a number of Negroes, Asiatics, and native Indians have been able to enter and succeed in most occupations. So, too, have individuals from white urban and rural slum areas. University training is becoming increasingly available to the children of the poor. Scholarship and fellowship aids as well as low-cost loans are providing more and more opportunities for students who are long on ability and short on means.

Not all of those who have opportunities for training take advantage of them. The development of one's physical and mental capacities requires more than the mere existence of opportunities. It requires initiative and drive on the part of the individual himself, and these traits differ considerably from person to person. But the fact remains that those born to parents farther up the income and social scale not only have more opportunities open to them but also grow up in an environment that is more likely to foster taking advantage of those opportunities.

Horizontal Differences

Within particular skill levels there are also income differences. These occur because of differences in the resource demand and supply conditions existing for different occupations. Engineering professors, for example, are generally paid higher salaries than professors of history. This is not because engineering professors are better trained or more highly skilled in their particular field but because there is a wider demand throughout the economy for engineers than there is for historians relative to their respective supplies.

There are at least two reasons why the supply of historians may have remained relatively large over time. First, personal preferences to work in the field of history rather than in the field of engineering may have induced many individuals to become historians even though they were well aware that their remuneration as historians would be lower. We can think of the historian in this case as taking a part of his pay in the form of on-the-job satisfaction.[4] Differences in pay attributable to differences in the desirability of jobs are referred to as *equalizing differences* and play a recognized role in the over-all pattern of wage and salary differences. Secondly, as individuals were in the process of choosing their professional field they may not have had complete information on comparative remuneration. Thus earnings possibilities may not have played a major role in their choice. Information of this kind is rapidly becoming more a part of common knowledge than it has been in the past. For example, it may have influenced your choice of what field to study.

Another common cause of income differences within a given profession has to do with experience or length of time in the field. Physicians, lawyers, and even schoolteachers find that their annual earnings rise as their experience increases, reaching a maximum some 20 or 30 years after entering the profession. Frequently the new entrant is as skilled as the old-timer—indeed on certain newly developed techniques he may be better. Yet the old-timer commands the premium. The difference here, of course, is on the demand side. Consumers place a premium on experience.

Differences in Capital Resources Owned

Differences in capital resources owned account for substantial differences in individual incomes. Some people own vast amounts of land, including the mineral deposits contained in it. Others own large amounts of corporate stocks and bonds. Still others own buildings or are direct owners of the plant and equipment of businesses. Some people own small amounts of the tools used in their regular occupations. As evidence of this difference, we shall consider in a general way how investment income-interest, dividends, rents and royalties, is distributed in Canada. Accord-

---

[4]*Another example of this principle is provided by the individual who sacrifices several thousand dollars per year in order to work for a university rather than for a private business or a government agency.*

ing to data collected by the Department of National Revenue for the year 1967, 210,351 persons derived their income mainly from investments. These taxpayers reported $1.4 billion of income. The distribution of incomes in which investment income predominates is summarized in Table 18–5.

TABLE 18–5

Percentage Distribution of Incomes Derived Mainly from Investments, Canada, 1967

Income Level	Percentage of Tax Returns in this Class	Percentage of Total Income Received by Individuals in this Class	Average Income in this class (dollars)
Under $10,000	86.7	57.2	3,945
$10,000-$15,000	6.6	13.2	12,081
Over $15,000	6.7	29.6	26,336
	100.0	100.0	5,984

Source: Based on data from Department of National Revenue, Taxation Statistics, *Ottawa, Queen's Printer, 1969 edition.*

As Table 18–5 indicates, individuals with incomes below $10,000 (86.7 percent of the group as a whole) received 57.2 percent of the $1.4 billion of income reported in 1967. Their average income was $3,945. On the other hand, persons with incomes above $15,000 (6.7 percent of the group) received 29.6 percent of the total and had average incomes of $26,336. What this analysis shows is that the degree of inequality is more extreme with respect to investment income than in all income. (Compare this table with Table 18–3.)

Now we must look at the factors that bring about wide disparities in the capital resources owned by different individuals. A list of the more prominent ones must include inheritance, luck, and the psychological propensity or will to accumulate.

Inheritance

If you want to be wealthy you will have made giant strides toward the achievement of your goal if you chose your parents wisely. Most people who own large amounts of capital—and who receive large incomes from capital—inherited much of what they have. Survey the wealthy families in your home community and you will find that by and large this is the case. Would the present generation of the Taylors, the Masseys, or the Eatons be as wealthy today as they are if they had been born in a slum off Spadina Avenue in Toronto? No one can say for sure, but it is highly unlikely that their capital holdings would approach their present magnitudes if this had been their lot.

Luck

Sometimes plain, old-fashioned luck brings about differences in the quantities of resources owned. A person may have purchased a piece of land for agricultural purposes, the price of the land being based on its expected net yield in producing farm products. Then the discovery of oil transforms the nature of the capital resource and makes its owner rich. Another familiar example of the same thing occurs from such things as a legislative decision to build a lake adjoining the property. To turn the example around, consider the initial impact of the relation between smoking and lung cancer on the value of capital used in cigarette production. In all of these examples there is an unexpected change in demand or marginal revenue product of the capital resources in question.

Propensities to Accumulate

Both of the factors just described attribute differences in quantities of capital owned to accidents of birth or chance; yet this is misleading. Many people with sizable holdings of capital resources built up most of their stocks over their own lifetimes. The starting point may have been a healthy endowment of labour resources—physical or mental or both. Many National Hockey League players have parleyed their initial salary earnings into bowling alleys, restaurants, sporting goods companies, real estate, and other kinds of capital. The original Timothy Eaton—the radical storekeeper—built one of the largest family-owned businesses in the world. Professional people often find it possible to set aside income from the use of their labour resources and to use what they have set aside to accumulate capital.

The personal characteristics that lead to capital accumulation vary widely among different individuals. Some who would like to accumulate capital are never able to do so because they have neither the requisite abilities nor the funds necessary for getting the whole thing started. Some whose incomes are large enough to permit some saving and investment in additional capital resources have no inclination to do so. Others have demonstrated marked capabilities of using up stocks of capital resources that they have inherited. Of one thing we can be sure, it is easier for people whose incomes are already large to accumulate additional capital resources than for those whose incomes are low. But a large income does not guarantee further capital accumulation.

Differences in Prices Paid for a Resource

Units of a given kind of resource are not always paid the same price, even when their qualities are more or less equal. These differences in price cause differences in the income earned by their owners. This may be so for several reasons. First, the differences may occur in the short-run, before forces inducing reallocation from lower-paying to higher-paying uses have had time to work themselves out. Second, the differences may be the consequences of price-fixing in some employments of the resource. Third, they may arise from supply restrictions or limitations on the quantity of the resource that can be used in certain employments of it. We met all of these phenomena in the three preceding chapters; nevertheless, they should be reviewed again in the context of their impact on income distribution.

Short-Run Differences

The conditions of demand for and supply of a resource in its different employment or in different geographic areas are constantly changing. With a shift in consumer demand from radios to television sets we expect that electronics technicians will be better paid in the latter field temporarily. Aircraft maintenance and repair shops catering to general aviation have experienced difficulty in retaining mechanics in recent years. With the relatively rapid growth of commercial air travel, rates of pay offered by the airlines have increased relative to those offered by the smaller general aviation shops.

Income differences of this kind are an integral and necessary feature of the price mechanism in the performance of its function of continually reallocating resources from uses where they contribute less to what consumers want to those where they contribute more. The income differences ordinarily indicate or reflect such differences. These provide the incentive for reallocation toward the higher-paying uses, and, in turn, the reallocation tends to wipe out the difference.

Price-Fixing

In Figure 18–1 we have a hypothetical free market demand for and supply of milk-wagon drivers in Winnipeg. The equilibrium wage rate is w and the level of employment is M. If all drivers work the same number of hours weekly, they will earn equal incomes.[5] Now suppose that through unionization and collective bargaining at wage rate of w_1 is put into effect. The employment level drops to M_1 and, of the number formerly employed, M_1M workers are now unemployed. The incomes of those who

[5]*Since milk-wagon drivers are essentially light truck drivers, their wage rates and incomes should be very close to those of other light truck drivers.*

retain employment will be higher, but those made unemployed have no income at all from their labour resources.

The picture probably will not be as dark as it has just been painted. The M_1M drivers who no longer are employed on the milk trucks will seek employment elsewhere, perhaps as light truck drivers or perhaps in other occupations. But it is almost certain that their incomes will be lower

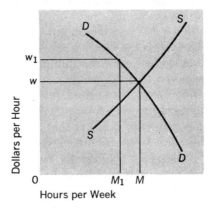

Figure 18-1
Effects of minimum price-fixing on income distribution.

in the new occupations than they were originally. Wherever else they go they increase the supply of labour in those employments, pressing those wage rates downward. And in most instances the occupations or employments into which they move were paying less than milk-wagon driving— otherwise they would have been in them before rather than on the milk trucks.

In general, we would expect minimum price-fixing, whenever it is effective, to create and to maintain income differences over time. Monopsony situations provide an exception to this statement for in these, if minimum prices are correctly set, not only will the wage rates and incomes of those originally employed be increased but the employment level will be increased as well.

Supply Control

Differences in incomes earned by units of a given resource are sometimes created or perpetuated through control of the supply that can be used in any specific employment. Supply controls may be imposed by organizations of suppliers or by the government. Where a union is able to restrict the number of members enrolled and is at the same time able to negotiate agreements with the major part of the employers using that specific kind of labour in which union membership must be a condition of employment, differences in earnings between union and non-union members in the trade may develop. Or, if the government limits the number of acres that can be planted to wheat, causing land that would otherwise have been planted to wheat to be put to some other use, differences in earnings between the land used for the former purpose and that used for the latter will occur. Analytically the case is very much the same as that of minimum price-fixing.

Measures to Help the Poor

No one seriously questions the desirability of alleviating poverty; the important consideration is what methods should be used toward this end. The preceding section noted that there has been relatively little change in the distribution of family income in Canada over the last 15 years. In particular the share of national income received by the lowest one-fifth of families—the group made famous by the Antipoverty Programs in the United States—has shifted upward only fractionally. But what are the policy measures that either concentrate specifically on the special problems of the poor at the present time or could do so in the future if we were inclined to move in that direction?

A Statistical Profile of the Poor

Before we can look intelligently at possible anti-poverty policies we must answer another question. Who are the poor? Table 18–6 provides some answers to the question for the year 1967. (It should be noted that data presented below are based on the following "poverty lines": unattached individuals with incomes below $1,740, families of two with less than $2,900, and families of three, four, and five or more with incomes of less than $3,480, $4,060 and $4,640 respectively.[6] Families and persons below these lines are referred to as being poor notwithstanding the fact that there is no existing official statistical concept of poverty in Canada.) A large proportion of households in which the head of the household was 65 years of age and over are poor. In this general category of families over 27 percent were poor. Clearly, age brings with it a strong possibility of poverty. Among households with a female head the incidence of poverty was high. Among families whose heads did not work during

[6]*For an explanation how these cut-off levels were established, see J. R. Podoluk* Incomes of Canadians. *Ottawa: Queen's Printer, 1968, p. 185. Cf. also Dominion Bureau of Statistics,* Income Distribution and Poverty in Canada, 1967, *October, 1969, p. 11.*

the year, approximately 46 percent were poor. Being unattached increases the likelihood that a person will be poor. Further, we find that the incidence of poverty is heavier on rural than on urban families. The table also confirms the earlier comment (see Chapter 17) that poor families are much more prevalent in the Atlantic provinces than in other regions of Canada. Yet, it is important to emphasize that although approximately 41 percent of rural families had low incomes, 55 percent of all low-income families lived in urban areas, and of this group more than one-third lived in metropolitan centres (30,000 and over). Additionally, although approximately 34 percent of families in the Atlantic provinces had low

TABLE 18-6

Incidence of Poverty (^{1}) Among Families and Unattached Individuals by Selected Characteristics, 1967

	Families	Unattached individuals
All units	18.6	39.0
By region of residence		
Atlantic provinces	33.7	52.5
Quebec	20.3	42.5
Prairie provinces	23.0	39.8
Ontario	12.4	32.5
British Columbia	16.2	40.5
By place of residence (^{2})		
Metropolitan centres	10.7	32.5
Other cities	15.6	50.2
Small urban areas	22.1	48.9
Rural areas	40.7	58.0
By sex of head		
Male	17.2	29.9
Female	35.6	47.7
By age of head		
24 and under	14.9	38.0
25-34	14.8	11.6
35-44	15.4	16.0
45-54	14.6	26.0
55-64	18.3	39.6
65-69	31.8	57.2
70 and over	43.2	68.4
By labour force status of head		
Paid worker	8.8	21.4
Self employed (^{3})	34.6	40.8
Not in labour force	46.4	70.7

^{1}*The percentage of all families or unattached individuals in a given category whose income in 1967 was below $1,740 for a single person, $2,900 for a family of two, $3,480 for a family of three, $4,060 for a family of four, and $4,640 for a family of five or more.*
^{2}*Classified according to size of population: metropolitan centres—30,000 and over; other cities—15,000—29,999; small urban areas—less than 15,000.*
^{3}*Includes farmers as well as professionals and owners of businesses.*
Source: Dominion Bureau of Statistics, Income Distribution and Poverty in Canada, 1967, Preliminary Estimates, *Ottawa, Queen's Printer, October, 1969, Table 6, p. 14.*

incomes, more than 54 percent of all low income families lived in Ontario and the Western provinces. It is thus clear that poverty in Canada is widely distributed geographically with a considerable proportion of it taking the form of relatively small pockets of poverty in otherwise high-income areas.

There are, of course, other characteristics contributing to poverty that are not indicated by Table 18–6. From 1961 Census data, not strictly comparable with that of the table, we can elicit some additional information on education that seems to be important.[7] Of nonfarm families using 70 percent or more of their incomes for food, clothing and shelter, 37 percent of the heads had eight years or less of education and another 20 percent had one to three years of high school.

Other characteristics also contribute to the chances of a household being poor, but we have identified the most important ones. To summarize, the chances are greatest if the household head is *65 years of age or over* or is *female* or is *not in the labour force* or is *lacking in education*. The last three characteristics are frenquently found either separately or together in slum areas.

One final remark should be made in concluding this section: some 840,000 families (including farm families) plus 586,000 unattached individuals (including farmers) were living below the statistical poverty lines (as defined above) in 1967. Or, to put the same point another way, nearly one-fifth of all Canadian families and two-fifths of unattached individuals were living in poverty in 1967.

Policies to Increase Earning Power

Armed with some idea of the characteristics of the poor we can examine the general types of actual and possible policy measures that may serve to alleviate poverty. Such measures fall into two broad, and over-lapping, categories. One includes those intended to increase the earning power of the poor. The other includes income supplements. We shall look at the first category in this subsection and at the second category in the next.

One of the most important sets of policy measures is that of providing *education and training* for the poor. Specifically, it is of prime importance in getting at the poor households in which the household head is under 65 years of age. The economic benefits to be derived are obvious. Education and training should enable its recipients to move upward into occupations more in demand by society. It should increase the quality of the labour resources owned by the poor and, consequently, their income levels.

[7]*Podoluk, loc. cit., p. 191.*

In Canada, responsibility for the organization and administration of public education is exercised by the provincial governments. However, the federal government helps to finance education and training. Direct financial support for education and training comprises three main elements. In the first place, the federal government provides per capita grants to each province to be disbursed among its universities and colleges. In this connection, the provinces have the choice of receiving either a grant amounting to $15 per head of population or 50 percent of the costs of the operations of post-secondary education, whichever is higher. Second, the federal government has assumed full financial responsibility for an expanded adult training program (Adult Occupational Training Act), including allowance to trainees to help offset the loss of earnings during training. Third, the federal government makes grants-in-aid for research personnel and equipment that assist educational institutions indirectly. In addition, the federal government operates a student loan program under the Canada Student Loans Act, shares equally with participating provinces in the costs of vocational rehabilitation services to handicapped persons (Vocational Rehabilitation of Disabled Persons Act, 1961), shares in the operating costs of the various programs conducted by employers in developing and operating approved training programs for their employees and participates to a considerable extent in informal education. It may be useful to add that the federal government is directly responsible for the education of the Eskimos in the Northwest Territories and the Indians on the reserves.

Other policy measures to increase the earning power of the poor are directed at increasing economic (and social) mobility. If we are to alleviate poverty, we need to eliminate the barriers that prevent the poor from moving to higher-paying occupations. The Manpower Mobility Program, which assists workers to explore job availabilities outside their local areas, to move their families and to buy or sell a house appears to have strengthened the possibilities for stimulating the movement of persons from lower to higher productivity employment both within and among the various regions in Canada. The Canada Fair Employment Practices Act, which came into effect on July 1, 1953, represents a further step to enhance labour mobility. It prohibits discrimination in employment based on race, colour, religion or national origin. It should be added, however, that it applies only to industries coming within federal jurisdiction. Since these industries employ, all told, only about 5 percent of Canada's paid labour force, the measure is unlikely to improve matters more than marginally. In addition to policy measures intended to eliminate discrimination in employment practices, others should point toward keeping occupations open to all qualified or potentially qualified persons interested in pursuing them. This means that, among other things, licensing laws, apprenticeship rules, resource price-fixing practices,[8] and other devices that may lead to controlled resource supplies should be continually evaluated to determine whether or not they inhibit mobility.

Policies to Maintain Income

Not all of the poor can take advantage of measures to increase their earning power. As we have seen, over 27 percent of the poor families are headed by individuals over 65 years of age. Another 14 percent are headed by females, some of whom find the double task of raising a family and being the family breadwinner impossible. Still others are ill or disabled. These who are necessarily outside the labour force must either be provided with income supplements or starve to death.

The most important income-maintenance measures administered federally are the Canada Pension Plan, old age security pensions, family allowances, youth allowances and unemployment insurance. Benefits under the Canada Pension Plan are classified under three main headings: Retirement Pensions which are payable to contributors[9] who have retired from regular employment at the age of 65; Disability Pensions for contributors who cannot engage in steady work, with additional benefits for their dependent children; and Survivors Benefits which are paid to or on behalf of the survivors of a deceased contributor. The old age security pension is payable to those age 65 and over. Until 1967 the pension amounted to $75 a month, but, beginning in 1968, the amount may be adjusted in line with changes in the Pension Index which, in turn, is based on the Consumer Price Index. Additionally, provision has been made for the payment of a monthly guaranteed income supplement to certain old age security pensioners who have little or no income other than the government pension. The maximum supplement is 40 percent of the old age security pension. Family allowances do not involve a means test and are paid at the monthly rate of $6 for each child under 10 years of age

[8]*In this context it is worth noting that the Female Employees Equal Pay Act, which came into effect on Oct. 1, 1965, prohibits an employer within federal jurisdiction from employing a female for any work at a rate of pay that is less than the rate at which a male is employed by that employer for identical or substantially identical work. Wage discrimination has been a particularly pernicious barrier to mobility for women.*

[9]*The Canada Pension Plan is universally applicable throughout Canada, except in the Province of Quebec where a comparable pension plan has been established. Contributions to the plan are made on earnings between $600 and $5,000 a year by both employees and self-employed persons. Employees contribute at the rate of 1.8 percent and a matching contribution is made by their employers; self-employed persons contribute at the rate of 3.6 percent.*

and $8 for each child age 10 or over but under 16 years. The Province of Quebec has its own family allowances program. Monthly allowances of $10 are payable in respect of all dependent youths age 16 and 17 who are receiving full-time educational training or are precluded from doing so by reason of physical or mental infirmity. Here again, the Province of Quebec has its own scheme. The unemployment insurance plan, which is financed very largely by compulsory contributions from employers and employees, provides for the payment of benefits to eligible unemployed persons. The total entitlement to the unemployed worker is related to his contribution history.

The Canada Assistance Plan was enacted in 1966 to complement other income maintenance measures. It provides that the provinces may at their option combine four separate federal-provincial assistance programs (for the aged, the blind, the disabled, and the unemployed) into a general program. Under this plan, aid is based on a more comprehensive and flexible assessment of recipients' budgetary requirements, and federal cost-sharing includes for the first time assistance to needy mothers and their dependent children. Rates of assistance and standards of eligibility are set by the individual provinces. Provision is made for federal contributions of 50 percent of the costs of assistance to needy persons and of the costs of certain welfare services. All provinces have signed agreements under the Canada Assistance Plan.

Other government policies are aimed at raising and/or maintaining income of certain groups. These groups are not always the poor, although in some cases they may be. Minimum wage laws and agricultural income supplements provide examples. The former are intended to help the poor, but it is questionable whether or not they really accomplish this objective. The latter, developed over time in the name of increasing the incomes of poor farmers, miss the mark almost entirely, as we indicated earlier. To press still further, what is the purpose of tariffs and import duties, government support of labour unions and collective bargaining, and other policies of a similar nature?

Some Questions and Problems

The cost of bringing every household above the poverty line as now defined would not impose an impossible burden on the economy. The continuing problem is that of *how* it should be done. The existing system has improved the income-generating capacities of the poor, but at the same time it has raised many problems and questions. Assistance to needy families, for example, has been said to encourage the breaking up of families by requiring that there be no employable male as a member of an eligible household. Often attempts by members of families to increase earnings have resulted in abrupt declines in or even the termination of income supplement or other social assistance.[10] On the other hand, are there cases in which income supplements are so high that incentives for recipients to seek employment are reduced significantly? Do we want cradle-to-the-grave social security coverage for *all* members of our society or are we concerned primarily with assistance to poor families? Are there alternatives to the present methods of making payments to the poor (and sometimes to those who are not poor) that promise to be superior to present methods? For example, is it possible—or desirable—to reduce the many programs that now exist to one simplified program? What are the advantages and disadvantages of new proposals for the elimination of poverty such as the negative income tax and other forms of guaranteed minimum income? Certainly at this point in time we do not have all the answers.

Within the framework of a free enterprise economic system, we can alter the distribution of income however we as a society wish. We can tax the wealthy to support programs to increase earning power and to maintain the incomes of the poor. Income transfers of this kind need not interfere with the *operation* of the price mechanism at all. They will, of course, decrease the purchasing power of those who are taxed and increase the purchasing power of those who benefit from the program, and these alterations in purchasing power may in turn change the structure of priorities that consumers as a group place on the range of goods and services available. And this is as it should be—unless we who pay the taxes are certain that we know more about what is good for the poor than they themselves know.

Summary

In a free enterprise economy the distribution of the economy's output among families and unrelated individuals depends basically upon the distribution of income earned. Income earned is frequently classified in two different ways. The functional distribution of income classifies it according to the amounts earned by capital resources and by labour resources. The personal distribution of income classifies families and unrelated individuals according to the size of their incomes regardless of whether the

---

[10]*An example cited by the Economic Council of Canada in its* Fifth Annual Review *might help make the above more precise. A family may be forced to move immediately out of subsidized housing into other accommodation at a substantial increase in rent which may exceed the increase in earnings. Under these circumstances, the incremental income is "taxed" at a marginal rate amounting to more than 100 percent.*

source is labour or capital. Over the last 20 years the share of income earned by labour resources has shown a tendency to increase. Conversely, there has been little change in the personal distribution of income since 1951.

Differences in family or individual incomes may arise from differences in labour resources owned. Vertical differences in labour resources owned refer to differences in skill levels. These account for the major differences in incomes at any given skill level. Horizontal differences refer to occupational differences at any given skill level. When labour is classified vertically and horizontally a number of labour markets emerge and differences in demand for and supply of labour among these markets result in differences in wages and salaries (prices) paid them.

Differences in capital resources owned may also account for substantial differences in family and individual income levels. These differences arise to a considerable extent as a result of inheritance. They result partly from luck on the part of capital owners, but they also arise from differences in the opportunities and in the propensities of people to accumulate.

In addition, income differences may be the result of differences in prices paid for different blocks of units of the same kind of resource. These differences in price may be short-run in character, stemming from changes in demand for the resource in its different employments. This may also be of a more permanent nature when a minimum price is fixed by private organizations or by the government in some uses of the resource but not in others. The same effect may be obtained when the supply of the resource that can be employed in some of its uses is controlled or fixed.

The major problem with respect to income distribution appears to be that of how to alleviate poverty, or how to get everyone up to some minimum income level. According to current definitions of poverty, nearly one-fifth of all families and two-fifths of unattached individuals in Canada are poor. In a large proportion of these cases, the household head is 65 years of age or older. The incidence of poverty is also high when the household head is female, or is not a member of the labour force or has only an elementary school education.

One category of policy measures to maintain incomes consists of attempts to increase the earning power of the poor. In this category we find measures to provide and improve conventional educational facilities at all levels. Additional special educational measures are aimed at the handicapped and at those in need of or desiring to upgrade their skills or learn new ones. In addition to educational measures, positive programs to eliminate barriers to the economic mobility of the poor are essential.

The other major category of policy measures designed to maintain income includes supplements to the incomes of families or individuals. Social security programs are in part intended for this purpose, as are minimum wage laws. Some programs to supplement incomes help the poor very little. These include payments to those in agriculture, tariffs to protect special groups of producers against foreign competition, and subsidies or other price-maintenance devices.

Exercises and Questions for Discussion

1. Why does labour receive a larger portion of national income than capital? Can this disparity be related to the productivity of each resource? Explain.
2. Incomes of families and of unrelated individuals have been moving upward over the past few years. What factors account for this rise? Explain how you think each has contributed.
3. There has been relatively little change in the distribution of family income in Canada since 1951. In particular the share of total income received by families in the lowest quintile has altered only fractionally. What factors account for this stability?
4. Why is investment income distributed more unequally than total income?
5. "Since the higher the price paid for a resource the greater the income will be for the owner of that resource, minimum prices for resources will increase income in the economy." Is this statement correct? Elaborate.
6. What measures are currently being used to alleviate poverty? What would you do to improve these policies? Be specific.
7. List the job opportunities that will be open to you upon graduation from college. What equalizing differences are there among the occupations? Is prospective income the major reason you have chosen the field in which you are now studying?

Selected Readings

Boulding, Kenneth E., *Economic Analysis*, Vol. I, *Microeconomics*, 4th ed. New York: Harper & Row, Publishers, Inc., 1966, pp. 90-105.

Economic Council of Canada, *Fifth Annual Review*. Ottawa: Queen's Printer, September 1968, Chaps. 6 and 7.

Economic Council of Canada, *Sixth Annual Review*. Ottawa: Queen's Printer, September 1969, Chap. 7.

Podoluk, Jenny R., *Incomes of Canadians*. Ottawa: Queen's Printer, 1968, Chap. 8.

Will, Robert E., and Harold G. Vatter, eds., *Poverty in Affluence*. New York: Harcourt, Brace & World, Inc., 1965, Section 8.

19

The Economics of Organized Labour

Any discussion of resource pricing, resource employment, resource allocation, and income distribution, would be seriously incomplete if organized labour were left out of the picture. Unionism as a movement has stirred emotions, both pro and con, and around its struggles a sort of folklore has been built up. Our purpose here is in no sense to provide a complete résumé of a fascinating area of study but rather to separate out those aspects of labour union activities that have important implications for the operation of the economy. We shall discuss in turn the structure of organized labour, unions and the government, the objectives of organized labour, the weapons used by unions, and the extent and effects of unionism.

The Structure of Organized Labour

Labour unions are organizations of workers, usually below the supervisory level, that attempt to improve the well-being of their members. Their activities are intended to enhance the social and political well-being of their members as well as their economic status; however, since the latter has taken precedence in North America, we shall be primarily concerned with it. We shall classify labour organizations in two ways—(1) according to the kinds of workers they enroll and (2) according to their positions in the organizational hierarchy.

Classification by Kinds of Workers

In classifying unions by kinds of workers we distinguish between craft unions and industrial unions. *Craft unions enroll* members of a particular skill or occupation, for example, plumbers. Other examples are furnished by carpenters' unions, bricklayers' unions, and printers' unions. Typically, but not exclusively, craft unions operate in industries characterized by small firms. Historically the craft type of organization was predominant until the 1930's.

Industrial unions include workers in a particular industry or in some cases a group of industries, regardless of skill levels or specific occupations. The United Steelworkers and the United Automobile Workers are outstanding examples. As big business developed during and after World War I, the craft type of organization in many ways became inadequate to serve the purposes of many workers. Large numbers of workers in each of several occupations working for a single employer, conflicting claims to specific kinds of work, and the difficulties inherent in securing co-ordination among several different unions in dealing with an employer or an employer group favoured the development of industrial unions in the mass-production industries typically populated by larger firms.

All unions in Canada do not fit neatly into one classification or the other. Some contain elements of both craft and industrial unionism but may be oriented toward one or the other pure type. The Teamsters Union, a case in point, consists predominantly of drivers but it also includes shipping clerks, mail room employees, retail clerks, and others.

Classification by Organizational Level

From the standpoint of the organizational hierarchy, there are three levels of unionism. These are local unions, national and international unions, and federations of unions. Their relations to one another are illustrated in Figure 19–1.

Local Unions

Local unions are the building blocks of organized labour. They are the organizations in which workers hold their memberships, and, as the name implies, they ordinarily embrace workers of a local geographic area. The local may be either craft- or industrially-oriented. A craft-oriented local frequently cuts across individual firm lines, having as members as many of those who ply the trade in the community as it can induce, or that it finds advantageous, to enroll, regardless of the firm for which they work. The plumbers of half a dozen or more plumbing establishments in your home community undoubtedly belong to a single plumbers' local. The

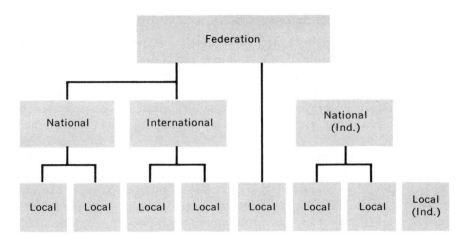

Figure 19-1
The organizational structure of labour unions

same is very probably true of the carpenters employed by most of your local builders. Frequently, though not necessarily, locals with an industrial orientation have as members the employees of a single company in a particular locality—for example, a General Motors Windsor local of the United Auto Workers. But wide differences exist from union to union and from area to area with respect to the precise coverage of any local union.

The officers of a local union are not ordinarily full-time union officials. Usually they are workers in the plant or craft where the local is located. In most cases they are not even paid as union officials, but frequently they are permitted time off for union duties although they are paid by the employer as full-time employees. The roster of officials includes at least a president, a secretary-treasurer, and shop or job stewards.

At the beginning of 1969 there were 9,310 local unions in Canada. Most local unions in Canada are relatively small, with not more than two or three hundred members. There are a few mammoth locals, however, with thousands of members. There are locals of national and international unions. locals directly chartered by a federation or central congress, and independent local organizations.

National and International Unions

National and international unions occupy the next level in the hierarchy. They are made up of groups of local unions, usually from the same craft or from the same industry, but sometimes they include locals from several related industries. In terms of structural units, the difference between national and international unions is a technical one only. Most locals of international unions are located in the United States, while all those of national unions are located in Canada. It should be added that all international unions operating in Canada have their main membership and central headquarters in the United States though the larger ones have Canadian head offices.

A national or international union is governed ultimately by a convention of delegates from its locals who meet in most cases annually or biennially. Officers are elected by the convention to carry on the business of the union throughout the year. The officers are full-time, paid, union officials and they exercise leadership of the national or international and of the locals composing it. As full-time, paid officials they are specialists in union business. Add to this the superior financial strength of the national or international as compared with most locals and it becomes apparent that much of the power of organized labour lies in the national and international unions. Normally the national or international receives its financial support from a designated portion of the dues that members of the locals must pay.

In 1969 there were 160 national and international unions active in Canada, of which 101 were international and 59 were national in scope. Among the latter the largest are the Canadian Union of Public Employees and the Public Service Alliance of Canada. The largest internationals include the United Steelworkers, the United Automobile Workers, the United Brotherhood of Carpenters and Joiners, the United Brotherhood of Teamsters and the International Brotherhood of Electrical Workers. As in the case of business firms, the great majority of unions in Canada are of modest size (three out of four have less than 10,000 members each), but the big unions account for a high proportion of the total membership. In 1969, the largest 10 accounted for 39 percent and the largest 18 took in more than 52 percent of all union members in Canada. These unions are shown in Table 19–1. Table 19–2 shows the distribution of membership by size and type of union.

The Federation or Congress

For most national and international unions in Canada (and in most other industrial nations), union organization does not stop at the national and international level but extends to the level of a federation (congress, league, coalition) of national and international unions. There are two of these federations in Canada today—the Canadian Labour Congress, and the Confederation of National Trade Unions. The Canadian Labour Congress (CLC) has close fraternal ties with the labour federation in the United States—The American Federation of Labor and Congress of

TABLE 19-1
Unions with 30,000 or more Members, 1969

Relative Position	Union	Canadian Membership
1.	United Steelworkers of America	150,000
2.	Canadian Union of Public Employees	124,500
3.	International Union, United Automobile, Aerospace and Agricultural Implement Workers of America	113,000
4.	Public Service Alliance of Canada	96,200
5.	United Brotherhood of Carpenters and Joiners of America	73,500
6.	International Brotherhood of Teamsters, Chauffeurs, Warehousemen and Helpers of America	56,200
7.	International Brotherhood of Electrical Workers	56,000
8.	International Association of Machinists and Aerospace Workers	52,700
9.	International Woodworkers of America	49,300
10.	Fédération Nationale des Services, Inc. — Service Employees' Federation	44,800
11.	Canadian Food and Allied Workers	40,000
12.	International Brotherhood of Pulp, Sulphite and Paper Mill Workers	39,900
13.	Labourers' International Union of North America	33,900
14.	Canadian Brotherhood of Railway, Transport, and General Workers	33,600
15.	Fédération Nationale des Syndicats du Bâtiment et du Bois, Inc. — Building and Woodworkers' Federation	31,100
16.	Fédération des Travailleurs de la Métallurgie, des Mines, et des Produits Chimiques — Canadian Federation of Steel, Mine and Chemical Workers	30,400
17.	United Association of Journeymen and Apprentices of the Plumbing and Pipefitting Industry of the United States and Canada	30,200
18.	Syndicat des Fonctionnaires Provinciaux du Québec — Quebec Government Employees	30,000
	Total Membership	1,085,000

Source: Canada Department of Labour, Labour Organizations in Canada, 1969, Ottawa, Queen's Printer, pp. viii and ix.

TABLE 19-2

Concentration of Union Membership, 1969*

Membership Range	International Unions No. of Unions	International Unions Membership	National Unions No. of Unions	National Unions Membership	Total No. of Unions	Total Membership
Under 500	19	2,677	7	1,592	26	4,269
500- 999	4	3,065	4	2,964	8	6,029
1,000- 2,499	14	23,348	12	19,987	26	43,335
2,500- 4,999	11	39,795	10	37,174	21	76,969
5,000- 9,999	15	115,729	11	83,262	26	198,991
10,000-14,999	10	121,166	4	46,825	14	167,991
15,000-19,999	7	110,462	3	46,854	10	157,316
20,000-29,999	10	235,167	1	20,591	11	255,758
30,000 and over	11	694,705	7	390,638	18	1,085,343
Total	101	1,346,114	59	649,887	160	1,996,001

Excludes local unions directly chartered by a federation and independent local organizations.

Source: Canada Department of Labour, Labour Organization in Canada, 1969. Ottawa, Queen's Printer, p. XIV.

Industrial Organization (AFL-CIO).[1] This relationship primarily results from the affiliations of the international unions which, as already mentioned, operate in both Canada and the United States.

Not all national and international unions are affiliated with one of the central Canadian federations. Some, such as the Brotherhood of Locomotive Engineers, have never seen fit to join the CLC or the CNTU, while others, such as the Teamsters Union, have been expelled from the CLC. These national and internationals operate independently. Some local unions are also independent, belonging neither to a national or international nor to one of the Canadian federations. Still other locals may

[1]*There were two labour federations in the United States from 1937 to 1955. One was the American Federation of Labor, dating from 1886, while the other was the Congress of Industrial Organizations, which split off from the AFL in 1937, with the craft versus the industrial type of union organization being a key issue in dispute. The CIO at the time of the split was composed of young, growing unions highly oriented toward industrial unionism, while the old-guard AFL unions were predominantly craft-oriented. The two federations merged as the AFL-CIO in 1955. It may be useful to add that the United Automobile Workers, which disaffiliated from the AFL-CIO in 1968, and the International Brotherhood of Teamsters, which was expelled from the Federation in 1957, formed a new organization in 1969 called the Alliance for Labor Action (ALA). Although the ALA, according to its constitution, does not perform the function of a federation, it has been branded "a dual labor organization, rival to the AFL-CIO" by the AFL-CIO's executive council. Clearly this new organization could have serious implications for the American labour movement.*

TABLE 19-3
Union Membership by Type of Union and Affiliation, 1969

Type of Affiliation	No. of Unions	No. of Locals	Membership Number	Membership Percent
International Unions	101	4,956	1,346,114	65.0
AFL-CIO/CLC	85	4,460	1,106,861	53.4
CLC only	4	141	127,538	6.2
AFL-CIO only	5	10	604	*
Unaffiliated Railway Brotherhoods	1	102	7,186	0.4
Other Unaffiliated Unions	6	243	103,925	5.0
National Unions	59	4,034	649,887	31.3
CLC	23	2,631	339,157	16.3
CNTU	11	940	200,877	9.7
Unaffiliated Unions	25	463	109,853	5.3
Directly Chartered Local Unions	196	196	22,201	1.0
CLC	152	152	15,095	0.7
CNTU	44	44	7,106	0.3
Independent Local Organizations	124	124	56,414	2.7
Total	480	9,310	2,074,616	100.0

*Less than 0.1 percent
Source: Canada Departmant of Labour, Labour Organization in Canada, 1969.
Ottawa, Queen's Printer, p. XIII.

belong to one of the Canadian federations but not to a national or international union. Table 19–3 shows, as of January 1969, the distribution of union membership in Canada by type of union and congress affiliation.

It may be seen from Table 19–3 that 76.6 percent of all union members in Canada were in organizations affiliated with the CLC in 1969; in most cases these unionists belonged to unions which were also affiliated with the AFL-CIO. Another 10 percent of the total union membership in 1969 was affiliated with the CNTU. Unaffiliated international and national unions accounted for 10.7 percent and 2.7 percent was in independent local organizations.

A federation engages primarily in education, promotion, and research in matters affecting unionism. Its officers and employees devote much time to lobbying for favourable legislation and to discussing with public officials the issues of concern to organized labour. It plays a role in setting standards of ethics in the labour movement and in establishing relations with organized workers internationally.[2] By and large a federation's power is limited by the fact that most large national and international unions can withdraw from it and operate on their own.

A federation, like a national or international, is governed by a convention. In the case of both the CLC and the CNTU, the Convention meets

[2]*The CLC is a member of the International Confederation of Free Trade Unions (ICFTU) and the CNTU of the International Federation of Christian Trade Unions (IFCTU).*

every other year. The convention is made up of representatives from member unions, and officers of the two central bodies are elected by the convention. They, like national or international union officers, are full-time, paid, union employees and are ordinarily highly skilled in the performance of their duties.

Unions and the Government

The attitude of the public as reflected by government policy toward unions has changed over time from one of hostility to one of positive encouragement. In recent years the policy of encouragement has been tempered in some degree by government regulations of unions (and employers) and their affairs. Government policy is expressed through court decisions and through legislation. A brief history of the relations between government and organized labour will go far toward explaining the development of unionism and collective bargaining in Canada.

Pre-World War II Policies

Labour unions in the nineteenth century faced adverse public opinion, hostile courts, and legislation inimical to their growth and development. As an example, the master carpenters in Montreal passed a resolution in 1834 condemning a combination of their employees since "such a body of men cannot be considered competent to what they have undertaken, neither are they likely to confine themselves to decent and becoming order, they are therefore dangerous to the peace and safety of good citizens". The outstanding manifestation of employer resistance happened in the spring of 1872, during the celebrated "printers' strike". The master printers in Toronto, headed by George Brown of the Globe, had all 24 members of the Typographical Union committee indicted on a charge of seditious conspiracy. These indictments (14 were subsequently arrested) brought out clearly the weakness of trade unions before the law in Canada. Labour leaders determined therefore, to secure new legislation, and in the same year a bill dealing with both the civil and criminal law with respect to trade unions was passed by the Dominion Parliament. This statute, modelled on the British Trade Union and Criminal Law Amendment Acts of the previous year, exempted registered trade unions from the Common Law's provisions regarding 'conspiracy in restraint of trade'. For such unions, the legality of organized action for such purposes as increasing wages or shortening hours was fully established. Unregistered unions, however, were freed of their Common Law disabilities only in 1892. Parenthetically, the machinery for operating the Trade Union Act of 1872 was not set up till many years later.

Following Britain's lead, the Canadian government enacted legislation designed to increase the effectiveness of collective bargaining. Under the Conciliation Act of 1900 the Minister of Labour was empowered to investigate the cause of any industrial dispute and to offer conciliatory assistance upon request by either labour or management. The principle and practice of *compulsory investigation* was introduced in the Railway Labour Disputes Act of 1903, which was passed by Parliament following a protracted railway strike in 1901. The act, which was limited in scope to railroad transportation, provided for a three-man *conciliation board*, but where it failed to bring agreement a *board of arbitration* might be set up if both parties agreed. However, the disputants were not required to accept an arbitration award, nor were strikes or lockouts prohibited once the provisions of the act had been complied with.

In 1907, following a coal strike in southern Alberta, the federal government enacted the Industrial Disputes Investigation Act (I.D.I. Act), a benchmark in the history of Canadian labour law. It introduced the idea that a *compulsory delay of work stoppages*—the so-called "cooling-off period",—accompanied by a thorough investigation, would so modify the perspective of the parties in a labour dispute that many strikes and lockouts would be avoided; and this concept has stood virtually unaltered in Canadian legislation ever since. The Act was applied compulsorily only to mines and public utilities; it was extended to other industries only when desired by both parties.

When the I.D.I. Act was declared unconstitutional in 1925, the Canadian Parliament amended the statute to make it apply only to disputes coming under Dominion jurisdiction, such as ocean, coastal and Great Lakes shipping, interprovincial rail and air transportation and communication. However, within a few years all provinces except Prince Edward Island enacted enabling legislation extending the Act's coverage to operations within provincial jurisdiction. Accordingly, the I.D.I. Act remained almost the sole piece of labour legislation in this country until 1937, when some of the provinces began to pass similar laws of their own.

In 1939, the federal government amended the Criminal Code to prohibit employers from discharging workers solely on account of union activity. While this change marked some improvement in the status accorded unions, the attitude of employers toward them was still far from favourable.

Wartime Policies

With the onset of the Second World War, the federal government, under its national emergency powers, extended the I.D.I. Act, with its compulsory delay and conciliation provisions, to cover all defence industries. This was followed by a series of Orders-in-Council, which were designed to overcome various deficiencies in existing labour legislation and to meet new situations as they developed. Canada adopted a two-vote conciliation process as part of its dispute settlement machinery: one vote was required to set up a conciliation board; and another, to authorize a strike. These provisions failed to minimize the number of work stoppages and were unsatisfactory to labour, which still maintained that employers had too much power. Consequently, the Cabinet passed Privy Council Order 1003, which brought the Canadian labour code more into line with the American pattern.

P.C. Order 1003 marked a major change in the policy of the federal government toward organized labour. Modeled on the National Labor Relations Act (Wagner Act), which was passed by the U.S. Congress in 1935 and approved by the U.S. Supreme Court in 1937, this piece of legislation threw the full support of the federal government behind the right of labour unions to engage in collective bargaining with their employers. Workers were guaranteed the right to form and join unions of their own choosing for this purpose. To prevent the kind of employer interference that had historically almost stopped unionism in its tracks, certain employer practices were designated as *unfair labour practices*. These included (1) failure of the employer to bargain with the union in good faith; (2) attempts to coerce workers to join or not join a union and with regard to what union to join if they chose to join one; and (3) discrimination against any worker for union activities.

The Canada Labour Relations Board was created as a quasi-judicial agency to carry out the provisions of the statute. The Board heard complaints of unfair labour practices and prescribed the appropriate remedies. It was also responsible for seeing to it that workers could form unions if they so desired and for certifying those unions as the *bargaining agent* for employees. Toward this end the Board had the power to determine what constitutes an appropriate employee bargaining unit—a department of a plant, an entire plant, all the machinists of a given employer, all the plumbers of a specific city, or some other unit. Once the appropriate bargaining unit was designated, the Board conducted an election, if necessary, among employees to determine whether or not they wanted to be represented by a union, and, if so, by what union. If a majority of employees of a designated bargaining unit indicated through an election a desire to be represented by a given union, that union was so certified by the Board and had to be so recognized by the employer.

At the same time, PC 1003 retained, in amended form, the machinery derived from the I.D.I. Act for preventing or settling industrial disputes: the familiar compulsory conciliation and delay; the two-stage conciliation process—a conciliation officer stage and a tripartite conciliation board stage. It also banned strikes during the life of a collective agreement and all unsolved grievances arising had to be submitted to arbitration for a final and binding solution. The votes previously required to get a conciliation board established and to authorize a strike were both abolished.

The upshot of these wartime policies was that management and labour became accustomed to a uniform labour code across the country.

Postwar Policies

After official termination of the wartime emergency, the federal government's power over the major portion of Canada's industrial economy came to an end. Consequently, Parliament in 1948 passed a new statute, the Industrial Relations and Disputes Investigation Act, which contained most of the provisions of P.C. 1003. It had, of course, the much more restricted jurisdiction over labour-management relations accorded Parliament in peacetime. The provinces, however, with the exception of Prince Edward Island, enacted labour relations legislation modeled largely along the lines of the federal Act of 1948. Subsequently, the legislature of Prince Edward Island passed a labour relations act likewise modeled mainly on the federal legislation. Thus, although government industrial relations policy in Canada today is represented by eleven different authorities, the various statutes are sufficiently similar to constitute a fairly uniform national labour code. All of these laws guarantee freedom of association and the right to organize, provide machinery (labour relations boards) for determining questions of representation, defining appropriate bargaining units and investigating unfair labour practices, and require negotiation between management and certified bargaining agents. Except in Saskatchewan, they require the parties in a labour dispute to comply with the conciliation procedures laid down in the Act before a strike or lockout may legally take place (two-stage conciliation is the normal procedure in all jurisdictions), and they provide also for compulsory arbitration of disputes that are not otherwise settled where collective agreements are in force. Furthermore, in most jurisdictions certain critical public servants, such as policemen and firemen, are forbidden to strike, and, in lieu of this right, have recourse to final and binding arbitration. Additionally, there are special provisions relating to hospital disputes in six provinces. Among the various statutes, however, there is a considerable variety in details regarding such matters as the basis for determining "appropriate" bargaining units, "unfair" labour practices of unions and employers, and time limits for the various stages of the conciliation process.

The impact of federal and provincial legislation on union membership from 1940 to 1960, as we shall see later, was little short of spectacular.

However, through the 1950's some disenchantment with certain union activities was becoming evident. In 1959 two provinces amended their labour laws so as to reduce union privileges. The legislature of Newfoundland passed two bills: one voided the certification of the province's two locals of the International Woodworkers of America, and abrogated all collective agreements in force between them and employers; the other authorized the government to dissolve any trade union in the province which was a branch of an international union, if a substantial number of the union's officers had ever been convicted of any grievous crimes.[3] The Act also made unions full-fledged entities for any proceeding before the courts, including civil actions for damages, and declared unlawful the use of secondary boycotts.[4] The British Columbia legislation was amended to prohibit secondary boycotts in all their forms; trade unions were declared to be legal entities and, as such, liable in damages for breaches of the new Trade-unions Act or under the common law. The Manitoba Act was amended in 1962 to specify that unions could sue or be sued in their own name. In the same year, Parliament passed the Corporations and Labour Unions Returns Act. It provides for the reporting of financial and other statistics relating to the affairs of business corporations and labour unions (except unions with fewer than 100 members resident in Canada) carrying on activities in Canada. The legislation is composed of two parts. Section A of the return required from trade unions contains the information which is to be made public. It includes the name and address of the union; the union constitution; the name, address and nationality of each officer resident in Canada; the position of each union officer and the manner of his election or appointment. Section B, which is confidential to the government, requires union financial statements, including assets and liabilities and income and expenditure. In addition, international unions are required to disclose total payments by Canadian members for initiation fees, dues, health, welfare and death benefit assessments; fines, work permit and strike benefit contributions. Unions that fail to file returns may be fined $50 a day for each day the return is in arrears.

Granted that the present system of labour relations legislation in Canada is still one of positive encouragement to the organizing of workers into unions for collective bargaining purposes, there can be little doubt that government policy toward organized labour has grown more restrictive since the late 1950's. It is also highly significant that the report of the *Task Force on Labour Relations in Canada* recently recommended "an

---

[3]*In 1960 an amendment to the Labour Relations Act of Newfoundland transferred the power to dissolve a trade union from the provincial Cabinet to the Supreme Court of the province acting upon an application of the Attorney General.*
[4]*See pp. 405-406 for a definition and example of a secondary boycott.*

increase in government involvement in collective bargaining".[5] Not surprisingly, both the Canadian Labour Congress and the Canadian Manufacturers' Association have quarrelled with the report on this point. It may be well to add that the federal government's reaction to the weighty (250 pages) Woods report was less than ecstatic. Thus, how much influence it will have on upcoming federal labour legislation remains to be seen.

The Objectives of Organized Labour

To say that unions try to increase the well-being of their members is not very helpful in describing the range of their activities. As one reads through the voluminous literature on the labour movement on the North American continent, it appears that unions have four areas of more concrete objectives. These are (1) to redistribute income, (2) to establish a system of job rights and to improve working conditions, (3) to preserve and extend the union as an organization, and (4) to focus the political power of workers, that is, to serve as a political pressure group. The specific objectives stressed by individual unions differ from union to union, but in Canada most can be considered *business unions*. They are more concerned with economic action centering around the first three objectives than with political and social action.

In the pursuit of the first three objectives listed above, union officials negotiate with employers over the terms and conditions of employment. The negotiation process is known as *collective bargaining*. Through collective bargaining a *collective agreement* or *contract* is reached by the negotiating parties, with the terms of agreement put into writing and signed by the responsible representatives of each party. Agreements may be negotiated to run for one year, two years, or even longer. Sometimes the longer-term agreements provide that certain key issues—particularly wage rates—will be negotiated annually.

[5]*Canada,* Canadian Industrial Relations: The Report of the Task Force on Labour Relations. *Ottawa: Queen's Printer, 1969, p. 138.*

This task force was set up in March 1967 to conduct the most thorough review ever of federal labour legislation. It was headed by Dean H. D. Woods of McGill University; the other members were Dean A. W. R. Carrothers of the University of Western Ontario, Prof. J. H. G. Crispo of the University of Toronto, and Abbé Gérard Dion of Laval University. After spawning 62 research projects, the task force submitted its final report on December 31, 1968.

Redistribution of Income

Probably the most important objective of unions is to redistribute income. The common argument made is that business firms earn too much and workers earn too little. The union desires to make the owners of business share their earnings with workers. Collective bargaining with respect to wages covers a whole range of issues—whether rates will be hourly or by the piece, the size of differentials for different skill levels, whether wage increases will be based on seniority, the extent of fringe benefits, and others—but above all else the union seeks wage increases for its members. To the extent that it is successful in raising wages, a transfer of income from others in the economy to employed union members occurs. But does it really come from the business firm with which the union bargains?

Employment and Transfer Effects

Under any market conditions other than monopsony in the purchase of labour, if a union succeeds in obtaining wage rates *above what their equilibrium levels would be* there will be a reduction in the number of union members employed.[6] Those excluded from the unionized employment will either be unemployed or will work in employments not covered by the union in question. Their exclusion from the unionized employment means that they are added to the labour supply in other employments, forcing wage rates down somewhat in the latter labour markets. They and other workers would thus earn less than they would earn had the union been less successful. The union in this case receives income gains at the expense of those excluded from the unionized employment.

Consumers also contribute to the higher income of the employed union members. Higher wage rates increase production costs, leading to a lower level of output of the product produced, and reduced supplies cause the prices paid by consumers to be higher than they would otherwise be.

Total Income of Union Members

We frequently hear it said that if a union secures a wage increase, the purchasing power of union members will be increased. This is not necessarily the case, unless the wage increase follows or accompanies an increase in demand for the labour of the union members. If there is no such increase in demand and a union succeeds in obtaining a wage increase, placing the wage rate above the equilibrium level, the total income (pur-

[6]*See p. 371.*

chasing power) of union members may increase, decrease, or remain the same, the direction depending upon the elasticity of demand for labour. If demand is inelastic, the total income of the union workers will increase. However, if demand is elastic, their total income will decrease. If demand elasticity is unitary, the total income of the union members will not change.

Monopsony

The consequences of wage levels set above equilibrium levels will be different when the labour in question is purchased under conditions of monopsony. Under these circumstances the union may be able to increase simultaneously wage rates and the level of employment. There are no adverse effects on the economy's output or price level nor on the earnings of other workers in the economy. The effect of a wage level arrived at through collective bargaining carefully set above the equilibrium monopsony wage level, will be to increase the employment level as well as the wage rate.[7]

Establishment of Job Rights

The establishment of job rights, or of a system of "industrial jurisprudence," has been one of the important objectives of labour unions. Unions have long sought to protect their members from arbitrary or capricious actions on the part of supervisory personnel. They have also sought to retain for their members what those members consider to be their vested rights in particular jobs or in opportunities for promotion. A system of job rights ordinarily consists of a grievance procedure, a seniority system, and a set of working rules.

The Grievance Procedure

The collective agreement negotiated between union and employer usually establishes the formal outlines of a *grievance procedure*. By means of the grievance procedure all sorts of problems, complaints, and alleged unfair treatment of individual workers can be brought into the open and discussed by union and management officials. Collective bargaining on grievance matters is not limited to the period of the contract negotiation; only the procedure itself is established at that time. Rather, it is a continuous process that takes place throughout the year. Typically a worker complaint is handled first at the lowest possible administrative level. Discussion takes place between a union shop steward and the worker's fore-

[7]*See pp. 331-332.*

man, and frequently the matter can be cleared up at this point. Otherwise the case is referred upward to a department superintendent and a higher union official, or eventually to top management and top union officials. Failing settlement here the case is then carried to arbitration. A smoothly functioning grievance procedure can do much to promote good worker-employer relations.

Seniority Systems

Seniority systems are more narrowly centred around individual rights to particular jobs. They establish the order, based primarily on length of service, in which workers will be laid off in slack times, rehired, promoted, and so on. The intent of the union is to eliminate arbitrary actions in these matters on the part of supervisory personnel. Usually management objects to a strict seniority system, claiming that it does not permit putting the best man on a particular job, since length of service and efficiency are not necessarily coincidental. The union counterclaim is that in the absence of a seniority system, favouritism rather than efficiency is likely to be the main criterion for the actions of supervisors. They also argue that length of service and efficiency are likely to be closely related even if they are not precisely coincident in specific workers.

Working Rules

Working rules, too, are an attempt on the part of workers to protect what they consider to be their rights to specific jobs. Frequently their purpose is to lessen the impact of technological change, and usually their purpose is to increase the number of workers needed to perform a certain job above the number thought necessary by the employer. Work rules take several forms. Some require unnecessary work to be done. The International Typographical Union, for example, used for many years the famous "bogus work rule," requiring that the same advertisement in several newspapers be set into type separately for each newspaper even though a mat can be made from the first setting and used for subsequent runs. In the case of railroads, larger crews than are necessary have been required by the unions to operate diesel locomotives. In the construction trades work rules have often forbidden the use of prefabricated materials. Such practices are generally referred to as *featherbedding*.

Preservation and Extension of Unionization

All unions devote much effort to keeping their organization intact. Most, but not all, are interested in organizing the unorganized. What are the reasons for activities of this sort? What forms do these activities take?

The Reasons

Unions have a direct economic interest in keeping their organizations strong and in most cases in extending membership to the unorganized workers of their particular occupational or industrial jurisdictions. Suppose that the workers of a garment factory are organized but that a great many of those in the trade are not organized. The union is thus limited in the pressure it can exert on the employer for higher wages or for other benefits for its members. The existence of good substitutes for the labour of the union members makes the demand curve for union labour highly elastic. Rather than submit to union pressure, the employer can seek out nonunion employees. If the union can extend membership to cover other workers in the trade, the employer is denied access to nonunion competitive sources of labour and the union can be successful in bringing much more pressure to bear on him.

Some craft unions, rather than desiring to extend their membership, prefer to keep their organizations small and strong. Their objective is to maintain control of all the jobs available in their occupation and to limit the number who can enter it. Again, the economic rationale of the union is to make the demand for the union members as inelastic as possible. Further, limits to the number of workers who can ply the trade mean higher wages and larger incomes for those in the occupation. (Can you show this using a simple demand and supply diagram for labour?)

Another factor inducing most unions to try to extend their membership is the valid principle that there is strength or power in numbers. The larger the proportion of the work force that unions can count as members, the greater will be their abilities to accomplish other objectives as well as to obtain higher wage rates. If unions contain 100 percent of the labour force below supervisory levels, there will be no alternative nonunion sources of labour open to any one employer. Neither would there be nonunion territory to which employers can move or where nonunion competitors to unionized business can operate. Any employer attempting to resist union demands finds a very important alternative closed off.

There is still another reason why unions work continuously to preserve and extend their organizations. In the labour movement there are many individuals—union officers as well as union employees—whose present jobs and whose future positions depend upon the preservation of their organizations. A sort of bureaucracy has been built up with vested interests at stake. In this respect the union is no different from other organizations that have paid officers and paid employees.

The Methods

Union efforts at preservation and extension of unionism are carried on primarily in two ways. The most obvious one consists of drives to organize the unorganized. Most national or international unions have or have had paid organizers who go into nonunion plants and nonunion territories to convince workers of the benefits of unionism and to enroll them in new locals. These efforts have met with varying degrees of success. From 1940 until the mid-1950's union membership grew rapidly, but it levelled off during the following decade. Since 1964 union membership has steadily advanced as the result of intensive organizing efforts, especially among government employees.

The second activity consists of *union security* clauses which ordinarily form an important part of any collective bargaining contract. The term "union security" refers to the degree to which union membership is to be required among the workers in any given bargaining unit. There are four primary types of arrangements between the union and the employer, any one of which may be established. These are the closed shop, the union shop, maintenance of membership, and the open shop.[8]

Under the *closed-shop* arrangement the employer agrees to hire no one who is not a member of the union. Expulsion from the union constitutes grounds for dismissal by the employer of any employee. A closed-shop arrangement places much power in the hands of the union and, of course, places a premium on union membership. The closed shop is legal in all jurisdictions in Canada, and is common in the building, printing, and transportation trades.

The *union shop* is a somewhat less exclusive type of arrangement. Under the union shop the employer may hire whomever he pleases, but within a certain short, specified time period, say 30 days, the employee must join the union and must remain in good standing thereafter. By reason of their nature, craft unions tend to seek the closed shop, and industrial unions, the union shop. The federal Act and all provincial Acts recognize union-shop arrangements. In the United States, the Taft-Hartley Act of 1947 (characterized by union leaders as a "slave-labour" law) outlaws the closed shop for unions and employers operating in interstate commerce. However, it permits the union shop and other forms of union security. On the other hand, individual states are permitted by the Taft-Hartley Act to pass so-called "right-to-work laws," making the union shop as well as the closed shop illegal in their particular jurisdictions.

A third type of union security arrangement is called *maintenance of*

[8]*The so-called Rand Formula, as a form of union security, will be discussed separately;* *see pp. 400-401.*

membership. Maintenance of membership provides that employees who are union members in good standing at the time the collective agreement is made must remain so during the life of the agreement in order to remain employed. It is obviously a compromise arrangement between no union security at all and the complete security of the closed or union shop.

Most, but not all, employers have traditionally sought the open shop. Under the open shop employers are free to employ either union workers or nonunion workers as they see fit. Collective bargaining relations are ordinarily maintained under open-shop conditions only if the union is able to keep a majority of the employees of a particular bargaining group in the union; that is, if it is able to keep the union certified by the appropriate Labour Relations Board.

No account of union security in Canada would be complete without mention of the "check-off" provision, and the "Rand Formula". As already indicated, union security is founded upon a stable and established membership. Membership means bargaining power and support. Support means money. To assure that union dues and other union obligations are paid promptly and regularly by union members, unions have attempted to have employers accept the "check-off", that is, an arrangement whereby the employer undertakes to deduct union dues and other assessments from the earnings of the workers and remit the funds thus collected to the treasurer of the union. This practice strengthens the union's control over members. The check-off, as a form of union security, has much broader coverage than membership-security provisions. The 1962 Canada Department of Labour study on *Collective Agreements Provisions in Major Manufacturing Establishments* showed that while a little less than one half of the total of employees covered by the study (it covered 274,660 non-office employees in 361 manufacturing establishments) were not under an agreement with a provision requiring membership in the union as a condition of employment, nine employees out of ten were covered by some clause providing for the check-off of union dues. Furthermore, it noted that half of the employees were in establishments where collective agreements contained a provision for some form of *compulsory* or mandatory check-off.

In 1945 a dispute between the Ford Motor Company of Canada and the United Automobile Workers largely about union security resulted in a strike which lasted from September 12 to December 20. The strike ended with a joint decision to submit outstanding issues to arbitration and Mr. Justice I. C. Rand of the Supreme Court of Canada was appointed arbitrator. On January 29, 1946, he issued his award, the union-security section of which has resulted in what is commonly known as the Rand Formula. In its simplest form, the Rand Formula means the compulsory check-off of regular union fees and dues on all employees in the bargaining unit, irrespective of union status. In practice the Rand Formula tends to encourage union membership since there is no longer the possibility of a "free-ride" at the union expense. The Rand Formula is widely used in the automobile and agricultural implements industry and has been adopted in others as well. On the whole, however, it is not as common as other kinds of union security.

Political Objectives

It is almost axiomatic that the objectives of labour unions cannot be met solely through collective bargaining. The need for labour standards— minimum wages, maximum hours, annual vacations and general holidays, safety and others working conditions of Canadian men and women— requires legislative support and thus unions have an interest in the activities of Canadian legislative bodies. In addition, union activities have broadened over the years to include an interest in social security, international affairs, and the welfare of workers in other parts of the world. At home they have recognized that the well-being of a union member is bound up with the general economic environment of the nation as a whole. Accordingly, for more than 80 years now unions have been presenting their opinions on these matters to the three levels of government in Canada.

From the earliest years, labour unions in Canada have attempted to provide a focal point for marshalling worker support for or against particular issues and candidates. Besides "rewarding friends and punishing enemies", some Canadian unions, like many European and unlike most American unions, have nominated "Labour" candidates in local, provincial and federal elections. And since the 1930's, some sections of the Canadian labour movement have explicitly endorsed the socialist program of the Co-operative Commonwealth Federation (CCF) and its successor the New Democratic Party (NDP). Although the Canadian Labour Congress has not itself affiliated with the NDP (notwithstanding the fact that it helped organize it), a number of its affiliated unions, with some 250,000 members, have.

One general remark should be made in concluding this section. As in the United States and unlike Britain, class consciousness has been weak in Canada. For the most part labour union members are not unionists first and foremost. As well as being unionists they are Anglicans, Presbyterians, Catholics and so on. They are members of the PTA. They go fishing, boating, and water-skiing. They play softball, tennis, poker, and bridge. Their sons and daughters have opportunities to complete high school and to attend universities. The union is not the sole source of economic, social or political opportunity. It is viewed by most workers as one of many sources. Consequently, Canadian unions, like their American counterparts, are apparently unable to "deliver the vote" of their rank-and-file members, let alone workers in general. Or to put the judgment another way, the trade union movement in Canada has not yet shown the solidarity that helped the British Labour party and the Swedish Socialist party win national power.

The Weapons of Organized Labour

As noted earlier, organized labour, except for its participation in government activities, pursues its objectives through collective bargaining with employers. However, employers are not usually inclined to make extensive concessions to union negotiators just for the asking—or vice versa for that matter. In support of their collective bargaining demands unions have traditionally used three methods of inducing employers to yield ground. These are strikes, boycotts, and the force of public opinion.

The Strike

A *strike*, or a work stoppage, on the part of employees is the main weapon in the union's arsenal. If it is to be effective, the union must be able to block the employer from obtaining an alternative supply of labour. Picket lines are thrown up around the premises to advertise that a strike is in progress and to prevent—sometimes forcibly—nonunion workers from coming on the job. Members of other unions almost always honour the picket lines in any given industrial dispute and, to a very large extent, so do non-union workers. The odious term "scab" is applied to those who work as strikebreakers.

Strikes are costly to an employer. His revenue from sales will be cut off unless he has accumulated substantial inventories that he can sell while the strike is in progress; this has sometimes been the case in strikes against automobile manufacturers. Variable costs of the firm are reduced to zero, but fixed costs continue, thereby involving the firm in losses if sales revenue is insufficient to cover fixed costs. Further, the strike may cost the firm the customers who must turn to competitors while the strike is in progress. Thus the demand curve facing the firm, even after the strike has ended, may be shifted to the left.

Union members also bear the burdens of a strike since they usually lose their pay cheques for the duration of the work stoppage. Most large national and international unions have accumulated strike funds that they use to offset partially the pay cheque loss, but few are able to pay strike benefits to a large number of strikers over a long period of time.

The duration of a strike depends upon each party's evaluation of what it has to gain or lose from continuing it. The employer must weigh the costs of prolonging the strike against the costs of a settlement that will be acceptable to the union. The union must weigh pay cheque losses against possible gains to be obtained. Each must attempt to evaluate the other's position. All of these calculations are quite nebulous, for immediate gains or losses are not the only ones involved. If the employer makes concessions, what effect will this have on future union demands, or if the union makes concessions, what effect will this have on future employer resistance? Further, emotions or "principles" enter into the picture. Unions have on occasion prolonged strikes to the point at which pay cheque losses were greater than any possible gains that could be obtained, and employers have refused settlements that would be less costly than permitting the strike to continue. All of these factors lend uncertainty to a strike's duration, but the mounting losses on both sides provide an increasing incentive for a compromise arrangement to be worked out.

Earlier, the point was made that Canadian unions are not allowed to strike over recognition, jurisdiction or grievances, because the law provides other channels to gain these ends—the certification procedure and compulsory arbitration. Thus, for all practical purposes, the strike is now confined to the settlement of "economic" disputes, which means the renegotiation of expiring contracts. It is nonetheless still a very powerful weapon.

An impression of the impact of work stoppages in Canada can be obtained by noting the number of strikes, the number of workers involved in strikes, the time lost in strikes measured in man-working days, and the percentage of man-days lost in relation to total man days of employment per annum from 1901 to 1969. All of this is shown in Table 19–4.

A noteworthy fact brought out by these statistics is that there have been wide fluctuations in the number of strikes and lockouts,[9] the number of workers involved, and the proportion of man-days lost over the last 50 years. Thus, it is very difficult to make an objective judgment on the size of the strike problem in Canada on the basis of averages. Additional data not shown in the table indicate that there has been an increase in the number of big strikes—over 1,000 workers involved—since 1945. These are lasting longer, and the dislocations caused by the largest walkouts

[9]*The lockout is a management bargaining tactic—the employer refuses to admit workers to their jobs. A true lockout is rarely encountered.*

TABLE 19-4
Strikes and Lockouts in Canada, 1901-1969

Year	Strikes and Lockouts Beginning During Year	Strikes and Lockouts in Existence During Year			
				Duration in Man-Days	
		Strikes and Lockouts	Workers Involved	Man-Days	Percent of Estimated Working Time
1901..	97	99	24,089	737,808	....
1902..	124	125	12,709	203,301	....
1903..	171	175	38,408	858,959	....
1904..	103	103	11,420	192,890	....
1905..	95	96	12,513	246,138	....
1906..	149	150	23,382	378,276	....
1907..	183	188	34,060	520,142	....
1908..	72	76	26,071	703,571	....
1909..	88	90	18,114	880,663	....
1910..	94	101	22,203	731,324	....
1911..	99	100	29,285	1,821,084	....
1912..	179	181	42,860	1,135,786	....
1913..	143	152	40,519	1,036,254	....
1914..	58	63	9,717	490,850	....
1915..	62	63	11,395	95,042	....
1916..	118	120	26,538	236,814	....
1917..	158	160	50,255	1,123,515	....
1918..	228	230	79,743	647,942	....
1919..	332	336	148,915	3,400,942	0.60
1920..	310	322	60,327	799,524	0.14
1921..	159	168	28,257	1,048,914	0.22
1922..	89	104	43,775	1,528,661	0.32
1923..	77	86	34,261	671,750	0.13
1924..	64	70	34,310	1,295,054	0.26
1925..	86	87	28,949	1,193,281	0.23
1926..	75	77	23,834	266,601	0.05
1927..	72	74	22,299	152,570	0.03
1928..	96	98	17,581	224,212	0.04
1929..	88	90	12,946	152,080	0.02
1930..	67	67	13,768	91,797	0.01
1931..	86	88	10,738	204,238	0.04
1932..	111	116	23,390	255,000	0.05
1933..	122	125	26,558	317,547	0.07
1934..	189	191	45,800	574,519	0.11
1935..	120	120	33,269	288,703	0.05
1936..	155	156	34,812	276,997	0.05
1937..	274	278	71,905	886,393	0.15
1938..	142	147	20,395	148,678	0.02
1939..	120	122	41,038	224,588	0.04
1940..	166	168	60,619	266,318	0.04
1941..	229	231	87,091	433,914	0.06
1942..	352	354	113,916	450,202	0.05
1943..	401	402	218,404	1,041,198	0.12
1944..	195	199	75,290	490,139	0.06
1945..	196	197	96,068	1,457,420	0.19
1946..	223	226	138,914	4,515,030	0.54
1947..	231	234	103,370	2,366,340	0.27
1948..	147	154	42,820	885,790	0.10
1949..	130	135	46,867	1,036,820	0.11
1950..	158	160	192,083	1,387,500	0.15
1951..	256	258	102,793	901,620	0.09
1952..	213	219	112,273	2,765,510	0.29

TABLE 19-4
Strikes and Lockouts in Canada, 1901-1969

Year	Strikes and Lockouts Beginning During Year	Strikes and Lockouts in Existence During Year			
			Duration in Man-Days		
		Strikes and Lockouts	Workers Involved	Man-Days	Percent of Estimated Working Time
1953..	166	173	54,488	1,312,720	0.14
1954..	155	173	56,630	1,430,300	0.15
1955..	149	159	60,090	1,875,400	0.19
1956..	221	229	88,680	1,246,000	0.11
1957..	238	245	80,695	1,477,100	0.13
1958..	251	259	111,475	2,816,850	0.25
1959..	201	216	95,120	2,226,890	0.19
1960..	268	274	49,408	738,700	0.06
1961..	272	287	97,959	1,335,080	0.11
1962..	290	311	74,332	1,417,900	0.11
1963..	318	332	83,428	917,140	0.07
1964..	327	343	100,535	1,580,550	0.11
1965..	478	501	171,870	2,349,870	0.17
1966..	582	617	411,459	5,178,170	0.34
1967..	498	522	252,018	3,974,760	0.25
1968..	559	582	223,562	5,082,732	0.32
1969*..	556	585	601,954	7,736,710	0.46

*Preliminary figures.
Source: *Canada Department of Labour*, Strikes and Lockouts in Canada, *1968*. Ottawa: Queen's Printer, pp. *10-11*.

(secondary unemployment and shutdowns in related industries) appear to be getting more serious. For example, in 1967, the data show that 12 major stoppages (1,000 or more workers each) involved 27 percent of the workers and produced 53 percent of the total idleness. From the standpoint of *duration*, strikes lasting a month or more were responsible for over a quarter (26 percent) of all man-days lost.[10] And the percentage for 1969 will likely be well over half of working time lost. The point is simply this: since averages understate the actual burden of strikes, the importance of work stoppages should be measured qualitatively, i.e., in terms of size and "impact" (concentration and industrial location), rather than quantitatively (over-all totals). Of course, this is easier said than done.

The Boycott

Boycotts are another means used by unions to put pressure on employers. A *primary boycott* refers to a situation in which members of the union refrain from using or consuming the product of the employer with

[10]*Canada Department of Labour*, Strikes and Lockouts in Canada, 1967. *Ottawa: Queen's Printer, pp. 5 and 22.*

which there is a dispute. Through picketing union members may attempt to persuade others not to buy the product. In this manner the union hopes to inflict costs on the employer sufficient to induce him to meet the union's requests.

A *secondary boycott* is a more complex activity. In its usual form it means that the union boycotts and pickets an employer not a party to the dispute in the expectation that this third party will in turn bring pressure to bear on the employer from whom the union hopes to gain concessions. Suppose, for example, that a union of bakery workers is seeking higher wages or other benefits for its members. It throws up picket lines around supermarkets or other grocery stores through which the bakery markets its products. The hope is that these third parties will be hurt enough to exert pressure on the bakery to settle the dispute. This technique has been highly effective in a variety of circumstances. The presumed injustice of economic injury to parties outside the labour dispute is the basis for the British Columbia Trades Unions Act and the Newfoundland Labour Relations Act prohibitions of most secondary activities of this kind. It should be added that the secondary boycott has always been under suspicion in Canada and has frequently been held illegal in all jurisdictions in this country.

Public Opinion

The third major weapon used by organized labour is the force of public opinion. This can be thought of in two contexts: (1) in terms of building a favourable public attitude toward labour organizations in general and (2) in terms of securing public support in any given dispute between a union and an employer.

Unions, like other organizations, thrive best in an atmosphere of public support. As we shall see in the next section, this has been the historical experience in Canada. Although there were bitter labour disputes of paramount importance to the parties concerned prior to 1944, unions had no widespread impact on economic activity before that time. Their greatest gains followed public and governmental acceptance of them as legitimate organizations. The fact that this turnabout in attitudes occurred is indicative of the abilities of organized labour to influence public opinion over time.

The Effects and the Extent of Unionism

How have labour organizations affected the growth of the Canadian economy and the participation of workers in that development? It is impossible to answer the question with any degree of completeness or finality. Ample as is the information available on the labour movement, wages and labour productivity, and on the economy's performance over time, there are no good measures of what impact the labour movement has had or now has on economic activity. In the absence of objective measurements, we can only infer from economic theory and from the information that is available what the impact has been.

Economic Effects of Unions

To the extent that unions are successful in the pursuit of their objectives, it appears likely that their impact on the performance of the economy is adverse. If they succeed in obtaining and holding wage rates for union members above what the equilibrium levels would be, the result will be either unemployment or a persistent misallocation of labour resources, with too much of it being blocked out of unionized employment. We would expect, also, that their interference with the introduction of new productive techniques, to the extent that it is successful, would increase costs and hold down output in the affected industries. It appears likely, since it is the more highly skilled and better-paid workers that are unionized, that rather than decreasing income inequality unions increase it.

But are these adverse economic effects of great consequence in our economy? We hear much debate pro and con containing generous portions of emotion and opinion and uncomfortably little factual information. Against the adverse economic effects, social and psychological benefits, if any, should be weighed. But beyond these it appears likely that the effects of unions are overstated both by their advocates and by their adversaries. For example, ask almost any non-economist to identify the most important factor responsible for bringing about the tremendous increase in wage rates since the early 1900's and unions will be named. Yet the facts of union membership indicate that this cannot be so. The proportion of the labour force that has been unionized over time has not been sufficient for unions to be able to exert this kind of pressure or influence.

Origin and Growth of the Canadian Labour Movement

Although unions have been a part of the labour scene since the early 1800's, they have made up a significant part of the labour force only since the mid-1940's. Table 19–5 and Figure 19–2 show the growth of union

TABLE 19-5

Total Union Membership, Selected Years, 1911—1969

Year[1]	Union Membership (Thousands)	Total Non-Agricultural Paid Workers (Thousands)[2]	Union Membership As a Percentage of Civilian Labour Force	Union Membership As a Percentage of Non-Agricultural Paid Workers
1911	133			
1913	176			
1919	378			
1921	313	1,956	19.4	16.0
1924	261	2,138	7.5	12.2
1930	322	2,451	7.9	13.1
1935	281	1,941	6.4	14.5
1938	382	2,075	8.3	18.4
1939	359	2,079	7.7	17.3
1940	362	2,197	7.9	16.3
1943	665	2,934	14.6	22.7
1944	724	2,976	15.9	24.3
1949	1,006	3,326	19.3	29.5
1954	1,268	3,754	24.2	33.8
1960	1,459	4,522	23.5	32.3
1962	1,423	4,705	22.2	30.2
1963	1,449	4,867	22.3	29.8
1964	1,493	5,074	22.3	29.4
1965	1,589	5,343	23.2	29.7
1966	1,736	5,658	24.5	30.7
1967	1,921	5,953	26.1	32.2
1968	2,010	6,068	26.6	33.1
1969	2,075	6,380	26.3	32.5

[1]*Data on union membership for all years up to and including 1949 are as of December 31. Data for subsequent years are as of January 1.*
[2]*Figures for all years up to and including 1952 are as of the first week in June. Data for subsequent years are as of January.*
Source: *Canada Department of Labour,* Labour Organizations in Canada, 1969. *Ottawa, Queen's Printer, pp. XI and XII.*

membership for selected years from 1911 to 1969. Figure 19–3 shows union membership as a percentage of non-agricultural paid workers for selected years from 1921 to 1969. The irregular year intervals are included to show extraordinary changes that occurred.

Good data are not available for the nineteenth century, but from what we have it appears that unions were not an important force in the economy during that period. Certainly union membership did not exceed 4–5 percent of non-agricultural employment at any time. Still, the groundwork was being laid for the increase in union power and prestige during the twentieth century. Some 30 international craft unions, notably the International Typographical Union, the four railway-running trades (BLE, BLF, ORC and BRT) and the building trades (carpenters, bricklayers, plasterers, painters, etc.), chartered locals in Canada during the last half of the 1800's. By 1897 there were about 320 locals of international unions

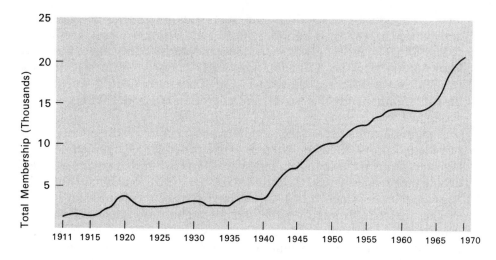

Figure 19-2
Union Membership in Canada, 1911–1969.

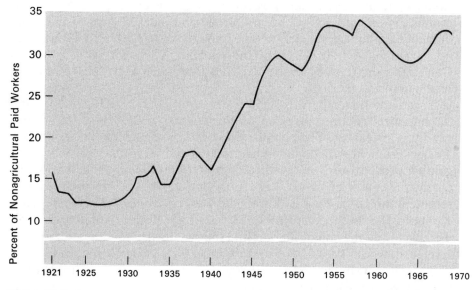

Figure 19-3
Union Membership as a Percentage of Nonagricultural Paid Workers, 1921–1969.

in Canada; by the end of 1902, there were well over 1,000. The year 1873 marks the advent of the first national central organization, the Canadian Labour Union, which held annual conventions until 1877. Following the lead of the Canadian Labour Union, the Toronto Trades and Labour

Council issued a call to all labour organizations to send delegates to a convention in 1883, to consider the formation of a new Canada-wide federation. The meeting was successful, and a new national central body, known initially as the "Canadian Labour Congress" but from 1886 on as the Trades and Labor Congress (TLC), was established on a permanent basis. Parenthetically the American Federation of Labor (AFL) was also set up in 1886.

The union influence on the economy has been markedly greater in the twentieth century. Membership rose from 1900 to 1919, sparked partly by vigorous industrial expansion and World War I, but these gains were lost during the prosperous 1920's and the Great Depression beginning in 1929. A low point was reached in 1934 at the depths of the depression.

The first real dispute over methods of organization occurred in 1902 when the TLC expelled 23 organizations that conflicted in jurisdiction with existing international unions of the AFL. The expelled unions, together with a number of purely Canadian "dual" (rivals of AFL unions) organizations promptly formed the National Trades and Labour Congress, which in 1908, became the Canadian Federation of Labour (CFL). Between 1901 and 1921, small clergy-organized French-speaking Catholic unions (*syndicats*) sprang up in Quebec and in 1921 formed the Canadian and Catholic Confederation of Labour. In 1927, the CFL and a few other national unions formed a new labour federation, called the All-Canadian Congress of Labour (ACCL), dedicated to national and industrial unionism.

Trade-union membership figures turned upward in 1936, and by 1937 the organized labour movement in this country was at the level attained twenty years earlier. The combination of improving economic conditions and government support and encouraging unionism and collective bargaining proved irresistible and trade union enrollment virtually doubled during the course of World War II. In doing so, it raised its proportionate representation of non-agricultural paid workers from 17.3 percent (about 1 out of 6) to 24.2 percent (about 1 out of 4). Rapid economic development followed the end of the war and the ensuing surge in union membership is shown in Table 19–5 and Figure 19–2. In 1959 the trade union movement in Canada had 1,459,000 members as compared to 711,000 thirteen years earlier. Union membership as a proportion of total non-agricultural paid employment reached a peak of 34.2 percent in 1958. Over the period 1960-1963 a slight decline in union membership occurred, but the growth has since resumed. Also deserving of mention is the fact that the percentage of union membership in relation to non-agricultural paid workers has generally been above 30 percent since 1949. Looked at the other way around, the non-union segment of the non-agricultural paid workers has generally never been less than two-thirds of the total.

The second phase in the continuing dispute over the relative merits of industrial and craft unionism came to pass early in 1939 when the Canadian branches of CIO international unions were expelled from the TLC, with a loss of more than 20,000 members. In 1940 the expelled unions merged with the ACCL to form the Canadian Congress of Labour (CCL). Contrary to most expectations, this new central organization not only survived but grew and waxed strong. In April 1956, only four months after the AFL and CIO merged in the United States, the CCL and the TLC amalgamated to form the Canadian Labour Congress (CLC). In 1960, the CCCL, after almost joining the CLC in September 1956, changed its name to the Confederation of National Trade Unions (CNTU).

Distribution of Union Membership

Although, relative to the total labour force, the significance of the union as reflected by union membership appears to be rather limited, are there areas in the economy that show relatively heavy concentrations of unionized workers? Certain broad trends in the distribution of union membership among sectors of the economy are shown in Table 19–6. The bulk of the membership has been split between the manufacturing sector and the non-manufacturing sector for the years shown, and a small fraction of it has been found in government employments. Both large sectors have

TABLE 19–6
Union Membership by Sector of the Economy 1959—1968[1]

	Manufacturing		Non-manufacturing		Government		Total	
	Number	Percent	Number	Percent	Number	Percent	Number	Percent
1959[2]	543	37.2	808	55.4	108	7.4	1,459	100.0
1960	561	38.5	799	53.9	99	5.5	1,459	100.0
1961	558	38.6	786	54.3	103	7.1	1,447	100.0
1962[3]	581	40.8	757	53.2	85	6.0	1,423	100.0
1963	590	40.7	774	53.4	85	5.9	1,449	100.0
1964	627	42.0	773	51.8	93	6.2	1,493	100.0
1965	676	42.5	819	51.5	94	5.9	1,589	100.0
1966	719	41.4	892	51.4	125	7.2	1,736	100.0
1967	759	39.5	955	49.7	207	10.8	1,921	100.0
1968	757	37.7	1,047	52.1	206	10.2	2,010	100.0

[1]*Thousands of persons.*
[2]*1959-1961 is based on the Dominion Bureau of Statistics,* Standard Industrial Classification *(1948).*
[3]*1963-1968 is based on Dominion Bureau of Statistics,* Standard of Industrial Classification *(1960).*
Source: Canada Department of Labour, Industrial and Geographic Distribution of Union Membership in Canada. *Ottawa: Queen's Printer, various years.*

TABLE 19-7
Union Membership by Industry, 1968

Industry Groups	UNION MEMBERSHIP		
	Number	Percent	
Manufacturing		757,463	100.0
Transportation equipment	123,201	16.3	
Pulp and paper	73,190	9.7	
Food processing	73,020	9.6	
Primary metals	72,577	9.5	
Electrical products	59,400	7.8	
Clothing	50,082	6.6	
Metal fabricating	45,376	6.0	
Wood	43,732	5.8	
Textiles	37,564	5.0	
Printing and publishing	31,916	4.2	
Machinery	29,933	4.0	
Chemical products	21,521	2.8	
Nonmetallic mineral products	21,191	2.8	
Rubber	15,380	2.0	
Furniture and fixtures	13,045	1.7	
Leather	12,133	1.6	
Beverages	11,873	1.6	
Tobacco products	6,247	0.8	
Petroleum and coal products	3,682	0.5	
Knitting mills	3,070	0.4	
Miscellaneous	9,330	1.2	
		100.0	
Nonmanufacturing		1,046,279	100.0
Transportation and utilities	354,905	33.9	
Construction	216,731	20.7	
Service	188,247	18.0	
Trade	82,711	7.9	
Mines	54,788	5.2	
Forestry	42,026	4.0	
Fishing and trapping	4,010	0.4	
Finance	785	0.1	
Agriculture	707	0.1	
Adjustment entry*	101,369	9.7	
		100.0	
Government		205,991	100.0
Federal	85,861	41.7	
Municipal	75,167	36.5	
Provincial	44,963	21.8	
		100.0	
Total membership	2,009,733	2,009,733	

*This entry represents the difference between total membership as reported in the CDL survey of union headquarters and the total obtained in the CDL survey of local unions.
Source: Canada Department of Labour (CDL), Industrial and Geographic Distribution of Union Membership in Canada, in 1968. Ottawa: Queen's Printer, p. 4.

experienced slight losses relative to total union membership, while the proportion of union members working for the government has been increasing.

A somewhat better perspective can be gained from an analysis of the data provided in Table 19–7. It is to be noted first of all that the largest number of union members in the manufacturing sector was employed in making transportation equipment—automobiles, locomotives, aeroplanes, and so on. Some 16 percent belonged to such unions as the United Automobile Workers and the International Brotherhood of Machinists. Other subsectors with a large number of union workers were pulp and paper, food processing and primary metals—steel, lead, zinc, copper, aluminum and others.

Electrical products, clothing, metal fabricating, wood, and textiles also contributed an appreciable number of members to the labour movement. In the non-manufacturing sector the largest numbers of organized workers were found in transportation and utilities, construction and service industries. These three groups accounted for 33.9, 20.7 and 18.0 percent, respectively, of total union membership within the non-manufacturing field. Wholesale and retail trade, mines, and forestry followed in that order. In finance and agriculture, unionization was virtually non-existent.

Geographically, as can be seen from Table 19–8, union membership is concentrated very heavily in three provinces, Ontario, Quebec and British Columbia. Why is this? A simple answer can be given to this question. These provinces are characterized by large cities and large industrial enterprises with indirect relationships between managers and workers. As a consequence of this impersonality, people are more willing to join a union.

TABLE 19–8
Union Membership by Province, 1968

Province	Number of Locals	Membership Number	Membership Percent
Newfoundland	163	24,295	1.2
Prince Edward Island	47	2,701	0.1
Nova Scotia	460	57,500	2.9
New Brunswick	395	39,493	2.0
Quebec	2,579	581,667	28.9
Ontario	3,202	716,162	35.6
Manitoba	370	72,914	3.6
Saskatchewan	378	44,497	2.2
Alberta	485	82,434	4.1
British Columbia	918	255,412	12.7
Yukon and Northwest Territories	29	1,061	0.1
Two or more provinces[1]	65	37,783	1.9
Adjustment entries	182[2]	93,814[3]	4.7
Total	9,273	2,009,733	100.0

[1]*Includes membership of Seafarers, Transportation—Communication Employees, United Telegraph Workers and Actors Equity.*
[2]*Represents difference between total membership as reported by union headquarters and that reported in the survey of local unions.*
[3]*Locals reported by union headquarters but for which separate membership data were not obtained.*
Source: Canada Department of Labour; Industrial and Geographical Distribution of Union Membership in Canada in 1968. *Ottawa: Queen's Printer, p. 6.*

In some areas of the economy, then, the bulk of the workers are organized. Where this is the case, one very astute student of labour economics in the United States estimates that the unions may be able to raise and hold the wage rates of their members by as much as 15-25 percent above what they would be in the absence of unions.[11] He suggests that this may be the case for the craft unions of the building and printing trades, railroads, and the entertainment industry. He also suggests that the strong industrial unions in such industries as steel or autos may be able to do the same thing. Another able American economist who has studied the labour movement extensively estimates that on the average the effect of unions on the wages of union members is no more than 4 percent, although in a very small group of industries it may be as high as 20 percent.[12]

International Unionism

No mention has been made so far of the effects that international unions —or, more accurately binational unions—have had on the Canadian trade union movement or on Canada as a whole. On the positive side, it would appear that international unions have played a prominent role in labour leadership in this country for more than a century. In consequence, the labour movement developed more rapidly in Canada than would otherwise have been the case. It would also seem that international unions have served to strengthen the bargaining power of their Canadian members, rendered substantial assistance in obtaining labour benefits based on high U.S. standards, frequently exerted a moderating influence on the sometimes excessive demands of individual locals, and prevented or tempered U.S. discriminatory moves against imports of certain commodities from Canada. On the other hand, the "demonstration effect" of U.S. wages may have impaired Canada's international competitiveness. Additionally, international unions, subject as they are to U.S. laws and controlled by U.S. citizens, may have served to lessen Canadian sovereignty.

While the general absence of reliable quantitative measures precludes categoric statements, a number of Canadian economists suggest that international unionism has conferred net benefits on organized labour in Canada and also on the Canadian economy.[13]

[11]*Albert Rees*, The Economics of Trade Unions. *Chicago: University of Chicago Press, 1962, pp. 77-80.*

[12]*H. G. Lewis*, Unionism and Relative Wages in the United States. *Chicago: University of Chicago Press, 1963, pp. 7-9.*

[13]*For a detailed discussion of the advantages and disadvantages of international unionism in Canada, see John Crispo,* International Unionism: A Study in Canadian-American Relations. *Toronto: McGraw-Hill, 1967. For a brief summary of this book, see review article by Frank Wildgen in* The Canadian Journal of Economics, *November 1969, pp. 628-30. See also, I. Brecher and S. S. Reisman,* Canada-United States Economic Relations. *Ottawa: Queen's Printer, 1957.*

It may be useful to add that Canadian locals of international unions appear to enjoy a wide and substantial measure of autonomy in the key areas of collective bargaining, including the use of the strike weapon. Moreover, analysis does not record a single case where a Canadian local has gone on strike under orders from international headquarters. Finally, most of the dues and assessments collected by Canadian locals are deposited in Canadian banks and used to cover their Canadian operations.[14]

Summary

Labour unions are organizations of workers that attempt to improve the well-being of their members, concentrating for the most part on economic well-being. Craft unions enroll workers of a given skill or occupation. Industrial unions enroll workers in a given industry or in related industries regardless of occupation or skill level. Union members hold their membership in local unions, whose jurisdiction is ordinarily a local firm, a local industry, or a local craft or occupation. Local unions from the same craft or industry or related industries usually band together to form a national or international union, these being the power centres of the labour movement. Most national and international unions, in turn, are joined together in a federation of unions, either the CLC or the CNTU.

Government policy toward labour unions is expressed in court decisions and in legislation. For most of the nineteenth century it was adverse to unions, often treating them as common law criminal conspiracies. It was not until 1872 that the Trade Union Act was passed by the Dominion Parliament declaring that unions were lawful entities. In 1900 Parliament passed the Conciliation Act, which authorized the Minister of Labour to investigate the cause of any industrial dispute and to appoint conciliation officers or conciliation boards upon request. Under the Railway Labour Disputes Act of 1903, provision was made for all railway disputes to be referred to a conciliation committee composed of three persons—one nominated by the employer, one by the union and a chairman chosen by these two—and (failing settlement) to voluntary and non-binding arbitration. The Industrial Disputes Investigation Act (I.D.I. Act) of 1907 introduced the principle of compulsory delay of work stoppages—the so-called "cooling-off period"—while investigation proceedings were underway. The I.D.I. Act was applied compulsorily only to industries held to possess the character of a public utility; it was applied to other industries

---

[14]*For some interesting comments on the U.S. influence on our unions, see Eugene Forsey, "The Influence of American Labor Organizations and Policies on Canadian Labor" in Duke University Commonwealth Studies Center,* The American Economic Impact on Canada. *Durham, N.C.: Duke University Press, 1959.*

only if both parties to a dispute consented. In 1925 the I.D.I. Act was declared by the courts to be *ultra vires* the Parliament of Canada whereupon the statute was amended, limiting its coverage to disputes occurring in works or undertakings solely under federal jurisdiction. Within a few years, however, all provinces except Prince Edward Island passed enabling legislation allowing the I.D.I. Act to be brought into force within their own jurisdictions. In 1944 the Government issued Privy Council Order 1003. Along with the familiar government policy on compulsory dispute settlement, PC 1003 provided for compulsory collective bargaining and also established a procedure for certifying unions. Parliament in 1948, after revoking the Wartime Labour Relations Regulations (PC 1003) and repealing the I.D.I. Act, passed a new statute, the Industrial Relations and Disputes Investigation Act, which was in effect a slightly amended version of PC 1003. Subsequently all provinces passed similar labour laws of their own. Thus the principles of the legislation in this field are essentially the same throughout Canada.

The activities of labour unions are aimed toward four general objectives: (1) a redistribution or transfer of income toward union members, (2) the establishment of job rights for union members, (3) preservation and extension of the union as an organization, and (4) the focusing of the political power of union members. They work toward the first three by negotiating with the employers for whom their members or prospective members work; the negotiating process is called collective bargaining. Terms and conditions of employment successfully negotiated form a collective agreement or contract. There are between 12,000 and 15,000 collective agreements in effect in Canada.

To the extent that unions are successful in raising wage rates for their members above equilibrium levels, a transfer of income to union members from those excluded from the unionized employment and from consumers occurs, except in the case of monopsony. Whether or not the total wage bill or purchasing power of union members increases or decreases depends upon the elasticity of demand for union labour.

Unions attempt to protect the job rights and working conditions of their members through a grievance procedure, a seniority system, and working rules. These are important parts of any collective agreement. Working rules that require the employer to hire more men than are necessary for the job at hand are generally referred to as featherbedding.

Preservation and extension of the union as an organization has a firm economic rationale. If it is successful, it denies employers substitute sources of labour, thus making the demand curve for union labour less elastic. Further, the greater strength of greater numbers induces most unions to attempt to bring additional workers under the union mantle.

Also, paid union officials have a vested interest—their jobs—in maintaining the organization intact and in expanding it. In order to obtain and hold workers as members, unions attempt to organize the unorganized and they bargain with employers for union security clauses for their agreements. The closed shop, in which only union members may be hired, is the strongest form of union security. Next is the union shop, in which the employer may hire whom he pleases but the employees must join the union within a specified time period. We sometimes find maintenance of membership arrangements, in which those who are union members at the time an agreement is reached must remain so for the duration of the agreement. Under an open-shop agreement the workers of a given employer may or may not be union members, depending upon their individual desires.

Politically, organized labour in North America has taken the position of "rewarding friends and punishing enemies" regardless of their political affiliation. However, some sections of the Canadian labour movement have taken direct political action since the 1870's. Political parties often woo the labour "vote", but they can never be sure that union leaders can deliver it for them.

Unions make use of three weapons in attempting to secure their collective bargaining objectives. These are strikes, or work stoppages; boycotts, or refusals to buy from the employer; and the force of public opinion. In all of these the union makes extensive use of picketing.

The impact of unions on economic activity is probably over-rated by most people. Union members made up less than 15 percent of non-agricultural paid workers until the early 1930's. With the improving economic conditions of the later 1930's, the active support of unions and collective bargaining by the federal government during the course of World War II, and the growing acceptance of unions by Canadians generally during the early years following the war, union membership rose rapidly from 1935 to the late 1950's. At this point, membership levelled off, the total number remaining almost stationary until 1965, when the upward trend was resumed. At its relative peak in 1958 union membership was 34.2 percent of total non-agricultural paid workers and has since declined slightly. Although unions are strong in certain sectors of the economy, the fact remains that about two-thirds of all non-agricultural paid workers in Canada are non-union. It may be useful to add, however, that many non-union workers are covered by collective agreements.

Exercises and Questions for Discussion

1. Suppose that in a certain city all public school teachers are encouraged to form and join a union. If this were accomplished, what would be the probable economic

impact on the number of teachers hired and the salary level on the quality of public education?

2. Earlier in the text it was stated that technological improvements increase employment. Unions, however, resist technological change because it will cause some of their members to become unemployed. Can these two statements be reconciled? Explain.

3. Discuss the pros and cons of unionism. Is the redistribution of income, as a result of unionization, equitable? Defend your answer.

4. Define the following: strike, primary boycott, secondary boycott. Under what circumstances do you think unions should be allowed to use each? When should they not?

Selected Readings

Forsey, E., "History of the Labour Movement in Canada," special article in Dominion Bureau of Statistics, *Canada Year Book*. Ottawa: Queen's Printer, 1967, pp. 773-781.

———; "The Movement Towards Labour Unity in Canada: History and Implications," *Canadian Journal of Economics and Science*, February, 1958, pp. 70-83.

Jamieson, S., *Industrial Relations in Canada*. Toronto: Macmillan Company of Canada, 1957.

———; "Labour Unionism and Collective Bargaining," in M. Oliver (ed.), *Social Purpose for Canada*. Toronto: University of Toronto Press, 1961, pp. 340-367.

Kovacs, A. E. (ed.), *Readings in Canadian Labour Economics*. Toronto: McGraw-Hill, 1961.

Logan, H. A., *Trade Unions in Canada: Their Development and Functioning*. Toronto: Macmillan Company of Canada, 1948.

Lorensten, E. and E. Wollner, "Fifty Years of Labour Legislation in Canada". *The Labour Gazette*, September, 1950.

Montague, J. T., "International Unions and the Canadian Trade Union Movement," *Canadian Journal of Economics and Political Science*, February, 1957, pp. 69-82.

Peitchinis, S. G., *The Economics of Labour: Employment and Wages in Canada*. Toronto: McGraw Hill, 1965.

Phelps, O. W., *Introduction to Labour Economics*. Toronto: McGraw Hill, 1961, Chaps. 8-10.

Phillips, W. G., "Government Conciliation in Labour Disputes: Some Recent Experience in Ontario," *Canadian Journal of Economics and Political Science*, November, 1956, pp. 523-34.

Quinet, Felix, *The Content and Role of Collective Agreements in Canada*. Don Mills: CCH Canadian Limited, 1969.

Woods, H. D. and S. Ostry, *Labour Policy and Labour Economics in Canada*. Toronto: Macmillan Company of Canada, 1962.

Index